Fodor's

LAS VEGAS

WELCOME TO LAS VEGAS

Las Vegas knows what everyone wants and delivers it in spades. Megaresorts fund their 45-foot bronze lions, half-size Eiffel Towers, and towering glass pyramids with the collective desires and dollars of more than 30 million annual visitors. From a Wolfgang Puck dinner to a Wolfpack-like adventure on the Strip, you're sure to find your perfect indulgence. Swim up to a blackjack table, chow down at a buffet, or chill out in an ultralounge. A Las Vegas vacation disorients and delights; when you're here, you're all-in, and the "real world" seems far out.

TOP REASONS TO GO

★ **Resorts:** Colossal hotels present exotic themes and over-the-top amenities.

★ **Dining:** Few cities in the world can claim a higher concentration of top restaurants.

★ **Gambling:** Novices and pros alike come to Vegas for legendary casino action.

★ **Shopping:** Lavish malls and bargain outlets provide retail options for every budget.

★ **Nightlife:** Master mixologists serve creative cocktails and famous DJs spin nightly.

★ **Shows:** Cirque du Soleil, international singers, and local stars perform day and night.

Fodor's LAS VEGAS

Editorial: Douglas Stallings, *Editorial Director*; Salwa Jabado and Margaret Kelly, *Senior Editors*; Alexis Kelly, Jacinta O'Halloran, and Amanda Sadlowski, *Editors*; Teddy Minford, *Associate Editor*; Rachael Roth, *Content Manager*

Design: Tina Malaney, *Associate Art Director*

Photography: Jennifer Arnow, *Senior Photo Editor*

Maps: Rebecca Baer, *Senior Map Editor*; David Lindroth, Mark Stroud (Moon Street Cartography), *Cartographers*

Production: Jennifer DePrima, *Editorial Production Manager*; Carrie Parker, *Senior Production Editor*; Elyse Rozelle, *Production Editor*; David Satz, *Director of Content Production*

Business & Operations: Chuck Hoover, *Chief Marketing Officer*; Joy Lai, *Vice President and General Manager*; Stephen Horowitz, *Head of Business Development and Partnerships*

Public Relations: Joe Ewaskiw, *Manager*

Writers: Joan Patterson, Heidi Knapp Rinella, Susan Stapleton, Matt Villano, Mike Weatherford

Editor: Douglas Stallings

Production Editor: Elyse Rozelle

Production Design: Liliana Guia

29th Edition

ISBN 978–1–101–88012–8

ISSN 1542–345X

All details in this book are based on information supplied to us at press time. Always confirm information when it matters, especially if you're making a detour to visit a specific place. Fodor's expressly disclaims any liability, loss, or risk, personal or otherwise, that is incurred as a consequence of the use of any of the contents of this book.

PRINTED IN THE UNITED STATES OF AMERICA

10 9 8 7 6 5 4 3 2 1

3 0646 00219 2932

CONTENTS

Fodor's Features

MAPS

ABOUT THIS GUIDE

Fodor's Recommendations

Everything in this guide is worth doing—we don't cover what isn't—but exceptional sights, hotels, and restaurants are recognized with additional accolades. Fodor'sChoice★ indicates our top recommendations. Care to nominate a new place? Visit Fodors.com/contact-us.

Trip Costs

We list prices wherever possible to help you budget well. Hotel and restaurant price categories from $ to $$$$ are noted alongside each recommendation. For hotels, we include the lowest cost of a standard double room in high season. For restaurants, we cite the average price of a main course at dinner or, if dinner isn't served, at lunch. For attractions, we always list adult admission fees; discounts are usually available for children, students, and senior citizens.

Hotels

Our local writers vet every hotel to recommend the best overnights in each price category, from budget to expensive. Unless otherwise specified, you can expect private bath, phone, and TV in your room. *For expanded hotel reviews, visit Fodors.com.*

Top Picks	Hotels &
★ Fodor'sChoice	Restaurants
	🖬 Hotel
Listings	⌁ Number of
✉ Address	rooms
✉ Branch address	⦿ Meal plans
☎ Telephone	✕ Restaurant
🖷 Fax	⟋ Reservations
⊕ Website	⋔ Dress code
✉ E-mail	▭ No credit cards
✉ Admission fee	ⓢ Price
◷ Open/closed	
times	**Other**
Ⓜ Subway	⇨ See also
⊹ Directions or	☞ Take note
Map coordinates	⃛ Golf facilities

Restaurants

Unless we state otherwise, restaurants are open for lunch and dinner daily. We mention dress code only when there's a specific requirement and reservations only when they're essential or not accepted. *For expanded restaurant reviews, visit Fodors.com.*

Credit Cards

The hotels and restaurants in this guide typically accept credit cards. If not, we'll say so.

EUGENE FODOR

Hungarian-born Eugene Fodor (1905–91) began his travel career as an interpreter on a French cruise ship. The experience inspired him to write *On the Continent* (1936), the first guidebook to receive annual updates and discuss a country's way of life as well as its sights. Fodor later joined the U.S. Army and worked for the OSS in World War II. After the war, he kept up his intelligence work while expanding his guidebook series. During the Cold War, many guides were written by fellow agents who understood the value of insider information. Today's guides continue Fodor's legacy by providing travelers with timely coverage, insider tips, and cultural context.

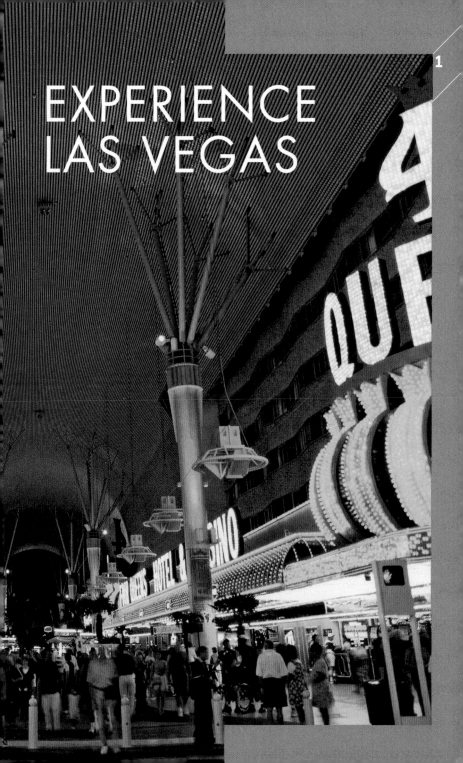

EXPERIENCE
LAS VEGAS

LAS VEGAS PLANNER

When to Go

Las Vegas doesn't have a high or low season by the standard definition, but you'll find it least crowded between November and January. Hotels are at their fullest July through October. Specific events—New Year's Eve, Super Bowl weekend, spring break, March Madness, major conventions—draw big crowds, so plan accordingly.

It's well known that summer highs often exceed 100°F, but with low humidity and ever-present air-conditioning, you can stay comfortable as long as you limit your time outside to short intervals. Even in the hottest months (late June through September) you can bear the heat, provided you stay hydrated and don't try to walk too far. And with more than 300 days of sunshine a year, the chances of a rain-out (or snow-out in winter) are slim (though when it does rain, it pours).

On the other hand, it does get chilly between late fall and early spring. There actually is a winter here, with nighttime temperatures of 40°F, and sometimes, though rarely, below; so bring a sweater or windbreaker for your evening strolls beneath the neon-bathed skies.

Getting Around

Bus Travel. Public bus transportation is available via Regional Transportation Commission of Southern Nevada (RTC). Tourist-friendly double-decker buses (dubbed "The Deuce") run up and down the Strip approximately every 15 minutes 24/7—a 24-hour pass is $8; a three-day pass is $20. The fare includes access to the "Strip and Downtown Express" (STX) and all RTC routes, which serve most of the Las Vegas Valley. Stops are near most resort properties, and are marked with signs or shelters. Visitors also can connect to and from McCarran International Airport via a 10-minute ride to the RTC's South Strip Transfer Terminal on Route 109. Buses from there connect to the Deuce, Strip and Downtown Express, and more. For detailed information about how to get around town using public transit, check out the RTC's special website (⊕ *www.ridethestrip.com*).

Car Travel. If you're exploring the Strip or Downtown, it's best just to park your car and walk. Parking at Strip casinos used to be free, but now most casinos charge hourly fees. If you think you'll be operating beyond the Strip during your stay, get a rental car.

Monorail Travel. The Las Vegas Monorail costs $5 per ride (or $12 for a one-day pass) and runs from the MGM Grand to Harrah's before making a jog out to the Convention Center and terminating at the Sahara Avenue Station near the SLS Las Vegas. It's no sightseeing tour; the train runs along the back sides of the resorts. But it's a fast way to travel the Strip, especially on weekends when even the Strip's backstreets are full of traffic. The trains run 7 am–midnight Monday; 7 am–2 am Tuesday through Thursday; and 7 am–3 am weekends. Discounts are available when you purchase tickets online (⊕ *www.lvmonorail.com*).

Ride Sharing. Ride-sharing services such as Uber and Lyft serve the Las Vegas market and now are allowed to pick up and drop off passengers anywhere in town.

Taxi Travel. Cabs cost $3.50 initial fare plus $2.76 per mile. They are convenient and worthwhile, especially if you're splitting a fare (no more than five people allowed in a cab). Note: Cab rides originating at McCarran International Airport include a $2 surcharge.

Safety Tips

Few places in the world have tighter security than the casino resorts lining the Strip or clustered together Downtown. Outside of these areas, Las Vegas has the same urban ills as any other big city, but on the whole, violent crime is extremely rare among tourists, and even scams and theft are no more likely here than at other major vacation destinations. Observe the same common-sense rituals you might in any city: stick to populated, well-lighted streets, don't wear flashy jewelry or wave around expensive handbags, keep valuables out of sight (and don't leave them in unattended cars), and be vigilant about what's going on around you.

Reservations

Many attractions don't require reservations; some places don't even accept them. But any activity with limited availability—a stage show, a restaurant, a guided tour—deserves a call ahead.

Use common sense. Ask yourself these questions:

■ Am I bringing a big party (six or more people) to this event?

■ Is this a weekend event at a popular time of day (6–9 pm for dinner, 10 am–2 pm for golf)?

■ Is the venue very popular?

■ Will I be disappointed if I arrive to find the venue full?

■ Will the people I'm traveling with hold me personally responsible for ruining their morning/day/evening?

If you answered "yes" to one or more of these questions, then you need to make a reservation, or you need someone to call ahead for you. Who would be willing to do such a thing? Your hotel's concierge, that's who. And don't wait until you check in; call the concierge before you leave home to get a jump on the crowd (just be sure to tip him or her accordingly).

Las Vegas Hours

Hoping for sushi at 4 in the morning, or looking to work out at a gym at midnight? Sounds like you're a night owl, and that means Vegas is your kind of town. There are all kinds of businesses that run 24/7 in this city of sin, from supermarkets to bowling alleys. Oh yeah, and they have casinos, too.

Attractions, such as museums and various casino amusements, tend to keep more typical business hours, but you can almost always find something to keep you entertained no matter the hour.

Visitor Centers

The Las Vegas Convention and Visitors Authority (LVCVA) runs a visitor center (☎ 702/892–0711 ⊕ www.lasvegas.com) at 3150 Paradise Road, open weekdays from 8 to 5. Stop by for brochures and advice on what to see and do in town.

The LVCVA also operates the Las Vegas Hotline (☎ 877/847–4858), with operators who are plugged into every major resort and restaurant in the region. Think of them as a concierge service for all of southern Nevada.

WHAT'S WHERE

1 South Strip. Between fight nights at the MGM Grand and concerts at T-Mobile Arena, the section of Strip between the Monte Carlo and Mandalay Bay could be considered the entertainment hub of Vegas. Rooms on this side of town generally are within 15 minutes of the airport and are slightly more affordable than their Center and North Strip counterparts.

2 Center Strip. The heart of the Strip is home to CityCenter and iconic resorts such as Caesars Palace. This section, a 20-minute cab ride from the airport, stretches north from CityCenter to The Venetian. Several of the Strip's largest shopping centers are in this area.

3 North Strip. The North Strip is defined by luxury. The Wynn Las Vegas and its neighbors have some of the swankiest rooms in town. About a 30-minute ride from the airport, the North Strip clubs and restaurants are some of the best in town.

4 Downtown. Experience the old Vegas tradition—dice and drinks. With some exceptions, rooms range from shabby to mediocre. Nightlife in this neighborhood has made a comeback with the opening of the Smith Center for the Performing Arts and others. The Downtown Project, powered by Zappos.com, has brought new life to the area.

5 Paradise Road and the East Side. Parallel to the Strip, a short drive or 15-minute walk east, is the mellower Paradise Road area, which includes the Convention Center. There's less traffic, and there's monorail service along one stretch. Hotel options include the Hard Rock Hotel. Beyond are the University District and Boulder Strip.

6 Henderson and Lake Las Vegas. Southeast of the Strip but west of Lake Las Vegas, this area's perhaps the most stereotypically "suburban" in the Valley. Still, its outlets are popular, and locals come from miles around to gamble at Green Valley Ranch Resort & Spa Casino. It also encompasses man-made Lake Las Vegas.

7 West Side. West of the Strip, on the other side of Interstate 15, are several large resort hotels. This isn't a glamorous area, and you'll be cabbing or driving to and from the Strip.

8 Summerlin and Red Rock Canyon. West of Downtown, this tony neighborhood looks out on the gorgeous Red Rock National Conservation Area. It's home to a couple of resorts as well.

9 South Side. Within a few miles' radius south of McCarran International Airport are some large resorts, a bunch of budget motels, economical time-shares, the huge shopping mall Town Square, and lots of chain restaurants. There are even some resorts far south of town.

10 North Side. This area, between Summerlin and Nellis Air Force Base (and north of Downtown), encompasses the neighborhood known on maps as North Las Vegas. It's home to the Las Vegas Motor Speedway, some locals casino hotels, and a host of up-and-coming restaurants.

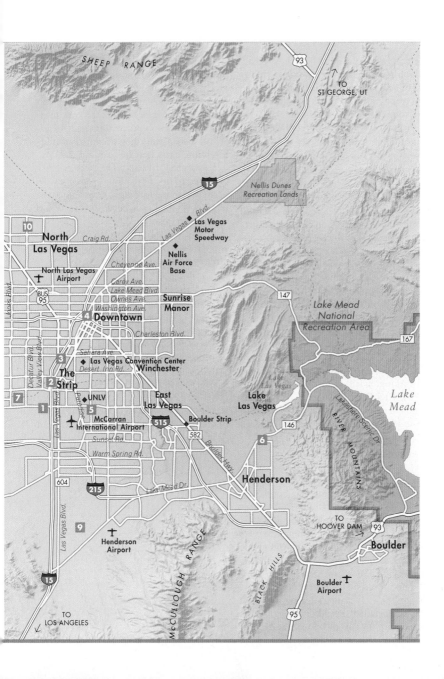

WHAT'S NEW

Life comes at you quickly in Las Vegas, and things around town always are changing. In addition to new attractions, some new trends around town have emerged, and some big changes are in store for the future. We've summarized the most important stuff for you here.

No more free parking
In the olden days of Las Vegas (read: back in 2015), visitors could drive into town and park indefinitely in casino resort parking garages for free. That all changed in 2016, when MGM Resorts became the first of the major casino companies to charge for parking. Fees to start were nominal, especially if you were a member of the company's M Life players' card program. And critics were vocal in opposition to the change. Gradually, however, as other casino companies saw that the new parking fees didn't really dissuade visitors from driving in, they added fees, too. Now it's a big deal to find casino resorts that DON'T charge for parking. Station Casinos, which owns Palms, Red Rock Casino, Green Valley Ranch, and a host of others, is one of the holdouts. Consider the trend a sign of the times.

Big changes at Wynn
Golfing at Wynn Las Vegas used to be a treat. The 18-hole course right behind the resort was the only golf course on the Strip, and it had 11 water features and a 37-foot waterfall. Though it cost travelers $500 to play, the place was jam-packed all the time. Perhaps this is why it came as such a surprise in the middle of 2016 when Steve Wynn himself announced he'd shutter the course by September 2017 to make way for a new attraction named Paradise Park. Details on the plan for this development are still sketchy, but on earnings calls, Wynn himself waxed poetic about a new theater, a new tower of rooms, a substantial expansion of Wynn/Encore's convention and meeting space, and related entertainment attractions and customer activities. Wynn also openly has dreamed of adding white-sand beaches and an Atlantic City–style boardwalk. The expansion is expected to open by 2020. More immediately, Wynn is building a new retail area named Wynn Plaza between the Wynn and Encore resorts. When complete, this new area will add more than 173,000 square feet of space to the shops that already exist at the resorts.

Down the road
Other casinos are in the works, particularly on the North Strip. The biggest of the bunch: Resorts World Las Vegas, is a continuation of the failed Echelon Place project, which Singaporean company Genting picked up from Boyd Gaming in 2013. When it opens, the casino will rival CityCenter in size and will comprise four different towers, a tremendous casino, a movie theater, a water park, and more. Plans are for the entire resort to have an Asian theme. The project is scheduled for completion in 2019.

FREE THINGS TO DO

Experience Fremont Street. The Downtown casinos' answer to the spectacle of the Strip is the Fremont Street Experience, played out on a 90-foot-high arced canopy that covers the entire street. Every hour between sunset and midnight it comes alive with an integrated video, graphics, and music show. Several different programs run each night and contribute to a festive outside-in communal atmosphere that contrasts with the Strip's every-man-for-himself ethic.

Watch a Free Show. You can easily spend $100 or more on seats at a typical Vegas concert or big-name production, but several casinos offer fabulous, eye-catching extravaganzas that won't cost you a penny. There's the erupting volcano at the Mirage, the graceful Fountains of Bellagio, and the Wildlife Habitat (with a flamboyance of flamingos!) at the Flamingo Las Vegas. People-watching is a free show of a different kind, too.

See the New Old Downtown. The Downtown casinos don't attempt to compete with the opulence of the Strip, but Fremont and connecting streets have their own charm. The Downtown Container Park is a collection of shipping containers that have been converted into an outdoor mall of shops, bars, and restaurants. Also, sip handcrafted cocktails at newer lounges, such as Commonwealth and Park on Fremont. Stroll through history as you tour old signs at the Neon Museum and check out the art deco–inspired Smith Center for the Performing Arts.

Preview a TV Show. Vegas is home to several preview studios, where you're asked to watch and offer feedback on TV shows. Some studios offer a small cash stipend for your time; for others you'll have to be satisfied with free refreshments, coupons, and the thanks of a grateful nation. We like **CBS Television City research center** (⌧ *3799 Las Vegas Blvd. S, South Strip* ☎ *702/891–5753* ⊕ *tvcityresearch.com* ☉ *Daily 10–8:30*) at the MGM Grand. ∎ TIP➜ No kids under 10.

Cruise the Strip. You haven't done Vegas until you've been caught—either intentionally or unwittingly—in the slow-mo weekend-night crawl of traffic down the Strip. You can handle the experience like a been-there local, or you can play the delighted tourist: relaxed, windows down, ready to engage in silly banter with the carload of players in the convertible one lane over. We suggest the latter, at least once. Just be mindful of all the pedestrians, who can crowd the crosswalks and are just as dazed as you are by the cacophony.

Seek History. Don't miss out on the opportunity to explore bits and pieces of bygone days. Downtown, drop by **The Mob Museum** (⌧ *300 E. Stewart Ave., Downtown* ⊕ *www.themobmuseum. org*), which examines the city's ties to the Mafia and resides in the formal federal courthouse and U.S. Post Office. Also check out the Neon Museum (⌧ *770 Las Vegas Blvd. N, Downtown* ⊕ *www. neonmuseum.org*), which curates a lot full of neon signs that fronted casinos of yesteryear. Beyond Downtown, Vegas is full of well-preserved examples of fine architecture, mid-century—we like the **Morelli House**—and modern, like the Frank Gehry–designed **Cleveland Center.** Wander through the older hotels on the Strip and Downtown that will, eventually and inevitably, be torn down to make way for new construction.

LAS VEGAS
TOP ATTRACTIONS

Spectacular Spectaculars
(A) Will it be an acrobatic Cirque du Soleil extravaganza? A standing act by a musical legend? An afternoon comedy show, or Broadway-lite (90-minute cut-downs of the original productions from the Great White Way)? A classic feather revue, or a spooky hypnotist show? Maybe you're just in the mood for a plain old lounge show where the microphones squeal, the singer is slightly out of tune, and a great time is all but guaranteed. It's practically against the law to be bored in Vegas.

World-Class Restaurants
(B) The $2.95 lobster dinner has gone into hiding, but those cheap chow deals of yesteryear are hardly missed; Las Vegas has become a foodie's dream destination. Every major resort offers at least half a dozen fine-dining options in addition to the ubiquitous snack bars and fast-food places. If you stayed in Vegas for a year, you'd never have to eat at the same place twice.

Hitting the Tables
(C) Never mind those buffets, swimming pools, spas, traffic jams, dancing girls (and boys, and water), wedding chapels, and circus acts. It's Vegas, baby, and the best action is always at the tables. Roll the bones, double down, or go all in.

Natural Wonders
(D) Consider heading out of the casino and taking in one of the many natural wonderlands surrounding Las Vegas. Explore Lake Mead or Red Rock Canyon. During the winter months, hit the ski slopes at Mt. Charleston. There's more to this area than neon.

The High Roller
(E) At 550 feet tall and 520 feet in diameter, this Observation Wheel at the back of the LINQ Promenade, off the Center Strip, is the largest in the world—larger than the Singapore Flyer and the London

Eye. Full rotations from the swanky wheelhouse take about 30 minutes. The views are unbeatable.

Crystals, CityCenter

(F) This chichi shopping and dining mall designed by Daniel Libeskind has taken the retail and culinary scene in Vegas to an even higher level. In addition to a stellar restaurant, this austere space contains dozens of fine stores, including Gucci, Fendi, and Tom Ford, as well as dozens of pieces of public art.

Legendary Nightlife

Sky-high bars with Valley-wide views. Thumping bass lines and flashing lights. Semi-clothed Adonises and Venuses swinging overhead. Whether you're looking for a wild dance club or a sophisticated lounge scene, Vegas comes alive after dark. So dress to the nines, grab a kamikaze shot, and join the 24-hour party.

Over-the-Top Pools

(G) The tanning booth is now a ubiquitous feature in the Anytown strip mall, but it still can't compare with the old-fashioned poolside sun soak—especially if that soak is in Las Vegas, land of toned bodies, cocktails, cabanas, Euro-style bathing, man-made beaches, and swim-up blackjack. Most pools also now offer both dayclub and nightclub options.

Hoover Dam and Lake Mead

(H) If you have time for just one trip outside of town, make it to this Depression-era concrete monstrosity, considered one of the seven wonders of the industrial world. You'll understand why when you tour the interior and see the massive turbines that make the lights go on in Pasadena. Combine the trip with a visit to nearby Lake Mead, where you'll enjoy boating, water-skiing, and other watery activities.

DID YOU KNOW?

The iconic "Welcome to Fabulous Las Vegas" sign was designed by Betty Willis and erected in 1959. It still sits in the median at 5100 Las Vegas Boulevard South (south of Mandalay Bay) at the unofficial southern end of the Las Vegas Strip.

HISTORY, VEGAS-STYLE

by Matt Vilano

Over the last few years, we've all heard the brilliant marketing slogan "What happens in Vegas stays in Vegas." But a whole lot has happened in Vegas in the last few hundred years, and most of the stories *have* made it into the history books.

Archaeologists believe civilization in the area now known as Sin City stretches back almost 2,000 years. This once lush area was home to numerous Native American tribes, including the Kawaiisu, Kitenamuk, and Serrano. In the 1820s, Spaniards traveling from Mexico to northern California on the Old Spanish Trail named the area "Las Vegas" (meaning "The Meadows"). When the area became part of the U.S. in 1855, the name stuck.

The railroad arrived in 1905, and, over the next decades, Las Vegas grew from a rail hub to a leisure destination. The Hoover Dam, built in the 1930s, played a large part in development, but gambling put the city on the map. Since 1940, Las Vegas has seen casinos rise, fall, and rise again—bigger than before. These casinos have launched some of the greatest names in show business, including Frank Sinatra, Dean Martin, and Wayne Newton.

Today, Las Vegas and its environs (population: more than 2 million) shelter those who make the casinos whir. And nothing here sits for long; the town becomes hipper, bolder, and more sophisticated every year. The city is now home to 11 of the 21 largest hotels in the world. From a place nicknamed Sin City, you'd expect nothing less.

TIMELINE

| | 1829: water-rich Las Vegas valley (the Meadow) gets its name. | 1855: Mormons build fort. | 1864: Nevada becomes 36th state. | 1885: State Land Act attracts farmers. |

Precolonial Era   1800   1850   1900

(left) Detail from poster for John C. Fremont 1856; (above) Las Vegas circa 1895; (right) construction workers working Hoover Dam spillway between 1936 and 1946.

COL. FREMONT

Native Occupation

1500s–1800s

Cultural artifacts indicate that human settlers including the Kawaiisu, Kitanemuk, Serrano, Koso, and Chemehuevi occupied the area as far back as the 100 or 200 A.D. Archaeologists have said the land would have been hospitable—the region's artesian wells would have provided enough water to support small communities, and skeletal remains indicate wildlife was prevalent. It also stands to reason that many of the earliest inhabitants took advantage of the lush meadows after which the region ultimately was named; excavated pieces of detailed weavings and basketry support these theories.

Early Settlers

1820s–90s

Spaniards settled the area in the 1820s, but John Fremont, of the U.S. Army Corps of Engineers, quickly followed on a scouting mission in 1844. After annexation, in 1855, Brigham Young sent a group of missionaries to the Las Vegas Valley to convert a number of modern Native-American groups, including the Anasazi. The missionaries built a fort that served as a stopover for travelers along the "Mormon Corridor" between Salt Lake City and a thriving colony in San Bernardino, California. Dissension among leaders prompted the Mormons to abandon Las Vegas by the 1860s, leaving only a handful of settlers behind.

Industrialization Arrives

1890s–1920s

Everything in Las Vegas changed in the 1900s. Just after the turn of the century, local leaders diverted the spring and resulting creek into the town's water system. The spring dried up and the once-vibrant meadows turned into desert. Then, in 1905, the transcontinental railroad came through on its inexorable push toward the Pacific. The city also began to serve as a staging point for all the area mines; mining companies would shuttle their goods from the mountains into Las Vegas, then onto the trains and out to the rest of the country. With the proliferation of railroads, however, this boom was short-lived.

| 1905: Las Vegas is founded as a city. | 1911: Divorce laws are liberalized in Nevada | 1931: construction begins at Hoover Dam sight. Population booms. Gambling is legalized. | 1941: El Rancho Vegas, first hotel and casino on the Strip. | 1951: First Atomic Bomb is detonated north of Las Vegas. |

1920   **1940**   **1960**

1

IN FOCUS HISTORY VEGAS-STYLE

(above) The Flamingo Hotel; (below) Bugsy Siegel; (top right) The Rat Pack.

1930s
Early Casinos

Las Vegans knew they needed something to distinguish their town from the other towns along the rails that crisscrossed the United States. They found it in gambling. The Nevada State Legislature repealed the ban in 1931, opening the proverbial floodgates for a new era and a new economy. Just weeks after the ban was lifted, the now-defunct Pair-O-Dice opened on Highway 91, the stretch of road that would later become known as the Las Vegas Strip. The city celebrated another newcomer—dedicating the Boulder (now Hoover) Dam on the Colorado River in 1935.

1940s–50s
Bugsy Takes Charge

No person had more of an impact on Las Vegas's gambling industry than gangster Ben "Bugsy" Siegel. The Brooklyn, New York native aimed to build and run the classiest resort-casino in the world, recruiting mob investors to back him. The result was the Flamingo Hotel, which opened (millions of dollars over budget) in 1946. Though the hotel was met with historic fanfare, it initially flopped, making Siegel's partners unhappy and suspicious of embezzlement. Within six months, Siegel was "rubbed out," but the Flamingo lived on—a monument to the man who changed Vegas forever.

1950s–60s
Rat Pack Era

Frank Sinatra, Dean Martin, Sammy Davis, Jr., Peter Lawford, and Joey Bishop were a reckless bunch; upon seeing them together, actress Lauren Bacall said, "You look like a goddamn rat pack." The name stuck. The quintet appeared in a number of movies—who can forget the original *Ocean's Eleven*?—and performed live in Las Vegas. Their popularity helped Sin City grow into an entertainment destination. They also played an important role in desegregation—the gang refused to play in establishments that wouldn't give full service to African-American entertainers, forcing many hotels to abandon their racist policies.

TIMELINE

1966: Howard Hughes arrives in Las Vegas.	1971: Hunter S. Thompson writes *Fear and Loathing in Las Vegas*.	1970s: Elvis Presley and Liberace are Las Vegas's top performers.	1980: MGM Grand catches fire. It's the worst disaster in the city's history.	1989: Steve Wynn opens The Mirage
	1970	1980		1990

(left) Howard Hughes; (center top) Frank Rosenthal interviewing Frank Sinatra; (center bottom) Elvis Presley; (top) Liberace; (right top) Steve Wynn; (right bottom) Siegfried and Roy; (right) Bellagio's dancing fountains.

1960s
A Maverick Swoops in

- Multimillionaire Howard Hughes arrived in Vegas in 1966 and began buying up hotels: Desert Inn, Castaways, New Frontier, Landmark Hotel and Casino, Sands, and Silver Slipper, to name a few. He also invested in land—then mostly desert—that today comprises most of the planned-residential and commercial community of Summerlin. Hughes also wielded enormous political and economic influence in Nevada and nearly single-handedly derailed the U.S. Army's plan to test nuclear weapons nearby. His failure in this matter led to a self-imposed exile in Nicaragua until his death in 1976.

1960s–80s
Mob Era

- Elvis Presley made his comeback in 1969 at The International (now the Las Vegas Hotel) and played there regularly until the middle of the next decade. In the same era, East Coast mobsters tightened their grip on casinos, prompting a federal crackdown and forcing some to return to the east when gambling was legalized in Atlantic City, New Jersey, in 1976. Frank "Lefty" Rosenthal, largely seen as the inventor of the modern sports book, narrowly survived a car bomb in 1982. Others, such as Tony "The Ant" Spilotro, were not as lucky—Spilotro and his brother, another casino gangster, were beaten and strangled to death in 1986 and buried in a cornfield in Indiana.

Late 1980s–90s
Era of Reinvention

- The years immediately following the mob crackdown weren't pretty. The nation was in a recession, and tourism was down. Large fires at major resorts such as MGM Grand, Aladdin, and Monte Carlo devastated the city's economy and image. Gradually, Las Vegas recovered. Big corporations purchased hotels off the scrap heap, and several properties underwent major renovations. With the help of clever marketing campaigns, properties began attracting tourists back to experience the "new" Vegas. In 1989, Steve Wynn opened the city's first new casino in 16 years—the Mirage—and triggered a building boom that persists today.

| 1993: Work begins on Fremont Street Experience. | 1996: Las Vegas Motor Speedway opens. | 2001: Green Valley Ranch Resort and Spa opens. | 2005: The Wynn opens; Las Vegas celebrates its centennial. | 2010: The new Las Vegas CityCenter is completed. | 2016: The T-Mobile Arena and Park Theater open. |

2000 **2010** **BEYOND**

1

IN FOCUS HISTORY, VEGAS-STYLE

1990s
Age of the Mega-Hotel

- In all, more than a dozen new mega-resorts opened in the 1990s. The Mirage, which opened in 1989, started the domino effect of new hotels up and down the Strip. It was followed by the Rio and Excalibur in 1990; Luxor and Treasure Island (now TI) in 1993; the Hard Rock Hotel in 1995; the Stratosphere and the Monte Carlo in 1996; Bellagio in 1998; and Mandalay Bay, the Venetian and Paris Hotel & Casino in 1999. These, coupled with the $72-million, 1,100-acre Las Vegas Motor Speedway, which took the city from exclusively gambling destination to a NASCAR destination, made the city incredibly visitor-friendly. Tourists obliged, arriving in record numbers.

2000s
Variations on a Theme

- Never fans of complacency, Vegas hoteliers have continued to innovate. Steve Wynn, of Mirage and Bellagio fame, opened arguably the city's most exquisite resort, Wynn Las Vegas, in 2005. Sheldon Adelson, CEO of Sands Corporation, countered by opening The Palazzo next door to the Venetian, giving the two properties 7,000 rooms combined. Off the strip, multimillion dollar mega-resorts such as the Palms and Red Rock offered more exclusive, intimate experiences. Then, toward the end of this decade, Vegas experienced a new trend: hotels without casinos of any kind, outfitted for nothing but complete relaxation.

2010s
Mixing It Up

By 2010 non-gaming revenue had exceeded gaming revenue on the Strip for more than 10 years, and every major resort had fully adapted to this new normal with ever-greater investments in clubs, restaurants, shows, and shops. The mega resorts mega-merged, with MGM Mirage becoming MGM Resorts International and Harrah's Entertainment becoming Caesars Entertainment in 2010, dominating the Strip with more than 20 properties between them. Mixed-use spaces such as the mammoth CityCenter and major attractions such as the High Roller and the Park ushered in a new age of visitor amenities that emphasized entertainment inside and outside the resorts.

TIE THE KNOT

Vegas wedding chapels: They're flowers and neon and love ever after (or at least until tomorrow's hangover). They're also mighty quick, once you get that marriage license.

Chapel of the Flowers. Enjoy a brief facsimile of a traditional ceremony at this venue, designed to be a turnkey wedding operation, with three chapels and an outdoor garden, as well as on-site flower shop, photography studio, and wedding coordinators. Sure, it's still Las Vegas, so an Elvis impersonator is available for all ceremonies. ✉ *1717 Las Vegas Blvd. S, North Strip* ☎ *800/843–2410, 702/735–4331* ⊕ *www.littlechapel.com.*

Clark County Marriage License Bureau. A no-wait marriage certificate can be yours if you bring $77 cash (no credit cards), identification (prison IDs are accepted on a case-by-case basis), and your beloved to the Clark County Marriage License Bureau. Unless the office is unusually busy, the process normally takes less than an hour. ✉ *201 E. Clark Ave., Downtown* ☎ *702/671–0600* ⊕ *mlic.vegas.*

Little Church of the West. This cedar-and-redwood chapel on the South Strip is one of the city's most famous. The kitsch is kept under control, and the setting borders on picturesque (it's even listed on the National Register of Historic Places—ah, Vegas). Since it opened in 1942, the church has been the site of more celebrity marriages than any other chapel in the world. ✉ *4617 Las Vegas Blvd. S, South Strip* ☎ *702/739–7971, 800/821–2452* ⊕ *www.littlechurchlv.com.*

A Little White Wedding Chapel. The list of ALWWC alums is impressive: Demi Moore and Bruce Willis, Paul Newman and Joanne Woodward, Michael Jordan, Britney Spears, and Frank Sinatra. Patty Duke liked it so much, she got married here twice. Try the Hawaiian theme, where the minister plays a ukulele and blows into a conch shell to close out the ceremony. Or, get hitched in a pink Cadillac while an Elvis impersonator croons. One of the five chapels is a drive-through, for the ultimate in shotgun weddings. ✉ *1301 Las Vegas Blvd. S, North Strip* ☎ *800/545–8111, 702/382–5943* ⊕ *www.alittlewhitechapel.com.*

Office of Civil Marriages. At the Office of Civil Marriages a commissioner will do the deed for $77.75 on a credit card. The catch: You must call ahead to make an appointment. At least one witness is required. ✉ *330 S. 3rd St., 6th fl., Suite 660, Downtown* ☎ *702/671–0577* ⊕ *www.clarkcountynv.gov/clerk/services/pages/civilmarriages.aspx.*

Viva Las Vegas Wedding Chapels. An endless variety of wedding themes and add-on shtick is available, ranging from elegant to casual to camp; say your vows in the presence of Elvis, the Blues Brothers, or Liberace. Live webcams stream nuptials on the chapel's website in real time. Of the six chapels, one has a Doo-Wop Diner theme. ✉ *1205 Las Vegas Blvd. S, North Strip* ☎ *702/384–0771, 800/574–4450* ⊕ *www.vivalasvegasweddings.com.*

EXPLORING
LAS VEGAS

Updated by
Matt Villano

Easter Island, Machu Picchu, and other celebrated wonders of the world are certainly impressive. But Las Vegas...Las Vegas is a land where jungles thrive and fountains dance in the middle of the desert. It's a place that unites medieval England and ancient Egypt with modern-day Venice, Paris, and New York. It's a never-ending source of irony and improbability where you can turn a chip and a chair into a million dollars, or celebrate your shotgun wedding by shooting machine guns. Where else does such a wonderland exist? Nowhere. But. Vegas.

The smallish city (geographically) is larger than life, with a collective energy (and excess) that somehow feels intimate. Maybe it's the agreeable chimes and intermittent cheers from the casino floor that fade to tranquillity when you enter a sumptuous spa. Maybe it's the fish flown in nightly from the Mediterranean that lands on your plate. For each individual, Vegas is an equation where you + more = more of you: more chances to explore aspects of your personality that may be confined by the routine of daily life. It's for this reason alone that the "what happens here stays here" phenomenon is shared by so many visitors.

The city itself has a number of different faces. For a dose of history, head Downtown and explore everything from old casinos to a museum that pays homage to the mobsters who built them. For fun, glitz, and glamour, head to the Strip, which itself has three distinct sections (South, Center, North). For outdoor adventure, head west and south, either to the Spring Mountains beyond Summerlin or out to Hoover Dam and Lake Mead—man-made accomplishments of an entirely different sort. Along the way, you can pamper yourself at world-class spas and restaurants, engage in retail therapy at some of the best shopping spots in the world, dance the night away at rocking nightclubs, or—of course—court Lady Luck long enough to strike it rich. With the right itinerary, Vegas even can work for families with young kids.

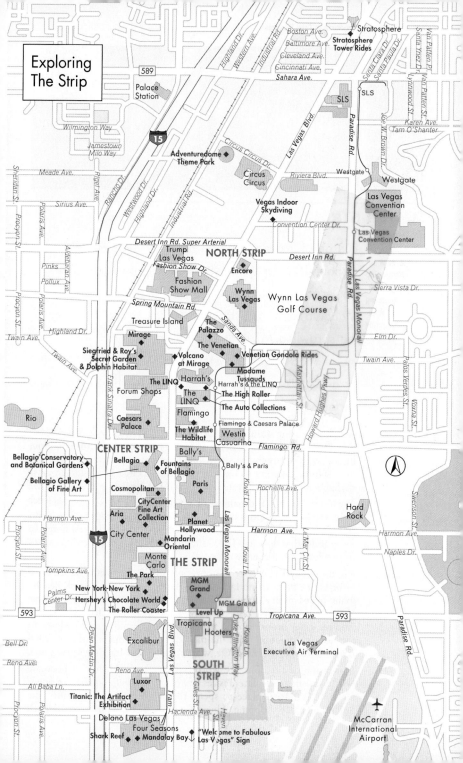

SOUTH STRIP

Dining
★★★★
Sightseeing
★★★★
Shopping
★★★
Nightlife
★★★

Fun and fantasy collide on the South Strip. Close to the airport, the resorts and attractions at this end of Las Vegas Boulevard go from New York–New York all the way to Mandalay Bay (and the Delano Las Vegas) and include the sprawling MGM Grand Resort. Whether it's a man-made beach lagoon, a glass pyramid, a medieval castle, or an Oz-like complex, imagination in these parts most certainly runs wild.

A first-time tour should start at the iconic "Welcome to Las Vegas" sign, just west of the runways at McCarran International Airport. From there, swing through the shark habitat at Mandalay Bay, check out the "Sphinx" in front of Luxor, and view the circa-1950 stained-glass skylights inside the renovated Tropicana Las Vegas.

The jousting in the Tournament of Kings at Excalibur is topped only by the gravity-defying loops of the roller coaster at New York–New York. Then, of course, there's the MGM Grand—one of the largest hotels in the world—that now has Top Golf, one of the swankiest driving ranges from which you'll ever swing.

Dig deeper and you start to appreciate the details of the South Strip resorts. The palm-frond fans inside Mandalay Bay. The South Beach–white of rooms at Delano Las Vegas. Even New Yorkers say the West Village–inspired food court at New York–New York feels like home. And the giant bronze lion in front of MGM Grand is a throwback to the hotel's affiliation with the movie company, but it's also a veiled reference to the *Wizard of Oz*, which inspired the building's green hue.

Noncasino destinations are worth visiting, too. Hershey's Chocolate World satisfies chocolate desires of every age. Town Square, an open-air mall, is a great place to spend the day to escape the casino vibe and spend a day shopping. Then there's The Park, with an arena that's home to Sin City's first professional sports franchise, the NHL's Golden Knights. Compared with the rest of the Strip, which is more modern and, at times, stuffy, the South Strip is whimsical and just plain neat.

GETTING HERE AND AROUND

Everything on the South Strip is relatively close. Most resorts are within a 10- or 15-minute cab ride from the airport, and all are accessible by public transportation. A monorail connects Mandalay Bay with Luxor and Excalibur. What's more, pedestrian bridges across Las Vegas Boulevard link Excalibur to Tropicana and New York–New York to MGM Grand (other bridges across Tropicana Avenue link Excalibur to New York–New York and the Tropicana to MGM Grand). If it's not July or August, a walking tour of this area is a fun activity (⇨ *see feature boxes*). From ground level, the heft of casinos never gets old.

The Las Vegas Monorail begins (or ends) on this part of the Strip at the MGM Grand station. The RTC (Regional Transportation Commission of Southern Nevada) services this part of the Strip with public buses and double-deckers (⇨ *see also Bus Travel in Travel Smart*).

TOP ATTRACTIONS

Luxor Las Vegas. Welcome to the land of the Egyptians—Vegas-style. This modern-world wonder is topped with a xenon light beam that burns brighter than any other in the world and can be seen from anywhere in the Valley at night; for that matter, it's supposedly visible even from space. The exterior is made with 13 acres of black glass. Forget elevators; climbing the slanted walls of the Luxor pyramid requires four "inclinators" to reach guest rooms. Above the casino is the world's largest atrium—you get the full impact of the space from the second floor, where "BODIES…The Exhibition" gives guests an eerie view of the human body. This atrium also is home to Fantasy, a seductive adult revue that's fun to share with your significant other, and Carrot Top, who—believe it or not—is still performing live shows in Vegas after nearly 20 years. For something entirely unique, head outside the casino, walk past the porte cochere, and follow the sidewalk inside a replica of the Great Sphinx of Giza. Only in Vegas. ⊠ *3900 Las Vegas Blvd. S, South Strip* ☎ *877/386–4658* ⊕ *www.luxor.com.*

Mandalay Bay. Mandalay Bay is famous for a few things: the House of Blues, which brings in some epic concerts throughout the year; the Shark Reef aquarium, which boasts a 1.6-million-gallon saltwater tank with more than 2,000 different animals; and an A-list of restaurants from celebrity chefs such as Charlie Palmer, Hubert Keller, Rick Moonen, and more. Technically the property is three separate brands: Mandalay, the Delano Las Vegas, and the Four Seasons Hotel Las Vegas. If you're into design, the lobby for the Delano incorporates natural features from around the Vegas Valley and is one of the sharpest lobbies you'll find in Nevada. Also worth noting: Minus 5 Ice Bar, which is located in the Mandalay Place shopping corridor that connects Mandalay Bay with the Luxor; for the price of admission you get to borrow a parka, waltz into a subzero drinking establishment, and throw back vodka from a glass made of ice. ⊠ *3950 Las Vegas Blvd. S, South Strip* ☎ *877/632–7800* ⊕ *www.mandalaybay.com.*

GREAT WALKS: SOUTH STRIP

Mummies to Big Apple: Inside Luxor's pyramid, follow the enclosed walkways to Excalibur. From there, it's an easy walk across a pedestrian bridge to New York–New York's gaming floor. Total time: 15 minutes.

All about M's: Inside the MGM Grand, resort guests can explore the grounds—both the MGM Grand and the area surrounding the Signature towers. Then you can join the masses and hit the Strip heading north toward M&M's World, one of the town's biggest candy stores. Total time: 30–40 minutes.

See an Icon: Head south on Las Vegas Boulevard from Mandalay Bay and you'll spot the famous "Welcome to Fabulous Las Vegas" sign. If you want to take a picture directly under the sign, be careful crossing the street; the sign sits in the center median and there's no crosswalk. Total time from Mandalay and back: about 40 minutes.

MGM Grand Hotel & Casino. A regal, bronze rendering of the roaring MGM lion mascot fronts the four emerald-green, fortresslike towers of the MGM Grand, one of the largest hotels in the world. Over the years, the property has become synonymous with big fights, most of which take place in the hotel's Grand Garden Arena. In recent years, the property also has added Hakkasan, an upscale restaurant and nightclub; Level Up, a hipster arcade with booze; Top Golf Las Vegas, a state-of-the-art driving range; and Brad Garrett's Comedy Club, where the beloved comic from *Everybody Loves Raymond* performs regularly. The hotel also has its share of restaurants from celebrity chefs, including Morimoto's first foray into Las Vegas. ⊠ *3799 Las Vegas Blvd. S, South Strip* ☎ *877/880–0880* ⊕ *www.mgmgrand.com.*

New York–New York Resort & Casino. The mini-Manhattan skyline that forms the facade of this hotel is one of our favorite parts of the Strip—there are third-size to half-size re-creations of the Empire State Building, the Statue of Liberty, and the Chrysler Building, as well as the New York Public Library, Grand Central Terminal, and the Brooklyn Bridge. Inside, portions of the casino floor have been made to look like neighborhoods of the real New York City. The Little Italy/Greenwich Village area is such an accurate replica many New Yorkers momentarily get confused. Without question, the big attraction is The Roller Coaster. A close No. 2: Hershey's Chocolate World. Then of course, there's The Park, which sits just north of the back side of the hotel and stretches from the Strip all the way to T-Mobile Arena. ⊠ *3790 Las Vegas Blvd. S, South Strip* ☎ *866/815–4365* ⊕ *www.newyorknewyork.com.*

FAMILY
Fodor's Choice
★

The Roller Coaster. There are two reasons to ride the Coney Island–style New York–New York roller coaster (aka Manhattan Express): first, with a 144-foot dive and a 360-degree somersault, it's a real scream; and second, it whisks you around the amazing replica of the New York City skyline, giving you fabulous views of the Statue of Liberty, Chrysler Building, and, at night, the Las Vegas lights—you climb to peak heights around 200 feet above the Strip. Get ready to go 67 mph over a dizzying succession of high-banked turns and camelback hills, twirl through a "heartline twist" (like a jet doing a barrel roll), and finally rocket along a 540-degree spiral before pulling back into the station. ⊠ *New York–New York, 3790 Las Vegas Blvd. S, South Strip* ☎ *866/815–4365, 702/740–6969* ⊕ *www.newyorknewyork. com/attractions* ⊠ *$14; all-day-ride pass $25.*

FAMILY   **Shark Reef.** Your journey through Mandalay Bay's long-running Shark Reef attraction begins in the mysterious realm of deep water at the ruins of an old Aztec temple. It's tropical and humid for us bipeds, but quite comfy for the golden crocodiles, endangered green sea turtles, and water monitors. Descend through two glass tunnels, which lead you deeper and deeper under the sea (or about 1.6 million gallons of water), where exotic tropical fish and other sea creatures swim all around you. The tour saves the best for last—from the recesses of a sunken galleon, sharks swim below, above, and around the skeleton ship. Elsewhere you'll find a petting zoo for marine life, a Komodo dragon exhibit, and a special jellyfish habitat. If you plan to visit other MGM Resorts attractions you can save with their three-for-$57 promotion. ⊠ *Mandalay Bay, 3950 Las Vegas Blvd. S, South Strip* ☎ *702/632–4555* ⊕ *www.sharkreef.com* ⊠ *$20.*

WORTH NOTING

FAMILY   **Hershey's Chocolate World.** Chocoholics rejoiced in 2014 when the two-story, West Coast flagship of Hershey's Chocolate opened as part of the streetscape fronting New York–New York. The attraction includes a retail store, a café, and a tester area where visitors can sample some of Hershey's newest confections. Visitors also can personalize Hershey's chocolate bar wrappers, or put together a bag of different-flavored Hershey's Kisses (almond, mint, and so on) chocolates wrapped in a variety of different colors. ⊠ *New York–New York, 3790 Las Vegas Blvd. S, South Strip* ☎ *702/437–7439* ⊕ *www.hersheyschoco-lateworldlasvegas.com.*

Level Up. Tucked just inside the main Strip entrance to the MGM Grand resort, this expansive space (which opened in the former Rainforest Cafe space at the end of 2016) is essentially an arcade for hipsters, along with a great bar. Games include everything from Pop-A-Shot and foosball to table hockey and more; most cost about $1 apiece. Beer pong tables are available and they're free, so long as you keep drinking beer (balls are 50 cents apiece). There's also a game that bills itself as the World's Largest Pac-Man. Golf fans love GolfStream Laser Golf, which essentially is virtual reality golf. Because it's Vegas, there's gambling here, too, in the form of electronic craps, roulette, blackjack, and baccarat. MGM even has moved its Sigma Derby horse-racing simulator to this new and exciting spot. ⊠ *MGM Grand, 3799 Las Vegas Blvd. S, South Strip* ☎ *702/891–7871* ⊕ *www.mgmgrand.com/en/nightlife/level-up.html* ⊠ *Free; games from $1.*

FAMILY
Fodor's Choice
★   **The Park.** Ever since the razing of The Boardwalk casino in the early 2000s, the space between New York–New York and the Monte Carlo sat vacant, a veritable eyesore on the south end of the Strip. Finally, in 2015, landowner MGM Resorts decided to do something about it.

The result, inventively dubbed The Park, is a small public park that runs from the Strip itself back west to the T-Mobile Arena, home to the city's first professional sports franchise, the Las Vegas Golden Knights hockey team. Along the way, The Park offers natural touches such as desert vegetation and rock from local quarries. It also has features such as a water wall, shade structures made to look like trees, and a 60-foot-tall statue of a dancing naked woman. Restaurants on the New York–New York side offer outdoor seating and games for patrons to play while they relax. On the Monte Carlo side, a brand-new theater (named the Park Theater) provides a new venue for intimate musical concerts. ⊠ *3784 Las Vegas Blvd. S, South Strip* ☏ *702/693–7275* ⊕ *www.theparkvegas.com.*

TAXI!

You're never far from a taxi in Las Vegas, but it's downright impossible to hail a cab on the Strip. Hotels welcome you to their taxi stand lines in the hope that you'll come back and play in their casinos. Ride-sharing services such as Uber and Lyft also are also available; drivers for these services pick up and drop off in the same areas as taxis.

FAMILY **Titanic: The Artifact Exhibition.** Travel down to the bottom of the North Atlantic where the "ship of dreams" rests after grazing an iceberg in 1912. The 25,000-square-foot exhibit inside Luxor Las Vegas includes a replica of guest compartments, the grand staircase, and a promenade deck that movie fans will recognize from a little film by James Cameron. Among the 250 emotionally arresting artifacts: luggage, clothing, a bottle of unopened champagne, and pieces of the ship, including a massive section of the iron hull, complete with bulging rivets and portholes. ⊠ *Luxor Las Vegas, 3900 Las Vegas Blvd. S, South Strip* ☏ *702/262–4000, 800/557–7428* ⊕ *www.luxor.com/entertainment* ⊠ *$32 adults, $24 kids 4–12.*

"Welcome to Fabulous Las Vegas" sign. This neon-and-incandescent sign, in a median of Las Vegas Boulevard south of Mandalay Bay, is one of Sin City's most enduring icons. The landmark dates back to 1959, and was approved for listing on the National Register of Historic Places in 2009. Young Electric Sign Company leases the sign to Clark County but the design itself was never copyrighted, and currently exists in the public domain. (This, of course, explains why you see so many likenesses all over town.) The parking lot in the median just south of the sign was expanded in 2015. If you prefer to go on foot, expect a 10-minute walk from Mandalay Bay. ⊠ *5100 Las Vegas Blvd. S, South Strip* ⊠ *Free.*

CENTER STRIP

Dining
★★★★★
Sightseeing
★★★★★
Shopping
★★★★★
Nightlife
★★★★★

It's fitting that this part of the Strip comprises the heart of today's Las Vegas. Even before the $8.5-billion CityCenter project was completed, this stretch captured the American consciousness like no other. It is, quite literally, where modern Vegas was born.

It began with the Flamingo more than 70 years ago, then The Mirage ushered in the age of the modern megaresort in the late 1980s. That renaissance gained momentum with Bellagio and snowballed from there. Today the stretch includes other classics such as Caesars Palace and Bally's, as well as thematic wonders such as Paris and Planet Hollywood. The centerpiece is, fittingly, CityCenter, a city-within-the-city that includes everything from public art to apartment-style living and more. Then, of course, there's the relative new kid on the block: the über-hip Cosmopolitan of Las Vegas.

There's no shortage of spectacles in this part of town. From the fountains in front of Aria and Bellagio to the Eiffel Tower at Paris and the volcano in front of The Mirage, the Center Strip truly is a feast for the eyes. Art is on display here as well; CityCenter has a $42-million public art collection for visitors to enjoy, and Bellagio has one of the most highly regarded galleries in town. Another popular pastime: shopping. A day of exploration here should include strolls through vast retail destinations such as Crystals, Miracle Mile, and The Forum Shops—all of which offer some of the finest boutiques and shops in the United States.

No visit to the Center Strip would be complete without a little pool time. For an intimate vibe, check out the Cosmopolitan's eighth-floor pool deck that looks down on the Strip. To live like royalty, check out the seven-pool Garden of the Gods Pool Oasis at Caesars Palace. Reclining on a lounger, soaking up the sun, you'll be experiencing Vegas the way countless others have over the years. The more things change, apparently, the more they stay the same.

GETTING HERE AND AROUND

CityCenter makes the Center Strip challenging to navigate; at some point, almost all pedestrian traffic along the west side of Strip must go near or through the Crystals Retail & Entertainment Center. Another bottleneck: the fountains at Bellagio, especially on weekend evenings when the biggest crowds gather. One way to avoid these backups is to take advantage of the Las Vegas Monorail between Monte Carlo and Bellagio. If you're traveling by cab, expect anywhere from 15 to 20 minutes to the airport, and 10 to 15 minutes to get to other parts of town.

Las Vegas Monorail stations here include the Bally's/Paris station, Flamingo/Caesars Palace station, and farthest north, the Harrah's/LINQ station. RTC services this part of the Strip with public buses and double-deckers (⇨ *see also Bus Travel in Travel Smart*).

TOP ATTRACTIONS

Aria. Glistening like a futuristic oasis in the heart of the Strip, Aria is a modern spin on the Las Vegas casino of old. Its soaring, three-story atrium is bathed in natural light (a novel concept in this town). The casino has windows, too. Many onlookers come to marvel at the artwork in the atrium, including Maya Lin's *Colorado River,* an 84-foot sculpture of reclaimed silver that mirrors the route of the eponymous waterway and hangs in the lobby behind the check-in desk. Much like the gardens at properties such as Bellagio and Wynn, the floral arrangements here change with the seasons. Other remarkable attractions include restaurant offerings on the Mezzanine, as well as the design of the high-limit rooms, which are masked from the rest of the casino by opaque stained glass. Aria remains one of the largest buildings in the world to achieve LEED Gold certification from the U.S. Green Building Council. ⊠ *3730 Las Vegas Blvd. S, City Center* ☎ *866/359–7757* ⊕ *www.aria.com.*

FAMILY
Fodor'sChoice
★
Bellagio Conservatory and Botanical Gardens. The flowers, trees, and other plants in Bellagio's soaring atrium are fresh and alive, grown in a 5-acre greenhouse. The artistic floral arrangements and ornamental landscaping here is breathtaking. Displays change each season, and the lighted holiday displays in December (for Christmas) and January (for Chinese New Year) are particularly dramatic. Live musical performances take place in the South Garden daily from 5 to 6 pm. ⊠ *Bellagio Las Vegas, 3600 Las Vegas Blvd. S, Center Strip* ☎ *702/693–7111, 888/987–6667* ⊕ *www.bellagio.com/attractions* ⊡ *Free.*

Bellagio Gallery of Fine Art. This gallery—one of the last of its kind inside Strip hotels—originally was curated from Bellagio founder Steve Wynn's private collection. Today, with Wynn long gone, the gallery operates independently, bringing in traveling exhibits from some of the most famous art museums in the world. Recent shows have featured works by Georgia O'Keeffe, Andy Warhol, and Claude Monet. But you're just as likely to see works by Picasso, Hopper, and others. Guides lead a daily tour at 2 pm. Also, once a month, the gallery pours select wines from Bellagio's cellar, and patrons can interact with the hotel's director of wine. ⊠ *Bellagio Las Vegas, 3600 Las Vegas Blvd. S, Center Strip* ☎ *702/693–7871, 877/957–9777* ⊕ *www.bellagio.com/attractions* ⊡ *$18.*

2

Fodor'sChoice ★ **Bellagio Las Vegas.** Sightseers come to Bellagio for three main reasons: the fountains out front, the Dale Chihuly installation of glass flowers in the lobby, and the conservatory gardens. Any one of these attractions is worth the trip. All three make the casino resort a must-see. The fountains are a spectacle in and of themselves: 1,200 jets in all, streaming and bursting in a choreographed water ballet across the man-made Bellagio lake. The conservatory gardens are particularly stunning during Christmas and Chinese New Year. The glass flowers are pretty amazing, as well; the sculpture is named Fiori di Como, and it continues to inspire almost two decades after it was created. But there are other reasons to spend some time at Las Vegas's first real destination resort. For starters, with restaurants from Michael Mina, Jean-Gorges Vong-erichten, and Julian Serrano, Bellagio still has one of the best restaurant rosters in town. Then, of course, there's the chocolate fountain from Jean-Philippe Maury; this is one of the largest of its kind in the world, and there's almost always a line to watch how it works. Finally, the Bellagio contains numerous luxe boutiques with names like Chanel, Dior, and Gucci. ⊠ *3600 Las Vegas Blvd. S, Center Strip* ☎ *888/987–6667* ⊕ *www.bellagio.com.*

Caesars Palace. The opulent entrance, fountains, Roman statuary, bas-reliefs, and roaming centurions all add up to the iconic, over-the-top Las Vegas hotel. Here you can get your picture taken with Caesar, Cleopatra, and the centurion guard; find the full-size reproduction of Michelangelo's *David*; or amble along Roman streetscapes in The Forum Shops to see replicas of iconic fountains from Italy. Vegas history is alive and well here, too, with the iconic main porte cochere and the old-school casino with crystal chandeliers. Renovations to the sports book in 2016 made the place more intimate, even though Caesars still has the largest-big screen in town. Shopping here, at The Forum Shops, is among the best in the city (especially considering the prevalence of animatronic shows). The hotel's pool complex, dubbed Garden of the Gods Pool Oasis, is arguably the nicest set-up on the Strip. ⊠ *3570 Las Vegas Blvd. S, Center Strip* ☎ *866/227–5938* ⊕ *www.caesars.com.*

CityCenter Fine Art Collection. CityCenter includes $42 million in public art. Pieces range from sculptures to paintings and elaborate fountains. Our favorite: *Big Edge*, an amalgam of kayaks and canoes by Nancy Rubins. ⊠ *CityCenter, Las Vegas Blvd. S, Center Strip* ⊕ *www.aria.com.*

Fodor'sChoice ★ **The Cosmopolitan of Las Vegas.** The Cosmopolitan is a truly different Las Vegas resort experience—a blend of arty sophistication and comfortable elegance. This is evidenced by the digital artwork on the columns near the registration desk, as well as the vending machines with wood-block paintings from local artists (the paintings are $5 apiece). Don't miss The Chandelier, a three-story bar that, as the name suggests, sits inside a giant chandelier. Mareina Mercer, the property mixologist, is an expert in edible cocktails and comes out with a brand-new menu for the bar twice a year. Elsewhere on property, hipsters love Marquee nightclub and dayclub. A slate of restaurants includes offerings from Scott Conant (Scarpetta, D.O.C.G.), José Andreas (Jaleo, China Poblano), and Costas Spilidas (Estiatorio Milos). There's also a Momofuku and a Momofuku Milk Bar, both of which have cult followings from

DID YOU KNOW?

One of the best places to view the Bellagio's famous dancing fountains is from the Eiffel Tower's observation deck, directly across the street.

across the country. Shopping at Cosmopolitan also is second to none. One-of-a-kind boutiques include Stitched (men's clothes), Retrospecs & Co. (eyewear), and CRSVR (sneakers). ✉ *3708 Las Vegas Blvd. S, Center Strip* ☎ *702/698–7000* ⊕ *www.cosmopolitanlasvegas.com.*

FAMILY **Fountains of Bellagio.** At least once on your visit you should stop in front
Fodor'sChoice of Bellagio to view its dazzling water ballet from start to finish. The
★ dazzling fountains stream from more than 1,000 nozzles, accompanied by 4,500 lights, in 27 million gallons of water. Fountain jets shoot 250 feet in the air, tracing undulations you wouldn't have thought possible, in near-perfect time with music ranging from Bocelli and the Beatles to "Billie Jean" and tunes from (DJ) Tiësto. Some of the best views are from the Eiffel Tower's observation deck, directly across the street (unless you've got a north-facing balcony room at the Cosmopolitan). Paris and Planet Hollywood have restaurants with patios on the Strip that also offer good views. ✉ *Bellagio, 3600 Las Vegas Blvd. S, Center Strip* ☎ *888/987–6667, 702/693–7111* ⊕ *www.bellagio.com/attractions.*

FAMILY **The High Roller.** Standing more than 100 feet taller than the iconic Lon-
Fodor'sChoice don Eye, the High Roller opened in 2014 as the largest observation
★ wheel in the world. The giant Ferris wheel at the east end of the LINQ features 28 glass-enclosed cabins, each of which is equipped to hold up to 40 passengers. One full rotation takes about 30 minutes; along the way, riders are treated to a dynamic video and music show on TV monitors in the pod, as well as one-of-a-kind views of Sin City and the surrounding Las Vegas Valley. The experience begins and ends in a state-of-the-art wheelhouse, where visitors can read about the engineering behind the project as they wait in line, buy drinks to take with them on the ride, or pick up souvenirs commemorating the spin. The best time to ride the wheel is nighttime, when 2,000 LED lights on the wheel itself create an otherworldly vibe. ✉ *3545 Las Vegas Blvd. S, Center Strip* ☎ *800/223–7277* ⊕ *www.caesars.com/linq/high-roller.html* 🎫 *$22–$47, depending on time of day.*

FAMILY **LINQ Promenade.** Yes, the name is confusing, but the LINQ Promenade, the shopping, dining, and entertainment complex between the Flamingo and the LINQ Hotel, is worth the trip. Some of the notable attractions include Sprinkles, where visitors can purchase cupcakes from an "ATM"; Purple Zebra, a Mecca to frozen margaritas; and Brooklyn Bowl, which is one-part bowling alley, one-part live music venue. Of course, there's also a new iteration of O'Shea's, the Irish-themed casino that was razed to create the new streetcape. The big draw, however, is the **High Roller,** a 550-foot-tall observation wheel with spectacular views of the city. ✉ *3545 Las Vegas Blvd. S, Center Strip* ☎ *800/223–7277* ⊕ *www.caesars.com/linq.*

Mandarin Oriental, Las Vegas. Most of the Mandarin Oriental's best features are open only to hotel guests. Still, one of the hotel's iconic experiences, the 23rd-floor Mandarin Bar, is open to all. Go for afternoon tea, and enjoy champagne and finger sandwiches as you watch the Strip play out below. Also worth experiencing: Twist, a fancy restaurant from Pierre Gagnaire, the father of modern fusion. ✉ *3752 Las Vegas Blvd. S, Center Strip* ☎ *702/590–8888* ⊕ *www.mandarinoriental.com/lasvegas.*

GREAT WALKS: CENTER STRIP

See the Fountains: Catch the dancing fountains outside Bellagio. Showtimes (basically) are every half hour. It's best to go at night, when the fountains are illuminated with spotlights. Total time: 20–30 minutes.

Retail Therapy: Start by circling the stores in Crystals at CityCenter, then hit the Miracle Mile Shops at Planet Hollywood. Stroll through the Grand Bazaar Shops in front of Bally's. Then, to wrap things up, cross the street and explore The Forum Shops at Caesars Palace. Total time: three hours, depending on stops and dressing-room time.

Molten Fun: The Mirage's volcano is worth a gander, but the best views are from the opposite side of the Strip. From the LINQ, head north and stop in front of the Casino Royale. It's best to go at night, when the "lava" glows like the real stuff. Total time: 25 minutes.

FAMILY **Mirage Las Vegas.** When Steve Wynn opened the Mirage in 1989, the $630-million property was the most expensive resort-casino in history; the hotel's distinctive gold windows got their color from actual gold used in the tinting process. Today the main attractions are *The Beatles: LOVE from Cirque du Soleil*, the dolphins at Siegfried & Roy's Secret Garden & Dolphin Habitat, and the volcano with breathtaking fire effects and music composed by Grateful Dead drummer Mickey Hart. Inside the casino, the sports book remains one of Vegas's finest. ✉ *3400 Las Vegas Blvd. S, Center Strip* ☎ *702/791–1111, 800/374–9000* ⊕ *www.mirage.com.*

FAMILY **Paris Las Vegas.** At this homage to the City of Light, replicas of the Arc de Triomphe, Paris Opera House, Hôtel de Ville, and Louvre, along with an *Around the World in Eighty Days* balloon marquee, are magnifique, but the crowning achievement is the 50-story, half-scale replica of the Eiffel Tower where guests are whisked 460 feet to the top for spectacular views of the Valley. Let go as an audience member of the *Anthony Cools Experience*, where volunteers are hypnotized to utterly hilarious and unpredictable effect. For a less intrusive escape, look up at the ceiling painted like a sky with clouds and pretend you're actually in France. ✉ *3655 Las Vegas Blvd. S, Center Strip* ☎ *702/946–7000, 877/796–2096* ⊕ *www.parislasvegas.com.*

Planet Hollywood Resort & Casino. Everything at Planet Hollywood is designed to make ordinary people feel like stars. Perhaps the main attraction in recent years: *Piece of Me,* a rollicking residency show from one of pop music's biggest names, Britney Spears. Because the property is obsessed with celebrities, it often hosts world-premiere events that attract stars from all over the world. There's something for everybody in the on-site Miracle Mile Shops, including clothing stores, restaurants, and more. Just be sure you bring a map, as the corridors of the mall wind around in circles and it's easy to get lost. ✉ *3667 Las Vegas Blvd. S, Center Strip* ☎ *702/785–5555, 866/919–7472* ⊕ *www. planethollywoodresort.com.*

2

FAMILY **Siegfried & Roy's Secret Garden & Dolphin Habitat.** The palm-shaded sanc-
Fodor's Choice tuary has a collection of the planet's rarest and most exotic creatures.
★ Animals are rotated regularly, but at any time you're likely to see
white tigers, as well as lions, a snow leopard, and more. Atlantic
bottlenose dolphins swim around in a 2.5-million-gallon saltwater
tank at the Dolphin Habitat. Pass through the underwater observation
station to the video room, where you can watch tapes of two dolphin
births at the habitat. In addition to the regular admission, there are
VIP edu-tours as well as a paint-with-the-dolphins experience, and a
deluxe trainer-for-a-day program. Spa patrons also can sign up for
an hour-long yoga class near the dolphin pool. ⊠ *The Mirage, 3400
Las Vegas Blvd. S, Center Strip* ☎ *702/791–7111* ⊕ *www.mirage.com/
attractions* ⤳ *$22.*

FAMILY **Volcano at Mirage.** This erupting volcano, a 54-foot mountain-fountain
surrounded by a lake of miniature fire spouts, is a must-see free attraction on the Strip. Two or three times a night the whole area erupts
in flames, smoke, and eerily backlit water that looks like lava. The
thundering island percussion sound track was created by Grateful
Dead drummer Mickey Hart. The best vantage point is near the main
drive entrance, or on the east side of Las Vegas Boulevard in front of
Casino Royale. ⊠ *The Mirage, 3400 Las Vegas Blvd. S, Center Strip*
☎ *702/791–7111* ⊕ *www.mirage.com/attractions* ⤳ *Free.*

WORTH NOTING

FAMILY **The Auto Collections.** Collectively billed as the "world's largest classic car
showroom," the 100 or so antique, classic, and special-interest vehicles
at this attraction on the fifth floor of the self-park garage of the LINQ
will keep gearheads entertained for hours. All the vehicles on the lot
are for sale, so the collection is constantly changing (there are about
250 cars in all). At any given time you might see "famous" cars, like
the Trans Am that acted as the pace car at the 1983 Daytona 500, or
cars that once belonged to famous people, like the '39 Chrysler the
late Johnny Carson rode in to his senior prom. Many of the cars are
just vintage rides: a supercharged '57 T-Bird, or the immaculate '29
Rolls-Royce Springfield Phantom I straight out of *The Great Gatsby.*
■ TIP➜ **Buy-One-Get-One admission coupons are available online.**
⊠ *The LINQ, 3535 Las Vegas Blvd. S, Center Strip* ☎ *702/794–3174*
⊕ *www.autocollections.com* ⤳ *$12.95* ☉ *Closed Sun.*

FAMILY **The Wildlife Habitat.** Just next to the pool area at Flamingo Las Vegas, a
flamboyance of live Chilean flamingos lives on islands and in streams
surrounded by sparkling waterfalls and lush foliage. Other animals on-
site include swans, ducks, koi, goldfish, pelicans, hummingbirds, and
turtles. The small habitat makes for a fun, brief stroll. Be sure not to
miss the daily pelican feeding at 10 am. ⊠ *Flamingo Las Vegas, 3555
Las Vegas Blvd. S, Center Strip* ☎ *702/733–3349* ⊕ *www.flamingolas-
vegas.com* ⤳ *Free.*

NORTH STRIP

Dining
★★★★★
Sightseeing
★★★★
Shopping
★★★★★
Nightlife
★★★★★

Like the best nights out, the North Strip is the perfect mix of luxury, fun, and debauchery—a blend of the very best that Vegas has to offer in high-end, low-brow, and laugh-out-loud diversion. Wynn, Encore, The Palazzo, and The Venetian are posh celebrity favorites. Carnival acts at Circus Circus and thrill rides at the Stratosphere entertain the masses. In between, SLS Las Vegas is where hipsters go to party.

Sister properties dominate the landscape in this part of town—resorts that complement each other wonderfully. One pair, The Venetian and The Palazzo, whisks visitors to Italy, where they can ride gondolas and marvel at indoor waterfalls. Another pair, Wynn and Encore, offer a different kind of luxury, one that Steve Wynn himself has sharpened after years in the business (and is expected to sharpen again in the coming years). Encore in particular is a one-of-a-kind blend of classic (authentic antiques pervade the property) and modern (windows in the casino). Also not to be missed: the Encore Beach Club, a thumping day-lounge experience.

Farther north, this part of the Strip embraces the circus. In the Adventuredome, behind Circus Circus, visitors can participate in an actual carnival, complete with cotton candy and midway games. On top of the Stratosphere tower the attractions aren't for the faint of heart, considering that they suspend you about 900 feet over the ground.

The North Strip has improved on a number of familiar Vegas experiences, too. Circus acts at Circus Circus are as campy as ever, and the "sports book" at Palazzo doubles as a casual restaurant from Emeril Lagasse. The North Strip presents a number of familiar sights; it just does them better.

GETTING HERE AND AROUND

The North Strip is far enough from the airport (up to 30 minutes) that if a cabby opts to take the interstate, it's probably not worth arguing for him to change course. A pedestrian bridge between The Palazzo and Wynn makes exploring these two properties easy. The journey from Trump and Encore to SLS, Circus Circus, and the Stratosphere is deceptively long; on hot days, it pays to take a cab or public transportation. Be warned: on foot from the Stratosphere, it's still 20 to 30 minutes to Downtown. And it's not the best neighborhood.

Las Vegas Monorail stations here include the Harrah's/LINQ station, the Las Vegas Convention Center station, the LVH station, and the SLS Vegas station. RTC services this part of the Strip with public buses and double-deckers (⇨ *see also Bus Travel in Travel Smart*).

TOP ATTRACTIONS

Fodor's Choice
★

Encore. Though smaller than its neighbor, Wynn Las Vegas, Encore pulls together some of the best touches from all of Wynn's. For that we owe thanks to Designer Roger Thomas, who invested in antiques from all over the world to decorate the resort. The other notable design element: sunlight, which streams in through window-lined corridors (a relative rarity in Vegas). Most people come to Encore for the partying, specifically the partying at Encore Beach Club, Surrender, and XS. A modest but beautiful shopping strip, the Esplanade at Encore, features Hermès, Chanel, and the first-ever Rock & Republic store. ⊠ *3131 Las Vegas Blvd. S, North Strip* ☎ *702/770–7000, 888/320–7123* ⊕ *www.encorelasvegas.com.*

The Palazzo Hotel Resort and Casino. The Palazzo certainly feels palatial. Wide, cavernous corridors give way to an expansive casino, which, in turn, fronts escalators to the Shoppes at Palazzo, a shopping area with 50 boutiques and a Barnes New York. Theater lovers flock to the property to experience *Baz,* the latest show from famed director Baz Luhrmann. The sports book doubles as a restaurant from Chef Emeril Lagasse, and, not surprisingly, it's got the best food of any book in town. With a top-quality energy conservation program and other green amenities, Palazzo has received LEED-Gold distinction from the U.S. Green Building Council. ⊠ *3325 Las Vegas Blvd. S, North Strip* ☎ *702/607–7777, 866/263–3001* ⊕ *www.palazzo.com.*

FAMILY
Fodor's Choice
★

Stratosphere Tower Rides. High above the Strip at the tip of the Stratosphere Tower are four major thrill rides that will scare the bejeezus out of you, especially if you have even the slightest fear of heights. Don't even think about heading up here if you have serious vertigo. People have been known to get sick just watching these rides. That said, hotel guests get complimentary admission to the Tower itself.

The **Big Shot** would be a monster ride on the ground, but starting from the 112th floor—and climaxing at more than 1,000 feet above the Strip—makes it twice as wild. Four riders are strapped into chairs on four sides of the needle, which rises from the Stratosphere's observation pod. With little warning, you're flung 160 feet up the needle at 45 mph, then dropped like a rock. The whole thing is over in less than a minute, but your knees will wobble for the rest of the day.

GREAT WALKS: NORTH STRIP

Viva Italy: The Strip has plenty of Italy to explore. To immerse yourself, stroll the canals around The Venetian's shops, then follow signs toward Barneys New York and The Palazzo. All told, you never have to step outside. Total time: 45 minutes.

Wynn Nature: Conservatory gardens in both Wynn Las Vegas and Encore feature seasonal flowers and trees—both rarities in the middle of the Las Vegas desert. To care for this greenery, Steve Wynn employs more than 50 gardeners. Total time: 40 minutes.

Mall and Trump: On superhot days, avoid the sun with a stroll through Fashion Show mall, then Uber to SLS for a few hours at the Foxtail Pool Club at SLS. Total time: 45 minutes.

The **X Scream** tips passengers 27 feet over the edge of the tower like a giant seesaw again and again. Sit in the very front to get an unobstructed view of the Strip, more than 800 feet straight down!

Another unobstructed view can be seen by dangling over the edge of the tower off the arm of **Insanity**. The arm pivots and hangs you out 64 feet from the edge of the tower; then it spins you faster and faster, so you're lifted to a 70-degree angle by a centrifugal force that's the equivalent of 3 g-forces.

The newest ride, **SkyJump Las Vegas,** is a controlled free fall that sends you careening off the side of the 108th floor. ⊠ *Stratosphere Tower, 2000 Las Vegas Blvd. S, North Strip* ☎ *702/380–7777* ⊕ *www. stratospherehotel.com/activities/thrill-rides* 🎟 *Tower $20; Big Shot, XScream, or Insanity $5 apiece; SkyJump $119 and up; unlimited rides (other than SkyJump) and tower day pass $36.*

Fodor'sChoice   **Vegas Indoor Skydiving.** This attraction, just north of Encore Las Vegas,
★   provides the thrill of skydiving without a plane. After 20 minutes of training you enter a vertical wind tunnel that produces a powerful stream of air. You'll float, hover, and fly, simulating three minutes of free fall. Airspeeds reach 120 mph. You can make reservations a minimum of 48 hours in advance for parties of five or more. The place closes for private parties from time to time, so it's wise to call ahead. ⊠ *200 Convention Center Dr., North Strip* ☎ *702/731–4768, 877/588–2359* ⊕ *www.vegasindoorskydiving.com* 🎟 *$75 for 1st flight, $50 per repeat flight.*

FAMILY   **Venetian Gondola Rides.** Let a gondolier "o sole mio" you down Vegas's rendition of Venice's Canalozzo. We love this attraction because it's done so well—owner Sheldon Adelson was obsessed with getting the canals *just right*: he had them drained and repainted three times before he was satisfied with the hue, and the colossal reproduction of St. Mark's Square at the end of the canal is authentic right down to the colors of the façades. The gondoliers who ply the waterway are professional entertainers and train for two weeks to maneuver the canals. It all makes for a rather entertaining way to while away an hour on the Strip. Outdoor gondola rides along the resort's exterior waterway are also available, weather permitting. Photo packages are available with all rides. ⊠ *The Venetian Las Vegas, 3355 Las Vegas Blvd. S, North Strip* ☎ *702/414–4300* ⊕ *www.venetian.com* ✉ *$29 per person in a 4-seater or $116 for a private 2-seater; photo packages from $22.*

The Venetian Las Vegas. This theme hotel re-creates Italy's most romantic city with meticulous reproductions of Venetian landmarks. As such, this gilded resort is a hit with foodies, shoppers, and high rollers alike. From the Strip you enter through the Doge's Palace, which stands on a walkway over a large lagoon. Inside, Renaissance characters roam the public areas, singing opera, performing mime, jesting, even kissing hands. Walking from the hotel lobby into the casino is one of the great experiences in Las Vegas: overhead, reproductions of famous frescoes adorn the ceiling; underfoot, the geometric design of the flat marble floor provides an Escher-like optical illusion of climbing stairs. On a lake in front of the casino visitors can take gondola rides and look out on the Strip; gondola rides also are available in the canals that adorn the Grand Canal Shoppes upstairs. The Venetian is known for its restaurant scene (hello, Mario Batali!), and the latest bar project, The Dorsey, has gotten rave reviews for its bourbon specialty. ⊠ *3355 Las Vegas Blvd. S, North Strip* ☎ *702/414–1000, 866/659–9643* ⊕ *www.venetian.com.*

Fodor's Choice ★ **Wynn Las Vegas.** In a city that keeps raising the bar for sheer luxury, the Wynn—monolithic in both name and appearance—offers a discreet turn for the tasteful. The resort is a best-of-everything experience—a playground for jet-setters, high rollers, or anyone who wants to feel like one. This excellence starts with the gardens near the front entrance; though smaller than Bellagio's, they are just as exquisite. It continues with the waterfall that pours from (man-made) rocks into a interior lake, both visible from the Parasol Up and Parasol Down lounges. Instead of booking another Cirque du Soleil show, Wynn created *ShowStoppers,* a new song-and-dance show that covers Broadway classics. On-site restaurants are just as appealing, with Wing Lei holding firm as one of the best Chinese restaurants in the entire city. High-end shopping options at Wynn Esplanade include Virtu, and LVNV, Wynn's own home furnishings brand. ⊠ *3131 Las Vegas Blvd. S, North Strip* ☎ *702/770–7000, 888/320–7123* ⊕ *www.wynnlasvegas.com.*

WORTH NOTING

FAMILY **Adventuredome Theme Park.** If the sun is blazing, the kids are antsy, and you need a place to while away a few hours, make for the big pink dome behind Circus Circus. The 5-acre amusement park has more than 25 rides and attractions for all age levels, and is kept at a constant 72°F. The newest roller coaster, El Loco, opened in 2014 and includes a barrel roll and a number of g-force drops. Also check out the Canyon Blaster, the world's largest indoor double-loop roller coaster, a huge swinging pirate ship, bumper cars, several kiddie rides, a mini-golf course, a laser-tag park, a rock-climbing wall, and much more. There are even attractions with computer-generated iterations of Dora and Diego and

FAMILY FUN

WILD TIMES

This may be Sin City, but there are plenty of great family-oriented activities. There's wildlife galore, starting with exotic birds at **Flamingo** and fish and reptiles at **Shark Reef at Mandalay Bay**. Next, head to **The Mirage** to see the white tigers of the **Secret Garden** and the eponymous mammals of the **Dolphin Habitat**.

FAST TIMES

If your family prefers adrenaline-based bonding, scream your way up the Strip, starting at the **Roller Coaster** at **New York–New York**. Continue north along the Strip (via the Monorail to SLS station), stopping at **Circus Circus**'s indoor theme park **Adventuredome** on your way to the **Stratosphere Tower**. Here the Big Shot, XScream, and Insanity–The Ride fly high above the Strip at 1,149 feet. Can't decide between wild animals and wild rides? Go Downtown for both at the Tank at **Golden Nugget**, where a three-story waterslide includes a ride through a glass tube into the heart of a 200,000-gallon shark tank.

DOWNTIME

For a mellower afternoon, head to The Venetian's **Madame Tussauds Wax Museum**. After posing next to Miley and J-Lo, check out the exploding volcano at **The Mirage**. Since you're at The Mirage, grab last-minute tickets for ventriloquist **Terry Fator**'s one-of-a-kind musical puppet act. You can minimize your kids' sinful intake by staying at the **Mandarin Oriental Las Vegas**, posh accommodations that are unusual for being casino-free.

SpongeBob SquarePants. ⊠ *Circus Circus, 2880 Las Vegas Blvd. S, North Strip* ☎ *702/794–3939, 866/456–8894* ⊕ *www.adventuredome. com* ⊟ *$6–$12 per ride, all-day pass $31.95.*

FAMILY **Madame Tussauds Las Vegas.** Audition in front of Simon Cowell or stand toe-to-toe with Muhammad Ali as you explore the open showroom filled with uncanny celebrity wax portraits from the worlds of show business, sports, politics, and everywhere in between. Crowd-pleasers include Lady Gaga, Tom Jones, Hugh Hefner, Miley Cyrus, Abe Lincoln, and the characters from *The Hangover*. An interactive segment lets you play golf with Tiger Woods, shoot baskets with Shaquille O'Neill, play celebrity poker with Ben Affleck, dance with Britney Spears, or marry George Clooney. Discount tickets are available online. ⊠ *The Venetian Las Vegas, 3377 Las Vegas Blvd. S, North Strip* ✛ *Outside the main hotel entrance* ☎ *866/841–3739* ⊕ *www.madametussauds. com/lasvegas* ⊟ *$17.97–$35.95.*

DOWNTOWN

Dining
★★★
Sightseeing
★★★★
Shopping
★★
Nightlife
★★★

There was a time not so many years ago when Downtown Las Vegas was filled with little more than tired casinos and hotels. Well, that's just not the case any longer. With neon lights—actually, make that a quarter-mile canopy of with 12.5 million synchronized LED modules—single-deck black-jack, and a host of new attractions that spotlight yesteryear (not to mention an influx of new businesses), old Vegas is alive and well Downtown.

This neighborhood revolves around Fremont Street, a covered pedestrian walkway through the heart of the Downtown gambling district. Originally, this attraction was nothing more than a place to stroll; today, however, the canopy sparkles with millions of lights, and outfitters have set up everything from zip lines to band shells on street level down beneath. Use Fremont Street to access resorts such as the Golden Nugget (our fave in this neighborhood), Four Queens, the Plaza Hotel and Casino, and others. Just be prepared for sensory overload.

Old is new again all over Downtown. The Mob Museum, which opened in 2012, pays homage to Las Vegas's Mafia years. Also on 3rd Street, the Downtown Grand has brought back some of the 1950s-era swagger. The Smith Center, a world-class performing arts center that opened in 2012, was designed to invoke the same art deco style that inspired the Hoover Dam. Then, of course, there's the Neon Museum, where visitors can behold the greatness (and, in a few cases, the glow) of original Las Vegas neon signs.

With the Downtown Container Park, Slotzilla and its zip lines, and the new Zappos.com headquarters in the (renovated) old City Hall, Downtown is undergoing an extended renaissance. A vibrant arts-and-mixology scene is emerging—the "First Friday" walkabout celebrates local art and artists on the first Friday of every month, and a burgeoning Arts District attracts fans of the avant-garde from all over the world.

No visit to Downtown Vegas would be complete without a pilgrimage to one of the neighborhood's most lasting legacies: Luv-it Frozen Custard. Flavors here change regularly, but cinnamon and almond chip are mainstays in the rotation. Try some in a homemade waffle cone with chocolate sauce on top.

GETTING HERE AND AROUND

Taxi and public transportation are the easiest ways to get to Downtown from the South, Central, and North strips, but be warned that city buses must stick to Las Vegas Boulevard and often get stuck in terrible traffic around rush hour. Once you're Downtown, everything is walkable. Don't stray from populated areas, and travel in pairs at night. And if you've had too much to drink, it's admirable but not advisable to walk back to the North Strip: it's more than an hour on foot. Best to take a taxi or a ride-share.

TOP ATTRACTIONS

Arts Factory. An intriguing concentration of antiques shops and galleries is found on East Charleston Boulevard and Casino Center Drive, anchored by the Arts Factory. This former warehouse houses studios and galleries for art of all types, including painting, photography, and sculpture. There's also a bistro on-site. The Arts Factory comes alive on "First Friday" with gallery openings, exhibits, receptions, and special events. "Preview Thursday," the day before First Friday, offers the same artwork with fewer crowds. Guided tours available on request (and with reservation). ✉ *107 E. Charleston Blvd., Downtown* ☎ *702/383–3133* ⊕ *www.theartsfactory.com* ⌧ *Free.*

Downtown Arts District. The emergence of the offbeat 18b Arts District (so called because it comprises 18 blocks bounded by South 7th, Main, Bonneville, and Charleston Streets on Downtown's southeastern corner) continues to generate excitement in the city's arts community and, increasingly, among visitors. With a number of funky, independent art galleries in its confines, the area, officially named in 1998, is a growing, thriving cultural hub—think of it as the Anti-Strip. In addition to the galleries—some of which contain impressive collections of locally known and world-famous artists—you'll find interesting eateries and dive bars to serve the alternative artists, musicians, and writers who have gravitated to the neighborhood. Each month the district hosts a First Friday gallery walk from 5 to 11 pm with gallery openings, street performers, and entertainment. It's an excellent time to come check out the still-nascent but steadily improving scene for yourself. ✉ *Downtown.*

Downtown Container Park. It turns out shipping containers—the same kinds you see on cargo ships and tractor trailers—can be pretty versatile. At this open-air mall, for instance, on the outskirts of the Fremont East neighborhood, the structures have been repurposed into food stalls, boutiques, offices, and even a three-story "tree house" complete with grown-up-friendly slides. The place also has an amphitheater stage fronted by real grass. Although the tree house is fun (especially with young kids), the highlight of the attraction is the large, fire-spewing praying mantis, which was originally constructed for use at the Burning Man festival in northern Nevada. The whole spot is part of the $350-million Downtown Project. ⊠ *707 Fremont St., Downtown* ☎ *702/637–4244* ⊕ *www.downtowncontainerpark.com.*

FAMILY **Fremont Street Experience.** If you're looking for something a little different, head to this ear-splitting, eye-popping show that takes place on the underside of a 1,450-foot arched canopy 90 feet overhead. The 12.5 million synchronized LED modules, 180 strobes, and eight robotic mirrors per block treat your eyes, and the 208 speakers combine for 550,000 watts of fun for your ears. The shows play five to seven times a night, depending on the time of year, and the six-minute presentations change regularly. Thrill-seekers can ride one of two zip lines ($) beneath the length of the canopy; the zips emerge from the face of the world's largest slot machine, appropriately dubbed Slotzilla. At street level, "entertainment" includes everything from break-dancers to (creepy) people in furry mascot costumes. ⊠ *Fremont St. from Main St. to 4th St., Downtown* ⊕ *www.vegasexperience.com* ⊠ *Free.*

Gamblers Book Club. This unassuming bookstore near Fremont Street Downtown is heaven for gambling nerds who want to stock up on research material for their next big run at the casino establishment. With more than 3,000 titles in stock, the place dubs itself the "World's Largest Gambling Bookstore," and we wouldn't argue here. Although sections on sports betting and poker are worthwhile, the best offerings spotlight books about Las Vegas history. Time your visit right and you might even score autographed copies of some of your favorite tomes. The store also carries a variety of gambling paraphernalia, including old card decks and dice. ⊠ *800 S. Main St., Downtown* ☎ *702/382–7555, 800/522–1777* ⊕ *www.gamblersbookclub.com.*

Gold & Silver Pawn Shop. Reality television fans flock to this run-of-the-mill pawn shop for a glimpse of owner Rick Harrison and the rest of the staff, all of whom appear regularly on the History Channel's *Pawn Stars* reality television show. On any given night, the line waiting to get in might be 30 or 40 people deep. Inside, dozens of glass cases are chock-full of jewelry, poker chips, and other curios. The merchandise area, which sells everything from G&S T-shirts to G&S shot glasses, is just as spacious. ⊠ *713 Las Vegas Blvd. S, Downtown* ☎ *702/385–7912* ⊕ *www.gspawn.com.*

The Mob Museum. It's fitting that the $42-million Mob Museum sits in the circa-1933 former federal courthouse and U.S. Post Office Downtown; this is where the Kefauver Committee held one of its historic hearings on organized crime in 1950. Today the museum pays homage to Las Vegas's criminal underbelly, explaining to visitors (sometimes with way too much exhibit text) how the Mafia worked, who was involved, how the law brought down local mobsters, and what happened to gangsters once they were caught and incarcerated. Museum highlights include bricks from the wall of the St. Valentine's Day Massacre in 1929, and a mock-up of the electric chair that killed a number of mobsters (as well as spies Julius and Ethel Rosenberg). ⊠ *300 Stewart Ave., Downtown* ☎ *702/229–2734* ⊕ *www.themobmuseum.org* ⊠ *$23.95.*

Exploring Downtown

FAMILY
Fodor's Choice
★

Neon Museum. Consider this Downtown museum the afterlife for old neon signs. The facility, which displays more than 150 signs that date back to the 1930s, opened to the public in 2012 on the site of the old La Concha Motel Downtown. The hotel's iconic lobby was renovated and now serves as the museum's entry point. The sign collection includes the original signs from the Stardust, the Horseshoe, and other properties. To get up close, visitors must take an educational and informative one-hour guided tour. Daytime tours, especially in summer, can be scorching. For an alternative, try one of the nighttime tours, where you can see four of the signs illuminated the way they were intended to be. ✉ *770 Las Vegas Blvd. N, Downtown* ☎ *702/387–6366* ⊕ *www.neonmuseum.org* ✆ *$19* ⚲ *Reservations essential.*

Slotzilla. It wouldn't be Vegas enough to build the world's largest slot machine and just leave it there. Now thrill-seekers can take off from a platform atop the 12-story slot machine and soar over Fremont Street. There are two options to zip: one that averages 70 feet above the ground and a second line that averages 110 feet. If you'd rather just play the big slot machine, you can do that, too. It is Vegas, after all. ✉ *425 Fremont St., Downtown* ⊕ *vegasexperience.com/slotzilla-zip-line* ✆ *$25–$45.*

WORTH NOTING

Antique Collection at Main Street Station. The hotel's collection of antiques, artifacts, and collectibles includes Louisa May Alcott's private railcar, stained glass from the Lillian Russell mansion, bronze doors and façade from the Kuwait Royal Bank, and a variety of Victorian chandeliers. There's even a piece of the Berlin Wall—where else—in the men's room off the lobby. ⊠ *200 N. Main St., Downtown* ☎ *800/713–8933, 702/387–1896* ⊕ *www.mainstreetcasino.com* ✉ *Free.*

FAMILY **DISCOVERY Children's Museum.** The DISCOVERY Children's Museum is one of the most technologically sophisticated children's museums in the entire country. The facility comprises nine themed exhibition halls, all of which are designed to inspire visitors—both children and adults—to learn through play. The star of the show: a 12-story exhibit dubbed "The Summit," with education stations on every level and a lookout that peeks through the building's roof. Parents of the smallest visitors will also love "Toddler Town," an area designed for those who are still crawling or just learning how to walk. ⊠ *360 Promenade Pl., Downtown* ☎ *702/382–5437* ⊕ *www.discoverykidslv.org* ✉ *$14.50* ☉ *Closed Mon.*

Gold Spike. Once a (seedy) casino, the Gold Spike has been resuscitated as part of Tony Hsieh's $350-million Downtown Project. In this case, that means gambling is out and free gaming is in. Gaming, as in shuffleboard, giant versions of Connect Four, and, on the back patio, life-size Jenga and beer pong with soccer balls and garbage pails. There's also a tiny house, which visitors can rent for parties or spend the night in. Sure, at times (especially on Thursdays after dark) it feels like the former casino floor is now a clubhouse for employees of Zappos.com. But the hot spot is open to the public and is becoming a popular place for locals, visitors, and hipsters to hang, too. Especially during weekday Happy Hour. ⊠ *217 Las Vegas Blvd. N, Downtown* ☎ *702/476–4923* ⊕ *www.goldspike.com* ✉ *Free.*

FAMILY **Las Vegas Natural History Museum.** If your kids are into animals (or taxidermy), they'll love this museum, where every continent and geological age is represented. You're greeted by a 35-foot-tall roaring T. rex in the dinosaur gallery that features Shonisaurus, Nevada's state fossil. From there, you can enjoy rooms full of sharks (including live ones, swimming in a 3,000-gallon reef tank), birds, cavemen, and scenes from the African savanna. Kids especially enjoy the various hands-on exhibits; the Young Scientist Center offers youngsters the opportunity to investigate fossils and animal tracks up close. After that, tour the Wild Nevada Gallery, where kids can see, smell, and even touch Nevada wildlife. Two-for-one ticket coupons are available online. ⊠ *900 Las Vegas Blvd. N, Downtown* ☎ *702/384–3466* ⊕ *www.lvnhm.org* ✉ *$10.*

FAMILY **Old Las Vegas Mormon Fort.** Southern Nevada's oldest historic site was built by Mormons in 1855 to give refuge to travelers along the Salt Lake–Los Angeles trail, many of whom were bound for the California goldfields. Left to Native Americans after the gold rush, the adobe fort was later revitalized by a miner and his partners. In 1895 it was turned into a resort, and the city's first swimming pool was constructed by damming Las Vegas Creek. Today the restored fort contains more than half the original bricks. Antiques and artifacts help to re-create a turn-of-the-20th-century Mormon living room. ⊠ *500 E. Washington Ave., Downtown* ☎ *702/486–3511* ⊕ *parks.nv.gov/parks/old-las-vegas-mormon-fort* ⊡ *$1.*

FAMILY **Springs Preserve.** This 180-acre complex defies traditional categories, combining botanical gardens, hiking trails, live animal exhibits, and an ultramodern interactive museum. The overarching theme of the facility is the rich diversity and delicate balance of nature in southern Nevada's deserts. Kids love the simulations of the flash-flood ravine, the re-created Southern Paiute Indian village (complete with grass huts!), and the trackless train, aboard which an engineer explains the role trains played in settling the West. The NV Energy Foundation Sustainability Gallery teaches about eco-friendly living, and a 2016 addition, Boomtown 1905, re-creates a streetscape designed to evoke turn-of-the-20th-century Vegas. There are also a few miles of walking trails that swing you by archaeological sites and may—if you're lucky—bring you face-to-face with some of the local fauna such as bats, peregrine falcons, and Gila monsters. The Springs Café provides famished eco-explorers with sustainable choices, like ethically raised cheeseburgers and environmentally mindful salads. The **Nevada State Museum,** with its famous fossil Ichthyosaur and a number of exhibits on local mining, is on the site (and included with admission) as well. ⊠ *333 S. Valley View Blvd., Downtown* ☎ *702/822–7700* ⊕ *www.springspreserve.org* ⊡ *$18.95.*

Vegas Vic. The 50-foot-tall neon cowboy outside the Pioneer Club has been waving to Las Vegas visitors since 1947 (though, truth be told, he had a makeover and was replaced by a newer version in 1951). His neon sidekick, Vegas Vicki, went up across the street in 1980. ⊠ *Fremont St. at N. 1st St., Downtown.*

PARADISE ROAD AND THE EAST SIDE

Dining
★★★
Sightseeing
★★
Shopping
★
Nightlife
★★★

The East Side of Las Vegas, an area that includes Paradise Road and stretches to the University District, is as eclectic as it is convenient. Much of the area is residential, save for a handful of (older) resorts. There is also a preponderance of restaurants, extensive medical offices, and most of the area's collegiate athletic facilities.

Paradise Road itself is the Strip's sister street. On the southern end the Hard Rock Hotel & Casino is one of the most popular off-Strip resorts in town, and has remained popular over the years. A number of other resorts, such as the Platinum, qualify as nongaming, but are still within walking distance of larger casinos. This stretch also comprises the heart of the area affectionately known as "Fruit Loop," Vegas's gay-friendly neighborhood. Especially on Friday and Saturday nights, the parties at the Piranha Nightclub (and other hot spots) are some of the biggest raves in town.

Though there aren't any resorts in the University District, UNLV (University of Las Vegas) and the Thomas and Mack Center provide plenty of things to see and do, from sporting events to (on-campus) museums and more. As with most college towns, the cost of living in this neck of the woods is considerably lower than it is elsewhere in town. In other words, you can find cheap meals and beer for less than $6.

GETTING HERE AND AROUND

Public transportation from the Strip to the East Side is actually pretty reliable, so long as you're not traveling in the middle of the night. Taxis know the area well, too, especially if you're heading from the Strip over to the Hard Rock or into the University District. As is the case with most of the Vegas suburbs, the best bets here are to opt for ride-sharing services or to rent a car.

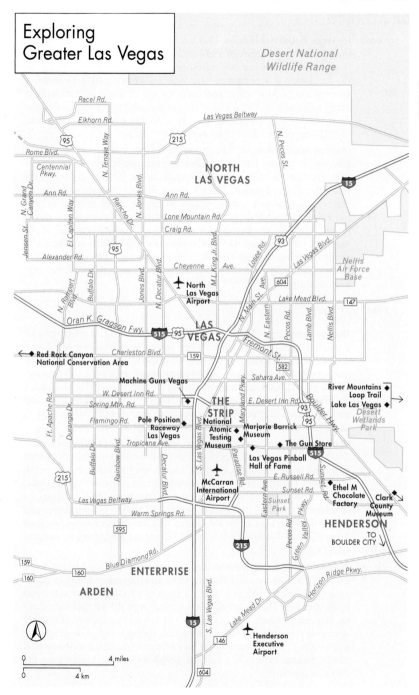

Exploring Greater Las Vegas

2

Desert National
Wildlife Range

Racel Rd.

Elkhorn Rd.

Las Vegas Beltway

95

215

N. Pecos St.

Rome Blvd.

Centennial
Pkwy.

N. Grand
Canyon Dr.

N. Tenaya Way

Jensen St.

El Capitan Way

Rancho Dr.

N. Jones Blvd.

N. Decatur Blvd.

**NORTH
LAS VEGAS**

15

Ann Rd.

Ann Rd.

Lone Mountain Rd.

Craig Rd.

M.L. King Jr. Blvd.

Losee Rd.

93

Las Vegas Blvd.

Alexander Rd.

95

Cheyenne Ave.

604

Nellis
Air Force
Base

N. Rampart
Blvd.

Buffalo Dr.

Jones Blvd.

North
Las Vegas
Airport

N. Main St. Ave.

N. Eastern Ave.

Pecos Rd.

Lamb Blvd.

Nellis Blvd.

Lake Mead Blvd.

147

Oran K. Gragson Fwy.

515 95

**LAS
VEGAS**

Fremont St.

Charleston Blvd.

159

582

← Red Rock Canyon
National Conservation Area

Sahara Ave.

River Mountains ◆
Loop Trail
Lake Las Vegas ◆

Machine Guns Vegas ◆

W. Desert Inn Rd.

Spring Mtn. Rd.

**THE
STRIP**

Maryland Pkwy.

E. Desert Inn Rd.

Boulder Hwy.

93

95

Desert
Wetlands
Park

Ft. Apache Rd.

Durango Dr.

Flamingo Rd.

Pole Position ◆
Raceway
Las Vegas

Tropicana Ave.

National ◆
Atomic
Testing
Museum

Marjorie Barrick ◆
Museum

◆ The Gun Store

515

Buffalo Dr.

Rainbow Blvd.

Decatur Blvd.

S. Las Vegas Blvd.

Paradise Rd.

Las Vegas Pinball
Hall of Fame

E. Russell Rd.

◆ Ethel M
Chocolate
Factory

Clark
County
Museum

215

McCarran
International
Airport

Eastern Ave.

Sunset Ave.

Sunset Rd.

Sunset Rd.

Pecos Rd.

Green Valley Pkwy.

HENDERSON

Las Vegas Beltway

Warm Springs Rd.

595

Sunset
Park

TO
BOULDER CITY ↓

Blue Diamond Rd.

ENTERPRISE

Horizon Ridge Pkwy.

159

160

160

ARDEN

Lake Mead Dr.

S. Las Vegas Blvd.

15

146

✈ Henderson
Executive
Airport

604

0 _____ 4 miles
0 _____ 4 km

TOP ATTRACTIONS

FAMILY **Las Vegas Pinball Hall of Fame.** This fun facility has more than 200 games that were created between 1947 to 2009, including the old wood-rail models. Though it may sound more like an arcade than a museum, the local club is a nonprofit organization whose goal is to preserve these pieces of Americana and share the joy of the silver ball with as many folks as possible. All quarters get donated to the local Salvation Army. ⊠ *1610 E. Tropicana Ave., East Side* ⊕ *www.pinballmuseum. org* 🖃 *Free entry, 25¢ or 50¢ per game.*

FAMILY **Marjorie Barrick Museum.** This museum on the University of Nevada Las Vegas campus has an excellent permanent collection of objects that predate the arrival of Europeans in the American Southwest and throughout Mexico. There's also a live reptile exhibit featuring regional lizards and snakes, plus a Xeriscape (they call it "Xeric") garden featuring drought-tolerant flora from the four corners of the Earth. For kids, the best experience is the "archaeology dig" in the museum lobby, where they can jump into a (glorified) sandbox and excavate cultural treasures. ⊠ *4505 S. Maryland Pkwy., University District* 🕾 *702/895–3381* ⊕ *barrickmuseum.unlv.edu* 🖃 *Free; suggested contribution $5* 🕾 *Closed Sun.*

WORTH NOTING

The Gun Store. Opened in 1988, the Gun Store puts you on the range with a machine gun of your choice. When you walk in, you're greeted with a wall full of weapons, most of which are available to rent. Pick your era; hose the target a steady diet of lead Cagney-style with a Thompson. World War II buffs might go for an MP40 Schmeisser. Have a flair for the international? Grab an Uzi or Sten. They've got handguns, rifles, and shotguns, too. ⊠ *2900 E. Tropicana Ave., East Side* 🕾 *702/454–1110* ⊕ *www.thegunstorelasvegas.com* 🖃 *From $89.95.*

Haunted Vegas Tours. As you ride through the streets of Las Vegas on this 2½-hour tour, your guide, dressed as a mortician, tells the tales of Sin City's notorious murders, suicides, and ghosts (including Bugsy Siegel, Elvis, and Tupac Shakur). A 30-minute *Rocky Horror*–like sideshow, called *Haunted Vegas*, runs before the 21-stop tour. Make reservations in advance and note that kids have to be 13 for the Haunted tour and 16 for the Mob tour. ⊠ *Royal Resort, 99 Convention Center Dr., East Side* 🕾 *702/677–6499, 866/218–4935* ⊕ *www.hauntedvegastours.com* 🖃 *$89.95.*

FAMILY **National Atomic Testing Museum.** Today's Las Vegas is lighted by neon and LCD, but during the Cold War, uranium and plutonium illuminated the area from time to time as well in the form of a roiling mushroom cloud in the distance. This museum, in association with the Smithsonian, commemorates southern Nevada's long and fascinating history of nuclear weapons research and testing with film footage and photographs of mushroom clouds; testimonials; and artifacts (including a deactivated bomb, twisted chunks of steel, and bomb-testing machinery from the Nevada Test Site).

Monthly group tours of the 1,375-square-mile **Nevada National Secu-rity Site**—an area that is larger than the state of Rhode Island and used to be the spot in the desert where the government tested atomic bombs—take you onto the terrain for visits to test-site craters and observation points. The site is 65 miles northwest of Downtown, and each tour usually covers a total of 250 miles. Tours leave from the Atomic Testing Museum; both sites are included with the price of admission, and shorts and sandals are not permitted. To register for a tour, contact the Nevada office of the National Nuclear Security Administration (⊕ *www.nnss. gov/pages/publicaffairsoutreach/nnsstours.html*). And be warned: Tours book up to a year in advance. ⊠ *755 E. Flamingo Rd., Desert Research Institute, East Side* ☏ *702/794–5151 museum, 702/295–0944 Nevada National Security Site tour reservations* ⊕ *www.nationalatomictesting-museum.org* ✑ *$22.*

HENDERSON AND LAKE LAS VEGAS

Dining
★★
Sightseeing
★★★★
Shopping
★★
Nightlife
★★

Suburbia stretches to the east and southeast of the Las Vegas Strip, and it continues to spread; Henderson is one of the fastest-growing cities in the entire nation. Much of this area is residential, with only a smattering of casinos. Some travelers may just pass through on their way to Lake Mead or Hoover Dam, but the resorts in the area are also worth a look.

One of those casinos—The M Resort—has commanding views of the Strip. Because the property is uphill from town, it literally looks down on the rest of the Valley. Another casino resort, Green Valley Ranch, is adjacent to one of the best shopping malls in the area. Both are worthwhile destinations for a weekend or an afternoon.

Out near Lake Las Vegas, the vibe is much more luxurious. Resorts such as the Westin Lake Las Vegas Resort & Spa and the Hilton Lake Las Vegas Resort & Spa dot the shoreline of a man-made lake, providing the perfect backdrop for golf and a variety of other outdoor activities. Bicyclists, joggers, Rollerbladers, and walkers will love the River Mountains Trail, a 36-mile loop that links Henderson, Lake Las Vegas, and Boulder City to the south. Pedaling over the sometimes-formidable mountains, it's hard to believe this deserted region is just a dozen miles from a major city.

Farther afield are the main attractions in this part of the Valley: Lake Mead National Recreation Area and Hoover Dam (⇨ *see also Side Trips chapter*). If you've got the time, rent a houseboat for a multiday vacation on the lake; it's the best way to explore the body of water at your own pace. At the dam, take the tour for an inside look (literally) at one of humankind's greatest engineering feats. These icons are packed in summer, so it's best to plan your trip for a shoulder season.

Green Valley Ranch, an elegant resort that rivals many big Strip properties, is a great place to explore in Henderson.

GETTING HERE AND AROUND

From the Strip, both Interstate 515 and Boulder Highway wind southeast toward Henderson, and Lake Mead Drive cuts due east toward Lake Mead. Public transportation serves this area, but the easiest way to get around is to rent a car. Once you're out by Lake Mead, bicycles are actually a great method of transportation. If you're philosophically opposed to exercise in Las Vegas, fear not—taxis are always just a phone call away.

TOP ATTRACTIONS

FAMILY **Ethel M Chocolate Factory.** Ethel M celebrated its 35th anniversary in 2016 and renovated its Henderson factory to commemorate the occasion. Today, watching gourmet chocolates being made on one of the weekend tours will make your mouth water; fortunately the self-guided tour is brief, and there are free samples at the end. You can buy more of your favorites in the store. Randomly, the factory also happens to be home to the largest cactus garden in the southwestern United States. ⌧ *2 Cactus Garden Dr., Henderson* ☎ *702/458–8864* ⊕ *www.ethelm. com* ✉ *Free* ☉ *Closed weekdays.*

FAMILY **River Mountains Loop Trail.** Stretching 36 miles around the River Mountains, this multi-use paved trail is perfect for hiking, biking, running, jogging, and horseback riding. For a stretch, the trail parallels the shores of Lake Mead, and connects with a historic spur that leads from the Lake Mead National Recreation Area to a parking lot just north of the Hoover Dam. The route runs through Boulder City, Henderson, and Lake Las Vegas. You can rent bikes at **JT's Bicycles** in Henderson

(⊕ *www.jtsbicycle.com*) and **All Mountain Cyclery** (⊕ *allmountaincyclery.com*) in Boulder City. The most popular trailheads are at the Alan Bible Visitor Center inside the recreation area and Bootleg Canyon Park, at the north end of Yucca Street in Boulder City. Access is also available at the eastern end of Equestrian Drive in Henderson, and the Railroad Pass Hotel & Casino, also in Henderson. ⊠ *Alan Bible Visitor Center trailhead, 8 Lake Shore Rd., Boulder City* ⊕ *www.rivermountainstrail.com.*

WORTH NOTING

FAMILY **Clark County Museum.** Step into the past (quite literally) at this modest museum, a 30-acre site that features a modern exhibit hall with a time-line exhibit about southern Nevada from prehistoric to modern times. The facility also offers a collection of restored historic buildings that depict daily life from different decades in Las Vegas, Boulder City, Henderson, and Goldfield. Other attractions include a replica of a 19th-century frontier print shop, and a 1960s wedding chapel that once stood on the Las Vegas Strip. There are also buildings and machinery dating from the turn of the 20th century, a nature trail, and a small ghost town. If you can't get to the Las Vegas Springs Preserve, on the North Side of town, this is a worthwhile substitute. ⊠ *1830 Boulder Hwy. S, Henderson* ☎ *702/455–7955* ⊕ *www.clarkcountynv.gov* ⌴ *$2.*

Lake Las Vegas. This 320-acre, man-made lake outside of Henderson is regarded for its golf courses, boating, fishing, and hotels. Two resorts sit on the lake shore: Hilton Lake Las Vegas Resort & Spa and the Westin Lake Las Vegas Resort & Spa. The lake was created by an earthen dam in 1991. ⊠ *Henderson* ⊕ *www.lakelasvegas.com.*

2

WEST SIDE

Dining
★★★
Sightseeing
★★
Shopping
★
Nightlife
★★★

The West Side of Las Vegas technically isn't a suburb (it's actually part of Las Vegas proper), but it sure feels like one. Big-box stores and fast-food chains abound. Housing developments sit on just about every major corner. Sure, resorts such as The Palms and The Rio do double duty as locals' joints and major tourist draws with vibes just as swanky as Strip properties. But for the most part, malls and tract houses in this stretch give way to a small number of locals' casinos here such as the long-standing Gold Coast.

There are hidden gems in this area, and most of them exist in the industrial section a stone's throw (west) from the Strip. Number one on the list: Machine Guns Vegas, a decidedly upscale shooting range. Pole Position Raceway Las Vegas, an indoor go-kart facility, is another favorite among visitors.

The West Side also has a small but thriving Chinatown. This three-block area has everything from ramen to vegan doughnuts to world-class Thai food. In particular, restaurants in a stretch of strip malls along Spring Mountain Road are known for their unpretentious and authentic experience. Not surprisingly, this is where many Strip chefs come to eat when they're not on the clock.

GETTING HERE AND AROUND
The Palms and The Rio are within easy taxicab distance from the Strip. The Rio is even walkable from the Center Strip—about 20 minutes west on Flamingo. As you venture beyond The Palms, you approach rental-car territory. Because the West Side is home to thousands of casino employees, public transportation blankets the area.

WORTH NOTING

*Fodor's*Choice ★ **Dig This.** This attraction is perfect for adults who like to play in a life-sized sandbox—and use big toys to do it. In this case, the toys are heavy construction machinery: bulldozers, excavators, mini-excavators, and skid-steer track loaders. Guests don hard hats and spend about 90 minutes driving the equipment on a big dirt lot, moving around giant tires, digging holes, and more. Dig This also partners with a number of other local businesses to get people off the Strip. ⊠ *3012 S. Rancho Dr., West Side* ☎ *702/222–4344* ⊕ *digthisvegas. com* ⚒ *$169–$249.*

Machine Guns Vegas. Swanky nightclub meets gun range in this only-in-Vegas addition to the scene. In an industrial neighborhood just west of the Interstate, "MGV" (as it's known) offers 10 indoor shooting lanes, including 2 in an ultra-exclusive VIP area, as well as a number of outdoor lanes. Many of the instructors are attractive women. Visitors have dozens of firearms to choose from, everything from "miniguns" and.22-caliber handguns up to an M-60 fully automatic machine gun. Package deals include multiple guns. Guests can select their targets; among the options are evil clowns and Osama bin Laden. ⊠ *3501 Aldebaran Ave., West Side* ☎ *800/757–4668, 702/476–9228* ⊕ *www.machinegunsvegas. com* ⚒ *From $99.*

FAMILY **Pole Position Raceway Las Vegas.** This is no putt-putting lawn-mower-engine powered go-kart. These miniature racers are electric (think: souped-up golf carts) and reach up to 45 mph. You and 12 competitors zip around the ¼-mile indoor track full of twists and turns. The Pole Position computers track your overall performance from race to race, and over multiple visits. You'll get a score sheet giving a detailed score breakdown to compare with your friends. Signing up for "membership" cuts the fees by about 20%. There's also a second location out near Summerlin. ⊠ *4175 S. Arville, West Side* ☎ *702/227–7223* ⊕ *www.polepositionraceway.com/las-vegas* ⚒ *$25.50* ☞ *Adults must be 56 inches tall to ride; kids must be 48 inches.*

NEED A BREAK **Ronald's Donuts.** The best doughnuts in Vegas are sold at this tiny Chinatown storefront tucked in a strip mall along Spring Mountain Road. Locals rave about the apple fritters, but more traditional selections, such as Boston creme, are addictive, too. Surprisingly, all of the offerings are vegan, a quirk that has put the hole-in-the-wall on the national map in recent years. Whenever you go, expect a line. ⊠ *4600 Spring Mountain Rd., West Side* ☎ *702/873–1032.*

2

SUMMERLIN AND RED ROCK CANYON

Dining
★★★
Sightseeing
★★★★
Shopping
★★
Nightlife
★★

There's a master plan behind the western suburb of Summerlin, and it shows. The town—which was founded by movie legend Howard Hughes—has been developed and built out according to a written-on-paper strategy, a "planned community" through and through. Today the neighborhood comprises dozens of gated communities, as well as a handful of epic golf courses and casino resorts such as the JW Marriott and Red Rock Casino, Resort & Spa.

Although the Red Rock Casino is hip and fun, the highlight of the region is the casino's namesake, the Red Rock National Conservation Area. This area, managed by the Bureau of Land Management (BLM), is an expansive open space that heads from civilization into the ocher-rock wilderness of the Spring Mountains beyond. Canyon walls boast some of the best rock climbing in the world. There are also petroglyphs, drawings by Native Americans who first inhabited this area more than 1,000 years ago.

One of the best ways to explore the wilderness outside Summerlin is, without question, on horseback. A number of outfitters run half- and full-day guided trips; some even include dinner. Just about every ride brings visitors up-close-and-personal with native flora and fauna, including Joshua trees, jackrabbits, and more. If possible, ask your guide to lead you to the top of the canyon for a one-of-a-kind glimpse of the Strip.

GETTING HERE AND AROUND

Public transportation to Summerlin exists from the Strip, but considering how long it would take you to get out there, the best bet is to rent a car. Interstate 215 winds around the outskirts of the Las Vegas Valley and ends in Summerlin; another option is to take service roads such as Charleston Boulevard and Spring Mountain Road.

The West Side of Las Vegas is the gateway to the Red Rock Canyon National Conservation Area at the base of the Spring Mountains.

Visitor Information Red Rock Canyon Visitor Center. ✉ *1000 Scenic Loop Dr., Summerlin South* ☎ *702/515-5350* ⊕ *www.redrockcanyonlv.org.*

FAMILY **Spring Mountains Visitor Gateway.** About an hour from Downtown—and about halfway up Kyle Canyon Road to the Spring Mountains National Recreation Area—you'll find this eco-friendly visitor center, which opened in 2015 and welcomes those heading to Mt. Charleston. Spend some time perusing the educational exhibits about the ecosystems and microclimates in the region's tallest mountains. Then hike one of the short interpretive trails for a sense of what the cactus- and bristlecone pine–strewn landscape is like. ✉ *2525 Kyle Canyon Rd.* ☎ *702/872-5486* ⊕ *www.gomtcharleston.com.*

TOP ATTRACTIONS

Downtown Summerlin. This open-air shopping mall with 125 stores and restaurants sits at the center of the Summerlin planned community, and, since it opened in 2014, has become the very heart of town. Locals are delighted to have name-brand stores such as Lululemon and Sur la Table around the corner, and on-site restaurants, including the suburban outpost of Downtown standard MTO Cafe, are always packed. On Saturday, the mall hosts a farmers' market from 9 am to 2 pm; other events are scheduled throughout the year. The mall has its own movie theater with luxury seats and a full bar, and is a short walk from Red Rock Casino, Resort & Spa. ✉ *Sahara Ave. and 215 Beltway, Summerlin South* ⊕ *www.downtownsummerlin.com.*

FAMILY **Red Rock Canyon National Conservation Area.** Red sandstone cliffs and
Fodor's Choice dramatic desert landscapes await day-trippers and outdoors enthu-
★ siasts at Red Rock Canyon National Conservation Area. Operated
by the BLM, the 195,819-acre national conservation area features
narrow canyons, fantastic rock formations, seasonal waterfalls, desert
wildlife, and rock-art sites. The elevated Red Rock Overlook provides
a fabulous view of the cream-and-red sandstone cliffs. For a closer
look at the stunning scenery, take the 13-mile, one-way scenic drive
through the canyon, open from dawn to dusk. Other activities including hiking, mountain biking, rock climbing, canyoneering, picnicking,
and wildlife-watching. A developed campground, 2 miles from the
visitor center, has 71 campsites, pit toilets, and drinking water for
visitors wanting to extend their stay. ⊠ *1000 Scenic Loop Dr., Summerlin South* ⊕ *www.blm.gov* ☷ *$7 per car, $3 per individual on a
bike, motorcycle, or on foot.*

WORTH NOTING

FAMILY **Kids Planet.** Considering that summer regularly brings temperatures of
115 degrees to the Las Vegas Valley, this indoor playground, on the
Summerlin/Spring Valley border, is a great place to take the kids for
a day. Attractions include an elaborate climbing structure, a ball pit,
a bouncy house, video games, and more. There's also a private room
for quiet time (or a birthday bash). Parents can play along with kids
or decompress in a comfortable waiting area. ⊠ *4215 S. Durango Dr.,
Summerlin South* ☎ *702/456–5454* ⊕ *www.kidsplanetlv.com* ☷ *$10
for 1st child, $8 for 2nd, $7 for 3rd.*

ELSEWHERE IN LAS VEGAS

NORTH SIDE

The swath of suburbia north of Downtown Las Vegas that stretches out past Nellis Air Force Base is vast and largely faceless. Some highlights: the Aliante Station Casino + Hotel, and Shadow Creek Golf Course, home to the Michael Jordan Celebrity Invitational golf tournament every spring. Because the region is so expansive, travel times vary widely, depending on where you're headed and where you're coming from. Our advice when traveling to or from this part of town: Rent a car.

SOUTH SIDE

This area, which loosely stretches from the McCarran Rental Car facility south of 215 to The M Resort, is a mix of stand-alone hotels (such as the Silverton, the South Point, and The M itself), big-box stores, and residential neighborhoods. It's also the first stretch of metropolitan Las Vegas that road-trippers from Los Angeles encounter on their approach. Without traffic, travel time from these parts to the South Strip is about 15 to 20 minutes. During rush hour, however, you might be better off dealing with traffic lights on Las Vegas Boulevard.

WORTH NOTING

Mermaid Restaurant & Lounge. Yes, those really are mermaids swimming in the giant fish tank that adorns the walls of this campy eatery inside the Silverton Casino Hotel. No, you don't have to worry about being lured to spend more money by their sirens' songs. Mermaid swims take place Thursday through Sunday during lunch and dinner; there are five different mermaids in all. In case you're wondering, there are other fish in this joint's sea, including sharks, stingrays, and about 4,000 other specimens. The standard pub food is pretty good, too. ⊠ *Silverton Casino Hotel, 3333 Blue Diamond Rd., South Las Vegas* ☎ *702/263–7777* ⊕ *www.silvertoncasino.com.*

GAMBLING
AND CASINOS

Updated by
Matt Villano

If the sum total of your gambling experience is a penny-ante neighborhood poker game, or your company's casino night holiday party, you may feel a little intimidated by the Vegas gambling scene. We're here to tell you that you don't need to be a gambling expert to sit and play.

All you need is a little knowledge of the games you plan on playing, the gumption to step up to the table, a bankroll, and the desire to have a great time. It would also be wise to remember that other than a very few extreme cases, the odds are always with the house. There are no foolproof methods, miracle betting systems, lucky charms, or incantations that will change this fact. So if you feel as though you can brave the risk, handle the action, and want to have some fun, roll up your sleeves and pull up a chair—it's gambling time.

GAMBLING PLANNER

CASINO RULES

Keep IDs handy. Dealers strictly enforce the minimum gambling age, which is 21 years everywhere in Nevada.

No kids. Children are allowed in gaming areas only if they're passing through on their way to another part of the resort.

No electronic distractions. As a general rule, casinos forbid electronic devices, or anything that distracts gamblers at the tables (for example, a phone or MP3 player). When you sit down at a table, make sure to remove any listening devices from your ears and set phones on silent mode. If you receive a call during a hand that you must answer, the dealer will generally allow you to finish the hand before asking you to step away from the table, and will hold your place while you take the call. For years cell phones and any two-way communication devices were prohibited in sports books, but most books have softened this position a bit in recent years, and some even allow gamblers to download apps they can use to place wagers in real-time (more on that in a bit).

Smoking. Smoke only in designated areas. Signs on the tables and around the casino will inform you whether it's OK to smoke in a specific area. Generally, smoking is permitted in all table games areas. In the slot machine/video poker and sports book areas, there are usually some nonsmoking-designated areas. (In the case of the MGM Grand, the entire sports book is smoke-free.) In almost every (live) poker room in Las Vegas, smoking is not permitted. If you're unsure, ask someone before lighting up.

3

CASINO STRATEGY

The right mind-set. There's nothing quite like the excitement you feel when you step into a Vegas casino for the first time. The larger-than-life sights and sounds draw you in and inspire fantasies of life-changing jackpots and breaking the bank on a game of chance. There's nothing wrong with dreaming about hitting it big. Plenty of folks win money every single day in Las Vegas, but most don't. Gambling should be entertainment, a pastime, a bonding activity with friends or family, and occasionally an intellectual challenge. It should never be an investment, a job, or a way of making a quick buck. If you approach gambling in this way, you may leave Las Vegas without a shirt (or thousands of dollars in debt).

The best approach. Learn enough about the games so that you aren't simply giving away your money. A little education will prevent you from making terrible bets or playing out of control. Bad bets (i.e., high-risk, high payout) can be some of the most exciting to play at the tables, and great fun if you like the action. Just remember that higher-risk games are much less likely to pay out over time.

Have fun! If you have reasonable expectations, set and keep to your financial goals, and play with proper strategy, you're bound to have a successful and enjoyable trip.

Notice how bets are advertised. A good rule of thumb for discerning good bets from bad bets at the tables is to look at how/if the bet is advertised. Good bets generally aren't posted (for example, odds in craps aren't even on the table, except for the long-shot proposition bets in the center of the table, such as the "Hardways" or "Any Seven" bets). Bad bets will be in flashing lights, and their big payouts will be prominently shown on the table or on large printed cards. Or they'll be "sold" by the dealer (like insurance in blackjack, and proposition bets in craps).

HOW NOT TO GO BROKE

Create solid goals on what you're willing to lose, and what would be a satisfying amount to win.

Consider what you can afford to lose and stick to this number, *no matter what.*

Pace yourself when you play, so you don't spend all your money too early in your trip.

Break your play into sessions.

If you lose your allotted goal during a session, quit playing and accept the loss. Many gamblers get deep into debt trying to "chase" a loss, and end up betting more than they can afford.

Never gamble with money borrowed on your credit card! Check out this sobering math: Say you want a $500 cash advance. The casino will charge a fee (it varies but for our example, 5%), which makes the total $525. Then the (credit-card) bank will charge you for the cash advance (usually 3%). You're now $45.75 in the hole before you even start playing. And if you're carrying a balance on previous purchases, the long-term costs of the *separate* finance charges on the cash advance can be staggering.

Make sure your winnings goal is realistic. If you wager $10 a hand at blackjack, it's not reasonable to think you'll win $5,000 in a session—$50–$100 would be a more obtainable goal. If you're fortunate enough to reach your realistic goal during one of your sessions, end that session immediately. You can put half of your winnings away, and gamble with the profit during another session.

Most important is to exercise discipline and not exceed your goals. Sticking to these basic rules, regardless of whether you're up or down, will contain your losses and preserve your winnings.

Go easy on the alcohol. We understand you want to let loose and have fun while you play, but overindulging at the tables can impair your judgment and cause you to make unwise decisions with your hard-earned money on the line. The only thing worse than a hangover is a hangover with an empty wallet.

THE GOOD, THE BAD, AND THE UGLY

Games you can actually beat under the right circumstances: Poker, sports betting, and video poker.

Games where you can lose money slowly: Baccarat (bank), single-deck blackjack, craps (Pass/Don't Pass, Come/Don't Come), Pai Gow Poker/Tiles, Single-Zero Roulette, Three-Card Poker, and some slot machines.

The rest: There are many more games offered in Vegas casinos (such as Blackjack Switch, Free Bet, Casino War), and new ones seemingly pop up every day. We won't discuss many of these games in the following pages because they're not considered to be "core" games, and aren't carried in the majority of the casinos. These games were created to increase profits that the better odds games don't provide, so if you choose to play them, do so with caution.

Games with worst odds: Keno and the Big Six Wheel. Avoid these two like the plague.

THE HOUSE EDGE

Think of a coin-flip game paying you $1 on heads and taking $1 on tails. Over time, you'd win as much as you'd lose. But a *casino*-hosted game might pay only $0.98 on heads while still taking $1 on tails. That difference is the "house edge." Two cents doesn't seem like much, but when enough people play, the casino earns millions over an extended period; it's a mathematical certainty. Another example: The "true odds" of rolling double sixes in craps is 1 in 36, but they pay you only 30 to 1, instead of $36 on a $1 bet. The extra $6 that should be paid to you is, in essence, kept by the house, making it a very bad bet. The house edge varies from game to game, so if you know the odds for each game, you can minimize your losses.

COMPS, CLUBS, AND COUPONS

Nearly every establishment has a rewards program, or Players Club, used to identify and reward its loyal gamblers. Members of the casino's Players Club will get regular mailings advertising specials, discounts, contests, and other information. When you sign up, you receive a card to present whenever you play. You may also get a PIN number so you can check your comp totals at one of the kiosks (a comp ATM) on the casino floor. The card is used to track your play at table games and slot machines. The amount of comps you're entitled to is based on factors such as the amount you buy in for, overall time played, average bet, and expected losses. Comps can be used for restaurants, gifts, rooms, or even cash in some places. In many cases one card is accepted at multiple casinos with the same owner. Sign up for a card at Harrah's, and use it at all of the Caesars-owned properties. Present your card every single time you play at a table or slot machine, and every time you move to a new one. Remember that comps are based on play, so don't expect to get a free meal if you sit at a game for only 15 minutes, and bet $10 a hand.

FUNBOOKS

Discount "funbooks" are another perk of joining a Players Club. Many casinos will offer you a book of coupons for discounts in their hotels, shops, and restaurants when you sign up. These books—yes, they're often still actual printed books—offer some excellent discounts of real value, and occasionally even freebies for drinks, food, or gift items, so it pays to take advantage of these while you are in town. Some hotels will give you the funbooks without signing up for the Players Card, but in others you will have to ask for them. However, some "books" exist in virtual form, and are accessible through a casino's app. Many of the best funbooks can be found at places that are off the Strip. The smaller casinos usually offer better deals in an attempt to lure you away from the big guys. You may also find some good coupon books in taxis, magazines in your room, and hotel gift shops, and even from people handing them out on the Strip.

TIPS FOR COMPS

Get a Players Club card. You *might* get a comp without a club card, but it's highly unlikely.

Don't forget to ask. No one is going to come up and offer you a comp. Even if you're not sure you've played enough for a comp, you should ask the floor person, or pit boss. The worst they can do is politely say no.

Buy in often, buy in big. Your initial cash stake, and average bet at a table is often what gets you noticed by the casino supervisors. They'll usually log your average bet based upon your opening few bets at the table, so make your first bets larger when the supervisor is paying attention, then reduce them when he or she moves away from the table. When you're finished at one table, cash in your chips at the cashier, and use those bills to buy in at the next table.

Consider the value of the comp. Never increase what you intended to gamble just to earn comps. It'll cost you *much* less to pay for dinner than to risk losing enough money to get a comp for that same dinner.

BETTER BETTOR ETIQUETTE

Know a little before you play. Dealers are available for questions, but you should learn the basics. Watch for a while, or ask the casino host or supervisor about beginner's classes. Even better, find an empty table and ask the dealer if he or she would be willing to walk you through the game.

Understand betting minimums before you sit down. Each table has a plaque or digital display with table minimums, maximums, and specific gaming rules.

Sympathy for the dealer. Dealers can't take cash directly from your hand, so lay it down on the table when you buy in. Place your bet in the proper area, and stack your entire bet in one pile, with the largest denomination chips on the bottom, and the smallest on the top.

Tip kindly. Dealers, like servers in restaurants, rely on tips as part of their salary. If a dealer is being particualrly nice, tip him or her by sliding a chip toward the rack or by betting for the dealer to the upper right of your betting circle.

Ask for change as you need it. The dealers have a limited number of chips in their rack for payouts and making change, so they prefer to give you enough small chips for 10 to 20 minimum bets at a time. If you're at a $10 table and you buy in with $300, they'll give you 20 $5 chips and 8 $25 chips. If you run out of $5 chips, just ask them to change your $25 chips as needed.

BEST BEGINNER CLASSES

The whole gambling scene can seem intimidating for the first-timer. But casinos have worked hard to help newbies feel comfortable playing the games, in the hopes that once they get a taste of the excitement, they'll be back for more.

Free lessons in Vegas are widely available. One place to look is in your hotel room; many resorts play a running loop of gaming lessons on TV. If you prefer the in-person format, most resorts offer free group lessons where would-be gamblers gather around a real table game while a dealer or supervisor explains how it works. Classes usually take place at scheduled times during low-traffic hours (just ask the casino host or one of the supervisors). Venues we like include these two:

Excalibur offers poker lessons at 11 am, roulette at 11 am and 7 pm, blackjack at 11:30 am and 7:30 pm, and craps at 12:30 and 8 pm.

Golden Nugget has daily lessons for the most popular games: poker and craps at 10 am, Pai Gow at 10:30 am, roulette at 11:30 am, and blackjack at noon.

HELPFUL WEBSITES

Perhaps the best time and place to learn how the games are played is before you leave for Las Vegas, on your home computer or tablet. There are tons of websites, and even phone and tablet applications that not only teach you how to play the games, but also provide simulations of the gaming experience. And unlike the brief lessons given at the casino, you can learn at your own pace and practice playing as much as you like, whenever you like.

Check your app store for free simulation game apps to download to your phone or tablet.

For roulette: **Roulette Edu** (⊕ *www.rouletteedu.com*).

For blackjack, Pai Gow Tiles, and video poker: **Wizard of Vegas** (⊕ *www.wizardofvegas.com/games*).

EASIEST GAMES TO PLAY

Roulette is considered the easiest table game, but it's also one with a high house edge. That's not a coincidence; players typically pay for easier games in the form of a larger advantage for the house. ■TIP➔ Play a single-zero wheel. It'll cut the house edge almost in half.

You can play **keno** while you eat in many casino coffee shops. Keno carries the worst odds in the whole casino, but it's extremely easy to play. You just mark numbers on a betting slip, give it to the keno runner with a buck or two, and watch the board on the wall to see if your numbers come up.

Bingo is also a fun, simple casino game. It's played in specialized parlors, mostly in the Downtown casinos, or off-Strip casinos (such as Station casinos), with a crowd of people sitting at tables in a large room listening for their lucky numbers to line up. The people you run into are often locals and casino workers, who like bingo's humble aesthetic after a long day filled with glitz and kitsch.

Newer **slot machines** are a little more complicated than traditional slots, but they still remain the easiest to play in the casino—put the money in (or bet your credits) and touch a button (or pull the handle if it's an older machine) and wait for the reels to stop spinning to see if you've won or lost.

BEST DEALERS

Dealers on the Strip keep the games moving fast and aren't prone to many mistakes, but they often don't go in for a lot of small talk. Many beginners feel more comfortable at tables that are social and lively. For that, try the folksy atmospheres of the locals' casinos off the Strip and away from Downtown, like Gold Coast or Sunset Station.

CLOSE UP

Las Vegas Lingo

Bank. A row or group of similar gaming machines.

Bankroll. The amount of money you have to gamble with.

Buy-in. The amount of cash you exchange for chips during a gaming session.

Cage. The casino cashier, where you can exchange your chips for cash.

Cheques (or Checks). The chips with money-equivalent values, used to place wagers at the tables.

Color Up. To exchange a stack of lower-denomination chips for a few high-denomination chips. Dealers will ask if they can "color you up" before you leave their table. Say yes.

Comp. Short for complimentary (i.e., a freebie). Can be a drink, room, dinner, or show tickets from the casino.

Cut. A ritual splitting of a deck of cards performed after shuffling.

Eye-in-the-Sky. The overhead video surveillance system and its human monitors in a casino.

Fill. When chips are brought to a table from the casino cage to refill a money rack that's low.

House. Another name for the casino's side of any bet, as in this sentence: "The house wins on any tie."

Layout. The printed felt covering of a particular table game, which states the game being offered, betting area, payout odds, and other pertinent information related to the playing of the game.

Marker. A player's IOU to the casino. Rather than buy in with cash, players who register for casino credit can sign a marker in exchange for chips.

Match Play. A one-time bet voucher for a table game, often given as a perk by casinos.

Pit. A subdivision of the casino floor, with several adjacent gaming tables.

Pit Boss. A senior casino employee who supervises the gaming tables in a casino pit, settles player disputes, and authorizes comps. The pit boss can usually be found at a computer console in the middle of the pit, or patrolling the entire pit he or she is assigned to.

Players Club Card. A card with a magnetic stripe on it used to track a gambler's activities in a casino.

Progressive. A special kind of jackpot, often available to multiple tables or game machines, that continues to grow until it's won.

Push. A Tie bet, where you neither win nor lose.

Rake. In poker, it's an amount the casino takes out of each pot as compensation for running the game. Usually it's 10% of the total pot (up to a certain limit, such as "10% up to $4"), or a flat fee per hour, depending on the game or casino.

Shoe. A small box in a table game from which cards are dealt.

Sports Book. The casino area for sports betting.

Table Games. All games of chance such as blackjack and craps played against the casino with a dealer.

Toke. A tip (short for token of your esteem). Usually given to dealers during play, to reward outstanding service, or celebrate a player's good fortune.

Before you sit down, make sure the game's moving at a speed you're comfortable with. Do the dealer and players look happy? Do the players have big stacks of chips? Is there a friendly vibe? If you're feeling especially chatty, locate a dealer from a familiar or interesting city (their hometowns are often printed on their name tags) and strike up some friendly banter. Vegas dealers are trained, skilled professionals who run their games like clockwork, but they're also customer service experts. It's their job to make sure you have a good time whether you win or lose. Don't hesitate to ask questions or seek advice if you're unsure of the rules, aren't sure what to do on a particular hand, or even want to know the best place to get a bite to eat. If you don't feel comfortable with a dealer for whatever reason, "color up" your chips and move on to another table. Conversely, don't hesitate to throw the dealer a toke (tip) if he or she enhances your overall experience.

> **LEARN BEFORE YOU GO**
>
> The Internet has resources galore: the *Las Vegas Advisor* (⊕ *lasvegasadvisor.com*) and *Gaming Today* (⊕ *gamingtoday.com*) are two publications that keep the rest of the world up to speed on the gaming industry, including where to find the best deals, promotions, and events. To find an in-depth discussion of game rules and odds, check out the Wizard of Odds (⊕ *wizardofodds.com*). Vegas visitors can stay informed on the latest news and tourism information from the two local newspapers' websites: the *Las Vegas Review-Journal* (⊕ *lvrj.com*) and the *Las Vegas Sun* (⊕ *lasvegassun.com*).

ELECTRONIC GAMING

So you feel like playing some blackjack, but it's a sunny day and you want to work on your tan? You can do both with certain handheld gambling devices known as PocketCasinos or eDecks. These tools are wireless portable devices that allow you to play certain games, such as blackjack, baccarat, and video poker, from places other than the casino floor. These devices are also revolutionizing sports book gambling. The devices are similar to computer games you play on your phone or tablet, with one major difference. Here, you're wagering real money, in the form of credits, that you deposit when you receive your device. The devices work only in certain areas of the casino, in order to prevent underage people from using them, so make sure you know where, and how to use it properly when you receive it. They're currently being offered at places such as **The Venetian, The Palazzo, Hard Rock, The M Resort, The Cosmopolitan,** and the **Tropicana,** to name a few. Other casinos, such as those owned by Station Casinos, offer a mobile app that enables you to bet right from your phone, so long as you're within the state of Nevada at the time you place your wager.

BLACKJACK

Blackjack, aka "21," anchors virtually every casino in America. It's one of the most popular table games because it's easy to learn, fun to play, and has potentially excellent odds for the player.

The object of this classic card game is simple. You want to build a higher hand than the dealer without going over 21—a *bust*. Two-card hands, from one deck of cards up to eight decks of cards, are dealt to everyone at the table, including the dealer, who gets one card face-down (the "hole" card) and one card faceup for all to see. Play then proceeds from gambler to gambler. You play out your hand by taking additional cards ("hitting") or standing pat ("staying"). When all the players have finished playing out their hands, the dealer then plays the house hand following preset rules. Once that's complete, the dealer pays winning players and rakes the chips of the losers.

PLAYING THE GAME

The value of a blackjack hand is the sum of all the cards; aces count as 1 or 11 (whichever is more advantageous to your hand), and face cards (jacks, queens, and kings) have a value of 10. Suit plays no role in blackjack. If you bust, you lose your bet immediately, no matter what happens with the dealer's cards. The dealer can also bust by going over 21, in which case all players remaining in the hand get paid off. If you're dealt a combination of a 10-valued card (a 10 or any face card) and an ace on your first two cards, it's called a *natural* blackjack. If this is the case, you're paid a bonus on your bet, unless the house also has a blackjack. The payout is either 3 to 2 on your original bet, or 6 to 5, depending on the house rules where you're playing. The dealers use a little mirror or other device at the table to check their hidden card for blackjacks before dealing out extra cards.

For those who aren't lucky enough to be dealt blackjack, play starts with the person sitting to the dealer's left. Everyone plays out his or her hand by motioning to the dealer whether they want to hit or stand. Players *must* make specific motions to the dealer about their intentions:

■ If the cards have been dealt faceup, which is the case at most casinos these days, you're not supposed to touch your cards, so you hit by tapping on the table with your finger(s) in front of your cards. To stand, you simply wave your hand side to side over your cards.

■ If the cards have been dealt facedown, pick them up and hold them (with one hand only!). To hit, you "scratch" on the table toward yourself with the corner of your cards. To stand, you slide the cards facedown under your chips. Don't fret if you knock over your chips in the process. The dealer will restack them for you if necessary. As long as your hand is less than 21, you can continue hitting and taking cards. If you bust, you must expose your cards immediately (if you are holding them), and the dealer will take your bet and remove your cards. At that point the dealer turns to the next player, who repeats the same hit/stand process. If you get a blackjack, expose your cards. You also should expose your cards if you wish to double-down or split (which we'll talk about in a bit).

■ Once every player has a chance to act on his or her hand, the dealer reveals his or her hidden card and plays out the hand according to the following rules:

■ Dealer shows 16 or less: dealer must hit.

■ Dealer shows 17 or more: dealer must stand (in most casinos). Note: In most casinos, the dealer must hit a "soft" 17 (Ace,6) until the hand reaches a total of 17 or higher.

Once the dealer's hand is complete, the bets are either paid (if the player's hand is higher than the dealer's) or raked (if the dealer's hand is higher than the player's). If the dealer has busted, all players remaining in the hand win their bets. In the event a player's hand value is equal to that of the dealer, it's a *push* (the dealer will knock on the table in front of the bet); the bet is neither paid nor raked.

DOUBLING DOWN

If your first two cards total 10 or 11, your chances of hitting and drawing a 10-value card to create a great hand are very good. To take full advantage of that, you can double down. It's a special bet you place after the hand has started, whose value can be any amount up to your initial bet. Doubling down for an amount not equal to your original bet is called "doubling for less," and the dealer will usually announce this when you do it. This confirms that you did not take the full amount of the double, so there are no discrepancies when you are paid. The upside of doubling is that you put more money in play for an advantageous situation. The downside is that you receive only a single card in lieu of the normal hit/stand sequence. Casino rules vary on which starting hands you can double down on, so ask the dealer before you slide a matching stack of chips beside your first bet. For years casinos let you double down on your first two cards; recently, however, the rules have changed to where you only can double when your first two cards total 9, 10, or 11.

SPLITTING

Splitting is another good way to raise your bet in a favorable situation. If your first two cards are of equal value (even two different face cards such as king and queen), you can split them apart and form two separate hands, then play each hand out separately as if it were a brand-new hand. When you want to split, push a stack of chips equal to your original bet into the betting circle, and tell the dealer your intentions. Never touch the cards yourself, unless you're playing a game that calls for it (like single deck), in which case you'll lay your cards down and place the extra bet. In some casinos you can re-split if you get another matching card for three or even four separate hands. You can draw as many cards as you want to make a hand when you split. In many casinos, you can't re-split aces and are allowed to draw only one card on each ace.

> ### BLACKJACK SWITCH
>
> Blackjack Switch is a Shuffle Master–owned game that started at Casino Royale but can now be found at just about every gambling hall in town. Instead of playing one hand, players are required to play two. Players can switch the second cards of their two hands to make two totally new hands. Standard splitting and doubling rules apply (though there is some strategy involved with switching into potentially lucrative hands). Think the switcheroo favors the players? Think again. Blackjack Switch pays only even money, and when the dealer busts with 22, all bets push.

INSURANCE AND EVEN MONEY

When the dealer's up card is an ace, he or she will ask if anyone wants to buy insurance. You can take insurance for up to half of your original wager. If the dealer makes blackjack, the insurance bet pays off at 2 to 1 odds; if the dealer doesn't, the insurance bet is lost and the hand is played normally. If you draw a blackjack when the dealer's up card is an ace, the dealer may ask if you want "even money" in some casinos. Taking even money is exactly the same as taking the insurance. It's offered this way to entice you to take the insurance (exactly what the house wants) instead of risking a push if the dealer has blackjack also. If you take even money, the dealer will pay you 1 to 1 on your bet instead of the normal 3 to 2, and lock up your cards before he or she checks her hidden card for blackjack. Experts consider both insurance and even money bad bets. Always pass on them.

STRATEGY

Although it's easy to learn, blackjack has varying layers of complexity that can be tackled, depending on your interest level. With practice and the perfection of basic strategy, you can reduce the house edge to about 0.5% (as opposed to about 2.5% for the average uninformed gambler), making blackjack one of the best bets of table games.

Basic strategy is simply the optimal way for a player to play his or her cards, based on the dealer's exposed card and a particular set of casino rules. We'll discuss these rules below *(The House Hedges)*, because basic strategy changes as certain rules change.

At its *most* basic, basic strategy is the assumption that the dealer's hole card is a 10. If the dealer's up card is a 9, he or she likely has a 10 underneath to make 19. If the dealer shows a 4, he or she likely has a 14. You then act accordingly, standing pat or hitting, depending on whether you can beat the dealer's hand. Learning and memorizing basic strategy is a must for professional gamblers, who can't afford to give up anything more to the house edge. For the casual or beginning gambler, the rules are printed on small charts *(example chart in this chapter)* that you can buy in any casino gift shop, or find and print online at one of the websites listed earlier. You're allowed to use these cards at the table for reference at any time, and you should every time you're not sure of whether to hit, stand, split, or double down on any given hand. You should, however, try to come with some basic knowledge of the game and strategy before you start playing, so you don't have to consult the card on *every* hand, which considerably slows down the game and enjoyment for other players at the table.

■ TIP➔ **To practice basic strategy, try ⊕ www.hitorstand.net. If you make the wrong decision on a hand, the program will tell you.**

If you don't have the patience to practice or memorize, or don't want to refer to a chart, you can always ask the dealer, who should have knowledge of basic strategy from his or her experience. Or, you can follow these basic rules-of-thumb based on the dealer's up card:

■ Ace, 10, 9, 8, 7—assume the dealer has a made hand (i.e., a hand totaling between 17 and 21 and will therefore not need to draw). If your hand is 17 or higher, stand. If your hand is 16 or lower, you should hit.

■ 2, 3, 4, 5, 6—assume that the dealer has an easily busted hand, so there's no need to take any risks. If your hand is 13 or higher, stand and hope the dealer busts. If your cards total 11 or lower, take a hit and then reevaluate using the same set of rules. If your hand totals 12, only hit against a dealer's 2 or 3.

■ If you have a "soft" hand (an ace with a value card; for example A,7) that totals less than 8 (or 18), you should always hit. If it totals 18, only hit against a dealer's 9, 10, or ace, and always stand on a soft total of 19 or 20.

■ If your hand total equals 11, you should consider doubling down against everything but a dealer ace. If your hand totals 10, you should consider doubling down against everything but a dealer 10 or ace.

■ Always split A,A, and never split 5,5. Some experts advise also always to split 8,8 and never to split 10,10, but those rules are up for interpretation and argument.

THE HOUSE HEDGES

The casinos know that their edge in blackjack is very small, especially against those who employ basic strategy, so they have come up with ways to hedge their bets by adding certain rules, or restrictions to the once-standard rules. These things not only increase the house edge against you, but can distort the odds for basic strategy decisions and make your chart much less effective by changing some variables of

Blackjack Table

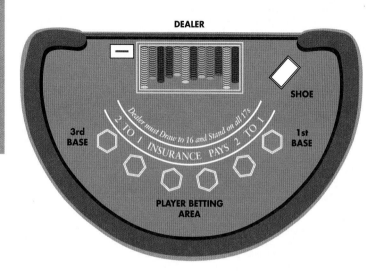

the games. Because the variables change from game to game, and casino to casino, you must be sure your basic strategy card matches the game you're playing.

CHOOSING THE BEST TABLE

Here are some general rules for choosing a good blackjack table and keeping the house edge low. Chances are you won't find a game with all of the following things in your favor. The trick is to find one that uses a combination of as many as possible. Choose a table that

■ pays blackjack at 3 to 2, not 6 to 5 or anything else.

■ uses a smaller number of decks in the game. The fewer decks, the better for you.

■ the dealer must stand on a soft 17 (A,6), instead of hitting.

■ allows you to double down on any hand. Some casinos will let you double only on 10 or 11.

■ allows you to split aces.

■ allows you to double down after splitting.

■ has surrender. This allows you to surrender a bad hand (usually a 15 or 16 against a dealer face-card) before drawing extra cards. The casino will charge you half your wager for this privilege. Sometimes it's a good idea, and basic strategy will let you know when.

THE SHUFFLE MATTERS

Some casinos now employ "continuous" shuffle machines at their blackjack tables. These machines recycle the used cards right back into the machine after every hand, where they're continuously shuffled

SAMPLE BLACKJACK BASIC STRATEGY CHART										
Your Hand	**Dealer's Up Card**									
	2	**3**	**4**	**5**	**6**	**7**	**8**	**9**	**10**	**A**
5–8	H	H	H	H	H	H	H	H	H	H
9	D	D	D	D	D	H	H	H	H	H
10	D	D	D	D	D	D	D	D	H	H
11	D	D	D	D	D	D	D	D	D	D
12	H	H	S	S	S	H	H	H	H	H
13	S	S	S	S	S	H	H	H	H	H
14	S	S	S	S	S	H	H	H	H	H
15	S	S	S	S	S	H	H	H	H	H
16	S	S	S	S	S	H	H	H	H	H
17	S	S	S	S	S	S	S	S	S	S
18	S	S	S	S	S	S	S	S	S	S
19	S	S	S	S	S	S	S	S	S	S
20	S	S	S	S	S	S	S	S	S	S
21	S	S	S	S	S	S	S	S	S	S
A,2	H	H	D	D	D	H	H	H	H	H
A,3	H	H	D	D	D	H	H	H	H	H
A,4	H	H	D	D	D	H	H	H	H	H
A,5	H	H	D	D	D	H	H	H	H	H
A,6	D	D	D	D	D	H	H	H	H	H
A,7	S	D	D	D	D	S	S	H	H	H
A,8	S	S	S	S	S	S	S	S	S	S
A,9	S	S	S	S	S	S	S	S	S	S
A,A	SP	SP	SP	SP	SP	SP	SP	SP	SP	SP
2,2	H	SP	SP	SP	SP	SP	H	H	H	H
3,3	H	H	SP	SP	SP	SP	H	H	H	H
4,4	H	H	H	D	D	H	H	H	H	H
5,5	D	D	D	D	D	D	D	D	D	H
6,6	SP	SP	SP	SP	SP	H	H	H	H	H
7,7	SP	SP	SP	SP	SP	SP	H	H	H	H
8,8	SP	SP	SP	SP	SP	SP	SP	SP	SP	SP
9,9	SP	SP	SP	SP	SP	S	SP	SP	S	S
10,10	S	S	S	S	S	S	S	S	S	S
H-Hit, S-Stand, D-Double Down, SP-Split										

and re-dealt nonstop directly from the machine, by the dealer. This should not be confused with an "automatic" shuffler, which uses a machine to shuffle the cards, but the cards are removed from the machine after the shuffle and placed in the shoe by the dealer. The difference? The continuous shuffler speeds up the game considerably, since there's no break for a shuffle, or a player cut. This increases the number of hands you'll play in your allotted session, and gives the house edge more chances to work against you. Remember, in blackjack, speed kills. If possible stick with the old-fashioned hand shuffle by the dealer, or even an automatic shuffler.

SHOE BREAK

If you see a sign on a table that reads "No mid-shoe entry," you can't enter play in the middle of the shoe. You have to wait until the shoe ends to start play. Some players have the belief (unsupported by mathematics) that new people can bring bad luck or change the cards. Or they feel it just ruins the flow of the game. Casinos mostly put these signs at high-limit tables to keep their highest-betting customers happy.

SIDE BETS AND VARIATIONS GAMES

Other strategies used by the casino to separate you from your money involve side bets and variation games. A side bet is a high-paying bet that's based on getting three 7s, a pair, a two-card 20, a three-card poker hand, and so on. This bet is usually placed before the cards are dealt, and isn't tied to the results of the main game—it's completely separate. Like the bonus bets in poker table games, these bets carry a hefty house edge and should be avoided.

Variation games like Double Attack Blackjack, Double Exposure Blackjack, or Spanish 21 use the rules of blackjack but change the dynamics of the game to stimulate more action and entice high-house-edge bets. For example, in Spanish 21 the deck has only 48 cards, because the 10s have been removed. Consequently, the rules allow players to do common blackjack things at strange times—you can surrender after your first two cards are dealt, or double down on any number of cards. Plus, hands like 6-7-8 and 7-7-7 pay automatic bonuses. There are many different variation games and side bets. If you're interested in learning them, you can take a course or ask the dealer, if he or she isn't busy. You should have a good understanding of how to play standard blackjack before attempting these games.

WHERE TO PLAY

For the best odds: Check out the blackjack survey at ⊕ *wizardofvegas. com/guides/blackjack-survey* for the latest info. According to a recent update, **Aria, Bellagio, The Cosmopolitan of Las Vegas,** and **Treasure Island** have 3-to-2 double-deck games with a house edge around 0.25, but you often must be willing to play $15 or $25 per hand. **To learn the game:** Downtown casinos are your best bet for low minimums. On the Strip **Circus Circus** and a handful of other casinos have $5 games.

3

POKER

Even after the poker boom of 2006–10, folks still can't seem to get enough of poker. The top players are celebrities, and poker is on TV more than hockey. If you've played, you know why: it's an intellectual challenge to suit any size brain. And it has an egalitarian quality that beginners love; sometimes the cards fall just right for rookies and they win a tournament, or take home a huge pot.

BASIC RULES

In poker you win by being the last player standing at the end of the hand. That happens one of two ways: by betting more than anyone else is willing to bet and forcing other players to "fold" (drop out until the next hand), or by having the best hand of all players remaining in the game after the final round of betting. The two twists that make poker great are that the hands of each player evolve as more cards are dealt or revealed, and that some or all of the cards are hidden from view, so you can only speculate on the hand values of other players.

The variations played in casinos—Seven-Card Stud, Texas Hold'em, Omaha, and a smattering of others like Razz and Pineapple—all demand that the player create the best five-card hand from a deal that originates from a single standard deck of 52 cards. Five-card hands are valued in order of their statistical rarity:

■ Straight Flush: Five cards of the same suit in consecutive rank. A 10-to-ace straight flush is called a "royal flush," the rarest and highest of all hands.

■ Four of a Kind: Four cards of equal rank plus one nonmatching card.

■ Full House: Three cards of equal rank, and two of a different equal rank (for example, 7-7-7-5-5). This hand is declared as "sevens full of fives." The value of the full house is dependent on the three equal cards, not the two. If two players both have full houses, the player whose three equal cards are higher value will win (for example, A-A-A-2-2 is better than K-K-K-7-7).

■ Flush: Five cards of the same suit, regardless of order.

■ Straight: Five cards in consecutive order, regardless of suit.

■ Three of a Kind: Three cards of equal rank, and two other nonmatching cards.

■ Two Pair: Two equal cards of one rank, two equal cards of a different second rank, with a fifth nonmatching card. Similar to the full house, the value of the highest-ranking pair wins (for example, 10-10-4-4 beats 7-7-6-6).

■ Pair: Two cards of equal rank, and three other nonmatching cards.

AT A GLANCE

Format: Multiplayer card game, dealt by house dealer.

Goal: Bet your opponents out of the game, or have the highest hand in the final showdown.

Pays: Varies; each pot is determined by the amount of betting.

House Advantage: None. The house "rakes" a small percentage of the total money played.

Best Bet: Tournaments are a great way to stretch your poker dollar, even for novices.

Worst Bet: Underestimating your competition.

■ High Card: Any five cards that don't fit into one of the *above* categories in which your highest card carries the value of your hand. If two hands have the exact same high card, the value of the next highest card is used, and so forth until the single largest-value high card is revealed.

The high card will also determine a winner when hands have the same value, such as a straight, flush, two pair, or a pair. For example, if two players have a pair of 9s, the player with the highest value of the remaining three cards wins (which is referred to as a "kicker, as in "I have a pair of 9s with an ace kicker"). Aces are the highest-ranked card with one exception: they can act as the low end of a straight (ace, 2, 3, 4, 5). The 5 card is considered the highest-ranked card for such a straight. In a final-round showdown that hand would lose to a 6-high straight (2, 3, 4, 5, 6). The suits are all equal in poker and totally identical hands split the pot.

The game starts when cards are dealt to all players at the table, who then take turns putting casino chips into a central "pot" during a predetermined number of betting rounds. When it's your turn to bet, you can decide to *check*, which means that you essentially pass your turn to the next player, or *fold*, which means you no longer participate in the hand. Any money you've already bet stays in the pot after you fold and will go to the winner of the hand. To stay in the game, each player must match, or *call*, the highest bet of that round to stay in the game. Players can also *raise*, which means that they are betting more than the round's current highest bet. After a raise, the betting round continues until everyone who wishes to stay in the game has contributed an equal amount to the pot.

Once all the betting rounds are over, if more than one player remains in the game, there's a *showdown* where all cards are revealed. In most games the highest-value hand wins, although some poker games pay players for having the lowest hand, as you will soon see.

GAME VARIATIONS

TEXAS HOLD'EM

Hold'em is the most popular form of poker. Each player (up to 10 can play one game) is dealt two cards facedown, followed by a betting round. Then five community cards are dealt on the table in three groups, each followed by a betting round. First is a group of three cards (the *flop*), and then there are two more rounds of one card each (the *turn* and the *river*). You can use any combination of your cards and community cards to create your best five-card hand.

Position is very important in Hold'em. The deal rotates around the table after every hand, and with it, the *blinds* (minimum opening bets used to stimulate the betting action). Depending on house rules, either one or two players must automatically bet in the first betting round, regardless of their cards (that's why they're called blinds; you have to bet without even seeing your cards). To stay in and see the three cards of the flop, the other players must match (or raise) the blind bet. This ensures that no player sees the flop for free, and adds heft to the pot. The later your position, the better—players have an advantage if they can see what the players before them decided to do, and can better judge whether the size of the pot justifies the risk of betting and staying in the game.

■ **TIP→** The dealer will hold your seat at a poker table for up to a half hour (for bathroom breaks, smoking, or just fresh air). Upon returning, you'll have to post the small and big blinds if you want to play immediately, or wait until the deal comes around to you naturally. If you don't return in the allotted time, you'll lose your seat at the table and your cheques will be collected and stored in the cashier cage until you claim them.

OMAHA

Omaha is dealt and played exactly like Hold'em except the player is given four cards instead of two, and *must* use two, and *only* two of the four cards, plus three of the community cards, to make his or her final hand. This adds another dimension to the game, as you must base your strategy on using only two of the four cards in your hand, and this strategy may change drastically from flop to river, because of the extra cards you're holding. You should have some experience playing Hold'em before taking on Omaha, in which reading hands is more complicated.

SEVEN-CARD STUD

In Seven-Card Stud there are no community cards; you're dealt your own set of seven cards over the course of five betting rounds: an initial batch of three cards (two down, one up); three more single up cards; and a final down card. By the showdown, every player remaining in the game has three down cards and four up cards from which to make his or her best five-card hand.

POKER BETTING LIMITS

Casino poker rooms list ongoing games and soon-to-start tournaments on a large video monitor at their entrance. Before you get into a game, you should understand the betting limit nomenclature. Here are the basics:

Limit Games. Also known as a "Fixed Limit" game, the amount you can bet is listed with two numbers, like "$3–$6." This means you must bet and raise $3 in the first two rounds of play and $6 in the third and fourth rounds. The amount of the "big" blind bet is equal to the low limit ($3).

Spread Limit. This type of game gives the player a range for betting and raising. An example would be a "$1–$4–$8" game, where your bets must be at least $1 and at most $4 for the first two rounds, and between $1 and $8 in the later rounds.

Pot Limit. Players are allowed to wager any amount up to the total of what's currently in the pot.

No Limit. These games are exactly what they sound like; they usually have low betting minimums (they're listed as "$1–$2NL") designed to jump-start the betting action every hand. If you've got the chips on the table, you can bet them. This is the style of play you see on television, where players go "All In." Don't get involved in a No Limit game if you don't know what you're doing.

HI-LOW GAMES

Sometimes you'll see Omaha and Seven-Card Stud listed with Hi-Low. These games are played with the same rules as their relatives with one big exception. To win the entire pot, you must have the best high hand *and* the best low hand. A low hand is basically the lowest value you can make for your five cards. For example 5, 4, 3, 2, A (or "wheel" as it's referred to) is the lowest possible hand. In a regular game of Omaha, this would be a straight, and a fairly high-ranked hand. In Hi-Low the straight rank used for the high hand isn't also assumed when determining the low hand. If one player has the high hand, and another has the low hand, the pot is split between them. If more than one player has an identical winning low, or high hand, then half of the pot is split between them and so forth.

STRATEGY

If you're a beginner, focus on learning how to play the game at low-stakes tables or tournaments before you invest any serious bankroll. The old adage "if you can't spot the sucker at the table, it's you" is never truer than at a Las Vegas poker table. Playing free poker online is a valuable tool for players who are trying to learn the game before a Vegas trip, but the style of play is different. Playing online ignores a lot of the subtleties of playing live, including the all-important *tells*, outward quirks that reveal the contents of your hand to observant opponents. Also, remember that you're not betting real money when you play online, and may be inclined to play bad hands that would be ill-advised to play in real money games.

Although bluffing and big showdowns are part and parcel of the TV poker phenomenon, casino poker success in limit games and small tournaments comes with a steady, conservative approach. The most important thing to learn is how to calculate *pot odds*. You compare the amount of money likely to be in the pot—your potential win—with the relative odds that your hand will be improved as more cards are dealt or revealed. As with everything in life, if the payoff is big enough, the price you pay to stay in the game is worth the risk.

There are no shortcuts to learning poker strategy. Each variation of the game has its nuances. Part of learning the game is to understand how good your hand has to become in order to win a hand, given a certain pot size and number of opponents. You can get lucky, but it takes study and repetition to become consistently good at poker over the long haul.

POKER DERIVATIVES

All of the following games are played like traditional casino table games that use the elements of poker at their core. These games are found in the main casino area with the other table games instead of the poker room. Although there are other variations of poker games around Vegas, these five are the most common. Most of these games carry high house advantages, but move at a slower, more relaxed pace, so you won't lose as quickly as you might at blackjack or craps. Most of them also have a jackpot or bonus bet that can carry a very high payout for rarer hands, which makes the hefty house advantage seem worth it to many players. The bonus hands and payouts are always clearly listed at the table, and you can always ask the dealer how to play these bets if you're feeling frisky.

THREE- AND FOUR-CARD POKER

Three- and Four-Card Poker are two of the most popular poker table games, and at least one table of either can be found in virtually every casino in Vegas. Because you have fewer than the standard five cards to make your final poker hand in both of these games, the odds of making certain hands change. As a result, the ranking system of hands is adjusted. For example, in Three-Card Poker, a straight beats a flush. The hand rankings will be listed clearly right on the table layout in front of you for your convenience. As always, if you're not sure of something, ask the dealer.

Three-Card Poker. First, place a bet in the "Ante" spot. You and the dealer get three cards facedown. After seeing your cards, you have the option to fold and surrender your Ante, or to play and make the "Play" wager (directly beneath the Ante). The Play will always be equal to your Ante. The dealer will then reveal his or her cards. If the dealer doesn't have a total hand value of queen-high or better, he or she doesn't *qualify*. If this is the case, the dealer will return your Play bet to you and you'll get paid even money on your Ante, *no matter what you have*. If you have a straight or better, you'll also get a bonus on your Ante for having a rare hand. If the dealer qualifies for the hand with a queen-high or better, and has a hand that's better than yours, he or she collects your Ante and Play bets. If he or she qualifies and your hand is better, you'll be paid even money on both your Play and Ante bets (and an Ante bonus if your hand qualifies).

POKER TOURNAMENTS

Poker tournaments are an excellent way for beginners to learn the game of poker in a real-life setting without the risk of losing large sums of money to more experienced players. Most casino poker rooms run tournaments in most of the popular games at different times throughout the day. Schedules can be found in the poker rooms, your room, or at the front desk. The listings will contain the game offered, the limits of the bets, if any, the amount it will cost you to enter plus the amount you pay the casino to run the game ($60+$15, for example), if you can rebuy any more chips when your first amount runs out (or add on any more chips when the rebuy period has ended), the time start, and any other pertinent information. The entry fees of all the players who play in the tournament are put into a prize pool that pays out to a top number of finishers, which is determined by how many players enter (for example, the top 10 finishers out of 100 that entered will get prize money). The tournament is played just like the live game except the players use fake poker chips instead of real ones, and the blinds increase at fixed time intervals to speed the game along. When you've lost all your chips and rebuys, you're out of the tournament. The one left with all the chips is the winner of the tournament, and wins the top money prize out of the pool.

Four-Card Poker. You start with an "Ante" wager and are dealt five cards, which you must use to make your best four-card hand. The dealer, however, will be dealt six cards to make his or her best four-card hand. Because of this extra card, there's no minimum hand needed for the dealer to qualify, as in Three-Card Poker, so you'll always have to beat the dealer to get paid. If you fold, you lose your Ante. If you decide to play, you can wager from 1 to 3 times your Ante wager in the spot marked "Play" (directly beneath the Ante). If your hand beats the dealer's when it's revealed, you'll be paid even money on both Ante and Play bets. You'll be paid a bonus on your Ante if your hand is three of a kind or better. If your hand isn't better than the dealer's, you lose both bets. Because the house has a large advantage by receiving an extra card in this game, it'll pay you if you push, or tie, the dealer's hand.

BONUS BETS

Both of these games have a stand-alone bet that has nothing to do with whether you win the hand or not. These bets are the real reason that these games are so popular, and even though they're optional, they're placed by most people who play the game. They pay high odds for rare hands, adding the excitement of potentially hitting a small jackpot. In Three-Card Poker it's called Pair Plus (above the Ante). If you choose this bet and get any hand that has a rank value of a pair or better, you get paid a bonus of up to 40 to 1 on your initial bet, depending on what the hand is. In Four-Card Poker the same bet is called Aces Up (also above the Ante). It pays if you get a hand that's at least a pair of aces or better, and like the Pairs Plus bet in Three-Card, it's paid at increasing odds, depending on how rare your hand is, up to 50 to 1. In both games the bonus hands, and what they pay, will be clearly marked on the table layout.

CARIBBEAN STUD

Caribbean Stud has waned in popularity as more exciting games like Three-Card Poker have emerged, so you might not find this game in every casino anymore. Each player places an initial Ante bet. You and the dealer are then dealt five cards facedown. The dealer will expose one of his or her cards to entice you to play. You must then decide whether to remain in the game, in which case you place an additional wager in the "Bet" square equal to double your Ante, or fold, in which case you lose your Ante.

After you've placed your additional bet, or folded, the dealer reveals the rest of his or her hand. If the dealer's hand isn't better than a minimum value of ace-king high, he or she doesn't *qualify,* and you're paid even money on your Ante wager, and push on your Bet wager, even if the dealer's nonqualifying hand is better than yours. If the dealer has a hand that's better than a value of ace-king high, it qualifies. If it's better than your hand, you lose both bets. If your hand is better than the dealer's *qualifying* hand, you're paid even money on your Ante wager, and your additional wager will get paid at even money, or at increasing odds, depending on what the hand is (for example, two pair pays 2 to 1, a straight pays 4 to 1). This game also offers a hard-to-resist $1 side bet for a progressive jackpot that pays bonuses for any hand better than a straight, and the jackpot (advertised in flashing lights) for a royal flush. This bet offers terrible odds, but adds to the excitement factor.

LET IT RIDE

You're dealt three cards; the dealer lays down two community cards. If your three cards plus the community cards make a five-card hand that's a pair of 10s or better, you win. You start by placing three bets of equal size. On the first two bets you have the option to take them back or let them ride, as the community cards are revealed. When the second community card is revealed, the dealer turns over your cards. If you don't have a pair of 10s or better, you lose your remaining bets. If you have the 10s or a better hand, you're paid even money, or at increasing odds based on what hand you have, on all the bets you let ride during the betting rounds. Like Caribbean Stud, there's a $1 bonus bet that will pay out if you get a hand that's three of a kind or better.

PAI GOW POKER

In this game you're dealt seven cards from which you make one five-card and one two-card poker hand. The two-card hand can *never* have a better rank value than the five-card hand, so set your cards carefully. There's a joker, which can be used as an ace in either hand, or a wild card to complete a straight or flush in your five-card hand. You play against the dealer, who also makes two hands from seven cards, and will always set them according to a strict set of house rules.

PAI GOW TILES

Many Vegas casinos offer Pai Gow Tiles, a distant cousin to poker. You'll recognize it right away because it's the only game in the house that uses a set of 32 dominoes (or "tiles") along with three dice. The goal of the game is to assemble a hand that beats the banker.

The dice are used to determine order of play, which begins with each player being given a stack of four tiles. The player then arranges them into two hands of two. Once everyone has set their pairs, the banker reveals the house hands and the players who beat both hands win even money, the players who win one and lose the other push, and the players who lose both hands lose their wager. There's also a 5% commission involved and a bank option for the players.

The twist, and what makes Pai Gow so addictive according to its adherents, is that there are different approaches to arranging your pairs. Because of this, and whether or not you bank the hand, the house edge can vary. What makes it a difficult game to learn is that the tile pairs have a specific—and nonintuitive—ranking system, which determines when hands win and lose.

If both of your hands are beat by the dealer's hands, you lose. If you lose one and win one, you push. If you win both hands, you win even money on your bet, minus a 5% commission to the casino. Some casinos now offer a "commission-free" version of the game, which is a slightly better bet.

WHERE TO PLAY

With the big boys: Bellagio, one of the oldest and most storied poker rooms on the Strip; and **Caesars Palace,** where the poker room is an open pit in the middle of the busy casino. **Best all-around poker room: Aria,** without question the most popular room in town among visitors, locals, and professionals alike.

3

SLOTS

Slot machines are the lifeblood of the Vegas casino, earning mountains of cash (roughly 80–85% of the total gambling handle on an average year). There's a reason why there are what seems like zillions of slot machines compared with table games—they guarantee a fixed rate of return for the casino with no risk. Some gamblers can't get enough of the one-armed bandits, and if you're one of them (a gambler, not a bandit), set yourself a budget and pray for those three 7s to line up.

BASIC SLOT PLAY

Playing slots is basically the same as it's always been: insert money, see what happens. Over the years the look and feel of the games have changed dramatically. Machines that dispense a noisy waterfall of coins have all but given way to machines that pay with printed, coded tickets—gone are the one-arm-bandits of yore. Tickets are inserted like cash and redeemed at the cashier's cage or at ATM-like machines that dispense cash. If you're a historian, or sentimental, you may still find a few coin-dispensing relics in some of the Downtown or off-Strip casinos. Nearly all games are digital. The mechanical spinning reels that physically revolved have been replaced by video touch-sensitive screens that are interactive. These screens offer fun bonus games for big bucks and excitement and make you feel like you played some role in the outcome. No matter which format you prefer, the underlying concept is still the same: you're looking for the reels—real or virtual—to match a winning pattern of shapes.

Each reel may have a few dozen shapes, creating an enormous number of possible patterns. The payout varies, depending on how rare the pattern is. The payout tables for each shape are usually posted above or below the "play" area of the machine. On some of the newer digital machines, there's a button marked "Payout Table."

STRATEGY

All slot machines, including every mechanical reel game, are run by onboard computers. The machine's computer brain generates a new random number thousands of times a second, which then determines where each reel will come to rest.

Although the casino can set the percentage an individual machine will retain for the house over the long term, each individual spin is an independent, random event. That means that if a jackpot reel pattern appears and pays a huge amount, the next jackpot is equally likely (or unlikely) to appear the very next spin. There's no such thing as an overdue machine, or a machine that's "tapped out."

Slot "payout" ranges can vary between 80% and 98%. A machine that pays out at 98% will, in the long

AT A GLANCE

Format: Bill- and ticket-operated electronic/mechanical machines.

Goal: Line up winning symbols on machine's reels according to payout schedule.

Pays: Varies by machine and casino.

House Advantage: Varies widely, depending on how the machine is set.

Best Bet: Playing "looser" higher-limit machines at the maximum coin bet.

Worst Bet: Playing "tight" machines at noncasino locations.

run, pay back 98 cents out of every dollar you put in, as opposed to the paltry 80 cents you'll get back on the 80% machine. Picking the right machine can make the biggest difference in how fast you lose. Of course, information on which slot machines are the loosest (the ones that pay out the most) is hard to obtain, and can change often. Play the games you enjoy, but never lose sight of the fact that the payout percentage of that machine will usually determine how much you win or lose.

■TIP→ Make sure you always insert your player card into the appropriate slot before you insert cash or tickets. Slot players often enjoy lucrative promotions and comps that table-game players don't.

CHOOSING A MACHINE

■ Higher-denomination machines tend to have higher payback percentages.

■ Look for machines that advertise a higher payout, but beware of the fine print. The machines with the high progressive jackpots are usually the tightest. Resist the temptation, and avoid them.

■ If you want to take a shot at the jackpot, you need to play the *maximum* coins with *every play*. If that means stepping down to a lower-denomination machine (e.g., from dollars to quarters) so you can afford it, then do it. After all, we know that hitting the jackpot is the "reel" reason you're in Vegas.

VIDEO POKER

Video poker attracts a large following. Many gamblers enjoy the solo play of a slot machine, but prefer a slightly more complex set of rules, like to have a say in the outcome, and can't get enough of that feeling when that fifth card completes a full house. Make no mistake, video poker is not "live poker on training wheels." People love video poker because it's fun and convenient, and because the house advantage can be relatively low under the right circumstances.

BASIC RULES

Casino visitors will find video poker in long rows of machines just like slot machines. And many casino bars feature video-poker consoles for patrons to play as they sip. To play, just feed in bills or tickets to buy credits, then play the game until those credits run out or you decide to take the money and run.

Unlike regular poker, with its multiple betting rounds, bluffs, and competing players, video poker is all about you making the best possible five-card hand as the computer deals. Video poker comes in many different flavors like "Jacks or Better," "Double Bonus," and "Deuces Wild." Each game has a slightly different gimmick but follows the same basic sequence. After your bet (usually from one to five credits), you get dealt five cards, faceup. You then have to choose which of the five cards to keep by either touching the card on the screen or by activating the appropriate button underneath each card. The cards you didn't keep are replaced with new cards. If it contains a winning combination, you get paid. It's that simple.

Or is it? Imagine you've bet one coin on a Jacks-or-Better game and you're dealt four hearts and one spade. Holding your four hearts and discarding your spade gives you a decent chance at making a flush (five cards of the same suit), which pays six coins. But before you throw it away, you realize the spade you hold is an ace, which matches your ace of hearts to make a pair. A pair pays only one coin, but it's a guaranteed payout, versus the possible payout of the flush. That dilemma—and others like it—is at the heart of video poker and is what makes it so much fun for so many.

3

UNSPOKEN RULE

Veteran players can be territorial about their machines and often play several at one time. If you're unsure whether a machine is "occupied," politely ask before you sit down. Casino personnel can direct you to open machines.

STRATEGY

The first priority for any video-poker player is finding the best machines. That's because even though two machines may be identical in the game or games they offer, slight variations in the payoff table make one far more advantageous to play than the other. Note: Most machines pay out with tickets instead of actual coins, and are multidenominational (that is, the machine will allow you to choose how much each "credit" is worth, from 1 cent all the way up to many dollars per credit). *In the following Payouts section, you can interchange the words "coins" or "quarters" with "credits," and it will mean the same thing.*

PAYOUTS

Video-poker enthusiasts identify games by certain key amounts in their payout tables (displayed on the machine). For example, with Jacks-or-Better (JOB) games, the important values to look for are those for the payout on a full house and flush. Put simply, what you want are what's known affectionately as full-pay machines, and for JOB that means a 9/6 payout. If your game pays nine coins on a full house and six coins on a flush, you've found a 9/6 machine (that is "nine six" machine, not "nine-sixths" machine) and it's the most advantageous you'll find. So if the JOB game you just bellied up to pays less than 9/6 on a full house and flush, you should take your coins elsewhere.

Full pay for Double Bonus games are 10 coins to 1 on a full house and 6 coins on a flush. So if that's your game, look for 10/6 machines (if

VIDEO POKER RULES

You'll find many video-poker variations in Vegas casinos, and a single machine can sometimes host several different game types, allowing the player to pick his or her poison from a menu. Here's a quick primer on the most popular:

Jacks-or-Better: The most common video-poker game, and the basis for many variations. The player must have at least a pair of jacks to be in the money.

Deuces Wild: Players must have three-of-a-kind to be in the money, but 2s are wild; that is, they become whatever card you need them to be to make your poker hand. Got two jacks, two queens, and a 2? The 2 can act as a jack or queen, so you've got a full house!

Double Bonus: Requires a pair of jacks or better to be in the money, but offers varied payouts on four-of-a-kind hands, with a bonus for getting four aces.

you're very lucky, you might find a rare 10/7 machine). Full pay for a Deuces Wild game is 9/5, but these numbers actually refer to the single coin payout for a straight flush and a four-of-a-kind. If that seems low for such stellar poker hands, remember that the presence of wild cards makes the likelihood of an outstanding hand quite a bit higher. In fact, some experts go so far as to list the five-of-a-kind payout and define full-pay Deuces Wild as 15/9/5. Such machines are rare these days on the Strip, and when they're found, it's often for higher bet denominations. Why? Read on.

Certain video-poker games are considered positive advantage games, meaning the potential exists for players to actually win money over the long term (unlike just about every other game in the casino). ■TIP→ To make the house edge negative, though, the player must bet the maximum coins and make the statistically optimum choice during every single hand. In a 25¢ game, you can choose to play any multiple of 25¢ up to five times that amount (five quarters or $1.25) per hand. If you examine the payout schedule for most video-poker games, you'll see that the payout on the highest-value hands is inflated for maximum bet games. This is the casino urging you to bet more per hand.

For example, if you get a royal flush with four quarters in a common Jacks-or-Better game, the payout is 1,000 quarters. Bump your bet up to five quarters per hand and your royal flush is worth 4,000 quarters. The occasional windfall of a royal flush can boost the game's return up over 100%. The casino is betting on human behavior here—expecting that many royal flush winners will have inserted less than the full bet. Nevertheless, the positive payout expectation is what makes video poker such an attractive game. However, the time and bankroll necessary to invest before hitting the full-pay royal flush can be prohibitive, so don't count on paying for your kid's college with video-poker proceeds.

3

ROULETTE

Roulette is an easy way to cut your teeth on the whole table game experience. You select and bet on numbers, groups of numbers, or a color (red or black); watch the dealer drop a ball on a spinning wheel; and hope that the ball lands on your space. It doesn't get more straightforward than this.

BASIC RULES

Most wheels are divided into red and black slots numbered 1 through 36 along with two green slots labeled 0 and 00 (zero and double-zero). The dealer (or croupier) drops a little white ball onto the spinning wheel, and as it loses momentum, it falls onto a series of randomizing obstacles until it settles into one of the numbered slots. You place your bet on a layout filled with numbers; the main betting area has 12 rows of three squares each, alternating red and black and covering numbers 1 through 36. There are also two green spaces for betting on 0 or 00. You can put chips on single numbers, or the lines that connect two, four, five (if 0/00 is involved), or six numbers together. You can also bet on entire categories of numbers, such as red/black, odd/even, and 1 through 18/19 through 36, or one of six different ways to bet on one-third of the numbers at one time.

INSIDE AND OUT

When you buy into roulette, you're issued specialty chips so that each player at the table has his or her own color. When you want to stop, trade your roulette chips for regular casino chips. ■TIP→ **Roulette chips are good only at the roulette table you bought them from. If you try to play at another table, or visit the cashier cage with them, you will be told to return them to the table you got them from.** As in any other game, you have to meet the table minimums when you're betting, but it gets a little confusing with roulette because the rules

Roulette Table

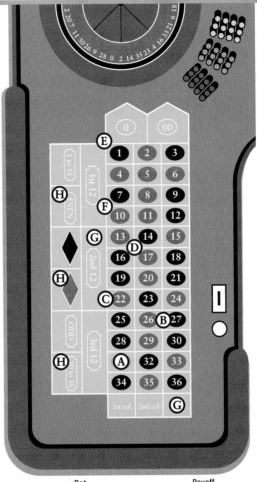

	Bet	Payoff
A	Single number	35 to 1
B	Two numbers	17 to 1
C	Three numbers	11 to 1
D	Four numbers	8 to 1
E	Five numbers	6 to 1
F	Six numbers	5 to 1
G	12 numbers (column)	2 to 1
G	1st 12, 2nd 12, 3rd 12	2 to 1
H	1-18 or 19-36	1 to 1
H	Odd or Even	1 to 1
H	Red or black	1 to 1

are different depending on what you want to bet on. Outside bets and inside bets are separate, and if you choose to bet on either or both, the table minimum rules apply independently. An "outside" bet is made anywhere but on the actual area of the layout that contains the numbers 0, 00, and 1–36. Even, Odd, Black, and Red would be outside bets. An "inside" bet is any bet placed within the numbered area. Betting the 1, 22, and 36 would be considered inside bets. A $5 minimum roulette table means you must bet $5 per bet if you bet on the outside, and $5 total if you bet inside. You may bet in smaller denominations on inside bets, but all inside bets must add

up to the minimum (even if you placed outside bets that make your total amount wagered over the table minimum).

So $5 on a single outside bet (like "Red") is legal, whereas five different $1 bets on the outside aren't. And regardless of whether you've placed an outside bet or not, a $1 inside bet is legal only if there are other inside bets that bring the total amount wagered inside to $5. So you could place $2 on your birth month, $2 on your birthday, then $1 on No. 21 in honor of your favorite movie.

Once betting is closed and the ball lands in its spot, the croupier places a marker on the winning number, on top of the stack of winning chips (if there are any). All the losing chip areas, inside and outside, are raked, and the croupier pays out each winning bet. Never reach for your winnings or start to make new bets until *all* the winning bets have been paid and the dealer has removed the marker from the table.

STRATEGY

Roulette is as simple a game as you'll find in the casino. The only complexity is in learning exactly where to place bets to cover the numbers you like. The odds, though, aren't good. The casino keeps more than 5% of the total amount wagered on American (or double-zero) roulette.

The best plan, if you're going to get serious about it, is to seek out the handful of "European" wheels in Las Vegas. The Euro wheel has only a 0, and no 00. Also, if the 0 is hit, you will lose only half of your even money bets. This will lower the house edge to 1.3% for even money bets, and 2.7% for all the rest. Unfortunately the few Euro wheels on the Strip usually reside behind the velvet ropes of the high-limit areas, so be sure to weigh the advantages of playing this type of wheel

against what you can afford to bet, and lose. Another option is the single-zero wheel. Like the Euro wheel, this wheel has only a 0, and no 00, but you lose 100% of your money on even money bets (unlike the Euro wheel). This wheel has a much better house edge (2.7%) than the double-zero wheel, and you can find these wheels in a few casinos on the main floor, with lower minimums.

RAPID ROULETTE

Rapid Roulette is an automated version of roulette. Instead of standing around a table, you sit at your own video terminal or a cluster of virtual terminals. Players give live dealers cash for credits, and make bets via the video screen. The ball is then spun on a live wheel, and the winning number is input into the machine. You're paid by credits for your winnings at your own terminal. When you cash out, the live dealer will give you chips for your winnings. You can find Rapid Roulette at many Strip casinos, including Luxor, Caesars, and MGM Grand.

WHERE TO PLAY

For low-limit games: Try Sam's Town (✉ *5111 Boulder Hwy., Boulder Strip* ☎ *800/897–8696* ⊕ *www.samstownlv.com*). **For single-zero games:** Most of the tables in town have disappeared, but **The Venetian** still offers single-zero games, both on the main casino floor and through its handheld electronic gaming device. **To go all night: Golden Nugget's** croupiers will hold your spot while you run to the 24-hour Starbucks in the South Tower for a jolt of gambling gasoline.

3

CRAPS

Even if you've never played this game, you may have heard the roar of a delighted crowd of players from across the casino floor. Craps is a fun and fast-paced game in which fortunes can be made or lost very quickly, depending on how smart you play.

It can look intimidating or complicated to the beginner, because there are so many bets that can be placed on every roll, but this shouldn't deter you from stepping up to the table to play. Craps offers a couple of the best odds bets in the casino.

BASIC RULES

At its core, craps is a dice game. A dice thrower—a "shooter"—tosses two dice to the opposite end of a table and people bet on what they think the outcome or future outcome of the dice will be. It's the job of the "stickman" (the dealer with the stick) to keep the game moving, and to call out the dice totals so everyone knows them no matter what their vantage point at the table is. Two other dealers place bets for you, pay the winners, and collect from the losers. A "box man" sits or stands in the middle and supervises the action. The main layout is duplicated on the right and left sides of the table, although the middle section (the betting area in front of the stickman) is common to both wings of the craps table.

To play, step up to the table wherever you can find an open space. You can start betting casino chips immediately, but you have to wait your turn to be the shooter. If you don't want to "roll the bones" (throw the dice) when it's your turn, motion your refusal to the stickman and he or she will skip you. To roll the dice, you must place a bet first. Then choose only two of the five dice offered by the stickman.

DO'S AND DON'TS OF SHOOTING

Do: Use one hand to pick up the two dice you have chosen. Use the same hand to throw them.

Don't: Move the dice from one hand to the other before you shoot. It arouses suspicion of cheating.

Do: Throw both dice at the same time, and be sure to hit the far wall. A roll that doesn't hit the far wall will not count, and the box man will make you retry.

Don't: Slide the dice during your toss.

Do: Follow table etiquette when someone else is shooting. Generally, this means that you should finish placing all of your bets before the dice is passed to the shooter.

Don't: Put your hands down into the table when someone else is shooting. If the dice hit your hand, it's considered bad luck. If a 7 "loser" is rolled after touching your hand, you may be blamed. To prevent this, again, make all of your bets before the dice are passed to the shooter.

AT A GLANCE

Format: Dice game played around a long, high-walled table.

Goal: Players bet that certain numbers or sequences of numbers will be rolled.

Pays: Even money on Pass/Don't Pass, Come/Don't Come, varies for other bets.

House Advantage: Varies according to what you bet.

Best Bets: Pass, Don't Pass/Come, Don't Come with full odds.

Worst Bets: Field bet, any proposition bet.

PASS LINE BETS

The game starts with the "come-out" roll. This is the first roll after someone rolls a 7, or if you happen to be the first one who comes to the table. The most common bet on the come-out roll is the Pass/Don't Pass Line, which can only be placed on the come-out roll, and which serves to illustrate the basic pattern the game follows.

RIGHT-WAY

Pass Line bettors bet *with* the shooter, or *right way*. If the come-out roll turns up a 7 or 11, it's an automatic win and they'll be paid even money on their Pass Line bet. If a total of 2, 3, or 12 (aka "craps") comes up on the come-out roll, they lose. The exact opposite applies for the Don't Pass bettor, who bets *against* the shooter, or *wrong way* (the exception to this is if a 12 rolls, which is a push for the Don't Pass/Don't Come bettor). For learning purposes, we'll focus more on right-way bets, which is the majority of bettors. Wrong-way bets are covered below.

If a shooter rolls a total of 4, 5, 6, 8, 9, or 10 on the come-out roll, it's known as hitting a "point." The point (5, for example) will be marked with a puck so everyone knows what it is. Once a point has been established, the players have the option to back up their Pass Line bets with "odds." The odds bet is probably the hardest bet for the beginner to understand. This is unfortunate because it's the best bet in the casino for the player, and it's not marked on the layout for this reason. The odds bet is placed directly behind the Pass Line bet. The maximum amount of odds you can take will be listed on the table, and it varies by casino. The term *5x odds* means you can bet up to 5 times your Pass Line bet. *The odds bet is so great because it's the only bet that has a 0% house edge.* Because of this, you should always play maximum odds, if you can afford to. Many other bets can be made at this point as well, but we'll cover them separately. Once all odds bets and any other bets are placed, the shooter keeps rolling the dice until he or she rolls the point again, or a 7. Any other rolls in the meantime won't affect the Line bets from winning or losing. If a point is hit before a roll of 7, it's called a *winner* and anyone who bet Pass will get paid even money on their Line bet, and the "true odds" on their odds bet. These are 2 to 1 for a roll of 4 or 10, 3 to 2 for a roll of 5 or 9, and 6 to 5 for a roll of 6 or 8. If the shooter rolls a 7 before he or she rolls the point, it's called a *loser,* and all Pass Line bets and the odds are lost. Once that happens, the dice are passed to the next player to "come out" and the sequence starts all over again.

OTHER BETS

In addition to Pass and Don't Pass bets, you can also make the following important wagers at craps:

COME BETS

Come bets can also be confusing for beginners, but if you understand how the Pass Line works, it's just as easy. The Come bet pays exactly the same as a Line bet and has the same great odds, so you should take the time to learn how to bet it. The main difference between a Line bet and a Come bet is that the Come bet is placed *after* the come-out roll, once a point has been established. Try to think of a Come bet as being just like its own little private Pass Line bet for you only, that you can place at any time during the roll (which you can't do with a Pass Line bet). Put your Come bet in the area marked "Come." The next roll is now the come-out roll for your Come bet only, which will win on 7 or 11, or lose on 2, 3, or 12. If the next roll is any other number, the dealer will put your Come bet on that number, and that number will now be the point for your Come bet only, not the Pass Line point (which has already been established). Now that the point has been established for your Come bet, you can take odds on it, just like the Line bet. This is done by placing your chips in the "Come" area and stating to the dealer that you want odds on your Come bet. The dealer will stack your Come odds on top of your Come point bet and a little offset, so he or she knows the amount of your original Come bet as opposed to your odds bet. Now that your Come bet has a point, it's subject to the same rules as the Pass Line. If your Come point is rolled before a 7, you win and the dealer will pay you in the "Come" area. If a 7 is rolled before your Come point, you lose.

PLACE BETS

If you want to bet on a number without subjecting to the rules of the Pass Line or Come, you can "place" it. The casino pays reduced odds for this bet, as opposed to true odds on the Line or Come. A Place bet can be wagered at any time on any number in the squared boxes. If that number is rolled before the 7, you win. Otherwise you lose. If you place the 4 or 10, it'll pay 9 to 5; the numbers 5 or 9 pay 7 to 5, and the numbers 6 or 8 pay 7 to 6. If you win the Place bet, the dealer will pay you your winnings only and leave your original bet on the number. Unlike a Come or Line bet, you can take down this bet at any time if

Craps Table

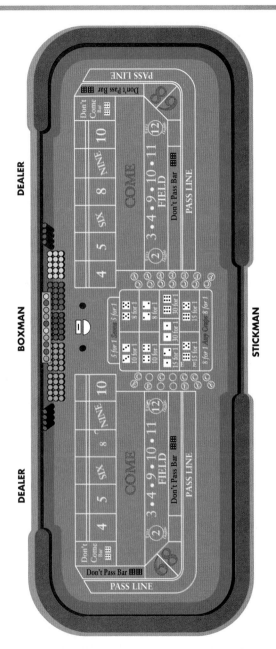

you want. To make it easier for the dealers to figure the payouts, you should bet in multiples of $5 for the numbers 4, 5, 9, and 10, and multiples of $6 for the 6 or 8. The house edge is a very reasonable 1.52% for a Place bet on the 6 or 8 and a good option, but this isn't true for the other numbers. If you must place the 4 and 10, then "buy" them and you'll reduce the house edge on those bets. A "Buy" bet is a Place bet in which you pay a 5% commission to the house to get true odds on your money (in the case of 4 or 10, that's 2 to 1). Make this bet at least $20 or it won't be worth it. Never buy the 5, 9, 6, or 8.

3

■TIP→ Betting the Big 6 and 8 is exactly the same as placing the 6 and 8 with one important difference. Big 6 and 8 pays you only 1 to 1, as opposed to the 7 to 6 you'll get when you place them. This is the reason this bet is printed so huge and is closer to you on the table layout. The casino wants you to bet here, instead of making the better Place bet. Just say NO to the Big 6 and 8.

ONE-ROLL BETS OR PROPOSITION BETS

One-roll bets are exactly that, bets that win or lose on one roll of the dice (for example, Field, Eleven, or Double Sixes). Basically you bet what you think the next roll will be. If you happen to guess right, you will be paid the odds listed on the table for that bet. These bets are located in front of you or the stickman, and you toss your wager in to him and tell him what you want. He or she will place your one-roll bet for you (except the Field, which you place yourself). One-roll and hard-way bets are also considered "proposition bets," so named because well-trained dealers will try to entice you to make these bets after every roll. The only proposition bet that's not a one-roll bet is a hard-way bet. A "hard" number is basically an exact pair on the dice (for example 2-2, 4-4). This bet will remain on the layout until a "soft" version of your number comes up (say 5-3 instead of 4-4), or a 7 is rolled. In this case you'll lose your hard-way bet. Hard-way bets can't lose on the come-out roll. Note: Hard-way bets are always live, or "working" on the come-out roll unless the player specifically calls them "off" (this will be announced by the stickman before the come-out roll). If you want to wait until a point is established before you put the hard-ways in action (and avoid a winner 7 from wiping out all of your hard-way bets at the same time), be sure to tell the stickman that your hard-ways are "off coming out." He or she will then place an "off" button on your bets to indicate that your bets are "off" until a point has been established. Proposition bets carry an abysmal house edge (as much as 16.67% for some bets). Avoid these like the plague.

DON'T PASS BETTORS
WRONG WAY

Don't bettors, or wrong-way bettors, as they're called, are betting against the shooter. They win when the shooter rolls a 7 (once the point is established), when everyone else at the table will lose. The wrong-way bets are the Don't Pass and Don't Come, and they work exactly opposite to the Pass and Come. You can "lay" odds on the Don't bets also, but since you have the advantage once the point has been established (because 7 is the most common roll), the casino will compensate for this by making you bet $6 to get $5 on the point of 6 or 8, $7 to get

CRAPS SAMPLE BETTING SEQUENCE

Here's a sample sequence of bets, starting with a new shooter coming out. You begin by placing a $10 chip directly in front of you on the Pass Line:

Roll 1. Come-out: shooter throws a 7, a winner for the Pass Line. The dealer pays you $10. Since no point was established by this roll, the dice are still in the come-out phase.

Roll 2. Come-out: shooter throws a 2—craps. Dealer takes your $10 Pass Line chip, which you must replace to keep playing. There's still no point, so the dice are still "coming-out."

Roll 3. Come-out: shooter throws a 4—a point. Pass Line bets now win only if another 4 is thrown before a 7. You take $10 odds behind your Pass Line bet, and decide to place a $10 chip in the "Come" betting area.

Roll 4. Shooter throws a 12—craps. Your Pass Line bet is unaffected, but your Come bet loses because it's still in the come-out phase. You replace it with another $10 Come bet.

Roll 5. Shooter throws a 9. Your Pass Line bet is unaffected. Dealer moves your Come bet chips onto the 9 square. You take $10 odds on your Come bet, and the dealer stacks it on top of your original $10 Come bet that's now in square 9, so you're now rooting for either a 4 (Pass Line bet) or a 9 (Come bet) to appear before any 7.

Roll 6. Shooter throws a 3—craps. Both of your bets are unaffected.

Roll 7. Shooter throws a 9. Your Come bet is a winner. The dealer will pay you $10 for your original bet, and $15 (3 to 2) for your odds bet, and place your winnings, original bet, and odds in the "Come" area for you to pick up. You now have no more Come bet.

Roll 8. Shooter throws a 7. Your remaining bet on the Pass Line loses.

$5 on the 5 or 9, and $2 to get $1 on the 4 or 10. Many people avoid wrong-way betting because they don't like the idea of betting more to get paid less, or they don't like to "go against" everyone else at the table. This is understandable, but wrong-way betting carries slightly better odds than right-way betting, and should be considered once you feel comfortable playing the game.

STRATEGY

Getting an education first is a good strategy for all the games, but it's essential for craps. Before you step up to a craps table, learn and understand the rules and mathematics of the game, as well as table etiquette, betting procedures and placement, and which bets to stay away from. Craps is by far the most complicated game to learn in the casino, and if you throw money blindly into it without understanding how it works, you'll lose fast. Our advice is to use the basics given here as a starting point, then build on that by getting a more advanced book, taking a lesson at a casino, or learning and playing online for free. Playing craps offers too much fun and excitement to be ignored, so take the next step and do your homework. You won't regret it.

At the craps table, the dice thrower is called the "shooter" and the dealer is the "stickman."

For those who don't mind playing "without a net" (you know who you are), or don't have the time or patience to sit for a class, you can enjoy the game using the basics above. Keep in mind that only a few bets carry a low house edge. They are

- Pass/Don't Pass Line with maximum table odds.
- Come/Don't Come bet with maximum table odds.
- Place bet on the 6 or 8.

Stick to these bets. It's best to bet the minimum on the Pass/Don't Pass line and then make the odds bet for the maximum the table allows, or as much as you can afford to comfortably. If you feel you must bet proposition bets for some extra action, limit the amount you bet to single dollars. Even if you get lucky and hit some of these on occasion, rest assured that over time these bad bets will eat a big chunk of your potential winnings.

WHERE TO PLAY **For the highest odds: Main Street Station** Downtown offers up to 20-times odds and several $5 craps tables. On the Strip, **Casino Royale** (✉ **3411 Las Vegas Blvd. S, Center Strip** ☎ **702/737–3500** ⊕ **www.** casinoroyalehotel.com**) has low minimums and generous 100-times odds on certain craps bets. For the friendliest dealers: The crews at **Treasure Island** or **The Mirage** will help you learn and keep your bets on track.

BACCARAT

Baccarat (pronounced bah-kah-rah) is a centuries-old card game played with an aristocratic feel at a patient rhythm. Baccarat is wildly popular around the world in all its varied forms and is gaining popularity in the United States. In fact, due to soaring popularity among whales, in many Vegas casinos baccarat has replaced blackjack as the most profitable table game for the house.

Although it's an easy game to play, baccarat has an air of mystery about it—perceived by many as a game played only by James Bond and powerful tycoons, behind closed doors with special access. Not so. The big version of the game may be the game of choice for many wealthy gamblers who like to play in roped-off areas or private rooms, and have very high betting limits, but the mini version of the game is becoming increasingly common in Vegas, because it's extremely easy to play. Like the big game, it has reasonable betting limits and carries a very good house edge for the casual gambler.

PLAYING THE "BIG BAC"

Up to 14 players can squeeze into a baccarat table, but the game is played out with just two hands. Before play starts, you place your bet on one of three possible outcomes: the Player hand will win, the Bank hand will win, or that play will result in a Tie. The Tie bet can be placed along with a Bank or Player bet, or by itself. When it's your turn, you can either accept the responsibility of representing the Bank, or you can pass the shoe on to the next player in line.

The dealers, with an assist from the Bank player holding the shoe, start the game by dealing two two-card hands facedown. The Player hand is dealt first and is traditionally placed in front of the gambler with the largest Player bet, who then turns them over and slides them back

Baccarat Table

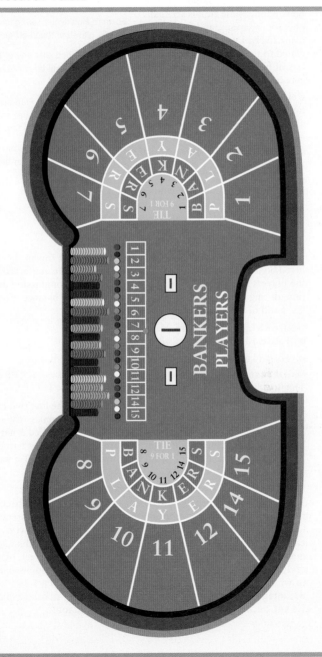

to the dealer. The player holding the shoe does the same with the Bank hand. These rituals are really only for ceremony, and to keep the game lively. Everyone at the table is tied to these two hands, regardless of how they're dealt and who gets to turn them over.

Depending on the value of the initial two-card hands, an extra card may be added to each hand according to a complicated set of drawing rules. Ask your dealer where you can get a copy of the rules when you sit down so you can follow the action. The winner of the hand is determined by which side has the higher total after all cards have been drawn. If you win on the Bank side, you must pay the house a 5% commission. The dealers keep track of this in the numbered boxes in front of them, which correspond to the numbered seats the players are sitting in. You can pay down this commission at any time during the shoe, but must pay any remaining balance after the last hand of the shoe has been played.

> ## AT A GLANCE
>
> **Format:** Multidealer card game usually played in roped-off areas.
>
> **Goal:** Player bets that one of two hands of cards will be closest to 9.
>
> **Pays:** Even money on Player and Bank bets; 8 to 1 (or more) on Tie bet. Bank bettors pay 5% fee.
>
> **House Advantage:** 1.06% on Bank bets, 1.24% for Player bets, 14+% for Tie bets.
>
> **Best Bet:** Bank bet.
>
> **Worst Bet:** Tie bet.

UNDERSTANDING THE HANDS

- Face cards and 10s equal zero.
- For any total more than 9, the first digit is ignored.

So if the cards are 7, 7, and jack, the total would be 14: $7 + 7 + 0 = 14$. The first digit [1] in 14 is ignored, so the final total is 4.

If you draw a total of 9 (a $10 + 9$, for example) on the first two cards, it's called a "natural" and is an automatic winner, unless the other side draws a natural 9 for a tie. A total of 8 is also called a natural, and can be beaten only by a natural 9 or tied with another natural 8. If a tie does occur, the Bank and Player bets push and the Tie wagers are paid at 8 to 1 (or more).

STRATEGY

There's no play strategy in the North American version of baccarat; the game is carried out according to immutable rules. In essence it's like choosing heads or tails, and flipping a coin to see who wins. Baccarat players enjoy looking for patterns in previously dealt hands that might give them a clue what will win next, by keeping track of them on little scorecards. But in the end your guess is as good as theirs as to who'll win the next hand. ■TIP→ The Bank bet, at a 1.06% house advantage, has good odds for such a simple game. Always avoid the Tie bet, because it has an excessive house advantage.

MINI-BACCARAT AND EZ-BACCARAT

The popularity of the big version of the game has waned over the years, and many casinos are removing the large tables altogether in favor of the smaller, more accessible version known as mini-baccarat. If you want to try baccarat, but can't handle the high minimum bets, the glacial pace, and the odd superstitious rituals of the big game, look

MISSING NUMBERS

You may notice that some of the baccarat layouts are missing numbers (usually 4, 13, and 14). This is because they're considered unlucky numbers in certain cultures.

for a mini-bac table. They're usually in the main pit of any casino with the rest of the table games, or sometimes in a separate or Asian-theme room. Mini-bac follows the same rules as its blue-blooded cousin, but it's played at a much smaller blackjack-style table. The minimums are lower and a single dealer dispenses the hands, without the players ever touching the cards. The players merely place their bets for each new hand dealt. Midi-bac, or Macau-style mini-bac, is a hybrid of the big and mini-bac games. It's played at a slightly larger mini-bac table. In Midi, one dealer handles the shoe, but the players get to handle and reveal the cards as in the big game. These games sometimes employ an extra bet called "Dragon Bonus" or "Emperor Bonus." As with most side bets on table games, this one has a high house edge and should be ignored.

EZ-Baccarat is another version of mini-bac that plays the same, except there's no commission charged for winning Bank bets. In this game the casino makes its money on the "Dragon" bet. If the bank wins the hand with a three-card 7 total, it's called a "Dragon." When this occurs, the Player hand and Tie lose, and all Bank bets are pushes. If you bet on the Dragon, you'll be paid 40 to 1 if it hits. Another side bet on this game is called the "Panda." If you bet the Panda, you'll be paid 25 to 1 if a three-card 8 on the Player side wins.

WHERE TO PLAY

Baccarat on a budget: Harrah's, The M Resort, and the Golden Nugget have tables with reasonable minimums. With the whales: Aria is baccarat nirvana. To be alone: Try wireless handheld electronic baccarat at The Venetian. Find a comfortable chair and play for stakes so low it makes the high rollers giggle.

SPORTS BETTING

Nevada remains the only place in America where you can physically, legally bet on sporting events. The betting takes place in a sports book, a dedicated area of a casino that accepts wagers on upcoming games. Here you can try your luck on all the major team sports in America, plus a few individual sports. You can place a wide variety of wagers— from the outcome of a single game to a combination of events. You can even place "futures" wagers on a game that won't kick off for several months.

Sports books make money by taking a small percentage of the total amount bet on both sides of a game; this is called vigorish, or vig for short. Casinos adjust the odds they offer on a game to attract a similar amount to be bet on both teams. That ensures that they get their cut risk-free, regardless of who actually wins the game.

BASIC RULES

Placing a bet in a sports book is simple. Pick a game where you like the betting odds, either in the form of a "point spread" or a "money line," *both of which will be explained below.* The sports book will have a betting window or counter with a cashier who'll take your wager (you have to pay up front) and issue you a ticket that states the details of your bet. Don't lose that ticket! If your wager is a winner, return to the betting window after the game, turn in your ticket, and you'll get your initial bet plus your winnings.

The most common bet in a sports book are 11-to-10 bets and involve a point spread. That means for every $11 you risk (or lay), you win a profit of $10. Place an $11 sports bet, and you get back $21 if your team beats the spread.

Nevada is the only state where you can legally bet on sporting events. Bets must be placed in sports books, which you'll find in almost every casino on the Strip.

POINT SPREADS

An 11-to-10 bet indicates a nearly even-money bet. But if the two teams aren't evenly matched, the casino needs some way to prevent the public from betting heavily on the superior team. That's what a point spread is for; it provides a scoring "handicap" to make both teams equally attractive to a bettor.

When you read a point spread listing, one team is usually the favorite (denoted with a negative number), and one is the underdog (with a positive number). Consider this point spread listing:

Sooners

Longhorns -6.5

The spread on this game is 6½. They sometimes use half points to eliminate the possibility of ties. The sports books have determined that the public believes the Longhorns are more likely to win the game. To lure bettors to wager on the Sooners, the casino is effectively agreeing to take away 6½ points from the Longhorns' final score (or add 6½ points to the Sooners' score, depending on which way you look at it) when it evaluates bets placed on that game. Sports bettors will say that the spread on this game is "the Longhorns minus 6½" or "the Sooners plus 6½"—the two phrases mean the same thing. If you bet on the Longhorns, they'll have to have won by a margin greater than the point spread for you to win your bet. If you bet on the Sooners, your bet wins if the Longhorns win by less than the spread (for example, the Longhorns win 21–17, a margin of victory less than the point spread) or lose the game outright. If your point spread wager ends in a tie, the sports book will return your original bet, minus the vig, which it always takes.

OVER/UNDER

Here you're betting on whether the combined final score of the game will be either over or under a designated total. The total is determined by the sports book and usually appears in the point spread listing like this:

Giants 42.5

Eagles -7

The negative number is the point spread, and it has no effect on over/under bets. The other number, 42.5, is the total for this game. Bettors are welcome to bet on the point spread, the over/under, or both. Over/under bettors would try to predict whether the combined score of the Giants and Eagles will be higher or lower than the total (in this case, 42.5). If the Giants won 24–20, the combined score would be 44, so the over bets win and the under bets lose. An over/under bettor wouldn't care who won the game, as long as either lots of points were scored (over bettors) or few points were scored (under bettors).

> **AT A GLANCE**
>
> **Format:** Wagering against the house at a dedicated betting counter.
>
> **Goal:** Correctly predict the outcome of sporting events.
>
> **Pays:** Varies by type of bet and casino. Standard is $10 won for every $11 bet.
>
> **House Advantage:** 4.55% on 11-to-10 bets, varies with other types of bets.
>
> **Best Bets:** NCAA basketball, NFL Over/Unders.
>
> **Worst Bets:** Proposition bets, Futures bets, Teasers.

■ TIP→ Betting odds vary from sports book to sports book, and they can change over time right up to the moment a sporting event starts. But once you place your bet, the point spread, money line, and/or payout odds are locked in place for that wager. Your bet is evaluated and paid according to the odds on your betting ticket.

THE MONEY LINE

Money Line bets have no scoring handicap attached to them (such as a point spread). The bet wins if the team wins on the field. Sports books use money lines to entice you to bet on the underdog by increasing the payout in the event that team wins. And they discourage bettors from taking the better team by reducing the payout if they win. Let's take a look at an example:

Astros +150

Cubs -170

The two numbers represent money lines. The underdog has a positive number and the favorite has a negative number. For underdogs, the amount shown is the amount (in dollars) you'd win on a $100 bet. In this case, if the underdog Astros won and you bet $100, you'd win $150. On the other hand, the Cubs money line represents the amount you have to risk to win $100. Because the Cubs are seen to be more likely to win, the sports book asks a bettor to pay a premium to bet on them—to win $100, you'd have to bet $170.

NUMBER OF TEAMS	PARLAY BETTING ODDS	PAYOUT ODDS
2	13–5	3–1
3	6–1	7–1
4	10–1	15–1
5	20–1	31–1
6	40–1	63–1
7	75–1	127–1
8	140–1	225–1
9	200–1	511–1
10	400–1	1,023–1

Note: You don't have to bet $100 at a time. The money line just represents the proportions of amount risked to amount won (and vice versa). Most casinos require a $5 or $10 minimum bet.

PARLAYS

A parlay bet is a combination bet where two or more bets must win in order for your wager to pay off. A single parlay bet might include several different sports, as well as point spread, money line, and over/under bets. You can even parlay two games being played simultaneously. Standard parlay odds vary by casino, *but the table is a good example of what to expect:*

If you get all wins plus a tie on your parlay, the bet will still pay, just at the next lowest level of odds. For example, if you bet a four-team parlay and three of the bets beat the spread but the final game tied against the spread, you'd be paid 6 to 1 as if it were a three-teamer. If you get a win and a tie on a two-team parlay, it pays as if it were a straight 11-to-10 bet.

■ TIP➜ Parlay cards are a quick way to bet on multiple games, but they sometimes have reduced payouts relative to normal parlay bets; sports books do not take vigs on parlay bets.

IN-GAME BETTING

In-game Betting is a relatively new and exciting way of making sports bets. The term *In-game Betting* describes a bet that you make on a game that's happening in real time. For example, you can make a bet on whether or not a player will make the next free throw in a basketball game that you're currently watching or which hockey team will score the next goal. Before this technology you had to make all of your final bets on a game before it started, and couldn't change or revise them once the game started. Players have two options for making In-game wagers. The first (and older) of the two revolves around a wireless, phone-size device known as an eDeck or PocketCasino; the second option comprises apps players can download to their mobile phones (but use only when they are in Nevada). Both of these iterations use similar technology to the software that runs the stock market; technology that can calculate and recalculate odds in real time. This enables the casino to change the odds tables, or lines, extremely quickly based on what's happening in the game being played at that time. How's this applied? Check out this scenario: You bet the "under" on a football game with an over/under of 40. At halftime the score is 27–10, which is already very close to the "over" of your original bet, and almost a certain loser. The computer has adjusted the over/under to 51 at halftime, enabling you to hedge (bet the other side to guard against a loss) your original bet, and now bet the "over." The benefit of this is that you have some information about how the game is being played because you're watching it as it's being played and can make better-educated guesses in the near future based on how the teams have already played in the past. The savvy bettor can also use information like momentum shifts, the resting of star players, and key injuries in real time to further enhance his or her chances. Of course, the downside is that you may still lose both bets and could get carried away placing too many bets to hedge your past losses as the game proceeds. Although this new type of betting may add some real excitement to watching and betting on sports, we recommend you have some knowledge and experience with sports betting, and know the sports you're betting on, before you try In-game Betting.

TIPS

■ Betting against a team is just as valid—and profitable—as betting for a team.

■ Pick a few teams, become intimately acquainted with them, and be prepared to bet for and against them based on your expertise. Don't try to learn the habits of the entire league.

■ Be realistic. Sporting events include innumerable random events, so even the best sports bettors are thrilled to win 60% of their 11-to-10 bets over the long haul.

■ Avoid exotic bets. Casinos let you bet on almost anything; don't take them up on it. Stick with the bets listed in this chapter.

■ Beware of hype. It's often wrong. Do your own homework and draw your own conclusions, and take joy in being a contrarian. The sports media have a way of making certain teams look utterly unbeatable. No team ever is. History is littered with examples.

■ Become an NCAA hoops fan. With so many teams in play leading up to March Madness, it's easy for odds-makers to get a point spread wrong, especially when smaller schools are playing each other.

■ Take a pass sometimes. Remember that a losing bet not placed is a win.

WHERE TO PLAY

For the best snacks: Every casino has plenty of eateries, but at Lagasse's Stadium, inside The Palazzo, the snacks are all gourmet and they're conceptualized by Emeril Lagasse. Reservations are required (usually with a $200 food-and-beverage minimum) for big events. **To watch the big game with your buddies:** Hands-down it's Caesars Palace, followed by The Mirage and The Wynn. If you're in the hinterlands, head to Red Rock.

CASINOS

Vegas casino floors can vary dramatically in motif and interior design, but the basic play of the table games and slots, whether they're under decorative awnings, faux garden trellises, or mirrored ceilings, is the same. Odds, table limits, and machine "looseness" *(see Blackjack and Video Poker sections)*, however, can vary greatly from casino to casino, so it pays (literally) to do a little research on the casino in which you wish to play.

Rewards and loyalty programs also vary. Of course, none of that may be as important to you as the overall setting and crowd. Here's the lowdown on some of Sin City's most popular casinos, and a few gamblers' choices, too.

SOUTH STRIP

Luxor Las Vegas. Although the casino at Luxor has lost almost all of its Egyptian flair, the new modern gaming floor delivers a vibe that's genuinely hip and exciting. The two main bars, Centra and Aurora, both open up to the casino, making them great spots to meet friends who'd rather not gamble. In the regular-limit area, table minimums are usually around $15 on weekends, but during the week you might find $10 tables. Free craps and blackjack lessons are offered daily at noon in the dice pit near the casino cage. If poker's your game, heads up; the Luxor's room has received awards from local newspapers and looks out on the sports book for easy bet-chasing after you fold. ⊠ *3900 Las Vegas Blvd. S, South Strip* ☎ *702/262–4444, 877/386–4658* ⊕ *www.luxor.com.*

Mandalay Bay Resort and Casino. Table limits start around $15 during the week, but often rise to $25 on the weekends, when crowds descend and throw particularly absurd amounts of money around on roulette. Pits of table games are spread out across 135,000 square feet, and with rows and rows of slot machines, the casino floor is sprawling. The high-limit area is one of the fanciest big-stakes parlors on the Strip, but it offers little other than baccarat; in the Lotus Room, gamblers can play Pai Gow and other Asian games while sipping tea. Toward the entrance to Delano Las Vegas, the sports book has high ceilings but a noticeable dearth of seats. The poker room occupies a corner of the sports book with great views of the big screens. ⊠ *3950 Las Vegas Blvd. S, South Strip* ☎ *702/632–7777, 877/632–7800* ⊕ *www.mandalaybay.com.*

MGM Grand Hotel & Casino. The biggest of the Las Vegas casinos, the MGM has a staggering amount of gaming space, which includes more than 3,500 slot machines and 165 different table games. Table minimums on blackjack, craps, and roulette mostly start at $15; on weekends nearly all jump to $25. The Strip entrance is all about the sports book (unless you consider gambling on beer pong at Level Up). Slots and pits of table games fan out from there. The Mansion, the casino's high-roller area (with mostly baccarat), exists in a separate wing with its own bar, kitchen, and entrance. You don't have to play to hang here; so long as you're respectful (and quiet), this casino-within-a-casino is home to some of the best whale-watching in Vegas. ⊠ *3799 Las Vegas Blvd. S, South Strip* ☎ *702/891–7777, 877/880–0880* ⊕ *www.mgmgrand.com.*

Monte Carlo. The Monte Carlo will change dramatically by the beginning of 2018, but the small-ish casino still is an appealing place to play. Two pits of traditional table games were removed in 2016 for electronic/virtual games from Interblock; customers seem to enjoy the newfangled options just as much. Hit Bar & Lounge, the high-limit area, is a swanky alternative to the main floor and offers mini- and Midi-baccarat and blackjack games up to $5,000 per hand. A high-limit slots room offers maximum bets up to $100 per pull. ⊠ *3770 Las Vegas Blvd. S, South Strip* ☎ *702/730–7777, 888/529–4828* ⊕ *www. montecarlo.com.*

New York–New York Hotel & Casino. The casino at New York–New York is just like New York City itself: loud, boisterous, and incessant. The gaming floor has a decor that can be described as art deco meets neon-futuristic. Table limits are a little lower than the high-end Strip casinos, with $5 blackjack available 24/7 and other table minimums starting at $10. Generally speaking, table games fan out from the Center Bar, and slot machines line the periphery of the casino. The oval-shape high-limit table games and slots area feature ornate Murano crystal chandeliers and wood paneling. Sports bettors will be disappointed by New York–New York's race and sports book—the area sits in a corner by the Sporting House, and barely has enough seats for a professional basketball team. ⊠ *3790 Las Vegas Blvd. S, South Strip* ☎ *702/740–6969, 800/689–1797* ⊕ *www.newyorknewyork.com.*

CENTER STRIP

Aria Resort & Casino. CityCenter's lone casino is at Aria. Oddly, however, whereas the rest of the hotel is bathed in sunlight, the main gaming floor (especially the middle table games pits) can at times feel too dark. Brighter gaming experiences can be had in the high-limit salons; there are separate rooms for American games (blackjack and roulette) and Asian games (mostly baccarat). Poker fans rave about Aria's spacious poker room, which has the private Ivey Room (named after Phil Ivey) for professionals. Perhaps the only disappointment is the sports book, which is oddly shaped and has sequestered horse betting in a closet-size satellite. ⊠ *3730 Las Vegas Blvd. S, Center Strip* ☎ *702/590–7757, 866/359–7757* ⊕ *www.aria.com.*

3

Bellagio Las Vegas. This roomy casino is luxurious and always packed. Under tassled, orange canopies you can sometimes spot high rollers betting stacks of black chips ($100 apiece) per hand. In Club Privé, the high-roller's area, wagers climb even higher. There are games for more typical budgets, too. Low-denomination slots are tucked in the back corners for low rollers, and excellent blackjack games are offered for mid- to high-level players (table minimums usually start at $15). If you can find them, the $10-minimum craps tables also can get lively. The casino's epicenter remains its now-famous poker room, which rose to national notoriety as a key element of the TV poker fad. Players such as Daniel Negreanu are regulars here, though they frequently hit Bobby's Poker Room, a private room behind a closed door. Elsewhere in the casino, the race and sports book is small but cozy; each leather seat is equipped with its own TV monitor. ⊠ *3600 Las Vegas Blvd. S, Center Strip* ☎ *702/693–7111, 888/987–6667* ⊕ *www.bellagio.com.*

Caesars Palace. Considering how huge Caesars Palace really is, the actual gaming area feels remarkably small. The Palace Casino retains its 1966 intimacy, with low ceilings and high stakes. The Colosseum Casino offers ShuffleMaster automated table games, and became home to the poker room in 2016. The Forum Casino boasts high ceilings, soaring marble columns, and graceful rooftop arches, and embraces the middle market with 5¢ and 25¢ slots and lower limits (but more stringent rules) on table games. The best place to gamble in Caesars Palace is in the race and sports book, which was refurbished in 2016 and now boasts the largest big-screen in town. A new bar at the back of the book has tightened the space a bit, but the area still has its signature armchairs for optimum viewing pleasure. ⊠ *3570 Las Vegas Blvd. S, Center Strip* ☎ *702/731–7110, 866/227–5938* ⊕ *www.caesarspalace.com.*

Casino Royale. The great odds are what make this no-frills casino (it's actually a Best Western!) across the street from The Mirage worth a visit. The place is famous for $3 craps and was the first casino in town to offer multiple Push-22 blackjack-derivative games, such as Blackjack Switch and Free Bet. Other options include $5 single-deck blackjack and a host of slot machines ranging in denominations from 1 penny to $5 a pull. With deals like these, Casino Royale isn't exactly known for top-shelf service; table-drink delivery can be painfully slow. Also, dining options are limited; if you're not into the Outback Steakhouse or Denny's, you're better off walking to The Venetian next door. ⊠ *3411 Las Vegas Blvd. S, Center Strip* ☎ *800/854–7666* ⊕ *www.casinoroyalehotel.com.*

Fodor's Choice
★

The Cosmopolitan. Even with windows that look out to the Strip (rare for casino game floors), the casino at the Cosmopolitan feels cozy; a sense of intimacy is created by its long, narrow layout. The vast majority of the table games here are blackjack, and the craps pit, toward the back of the casino, often gets lively after dark. Also, most slot banks have their own television monitors. The belle of the ball here is the sports book, which debuted in a new space at the front of the casino in 2016. TV screens are everywhere, and a ticker that runs along the top of the bar provides up-to-the-minute scores and odds. ⊠ *3708 Las Vegas Blvd. S, Center Strip* ☎ *702/698–7000* ⊕ *www.cosmopolitanlasvegas.com.*

The Cosmopolitan's glitzy gaming floor

The Mirage Hotel and Casino. The casino at The Mirage can be described as old-school fun. Blackjack and craps tables with $10 minimums are alongside tables with $500 minimums, bringing low rollers and high rollers together on the same gaming floor. The poker room boasts some of the most active games in all of Vegas. Slots abound in just about every direction on the gaming floor. There's a high-limit lounge that offers blackjack, baccarat, and video poker. True gamblers come to The Mirage for its race and sports book. The book, to your left when you enter from the Caesars Palace side of the Strip, brags about 10,000 square feet of big-screen action and, well, it should—it resembles NASA's mission control. ⊠ *3400 Las Vegas Blvd. S, Center Strip* ☎ *702/791–7111, 800/374–9000* ⊕ *www.mirage.com.*

Paris Las Vegas. Dealers in this casino are trained to wish players *bonne chance,* which loosely translates into "good luck" in English. This catchphrase, coupled with the psychedelic sky-painted ceiling, conveys a dreamlike feeling that might distract you from the fact that some table rules are poor for the player. (Hint: stay away from those single-deck blackjack tables; they pay only 6-to-5 for natural blackjacks.) Livelier pits include the craps and baccarat sections; roulette is prevalent here, too—perhaps in keeping with the French theme. Slot machines are plentiful, though waitress service away from the tables can be spotty at best. The race and sports book is quaint but smoky. ⊠ *3655 Las Vegas Blvd. S, Center Strip* ☎ *877/796–2096* ⊕ *www.parislasvegas.com.*

Planet Hollywood Resort & Casino. Slots abound in the casino at Planet Hollywood; fittingly it was one of the first casinos on the Strip with Elvis-themed one-arm bandits. Table-game pits are clustered under Swarovski crystal chandeliers in the center of the main casino floor, and some feature scantily clad go-go dancers starting at 8 pm in the Pleasure Pit. On weekends the low-limit blackjack and Pai Gow tables stay busy for hours on end. The poker room, which sits on the main casino floor, is clean and spacious, and is outfitted with plenty of TVs to catch the big game when you're not staked in a pot. The Heart Bar, at the center of the casino, is a great spot from which to people-watch during breaks in the gambling action. ☒ *3667 Las Vegas Blvd. S, Center Strip* ☏ *702/785–5555, 866/919–7472* ⊕ *www.planethollywoodresort.com.*

NORTH STRIP

Encore. Instead of occupying one giant space, Encore's gaming floor is broken up into tiny salons, separated by columns and exquisite red curtains. Thanks to floor-to-ceiling windows, each of the parlor-style casino areas has a garden or pool view. The gaming is surprisingly diverse, with a variety of low-minimum tables and slots (yes, you can play $10 blackjack here). The main-floor high-limit room features mostly baccarat; upstairs, an even more exclusive area named the Sky Casino features tables with betting limits in the stratosphere. Encore has the poker room for the interconnected Wynn properties; to place sports bets, head to Wynn Las Vegas. Guest room keys double as players' cards and track play over the duration of each stay. ☒ *3131 Las Vegas Blvd. S, North Strip* ☏ *702/770–7000, 888/320–7123* ⊕ *www.wynnlasvegas.com.*

Fodor's Choice ★ **Lucky Dragon.** This casino, which opened in late 2016 on Sahara Avenue just west of the Las Vegas Strip, has an overwhelmingly Asian theme. That explains the giant crystal dragon that hangs two stories above the gaming floor, and all the signs that appear in both English and Mandarin. It also explains why most of the games are Asian in nature: various forms of Pai Gow and baccarat. Sure, you can find a table or two of blackjack and roulette, but you've got to look pretty thoroughly to do so. The four gaming pits ring a center bar, which can get lively (and smoky!) on weekend nights. Not surprisingly, the Asian food here is spectacular. The casino also is one of the few properties in town to offer rolling chip baccarat (which basically is a game where high rollers call the shots). ☒ *300 W. Sahara Ave., North Strip* ☏ *702/889–8018* ⊕ *www.luckydragonlv.com.*

The Palazzo Hotel Resort Casino. Whereas The Venetian's casino can be described as busy and buzzing, The Palazzo's has a more composed vibe. Higher ceilings and wider walkways create a much slower pace on the casino floor; people are always gambling, but there's just more space to absorb their exuberance. Table games include roulette, Pai Gow poker, and Caribbean Stud; a separate high-limit room houses baccarat tables, assuming the biggest bettors will go here. There's blackjack, too, but odds on blackjack payouts vary, so be careful were you sit. The sports book, part of Lagasse's Stadium, is one of the most rollicking game experiences in Vegas. Slots here are plentiful but otherwise nondescript. ☒ *3325 Las Vegas Blvd. S, North Strip* ☏ *702/607–7777, 877/283–6423* ⊕ *www.palazzo.com.*

Treasure Island Hotel & Casino. T.I. has a reputation for being one of the best places to learn table games. Dealers are patient and kind, and just about every table game has an hour of free lessons every day. The best tutorials are in craps, where some pit bosses will go so far as to explain odds on certain bets. T.I.'s slot machines aren't nearly as enticing; despite machines at just about every denomination, the mix is oddly generic. Still, members of the casino's players club get huge deals on slots. The sports book was renovated in 2014. The poker room offers free Wi-Fi. ⊠ *3300 Las Vegas Blvd. S, North Strip* ☎ *702/894–7111, 800/288–7206* ⊕ *www.treasureisland.com.*

The Venetian Las Vegas. The Venetian's casino is a sprawling, bustling nexus of energy at just about every time of day. All told, the gaming floor boasts more than 120 games. Most table limits start at $25, though on weeknights you might find some with minimums of $15. The blackjack tables in particular have very good odds for high-level players—3-to-2 payouts in some cases. What's more, the casino offers a higher-than-typical progressive jackpot, but you've got to buy in for $5 per hand instead of the usual $1. If you like slots, you're in luck—progressive machines abound. The Venetian has kept up with the poker craze and has a tremendous poker room. With more than 50 tables and daily deep-stack tournaments, it's currently the largest poker spot in town. Poker guests even get free valet parking. ⊠ *3355 Las Vegas Blvd. S, North Strip* ☎ *702/414–1000, 866/659–9643* ⊕ *www.venetian.com.*

Fodor's Choice
★

Wynn Las Vegas. Wynn's casino is a gorgeous, inviting place to play (and a great place to spot celebrities). Table limits can be dauntingly high, most starting at $25, and it's not uncommon to spot $500-minimum blackjack tables on the regular casino floor. Lest you dismiss Wynn Las Vegas as exclusively opulent, rest assured that a healthy number of 1¢ slots are out in a prominent area, rather than relegated to some remote corner. It may also surprise you that the coin games have some of the best pay schedules in town. Wynn also offers a variety of push-22 blackjack-derivative games such as Blackjack Switch. There's a nice bar area next to the sports book, where plush chairs line individual viewing cubicles. The poker room for the interconnected Wynn properties now resides at Encore. ⊠ *3131 Las Vegas Blvd. S, North Strip* ☎ *702/770–7000, 888/320–7123* ⊕ *www.wynnlasvegas.com.*

DOWNTOWN

The D Casino Hotel. Old meets new on the gaming floor at The D. The old: an entire floor of vintage slot-machine games, including Sigma Derby, a quarter-powered contest in which plastic horses race around a plastic track. The new: points of sale around the casino that accept Bitcoin. The main gaming area is kitschy; female dealers tap out from behind table games and stand on tables to dance suggestively in lingerie. Thankfully, 3-to-2 payouts on blackjack and 10x odds at craps make the distractions worthwhile. ⊠ *301 Fremont St., Downtown* ☎ *702/388–2400* ⊕ *www.thed.com.*

Downtown Grand Hotel & Casino. In the olden days, the casino at the Lady Luck Hotel & Casino was considered one of the most happening spots in town. When the Downtown Grand opened on the same site in 2013, they sought to create a similar buzz. Results are mixed. The preponderance of low-minimum table games and low-denomination slot machines is a home run. Design, however, with exposed brick and HVAC ducts, is curious and feels like just about any microbrewery in any city in the U.S. The small sports book is operated by William Hill. ⊠ *206 N. 3rd St., Downtown* ☎ *702/719–5100* ⊕ *www.downtowngrand.com.*

El Cortez Hotel & Casino. It's fitting that one of the oldest casinos in Las Vegas (circa 1941, to be exact) still offers blackjack the way it should be played: with natural blackjacks paying 3 to 2. Elsewhere on the gaming floor, you'll find single-zero roulette and stickmen offering up to 10x odds on craps. Slots here are plentiful. The sports book, however, is cramped and in desperate need of the same kind of overhaul the Cortez gave its rooms in 2012. ⊠ *600 E. Fremont St., Downtown* ☎ *702/385–5200, 800/634–6703* ⊕ *www.elcortezhotelcasino.com.*

Fodor's Choice
★

Four Queens Resort & Casino. This isn't the fanciest casino in town, but locals and tourists (especially those from Hawaii, for some reason) love it for its approachable style and low table limits. At certain times of day, this means $3 blackjack (with single-deck games that pay 3 to 2 for blackjack), and 5x odds on craps. The casino also is home to a host of video poker options that pay out at 100%. The modest sports book is rarely crowded, making it a better option than some of the others in town. ⊠ *202 Fremont St., Downtown* ☎ *702/385–4011, 800/634–6045* ⊕ *www.fourqueens.com.*

Fodor's Choice
★

Golden Nugget. This is one of the most celebrated casinos in Downtown Vegas, and the place is as lively as ever. The biggest crowds tend to congregate in the older sections of the gaming floor, which are teeming with slot machines and lower-limit table games. This is also where companies such as ShuffleMaster like to pilot new games. The poker room, in a corner of the main casino floor, holds regular daily tournaments and offers free lessons daily at 10 am. Perhaps the only disappointment is the sports book, which is small and cramped. ⊠ *129 E. Fremont St., Downtown* ☎ *702/385–7111, 800/634–3454* ⊕ *www.goldennugget.com/lasvegas.*

Main Street Station Casino Brewery Hotel. Sure, Main Street grabs headlines for its brewery and antiques collection, but the gaming floor isn't too shabby either. The Victorian-themed 28,000-square-foot casino has the usual suspects of live-action tables, a bingo hall, and more than 800 of the latest video and reel machines. There's also an area of penny slots, as well as a daily slot tournament that usually draws a (surprisingly) large number of entrants—this tournament is what has prompted readers of *Strictly Slots* to vote Main Street's slot offerings best in Vegas. ⊠ *200 N. Main St., Downtown* ☎ *702/387–1896, 800/713–8933* ⊕ *www.mainstreetcasino.com.*

PARADISE ROAD AND THE EAST SIDE

Hard Rock Hotel & Casino. A favorite among the young and wealthy crowd, this hip casino revolves around table games, offering limits that are generally lower than elsewhere in town (which means you can stretch bankrolls longer). Slot machine offerings, which once were scant, now are plentiful. Hard Rock has spent gobs of money in recent years on a cavernous poker room and a new mobile system that enables bettors to wager on sports anywhere on the property. There also is swim-up blackjack in the Palapa Bar at Rehab Beach Club. If you've got the cash, the Peacock high-limit room and the Dragon Salon of Asian games are worth exploring, too. ✉ *4455 Paradise Rd., Paradise Road* ☎ *702/693–5000, 800/473–7625* ⊕ *www.hardrockhotel.com.*

WEST SIDE

Palms Casino Resort. This casino is geared toward locals, with regular and generous promotions for those who sign up for the Club Palms players card program. Slots are plentiful, with more than 1,300 machines total. On weekend nights the casino floor takes on a Strip-like vibe (and table limits rise accordingly). The best value on this floor is craps, with standard $10 minimums. The casino's sports book enables gamblers to bet right from their terminals, or from anywhere on property with a mobile app. Social, the open bar in the center of the casino, has one of the best cocktail menus in town. ✉ *4321 W. Flamingo Rd., West Side* ☎ *866/942–7770* ⊕ *www.palms.com.*

Rio All-Suites Hotel and Casino. The casino floor at The Rio is one of Vegas's liveliest places to play. The casino is perhaps best known for hosting the annual World Series of Poker, six weeks' worth of poker tournaments that culminate with the "Main Event" in which one pro takes home millions of dollars in cash. Elsewhere, the gaming floor serves up spontaneous performances by sexy "bevertainers" (cocktail waitresses who double as dancers), which provide a pleasant enough diversion for you to overlook the house edge. The Rio remains one of the only Vegas casinos to spread Mississippi Stud. There are also more than 1,200 slot machines, including dozens of different statewide progressives. ✉ *3700 W. Flamingo Rd., West Side* ☎ *702/777–7777, 866/746–7671* ⊕ *www.riolasvegas.com.*

SUMMERLIN AND RED ROCK CANYON

Red Rock Casino Resort Spa. Without question, this locals casino in Summerlin is one of the best-kept secrets in the entire Las Vegas Valley. Swarovski crystals sparkle over gamblers who wander around the circular gambling hall, creating a vibe of opulence and swank. There's even more bling inside the open-walled Lucky Bar, in the center of the casino. Despite all of these sparkles, betting minimums are low; it's not uncommon to stumble upon $5 craps and blackjack tables at peak hours. The real "gem" of the casino is the sports book, with its comfy chairs and giant big-screens. A cozy poker room, cavernous bingo hall, and ornate high-limit room (which promises blackjack as low as $25 per hand) also are worth a look. ✉ *11011 W. Charleston Blvd., Summerlin South* ☎ *702/797–7777, 866/767–7773* ⊕ *redrock.sclv.com.*

WHERE TO EAT

BEST BUFFETS IN VEGAS

Buffets originated in the late 1940s as an attention-grabbing loss leader that would attract hungry gamblers to the casinos (and keep them there). Now the buffet concept has grown into an important tradition at virtually every resort.

At the same time, the city's upscale culinary makeover has raised the quality of food in the buffets as well, and they continue to be famous and fabulous. Besides, who doesn't love that uniquely American obsession—unlimited gorging for one set price? Bargain-hunters will still find plenty of deals, but the top buffets typically charge upward of $30—or even $55—per person at dinner. Hey, there are lobster tails, Kobe beef, and unlimited champagne at some of these spreads—you get what you pay for.

OUR FAVORITES

Bacchanal Buffet, Caesars Palace. Named for a famously indulgent (long-gone) Caesars landmark restaurant, Bacchanal reflects the theme of plenty while raising the culinary bar. Therefore you'll find baked-to-order wood-fired pizzas, custom sushi, and daily chef's specials prepared while you watch. ⊠ *3580 Las Vegas Blvd., Center Strip* ☎ *702/731–7928* ⊕ *www.caesarspalace.com/restaurants.html.*

The Buffet at Bellagio. The Bellagio buffet became the first of the "premium" buffets under the ownership of Steve Wynn, bringing game, sushi, and exotic seafoods to the table. A recent introduction is caviar, served with blini, buckwheat waffles, or ahi cones with traditional accompaniments. Bellagio's buffet also has adopted a recent Las Vegas trend toward "bottomless" beverages with weekend brunch, so you can drink as much sparkling wine as you can handle. ✉ *3600 Las Vegas Blvd. S, Center Strip* ☎ *702/693–7111* ⊕ *www.bellagio.com.*

The Buffet at TI. This traditional buffet still provides lots of surprises, such as special desserts and other dishes to celebrate holidays. Weekend visitors also will find prime rib and a wide selection of seafood. ✉ *3300 Las Vegas Blvd. S, North Strip* ☎ *702/894–7111* ⊕ *www.treasureisland.com.*

The Buffet at Wynn Las Vegas. After he sold Bellagio and opened his eponymous resort, Steve Wynn continued remaking the face of Las Vegas with another superlative buffet, this time with dozens of dishes, rotisserie beef, seafood from around the world, and traditional touches like a rich and custardy home-style bread pudding. ✉ *3131 Las Vegas Blvd. S, North Strip* ☎ *702/770–3463* ⊕ *www.wynnlasvegas.com.*

Carnival World & Seafood Buffet, Rio Las Vegas. The Rio has consolidated its traditional and seafood buffets, which means you'll find endless oysters, crab, and more and still be able to have more traditional buffet favorites. Live cooking and carving stations provide a personal touch. ✉ *3700 W. Flamingo Rd., West Side* ☎ *702/777–7757* ⊕ *www.riolasvegas.com.*

Cravings Mirage. Eleven international cooking stations make it easy to find what's where at this traditional buffet, and serve-yourself beverage stations and unlimited beer and wine mean you'll never be thirsty. ✉ *3400 Las Vegas Blvd. S, Center Strip* ☎ *702/791–7111* ⊕ *www.mirage.com.*

Le Village Buffet, Paris Las Vegas. The popular buffet at Paris Las Vegas is divided into sections to reflect the regions of France, which means, for example, rotisserie chicken in Burgundy and buttery fresh crepes in Brittany that are cooked to order. ✉ *3655 Las Vegas Blvd. S, Center Strip* ☎ *702/946–7000* ⊕ *www.parislasvegas.com.*

Wicked Spoon, Cosmopolitan Las Vegas. Wicked Spoon shook up the world of Las Vegas buffets by eschewing the traditional steam-table pans for individual cooking vessels for some foods, such as mini-baskets of french fries and tiny pots of cassoulet; breakfast and lunch are combined into a daily brunch. ✉ *3708 Las Vegas Blvd. S, Center Strip* ☎ *702/698–7000* ⊕ *www.cosmopolitanlasvegas.com.*

Updated by
Heidi Rinella

Las Vegas is one of America's hottest restaurant markets. Nearly every big Strip property has at least one and often two or more celebrity-chef restaurants. Away from the Strip, the unprecedented population growth in the city's suburbs has brought with it a separate and continuous wave of new eateries, both familiar chains and increasing numbers of legitimate destination restaurants.

Casino-resort dining basically falls into one of three categories. In the top echelon are the properties that have a half dozen or more bona fide star-status restaurants: Aria, Bellagio, Caesars, The Cosmopolitan, Mandalay Bay, MGM Grand, Venetian/Palazzo, and Wynn/Encore. At the next level are those resorts with one or two stellar restaurants and a smaller range of worthwhile but not quite top-of-the-line options. On the Strip, these include The Cromwell, Mandarin Oriental, Mirage, Monte Carlo, New York–New York, Paris, Planet Hollywood, SLS Las Vegas, and Treasure Island. Off the Strip, you can add the Lucky Dragon, Palms, the Hard Rock, M Resort, The Rio All-Suite Hotel, Green Valley Ranch, the JW Marriott, and Red Rock Resort. Then there's everybody else: casino-resorts with maybe a decent eatery or two but that simply aren't known for great food.

Downtown Las Vegas has seen a big revitalization in the past several years, and that extends to restaurants. Although Downtown still lacks a destination restaurant, notable spots are Carson Kitchen, Therapy, Turmeric, Le Thai, and La Comida in Fremont East; and Pizza Rock and the older Triple George Grill in the Downtown 3rd District. There also are a number of good restaurants in the Downtown Container Park.

Outside the tourism corridor, Las Vegas has a number of marquee restaurants with increasing cachet among foodies from out of town—places such as Todd's Unique Dining, Marché Bacchus, Nora's Italian Cuisine, and Lotus of Siam. There's great food to be had off the beaten path in Las Vegas, and you'll pay a lot less in these areas, too.

If you haven't been to Vegas in a few years, you'll notice some major changes. Names like Wolfgang Puck, Michael Mina, and Emeril Lagasse still have plenty of pull in this town, but the Vegas chefs commanding the most attention are French imports such as Pierre Gagnaire, Joël Robuchon, and Guy Savoy, along with vaunted U.S. chefs like Giada De Laurentiis, Charlie Palmer, and Mario Batali.

There's also a trend toward high-minded restaurants with exclusive-nightclub vibes. Note the success of see-and-be-seen Pan-Asian hot spot Hakkasan and Tao Asian Bistro & Nightclub, the youthful late-night haunts LAVO and FIX, and bordello-chic establishments such as Strip House—to name just a few. Elsewhere in town, Las Vegas's growing international—and especially Asian—population has created a market for some of the best Chinese, Thai, Vietnamese, and Pan-Asian restaurants in the country.

4

LAS VEGAS DINING PLANNER

RESERVATIONS

As the Vegas dining landscape has become rife with showstopping, one-of-a-kind restaurants, reservations at dinner (and occasionally even at lunch) have become a necessity in many cases. Generally, if you have your heart set on dinner at any of the celeb-helmed joints at the bigger Strip casinos, you should book several days, or even a couple of weeks, ahead. On weekends and during other busy times, even at restaurants where reservations aren't absolutely essential, it's still prudent to phone ahead for a table.

WHAT TO WEAR

Although virtually no Vegas restaurants (with the exception of Joël Robuchon at the Mansion inside MGM Grand) require formal attire, men will likely feel a bit out of place at some of the top eateries on the Strip if not wearing a jacket—at the very least, avoid jeans in these spots. Dressing according to the mood of the restaurant (smart, stylish threads at the better ones) will generally help you out in terms of how you're treated and where you're seated. Casual attire is the norm at lunch, at less fancy venues, and virtually anywhere off the Strip or outside upmarket resorts.

HOURS

The majority of the top restaurants on the Strip are dinner only, although there are plenty of exceptions to this rule. Unless otherwise noted, the restaurants *listed in this guide* are open daily for lunch and dinner. Hours vary greatly from place to place, with 5 to 10 pm typical for dinner hours, but many of the more nightlife-driven venues serve until after midnight or even around the clock. Las Vegas is definitely a city where it's best to phone ahead and confirm hours.

TIPPING AND TAXES

In most restaurants, tip the waiter 16%–20%. (To figure the amount quickly, just double the tax noted on the check and add a bit more.) Bills for parties of eight or more sometimes include the tip already. Tip at least $1 per drink at the bar.

CHILDREN

Although it's unusual to see children in the dining rooms of Las Vegas's most elite restaurants, dining with youngsters doesn't have to mean culinary exile. *Some of the restaurants reviewed in this chapter are excellent choices for families, and are marked with "Family."*

PRICES

Las Vegas's status as a bargain-food town has evaporated steadily, even rapidly, as the restaurant scene has evolved and the city has been thrust into the gastronomic spotlight; it's now ranked as the most expensive restaurant city in the country. At top restaurants in town it's unusual to experience a three-course meal (including a bottle of wine, tips, and tax) for less than $100 per person, and prices can be two to three times that at many establishments. You can save money by trying lunch at some of the top eateries, and by checking out the increasingly noteworthy crop of restaurants that have developed off the Strip. Credit cards are widely accepted, but some restaurants (particularly smaller ones off the Strip) accept only cash. If you plan to use a credit card, it's a good idea to double-check its acceptability when making reservations or before sitting down to eat.

WHAT IT COSTS				
	$	$$	$$$	$$$$
Restaurants	under $12	$12–$20	$21–$30	over $30

Prices are the average cost of a main course at dinner or, if dinner isn't served, at lunch.

RESTAURANT REVIEWS

Restaurant reviews have been shortened. For full information, visit Fodors.com.

SOUTH STRIP

$$$$
AMERICAN

✕ **Aureole.** Celebrity-chef Charlie Palmer re-created his famed New York restaurant for Mandalay Bay. It was extensively renovated in late 2016 but retains designer Adam Tihany's four-story wine tower, which holds more than 60,000 bottles that are reached by "flying wine angels," who are hoisted up and down via a system of electronically activated pulleys. **Known for:** Charlie Palmer's innovative cuisine; wine tower with "angels" on cables; scenic swan court and room adjoining. Ⓢ *Average main: $41* ✉ *Mandalay Bay Resort & Casino, 3950 Las Vegas Blvd. S, South Strip* ☎ *702/632–7401* ⊕ *www.charliepalmer.com* ⊘ *Closed Sun. No lunch.*

$$$
SOUTHWESTERN
FAMILY

✕ **Border Grill.** Mary Sue Milliken and Susan Feniger are the popular, green-minded chefs who created this cheery, sophisticated outpost of their Santa Monica restaurant. Service is snappy, and you'd be hard-pressed to find a tastier margarita in town—particularly the mango-cilantro and raspberry-chipotle versions. **Known for:** urban Mexican cuisine; fun, flavored margaritas; patio next to Mandalay Bay Beach. $ *Average main: $25* ✉ *Mandalay Bay Resort & Casino, 3950 Las Vegas Blvd. S, South Strip* ☎ *702/632–7403* ⊕ *www.bordergrill.com.*

$$
BURGER
FAMILY
Fodor's Choice
★

✕ **Burger Bar.** There's a burger joint in every resort, but Hubert Keller's Burger Bar is truly a standout. You build your own burger at this jovial restaurant with marble tables and wood-paneled walls. **Known for:** burgers with a variety of ground meats; fun atmosphere during sports events; dessert burgers. $ *Average main: $20* ✉ *Mandalay Place, 3930 Las Vegas Blvd. S, South Strip* ☎ *702/632–9364* ⊕ *www.burger-bar.com.*

$$$$
STEAKHOUSE

✕ **Charlie Palmer Steak.** Charlie Palmer understood that the Four Seasons, a quiet enclave within a busy hotel-casino complex, needed a similar restaurant. Although his Aureole at Mandalay Bay can be something of a scene, this nearby steak house is easygoing and understated. **Known for:** top-quality steaks; great "cut of the week" deal; quiet refuge from the hubbub. $ *Average main: $42* ✉ *Four Seasons Hotel, 3960 Las Vegas Blvd. S, South Strip* ☎ *702/632–5120* ⊕ *www.charliepalmer.com* ☺ *Closed Sun. No lunch.*

$$$
AMERICAN
FAMILY

✕ **Citizens Kitchen & Bar.** This 24-hour pub serves up some of the best comfort food Vegas has to offer. Dishes include beer-braised bratwurst, brick chicken, and "disco" fries with cheddar, mozzarella, bacon, and gravy. **Known for:** 24/7 service; convenient location right off the casino; fun food like disco fries smothered in cheese, bacon, and gravy. $ *Average main: $25* ✉ *Mandalay Bay, 3950 Las Vegas Blvd. S, South Strip* ☎ *702/632–7000* ⊕ *www.mandalaybay.com/dining.*

$$$
AMERICAN

✕ **Della's Kitchen.** Della's is of the new school of updated, farm-to-table resort coffee shops. Both breakfast and lunch are available all day. **Known for:** best casual breakfast and lunch spot at the Delano; regional specialties like Portuguese sausage; quiet atmosphere for a coffee shop. $ *Average main: $25* ✉ *The Delano Las Vegas, 3940 Las Vegas Blvd. S, South Strip* ☎ *702/632–9444* ⊕ *www.delanolasvegas.com* ☺ *No dinner.*

$$$$
SOUTHERN
FAMILY

✕ **Emeril's New Orleans Fish House.** Chef Emeril Lagasse's first restaurant in Las Vegas has been joined by three others, but it's still a popular choice and has been periodically updated. The menu still puts the spotlight on the chef's Creole-inspired cuisine, such as barbecued shrimp, Louisiana-style jambalaya, and oysters on the half shell with watermelon mignonette. **Known for:** Creole and Cajun specialties; lively, family-friendly atmosphere; killer banana cream pie. $ *Average main: $38* ✉ *MGM Grand Hotel & Casino, 3799 Las Vegas Blvd. S, South Strip* ☎ *702/891–7374* ⊕ *emerilsrestaurants.com.*

$
AMERICAN

✕ **Fatburger.** Billing itself immodestly "the Last Great Hamburger Stand," this fast-food joint across from Monte Carlo cooks up toothsome charbroiled burgers, hefty chili dogs, and crispy "fat fries." The Strip location is open 24 hours and serves alcohol. **Known for:** simple charbroiled burgers; long history in the West; full bar in this location. $ *Average main: $9* ✉ *3763 Las Vegas Blvd. S, South Strip* ☎ *702/736–4733* ▭ *No credit cards.*

$$$$
ITALIAN

✕ **Fiamma Trattoria.** A beautiful, modern space with a split-level dining room that's done in rich chocolate, copper, and tan tones, this trattoria sits along MGM's booming restaurant row, the District, and turns out deftly seasoned Italian food, such as a crispy calamari appetizer with

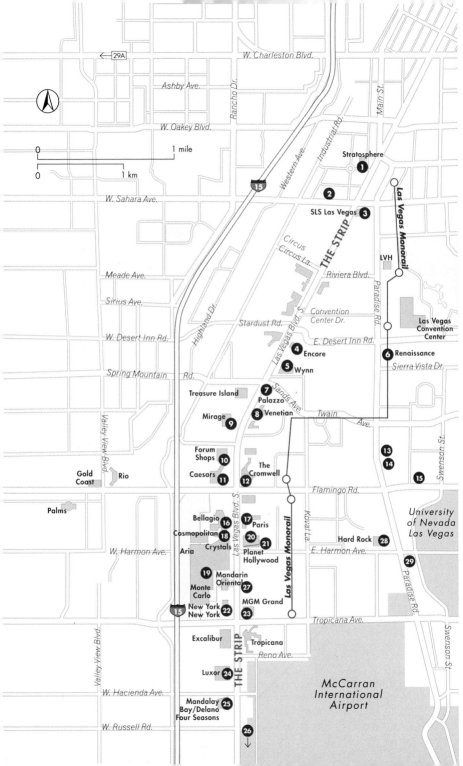

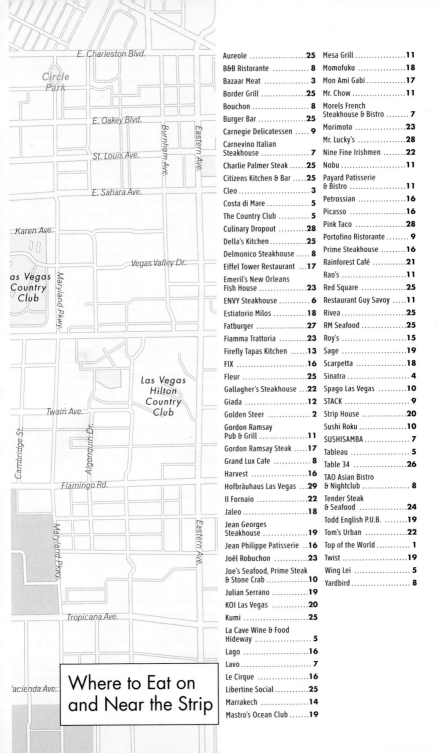

Where to Eat on and Near the Strip

zucchini and zesty pepperoncini. Several fish, poultry, and beef entrées are on the menu, such as grilled Mediterranean sea bass or spaghetti chitarra. **Known for:** house-made pasta; unusual two-floor dining room; cozy fireside lounge. $ *Average main: $45* ✉ *MGM Grand Hotel & Casino, 3799 Las Vegas Blvd. S, South Strip* ☏ *702/891–7600* ⊕ *www. mgmgrand.com* ☉ *No lunch.*

$$$$
INTERNATIONAL

✕**Fleur.** Chef Hubert Keller's Fleur has two dining spaces, one fairly intimate and one open to Mandalay Bay's restaurant row, so you can watch the world (or at least Las Vegas) go by. Small plates themed to various cuisines around the world can be enjoyed à la carte or as a tasting menu for two or four. **Known for:** upscale yet fun menu of small plates; indulgent Wagyu "Burger 5000" with foie gras, truffles, and Chateau Petrus; great people-watching on the indoor patio. $ *Average main: $37* ✉ *Mandalay Bay Resort & Casino, 3950 Las Vegas Blvd. S, South Strip* ☏ *702/632–9400* ⊕ *www.mandalaybay.com.*

$$$$
STEAKHOUSE
FAMILY

✕**Gallagher's Steakhouse.** This credible remake of the famed 1927 Manhattan original offers an old-school carnivore experience inside the cleverly decorated New York–New York casino. The convivial tavern's walls are lined with black-and-white photos of sports stars, actors, and politicos, and the hardwood floors and tray ceilings transport guests directly to Gotham. **Known for:** aged meat display near entrance; old New York atmosphere; sublime sauces. $ *Average main: $55* ✉ *New York–New York Hotel & Casino, 3790 Las Vegas Blvd. S, South Strip* ☏ *702/740–6450* ⊕ *www.newyorknewyork.com.*

$$$$
ITALIAN
FAMILY

✕**Il Fornaio.** This soothingly neutral Italian restaurant will satisfy carb cravings as well as yearnings for dishes that Grandma used to make. Crusty loaves of freshly baked bread, pasta, and dough for its excellent thin-crust, wood-oven pizzas are all made in-house. **Known for:** freshly made breads and pastries; wood-oven-baked pizzas; people-watching from indoor terrace. $ *Average main: $35* ✉ *New York–New York Resort & Casino, 3790 Las Vegas Blvd. S, South Strip* ☏ *702/650–6500* ⊕ *www.ilfornaio.com.*

$$$$
FRENCH
Fodor's Choice
★

✕**Joël Robuchon.** Chef Joël Robuchon employs his haute cuisine at two gorgeous, side-by-side restaurants. The more glamorous manse that bears his name offers the ultimate gastronomical rush, with elaborate dishes and luxurious ingredients in several multicourse menus. **Known for:** elegant, formal atmosphere; elaborate tasting menus; small plates in the Atelier. $ *Average main: $200* ✉ *MGM Grand Hotel & Casino, 3799 Las Vegas Blvd. S, South Strip* ☏ *702/891–7925* ⊕ *www.mgmgrand.com* ☉ *No lunch* 👔 *Jacket required.*

$$$$
JAPANESE
FUSION

✕**Kumi.** Chef (and former professional snowboarder) Akira Back presents a Japanese menu with a slight Korean twist in a sleek space with natural woods and hammered steel. Menu items include dishes such as Jidori chicken with kimchee green beans and hirami carpaccio with dried shallots, as well as more conventional tataki, tempuras, and a wide variety of rolls and sushi. **Known for:** Japanese food with a Korean twist; sleek, contemporary decor; artisanal cocktails. $ *Average main: $45* ✉ *Mandalay Bay, 3590 Las Vegas Blvd. S, South Strip* ☏ *702/632–7777* ⊕ *www.kumilasvegas.com* ☉ *No lunch.*

DINING WITH KIDS

Although Vegas isn't exactly a family destination, there are plenty of spots around town—both on and off the Strip—that happily welcome kids. Here's a look at several restaurants worth a trip if you have kids in tow.

Big Ern's. At locations in the Downtown Container Park and Fiesta Rancho on the East Side, this draw is fantastic barbecue, with the added attraction of a huge play structure in the center of the plaza at Container Park.

Grimaldi's. Exceptionally tasty pizza and a casual dining room draw crowds to this cheery restaurant at The Palazzo (where there's a little outdoor patio that's good fun on a nice day) and Henderson.

Jean Philippe Patisserie. With locations in both Aria and Bellagio, the draws here are beautifully displayed cakes, cookies, gelato, and dessert crepes, and a fanciful Wonka-esque ambience, with a chocolate fountain at the Bellagio location.

Honey Salt. The menu at this Summerlin restaurant was created by kids for kids (age 10 and under), with both delicious (mac and cheese, Coley's Buttery Pasta and Parm) and nutritious (steamed broccolini) offerings. There are Brookies for dessert and a Grow-Your-Own Sundae, where magic seeds (chocolate-covered sunflower seeds) grow a plant (scoop of vanilla ice cream) sprinkled with dirt (crushed cookies) and (gummy) worms, served with a squeezable dispenser of warm chocolate fudge.

Rainforest Cafe. If you want to be sure the kids won't fuss during dinner, take them to this popular spot in the Harmon Retail Center so they can dine among animatronic animals and listen to (faux) weather reports.

Village Eateries. The indoor food court at New York–New York is designed to resemble the Big Apple's Greenwich Village—with pizza, hot dogs, burgers, cheesesteaks, deli sandwiches, quesadillas, fried shrimp, and ice cream among the many offerings.

$$$$ ✕ **Libertine Social.** This casual spot from James Beard Award–winning
AMERICAN chef Shawn McClain and modern mixologist Tony Abou-Ganim puts the emphasis on "social." The food's fun but seriously good, such as the Modern Fried Egg, in which an empty egg shell is filled with corn pudding, a fluffy egg and caviar, or the social toasts and dips, flatbreads, and charcuterie and cheese boards. **Known for:** serious but fun menu; updated versions of historic cocktails; emphasis on the "social". $ *Average main: $35* ⊠ *Mandalay Bay, 3950 Las Vegas Blvd. S, South Strip* ☎ *702/632–7200* ⊕ *www.mandalaybay.com* ☉ *No lunch.*

$$$$ ✕ **Morimoto.** "Iron Chef" Masaharu Morimoto has opened his a restau-
JAPANESE rant in what he proudly called "the most famous city in the world,"
FUSION and it marked his first foray into teppanyaki, sure to be popular with conventioneers. There's also sushi, of course, and some of his standbys. **Known for:** food by the original Iron Chef; sushi, teppanyaki, and conventional dining; dramatic black-and-white interior. $ *Average main: $40* ⊠ *MGM Grand, 3799 Las Vegas Blvd. S, South Strip* ☎ *702/891–3001* ⊕ *www.mgmgrand.com.*

$$$ ✕ **Nine Fine Irishmen.** Irish craftspeople and materials were used to
IRISH   construct this authentic-feeling pub and restaurant. Live bands and
Irish dancers perform as patrons down draught Guinness, Harp Lager,
Killian's Red, or Irish-whiskey-spiked coffee and dine on a menu of
hearty Irish fare. **Known for:** fun, Irish-themed cuisine; lots of Irish
whiskey; location overlooking the "Brooklyn Bridge". ⑤ *Average main:
$30* ✉ *New York–New York Hotel & Casino, 3790 Las Vegas Blvd. S,
South Strip* ☎ *702/740–6463* ⊕ *www.nynyhotelcasino.com/restaurants/
nine-fine-irishmen.aspx.*

$$$ ✕ **Rainforest Cafe.** The Rainforest Cafe moved out of its longtime berth in
AMERICAN   the MGM Grand in 2015, but its new location just up the Strip on Har-
FAMILY   mon Avenue still has plenty of animatronic animals. The menu offers
an eclectic mix of classic American food like fried chicken and pot roast
with a mix of pastas, burgers, and Caribbean and South American influences. **Known for:** animatronic wildlife; periodically changing (indoor)
weather; family-friendly food. ⑤ *Average main: $25* ✉ *Harmon Retail
Center, 3717 Las Vegas Blvd. S, South Strip* ☎ *702/891–8580* ⊕ *www.
rainforestcafe.com.*

$$$$ ✕ **Red Square.** Red Square marks its entrance with a headless statue
RUSSIAN   of N. Lenin, and the interior has an imperial opulence with soaring
ceilings and intricate chandeliers as well as a bar made of ice. Start
with a Red Dawn or Moscow Mule cocktail and choose among a
five caviars or the salmon pizza with caviar and pickled red onions.
Known for: ice bar; lush atmosphere; Russian-tinged food. ⑤ *Average main: $40* ✉ *Mandalay Bay Resort & Casino, 3950 Las Vegas
Blvd. S, South Strip* ☎ *702/632–7407* ⊕ *www.mandalaybay.com/
dining* ⊘ *No lunch.*

$$$$ ✕ **Rivea.** Culinary lion Alain Ducasse replaced his 64th-floor Mix with
FRENCH FUSION   the equally stunning Rivea, offering unparalleled views of the Strip and
Riviera-style interpretations of his cuisine. It's suitably more casual fare,
with such shared plates as paccheri pasta with ox cheek, and sautéed
calamari and prawns. **Known for:** Riviera spin on Alain Ducasse's cuisine; 64th-floor location; unparalleled views up the Strip. ⑤ *Average
main: $50* ✉ *Delano Las Vegas, 3940 Las Vegas Blvd. S, South Strip*
☎ *877/632–5400* ⊕ *www.delanolasvegas.com* ⊘ *No lunch.*

$$$$ ✕ **RM Seafood.** Rick Moonen is one of the culinary world's leading
SEAFOOD   sustainability advocates, and in the downstairs portion of Rx Boiler
Room he operates RM Seafood, a casual space complete with raw
bar. The menu focuses solely on sustainable fish. **Known for:** creative
menu dedicated to seafood; sustainable fish and shellfish; casual spot
in shopping area. ⑤ *Average main: $45* ✉ *Mandalay Bay Resort &
Casino, 3950 Las Vegas Blvd. S, South Strip* ☎ *702/632–9300* ⊕ *www.
rmseafood.com.*

$$$$ ✕ **Tender Steak & Seafood.** Tender is the steak house that it seems every
SEAFOOD-   Las Vegas hotel-casino is required to have, but it offers a menu that
STEAKHOUSE   veers off the beaten path. In addition to the typical steak offerings,
you'll find a wide selection of fish and even wild game. **Known for:**
dry- and wet-aged steaks; selection of wild game; classic steak-house
styling. ⑤ *Average main: $55* ✉ *Luxor Las Vegas, 3900 Las Vegas Blvd.
S, South Strip* ☎ *702/262–4852* ⊕ *www.luxor.com* ⊘ *No lunch.*

CLOSE UP

Las Vegas Hamburger Roundup

A number of casino resorts have opened eateries dedicated to that most quintessentially American of cuisines—the compact and delicious hamburger. All of these restaurants are casual affairs; most don't even accept reservations.

B&B Burger & Beer. How American is this? You can actually nosh a burger and quaff an icy craft brew while overlooking the outdoor canals at The Venetian—or take in the indoor action in the resort's poker room. ⊠ *The Venetian, 3355 Las Vegas Blvd. S, North Strip* ☎ *702/414–2220*

Bobby's Burger Palace. Bobby Flay is the original grillmaster, and he proves it at this colorful spot that serves not only burgers but also salads and drinks and shakes, many of them spiked. ⊠ *Residences at the Mandarin Oriental, 3750 Las Vegas Blvd. S, Center Strip* ☎ *702/598–0191*

Burger Bar. Chef Hubert Keller started the burger trend with this modest restaurant in 2004; the simple build-your-own-burger menu features a variety of different meats (beef, buffalo, lamb, turkey) and toppings. The creamy cheesecake and chocolate burgers are sweet dessert treats. ⊠ *Mandalay Place, 3930 Las Vegas Blvd. S, South Strip* ☎ *702/632–9364.*

Gordon Ramsay Burger. The volcanic Scottish chef now has four restaurants in Las Vegas and his burger spot, where the main attraction is cooked over an open flame, is among the most popular. ⊠ *Planet Hollywood, 3667 Las Vegas Blvd. S, Center Strip* ☎ *702785–5462*

LVB Burgers and Bar. Burger choices in this restaurant near the Mirage sports book include duck, salmon, lamb, and turkey. Spiked milk shakes—including "rum in the coconut," with Myers's rum, coconut, pineapple, and vanilla ice cream—make great accompaniments. ⊠ *Mirage Las Vegas, 3400 Las Vegas Blvd. S, Center Strip* ☎ *702/792–7888.*

Shake Shack. These branches of the New York original offer the famous burgers made with a proprietary blend of meat. There's a second location in downtown Summerlin. ⊠ *New York-New York, 3970 Las Vegas Blvd. S, South Strip* ☎ *725/222–6730*

$$$ ✕ **Tom's Urban.** From restaurant-industry veteran and Smashburger
AMERICAN founder Tom Ryan, this gastropub bridges a space at New York–New
FAMILY York between the casino and the Brooklyn Bridge, which gives it great views of the action. The large menu of drinks and beers is matched by an extensive food menu, including burgers, pizzas, and other entrées. **Known for:** varied menu of gastropub favorites; huge selection of drinks; seasonal specialties. $ *Average main: $25* ⊠ *New York–New York, 3790 Las Vegas Blvd. S, South Strip* ☎ *702/740–6766* ⊕ *www. tomsurban.com.*

CENTER STRIP

$$$
DELI
FAMILY
×**Carnegie Delicatessen.** The famed NYC source of matzoh-ball soup and mammoth sandwiches may have closed, but the famous corned beef lives on at the Mirage. The prices for the sandwiches are sky-high as the meat is stacked, but it's not so much if you consider the cost by the pound. **Known for:** stacked-to-here sandwiches; stands in for now-closed New York landmark; open for late noshing. $ *Average main: $25 ✉ The Mirage, 3400 Las Vegas Blvd. S, Center Strip ☎ 702/791–7310 ⊕ www.mirage.com/restaurants.*

$$$$
FRENCH
×**Eiffel Tower Restaurant.** This Paris Las Vegas Resort restaurant is a room with a view, all right—it's about a third of the way up the hotel's half-scale Eiffel Tower replica, with vistas from all four glassed-in sides (request a Strip view when booking for the biggest wow factor—it overlooks the fountains at Bellagio, across the street). But patrons are often pleasantly surprised that the food here measures up to the setting. **Known for:** view overlooking Bellagio fountains; fine French cuisine; caviar by the ounce. $ *Average main: $50 ✉ Paris Las Vegas, 3655 Las Vegas Blvd. S, Center Strip ☎ 702/948–6937 ⊕ www.eiffeltowerrestaurant.com.*

$$$$
MEDITERRANEAN
×**Estiatorio Milos.** The first Greek restaurant on the Las Vegas Strip certainly doesn't disappoint, although you'll pay well for the experience. Chef Costas Spiliadis flies in fresh fish from the Mediterranean; you pick out the piece of fish at market price and select how you'd like it prepared. **Known for:** fish from the Mediterranean; updated Greek classics; terrace overlooking the Strip. $ *Average main: $60 ✉ The Cosmopolitan, 3708 Las Vegas Blvd. S, Center Strip ☎ 702/698–7000 ⊕ www.cosmopolitanlasvegas.com.*

$$$$
AMERICAN
×**FIX.** The ceiling, constructed almost entirely of Costa Rican padouk wood, curves like a breaking wave at this upscale comfort-food restaurant, where childhood favorites get updated twists. You'll find modern takes on grilled cheese, mac and cheese, and eggs Benedict. **Known for:** menu of fun hipster favorites; undulating wooden ceiling; late-night menu. $ *Average main: $45 ✉ Bellagio Las Vegas, 3600 Las Vegas Blvd. S, Center Strip ☎ 702/693–8865 ⊕ www.bellagio.com/restaurants ⊘ No lunch.*

$$$$
ITALIAN
×**Giada.** The only restaurant, anywhere, from TV personality and classically trained chef Giada de Laurentiis sits on a prime piece of real estate at the intersection of the Strip and Flamingo Road. The wide expanse of floor-to-ceiling windows provide commanding views, and the food's pretty impressive, too. **Known for:** Giada's only restaurant; expansive view of Strip; huge dessert cart. $ *Average main: $50 ✉ The Cromwell, 3595 Las Vegas Blvd. S, Center Strip ☎ 855/442–3271 ⊕ www.caesars.com/cromwell.*

$$$$
BRITISH
FAMILY
×**Gordon Ramsay Pub & Grill.** Three things stand out at this comfortable, casual restaurant, conceptualized by tyrannical celeb chef Gordon Ramsey: the libations, the cheery across-the-pond ambience, and the elevated British pub grub—in that order. The cocktails are strong and diverse, but it's the beer here that's to die for. **Known for:** Ramsay's pub favorites; fun, lively atmosphere; across from Coliseum. $ *Average main: $35 ✉ Caesars Palace, 3570 Las Vegas Blvd. S, Center Strip ☎ 702/731–7410 ⊕ www.caesarspalace.com.*

$$$$ ✕**Gordon Ramsay Steak.** Gordon Ramsay's heavily British-theme Las
BRITISH Vegas flagship bridges the geographic gap with a Chunnel-like entrance
STEAKHOUSE connecting it to Paris Las Vegas. It bridges the culinary gap with a
wide variety of cuts of beef, showcased before dinner on a rolling cart.
Known for: classic steak-house favorites with Ramsay flourish; meat
displayed on carts; entryway that bridges Paris to London. ⑤ *Average
main: $50* ✉ *Paris Las Vegas, 3655 Las Vegas Blvd. S, Center Strip*
☎ *877/346–4642* ⊕ *www.parislasvegas.com* ◎ *No lunch.*

$$$$ ✕**Harvest.** It's no easy feat coming up with a truly original restaurant in
ECLECTIC Las Vegas that offers more than just a gimmicky theme or celebrity-chef
Fodor'sChoice pedigree. Harvest, a casual but cosmopolitan spot that's secluded from Bel-
★ lagio's noisy gaming areas, succeeds on all counts by presenting a locally
sourced, sustainable menu. **Known for:** farm-to-table menus; snack and
dessert carts; interior evokes the outdoors. ⑤ *Average main: $49* ✉ *Bel-
lagio Las Vegas, 3600 Las Vegas Blvd. S, Center Strip* ☎ *702/693–8865*
⊕ *www.bellagio.com/restaurants* ◎ *Closed Mon. No lunch.*

$$$$ ✕**Jaleo.** Chef José Andres was one of the first to capitalize on the tapas
SPANISH concept in the United States (at the Washington, DC, version of Jaleo),
FAMILY and small plates are the highlights of the menu here, too. You haven't
thoroughly explored the menu until there are stacks of plates on your
table. **Known for:** Spanish and other tapas; fun atmosphere; tiny dining
space. ⑤ *Average main: $49* ✉ *The Cosmopolitan, 3708 Las Vegas Blvd.
S, Center Strip* ☎ *702/698–7000* ⊕ *www.cosmopolitanlasvegas.com.*

$$$$ ✕**Jean Georges Steakhouse.** This steak house, named for famed chef
STEAKHOUSE Jean-Georges Vongerichten, serves up a modern spin on the traditional
meat and potatoes. To wit: dishes such as the soy-glazed short rib
with Granny Smith apple and Dungeness crab dumplings. **Known for:**
Vongerichten's latter-day spins; fine dry-aged steaks; newly renovated.
⑤ *Average main: $60* ✉ *Aria, 3730 Las Vegas Blvd. S, Center Strip*
☎ *877/230–2742* ⊕ *www.arialasvegas.com/dining* ◎ *No lunch.*

$$ ✕**Jean Philippe Patisserie.** Chocolate—dark, white, and milk—flows from
CAFÉ a tall glass fountain at the entrance of this stunning pastry shop just
FAMILY off the Bellagio's iconic conservatory. This artful homage to chocolate
Fodor'sChoice has decadent desserts, including cakes, cookies, gelato, hand-dipped
★ chocolate candies, and particularly memorable crepes (try the one filled
with mango, coconut, passion fruit, and pineapple sorbets). **Known for:**
three-tier chocolate fountain; indulgent pastries and chocolates; amusing
seasonal sculptures. ⑤ *Average main: $15* ✉ *Bellagio, 3600 Las Vegas
Blvd. S, Center Strip* ☎ *702/693–7111* ⊕ *www.bellagio.com/restaurants.*

$$$$ ✕**Joe's Seafood, Prime Steak & Stone Crab.** Drop by this bustling branch
SEAFOOD of the famed South Miami Beach restaurant for, at the very least, a pile
of fresh stone crabs and a beer. But Joe's is worth a try whether for a
light lunch or snack (or a full meal) to remember. **Known for:** stone crab
year-round; lots of steaks and chops; table-side service. ⑤ *Average main:
$45* ✉ *The Forum Shops at Caesars, 3500 Las Vegas Blvd. S, Center
Strip* ☎ *702/792–9222* ⊕ *www.joes.net/las-vegas.*

$$$$ ✕**Julian Serrano.** Chef Julian Serrano—renowned for Picasso at Bel-
SPANISH lagio—chose to honor his homeland's tapas and paella traditions at
his eponymous restaurant in Aria. Tapas include classics as well as
those with Serrano's special touch. **Known for:** authentic tapas; creative

4

Julian Serrano twists; people-watching in Aria lobby. $ *Average main: $40* ⊠ *Aria Hotel & Casino, 3730 Las Vegas Blvd., Center Strip* ☎ *877/230–2742* ⊕ *www.arialasvegas.com/dining.*

$$$$
ASIAN
✕ **KOI Las Vegas.** KOI has garnered a reputation as a see-and-be-seen restaurant in New York, Bangkok, Los Angeles, and Las Vegas. The cavernous 220-seat Las Vegas outlet offers sublime Asian-fusion fare. **Known for:** inventive sushi rolls; loud dining room; drinks in the lounge. $ *Average main: $45* ⊠ *Planet Hollywood Resort & Casino, 3667 Las Vegas Blvd. S, Center Strip* ☎ *702/454–4555* ⊕ *www.planethollywood-resort.com* ⊗ *No lunch.*

$$$$
ITALIAN
✕ **Lago.** Renowned chef Julian Serrano, who long has had the award-winning Picasso at Bellagio (and an eponymous tapas spot at Aria), has added more frontage on the resort's lake with his first Italian restaurant, which specializes in small plates. There's a three-course tasting menu as well as à la carte choices at lunch, an intermezzo menu for late afternoon, and the à la carte dinner, with such standards as Caesar and caprese salads and more esoteric choices like risotto with tripe and tomato, and shrimp-stuffed squid with lemoncello dressing. **Known for:** Italian-style small plates; tasting menus; view of Bellagio fountains. $ *Average main: $40* ⊠ *Bellagio, 3600 Las Vegas Blvd. S, Center Strip* ☎ *702/693–8865* ⊕ *www.bellagio.com.*

$$$$
FRENCH
✕ **Le Cirque.** This sumptuous restaurant, a branch of the New York City landmark, remains one of the city's true temples of haute cuisine, despite increased heavy-hitting competition. The mahogany-lined room is all the more opulent for its size: in a city of mega-everything, Le Cirque seats only 80 under its draped silk-tent ceiling. **Known for:** tiny, jewel-box room; food not often found elsewhere; fine, attentive service. $ *Average main: $65* ⊠ *Bellagio Las Vegas, 3600 Las Vegas Blvd. S, Center Strip* ☎ *702/693–8865* ⊕ *www.bellagio.com/restaurants* ⊗ *Closed Mon. No lunch.*

$$$$
SEAFOOD
✕ **Mastro's Ocean Club.** In addition to food that is upscale and delicious, this impressive restaurant has two other attractions. The first is a piano lounge that serves stellar martinis; the second is the "Tree House," a two-story wooden sculpture that rises from the ground level and houses the main dining room 30 feet above the ground. **Known for:** warm, welcoming service; "tree house" structure; warm butter cake. $ *Average main: $45* ⊠ *Crystals, 3270 Las Vegas Blvd. S , Suite 244, Center Strip* ☎ *702/798–7115* ⊕ *www.mastrosrestaurants.com* ⊗ *No lunch.*

$$$$
SOUTHWESTERN
✕ **Mesa Grill.** Playful splashes of green, blue, red, and yellow offset the swanky curved banquettes and earth tones at the first restaurant outside New York City from Iron Chef and grill-meister Bobby Flay. The menu is decidedly Southwestern, but with plenty of contemporary twists. **Known for:** stand-in for the long-gone NYC original; colorful interior; weekend brunch. $ *Average main: $44* ⊠ *Caesars Palace, 3570 Las Vegas Blvd. S, Center Strip* ☎ *702/731–7731* ⊕ *www.caesarspalace.com/restaurants.*

$$$$
ASIAN FUSION
✕ **Momofuku.** David Chang's budding New York–based restaurant empire went way west for the first time with this spot at The Cosmopolitan. It offers a mix of Momofuku favorites and only-in-Vegas

choices, like the oysters broiled with kimchee, spinach, and bacon. **Known for:** classics honed at New York original; some only-in-Vegas choices; fried chicken and caviar for large parties. $ *Average main: $35* ✉ *Cosmopolitan of Las Vegas, 3708 Las Vegas Blvd. South, Center Strip* ☎ *702/698–7000* ⊕ *www.cosmopolitanlasvegas.com.*

$$$$ ✕ **Mon Ami Gabi.** This French bistro and steak house that first earned
FRENCH acclaim in Chicago has become much beloved here in Las Vegas, in large part because it was the first restaurant to have a terrace overlooking the Strip. For those who prefer a quieter environment, a glassed-in conservatory conveys an outdoor feel, and still-quieter dining rooms are inside, adorned with chandeliers dramatically suspended three stories above. **Known for:** view of Strip from outdoor patio; lots of steak frites variations; great for breakfast or brunch. $ *Average main: $35* ✉ *Paris Las Vegas, 3655 Las Vegas Blvd. S, Center Strip* ☎ *702/944–4224* ⊕ *www.monamigabi.com.*

$$$$ ✕ **Mr. Chow.** It was a long time coming, but the venerable celebrity
CHINESE magnet Mr. Chow opened its Las Vegas branch in Caesars Palace in 2015. On the second floor overlooking the Garden of the Gods pool complex, the predominantly white restaurant is centered by a circular suspended "kinetic sculpture" that periodically descends and opens itself to the room. **Known for:** kinetic sculpture centerpiece; lots of Mr. Chow classics; superb, friendly service. $ *Average main: $42* ✉ *Caesars Palace, 3570 Las Vegas Blvd. S, Center Strip* ☎ *702/731–7888* ⊕ *www.caesars.com* ☾ *No lunch.*

$$$$ ✕ **Nobu.** Celebrity chef Nobu Matsuhisa established a foothold in the
SUSHI Vegas market with a namesake restaurant at the Hard Rock Hotel, but later added this modern location at the base of his hotel tower at Caesars Palace. The result: one of the hottest tables in town. **Known for:** Nobu classics like black cod miso; extensive sushi and sashimi list; imported Japanese Wagyu. $ *Average main: $40* ✉ *Nobu Hotel, 3570 Las Vegas Blvd. S, Center Strip* ☎ *702/785–6628* ⊕ *www.caesarspalace. com* ☾ *No lunch.*

$$$ ✕ **Payard Patisserie & Bistro.** Dessert is king at this Las Vegas outpost
CAFÉ of the New York–based restaurant from celebrated chef François
FAMILY Payard. Tourists and business travelers queue during lunch at the counter for made-to-order crepes and treats that might include the Apple Tatin Crepe, with ginger and caramel sauce. **Known for:** crepes and pastries; classic French dishes; intimate atmosphere. $ *Average main: $25* ✉ *Caesars Palace, 3570 Las Vegas Blvd. S, Center Strip* ☎ *702/731–1292* ⊕ *www.caesarspalace.com* ☾ *No dinner Sun.–Thurs.*

$$$$ ✕ **Petrossian.** This elegant bar with dark-wood paneling and a baby
ECLECTIC grand piano sits just off Bellagio's lobby, near the famous Dale Chihuly glass ceiling. It's open for cocktails 24/7, but the best time to visit is during the lavish afternoon tea, held daily from 1 to 4 pm. **Known for:** numerous caviar choices; afternoon tea; soothing piano music. $ *Average main: $35* ✉ *Bellagio Las Vegas, 3600 Las Vegas Blvd. S, Center Strip* ☎ *702/693–7111* ⊕ *www.bellagio.com.*

$$$$
EUROPEAN
Fodor's Choice
★

✕ **Picasso.** Adorned with some original works by Picasso, this restaurant raised the city's dining scene a notch when it opened in Bellagio in 1998. Although some say Executive Chef Julian Serrano doesn't change his menu often enough, the artful, innovative cuisine—based on French classics with strong Spanish influences—is consistently outstanding. **Known for:** artworks by the master; Julian Serrano's award-winning food; overlooking Lake Bellagio. ⑤ *Average main: $125* ⊠ *Bellagio Las Vegas, 3600 Las Vegas Blvd. S, Center Strip* ☎ 702/693–8865 ⊕ *www. bellagio.com/restaurants* ⊘ *Closed Mon. No lunch.*

$$$$
ITALIAN

✕ **Portofino Ristorante.** Decorated in soothing pale neutrals that, suitably, evoke a village in Genoa, Portofino is a signature Italian restaurant of the Mirage, having replaced Onda in 2014. The classics are still here— the lasagna and pasta e fagioli and veal osso buco—as well as updated dishes. **Known for:** Italian coastal cuisine; veal osso buco; quiet enclave. ⑤ *Average main: $35* ⊠ *The Mirage, 3400 Las Vegas Blvd. S, Center Strip* ☎ 866/339–4566 ⊕ *www.mirage.com/restaurants* ⊘ *Closed Tues. and Wed. No lunch.*

$$$$
STEAKHOUSE

✕ **Prime Steakhouse.** Even among celebrity chefs, Jean-Georges Vongerichten has established a "can't touch this" reputation. Prime—with its gorgeous view of the fountains—is a place to see and be seen at Bellagio. **Known for:** excellent prime steaks; sophisticated decor; view of Bellagio fountains. ⑤ *Average main: $55* ⊠ *Bellagio Las Vegas, 3600 Las Vegas Blvd. S, Center Strip* ☎ 702/693–8865 ⊕ *www.bellagio.com/ restaurants* ⊘ *No lunch.*

$$$$
ITALIAN
FAMILY

✕ **Rao's.** Whereas its 10-table New York counterpart is notorious for a never-changing reservation list, this 200-seat outpost at Caesars Palace lets someone besides the regulars eat, too. Hearty portions of family-style, rustic, southern Italian cuisine are featured on the menu. **Known for:** accessibility, unlike NY original; traditional red-sauce dishes; bocce court. ⑤ *Average main: $40* ⊠ *Caesars Palace, 3570 Las Vegas Blvd. S, Center Strip* ☎ 702/731–7267 ⊕ *www.caesarspalace. com* ⊘ *No lunch.*

$$$$
FRENCH
Fodor's Choice
★

✕ **Restaurant Guy Savoy.** In an ultraswank dining room on the second floor of the Augustus Tower, Michelin three-star chef Guy Savoy introduces diners to his masterful creations, such as roasted turbot with bean sprouts and green curry. The 14-course, jumbo-priced "Innovation Menu" is the restaurant's crown jewel, featuring signature dishes such as artichoke-and-black-truffle soup, and pan-seared quails. **Known for:** one of Las Vegas's best; caviar room; Krug chef's table. ⑤ *Average main: $75* ⊠ *Caesars Palace, 3570 Las Vegas Blvd. S, Center Strip* ☎ 877/346–4642 ⊕ *www.caesarspalace.com* ⊘ *Closed Mon. and Tues. No lunch.*

$$$$
AMERICAN
Fodor's Choice
★

✕ **Sage.** Farm-to-table produce and artisanal meats flavored with innovative concepts from the Mediterranean are presented at Chef Shawn McClain's swanky Aria restaurant. Exciting fare includes spice-crusted venison loin with salsify and Kusshi oysters with piquillo peppers. **Known for:** award-winning chef Shawn McClain; innovative seasonal dishes; huge absinthe selection. ⑤ *Average main: $50* ⊠ *Aria Hotel & Casino, 3730 Las Vegas Blvd., Center Strip* ☎ 877/230–2742 ⊕ *www. arialasvegas.com/dining* ⊘ *No lunch.*

$$$$ ✕ **Scarpetta.** In Italian, *scarpetta* refers to the process of using bread
ITALIAN to soak up every last morsel of a dish, and Chef Scott Conant inspires
diners to do just that when they eat at his casual and festive modern
Italian eatery. Conant makes all of his own pasta, which takes front and
center on the eclectic menu (the simple spaghetti with tomato and basil
is, in a word, divine). **Known for:** riffs on Italian classics; house-made
pasta; view of Strip. Ⓢ *Average main: $45* ✉ *The Cosmopolitan, 3708
Las Vegas Blvd. S, Center Strip* ☎ *702/698–7000* ⊕ *www.cosmopoli-
tanlasvegas.com* ☽ *No lunch.*

$$$$ ✕ **Spago Las Vegas.** Just as Steve Wynn ushered in the age of the Vegas
AMERICAN megaresort with the Mirage, Wolfgang Puck sparked the celebrity-chef
boom when he opened a branch of his famous Beverly Hills eatery at
Caesars' Forum Shops in 1992. Spago Las Vegas has remained a fixture
in this ever-fickle city, and it remains consistently superb. **Known for:**
the city's first celebrity-chef restaurant; Wolfgang Puck classics; indoor
patio for people-watching. Ⓢ *Average main: $40* ✉ *The Forum Shops
at Caesars, 3500 Las Vegas Blvd. S, Center Strip* ☎ *702/369–6300*
⊕ *www.wolfgangpuck.com.*

$$$$ ✕ **STACK.** Curvy strips of exotic wood form the "stacked" walls of this
AMERICAN beautiful restaurant, owned by nightclub impresarios The Hakkasan
Group. Inventively prepared comfort classics dominate the menu.
Known for: grown-up comfort foods; undulating wooden walls; sir-
loin on hot rock. Ⓢ *Average main: $40* ✉ *The Mirage, 3400 Las Vegas
Blvd. S, Center Strip* ☎ *866/339–4566* ⊕ *www.mirage.com/restaurants*
☽ *No lunch.*

$$$$ ✕ **Strip House.** This lavish but cheeky steak joint with sisters in New
STEAKHOUSE York wears its bordello-chic atmosphere with a healthy touch of irony.
The red-flocked wallpaper and other decor may suggest you're inside
an early-20th-century house of ill repute, but the menu of artfully presented chops and classic American foods reflects a highly skilled, contemporary kitchen. **Known for:** bordello-chic interior; indulgent steaks
and chops; 24-layer chocolate cake. Ⓢ *Average main: $50* ✉ *Planet
Hollywood Resort & Casino, 3667 Las Vegas Blvd. S, Center Strip*
☎ *702/737–5200* ⊕ *www.planethollywoodresort.com* ☽ *No lunch.*

$$$$ ✕ **Sushi Roku.** On the top floor of the towering atrium at the Strip
JAPANESE entrance to The Forum Shops, Roku occupies an airy dining room
lined with bamboo stalks and tall windows facing the Strip. Sushi is
the main draw, but there's much more. **Known for:** huge selection of
sushi; many seasonal dishes; view of the Strip. Ⓢ *Average main: $40*
✉ *The Forum Shops at Caesars, 3500 Las Vegas Blvd. S, Center Strip*
☎ *702/733–7373* ⊕ *www.sushiroku.com.*

$$$ ✕ **Todd English P.U.B.** This sports bar represents four-time James Beard
BRITISH Award winner Todd English's first pub concept—*pub*, in this case,
stands for "public urban bar"—and it has become one of the Strip's
most popular casual spots. The menu takes playful approaches to tra-
ditional bar food. **Known for:** freshly carved meats; updated, upscale
bar food; large selection of beers. Ⓢ *Average main: $25* ✉ *The Shops at
Crystals, 3720 Las Vegas Blvd. S, CityCenter, Center Strip* ☎ *702/489–
8080* ⊕ *www.toddenglishpub.com.*

$$$$ ✕ **Twist.** The 23rd floor of the Mandarin Oriental is the only place in
FRENCH the United States to experience food from renowned French chef Pierre
Gagnaire. He pioneered the "fusion" movement in cooking, and every
dish blends flavor and texture in surprising ways. **Known for:** Pierre
Gagnaire's only U.S. restaurant; fusion-dominated menu; expansive
views. ⑤ *Average main: $65 ⊠ Mandarin Oriental, 3752 Las Vegas
Blvd. S, Center Strip* ☎ *888/881–9367* ⊕ *www.mandarinoriental.com/
lasvegas* ☉ *Closed Mon. No lunch.*

NORTH STRIP

$$$$ ✕ **B&B Ristorante.** Ubiquitous food personality Mario Batali and his
ITALIAN trusty business partner and wine pro Joe Bastianich are the owners
of this inviting tribute to the rustic foods of the Italian countryside.
Along The Venetian's "restaurant row," B&B glows from within its
dark-wood and leather confines (look for the bright orange Crocs on the
host's podium). **Known for:** cuisine by Mario Batali; beef cheek ravioli
with truffles; wines by the quartino. ⑤ *Average main: $40 ⊠ The Vene-
tian, 3355 Las Vegas Blvd. S, North Strip* ☎ *702/266–9977* ⊕ *www.
bandbristorante.com* ☉ *No lunch.*

$$$$ ✕ **Bazaar Meat.** José Andres's restaurant, the crown jewel of the SLS
ECLECTIC Las Vegas, is decorated in a subtle jungle motif and is clearly all about
meat. Choose from the steaks sold by the pound to suckling pig (by
the quarter or whole, which you'll have to order ahead), and every
other type you can imagine. **Known for:** meat in every form possible;
whole suckling pig; jungle-themed atmosphere. ⑤ *Average main: $60
⊠ SLS Las Vegas, 2535 Las Vegas Blvd. S, North Strip* ☎ *702/761–7610*
⊕ *www.slslasvegas.com* ☉ *No lunch.*

$$$$ ✕ **Bouchon.** When chefs name their idol, more than a few will cite French
FRENCH Laundry chef Thomas Keller, the star behind this stunning, capacious
French bistro and oyster bar in The Venezia Tower. Soaring Palladian
windows, antique lighting, a pewter-topped bar, and painted tile lend a
sophisticated take on French country design, a fitting setting in which to
dine on savory, rich cuisine. **Known for:** Thomas Keller's bistro interpretations; classic French-bistro atmosphere; patio overlooking Venezia pool.
⑤ *Average main: $33 ⊠ The Venetian, 3355 Las Vegas Blvd. S , Venezia
Tower, 10th fl., North Strip* ☎ *702/414–6200* ⊕ *www.bouchonbistro.com.*

$$$$ ✕ **Carnevino Italian Steakhouse.** The giant bronze steer just inside the front
STEAKHOUSE door of Chef Mario Batali's handsome restaurant attests to the primary
offering: melt-in-your-mouth beef. Steaks here are dry-aged, grilled until
the crust is slightly charred, then carved table-side by knowledgeable, attentive servers. **Known for:** opulent dry-aged steaks; lardo served with bread;
sophisticated decor. ⑤ *Average main: $40 ⊠ The Palazzo, 3325 Las Vegas
Blvd. S, North Strip* ☎ *702/789–4141* ⊕ *www.carnevino.com* ☉ *No lunch.*

$$$ ✕ **Cleo.** Middle Eastern is rare on the Strip. Cleo is a worthy interpreter,
MIDDLE EASTERN with such dishes as a vast variety of mezze, some of them prepared in the
FAMILY wood-burning oven, plus specialties like lamb tagine and grilled octo-
pus. **Known for:** best Middle Eastern on Strip; accommodating service;
updated riff on Middle Eastern decor. ⑤ *Average main: $30 ⊠ SLS Las
Vegas, 2535 Las Vegas Blvd. S, North Strip* ☎ *702/761–7612* ⊕ *www.
slslasvegas.com* ☉ *Closed Sun. and Mon. No lunch.*

$$$$
MEDITERRANEAN

✕**Costa di Mare.** Longtime Wynn Las Vegas chef Mark LoRusso was given a new showcase in this Mediterranean seafood spot in the space formerly occupied by Bartolotta Ristorante di Mare. Costa continues the tradition of freshly flown-in Mediterranean fish sold by the ounce, plus dishes such as cuttlefish with cuttlefish-ink pasta, and several raw-fish appetizers. **Known for:** fish flown in daily from Mediterranean; many choices sold by the gram; private cabanas overlooking lagoon. $ *Average main: $50* ⊠ *Wynn Las Vegas, 3131 Las Vegas Blvd. S, North Strip* ☎ *702/770–3305* ⊕ *www.wynnlasvegas. com* ☾ *No lunch.*

$$$$
AMERICAN

✕**The Country Club.** Removed from the din, this über-elegant, dark-wood dining room is tucked down a corridor off the main casino floor. This clubby restaurant caters to golfers and is a locals' power-lunch spot, but it's a place every person can enjoy, especially when the weather is conducive to dining on the patio. **Known for:** fine steaks and seafood; Las Vegas's power-lunch spot; lovely view of golf course. $ *Average main: $45* ⊠ *Wynn Las Vegas, 3131 Las Vegas Blvd. S, North Strip* ☎ *702/248–3463* ⊕ *www.wynnlasvegas.com/restaurants* ☾ *No dinner Sun.–Tues.*

$$$$
STEAKHOUSE

✕**Delmonico Steakhouse.** Chef Emeril Lagasse gives a New Orleans touch to this big city–style steak house at The Venetian. Enter through 12-foot oak doors to find a sedately decorated, modern room in which to relax and enjoy your Little Tokyo, made with tea and Japanese whiskey, along with appetizers such as truffle and Parmesan potato chips; Lagasse's signature barbecue shrimp, served with a fresh-baked rosemary biscuit; or the Caesar salad, prepared table-side for two. **Known for:** Emeril's steak interpretations; Japanese whiskey selection; contemporary decor. $ *Average main: $50* ⊠ *The Venetian, 3355 Las Vegas Blvd. S, North Strip* ☎ *702/414–3737* ⊕ *www.emerilsrestaurants.com.*

$$$$
STEAKHOUSE

✕**Golden Steer.** In a town where restaurants come and go almost as quickly as visitors' cash, the longevity of this steak house, opened in 1958, is itself a recommendation. Both locals and visitors adore this classic steak house with red-leather seating, polished dark wood, and stained-glass windows for the huge slabs of well-prepared meat. **Known for:** Rat Pack–era vibe; dark, opulent atmosphere; table-side preparations. $ *Average main: $45* ⊠ *308 W. Sahara Ave., North Strip* ☎ *702/384–4470* ⊕ *www.goldensteersteakhouselasvegas.com* ☾ *No lunch.*

$$$
AMERICAN
FAMILY

✕**Grand Lux Cafe.** Warm earth tones, soft music and lighting, cloth napkins, and marble-topped tables are an elegant milieu in which to enjoy a glass of wine and mélange of appealing, freshly cooked flavors and textures—Asian nachos, double-stuffed potato spring rolls, stacked chicken quesadilla—24 hours a day. Located right off the main casino floor, this convenient chain eatery offers eclectic menu items and familiar crowd-pleasers: pizza, pastas, barbecue ribs, burgers, BLTs, and even wood-grilled filet mignon or rib eye. **Known for:** varied, eclectic menu; Cheesecake Factory desserts; open 24/7. $ *Average main: $25* ⊠ *The Venetian, 3355 Las Vegas Blvd. S, North Strip* ☎ *702/414–3888* ⊕ *www.grandluxcafe.com* ☞ *Also in The Palazzo.*

4

$$$$
MEDITERRANEAN
FAMILY

✕ **La Cave Wine & Food Hideaway.** This intimate, casual restaurant focuses on wine and Mediterranean-inspired small plates such as sweet and salty bacon-wrapped dates with blue-cheese fondue and beef carpaccio with mushrooms and truffle aioli. The remarkable wine list reflects global selections, with an emphasis on Europe. **Known for:** innovative, varied menu; cozy spot; scenic view from patio. ⑤ *Average main: $35* ✉ *Wynn Las Vegas, 3131 Las Vegas Blvd. S, North Strip* ☎ *702/770–7100, 877/321–9966* ⊕ *www.wynnlasvegas.com.*

$$$$
ITALIAN

✕ **Lavo.** The food at this Roman-styled see-and-be-seen restaurant/nightclub often is overshadowed by the roaring club scene, but it's worth a stop—especially if you go early to avoid the *thump thump* of the music upstairs. Many of the dishes are meant to be shared. **Known for:** celebrity sightings; funky atmosphere; menu far beyond red-sauce choices. ⑤ *Average main: $40* ✉ *The Palazzo, 3325 Las Vegas Blvd. S, North Strip* ☎ *702/791–1800* ⊕ *www.lavolv.com* ☽ *No lunch weekdays.*

$$$$
FRENCH

✕ **Morels French Steakhouse & Bistro.** Relaxed and dapper, Morels is Palazzo's upscale yet unfussy all-day dining option. Its specialty is both traditional Parisian-inspired bistro fare and steak-house victuals. **Known for:** iced seafood bar; extensive cheese selection; view from patio. ⑤ *Average main: $40* ✉ *The Palazzo, 3325 Las Vegas Blvd. S, North Strip* ☎ *702/607–6333* ⊕ *www.palazzo.com/restaurants.html.*

$$$$
ITALIAN

✕ **Sinatra.** Encore recalls the panache of vintage Vegas by dedicating one of its fine-dining venues to Frank Sinatra; a photo of the Chairman of the Board with the "other" chairman—Wynn/Encore owner Steve Wynn—even adorns one of the dining rooms. Chef Theo Schoenegger, formerly of L.A.'s celebrated Patina, turns out simple, elegantly presented Italian cuisine, such as Frank's spaghetti and clams and Ossobuco "My Way." Framed photos of Ol' Blue Eyes (as well as his Academy Award for *From Here to Eternity*) adorn the ivory-and-ruby-hued indoor dining room. **Known for:** menu includes Frank's favorites; Ol' Blue Eyes decor and music; outdoor seating with fireplaces. ⑤ *Average main: $48* ✉ *Encore, 3131 Las Vegas Blvd. S, North Strip* ☎ *702/770–3463* ⊕ *www.wynnlasvegas.com/restaurants* ☽ *No lunch.*

$$$$
ASIAN

✕ **SUSHISAMBA.** Come to this trendy, tricolor restaurant for its fresh sushi and sashimi, beautifully prepared and presented, with delightful dipping sauces and edible garnish. Dim lighting, hip music, voluptuous decor, and excellent cocktails complement the exotic fusion of flavors from Japan, Brazil, and Peru. **Known for:** Japanese-Peruvian fusion; extensive cocktail selection; lively atmosphere. ⑤ *Average main: $33* ✉ *The Palazzo, 3325 Las Vegas Blvd. S, North Strip* ☎ *702/607–0700* ⊕ *www.sushisamba.com.*

$$$
AMERICAN
FAMILY

✕ **Tableau.** Isolated from the busier parts of the Wynn, this bright, airy breakfast-and-lunch restaurant overlooks a serene pool and well-manicured garden off the gleaming Tower Suites lobby. It also offers a splurge-worthy weekend brunch. **Known for:** quiet refuge; opulent breakfasts and brunches; view of resort pool. ⑤ *Average main: $25* ✉ *Wynn Las Vegas, 3131 Las Vegas Blvd. S, North Strip* ☎ *702/770–3463* ⊕ *www.wynnlasvegas.com/restaurants* ☽ *No dinner.*

CHEAP EATS

Don't forget about Sin City's terrific hole-in-the-wall dives, inexpensive regional chains, and cheap-and-cheerful take-out counters that serve tasty treats at rock-bottom prices.

Fatburger. There are a dozen branches of this popular California chain around Las Vegas, but only one on the Strip: across from the Monte Carlo. ⌧ *3763 Las Vegas Blvd. S, South Strip.*

In-N-Out Burger. Visitors need no longer need a car or taxi for an In-N-Out fix, now that there's a location at The LINQ on the Strip. ⌧ *3545 Las Vegas Blvd. S, Center Strip.*

Jason's Deli. Jason's offers all manner of deli food, and free ice cream for dessert! And there's a convenient location Downtown. ⌧ *100 N. City Pkwy., Downtown.*

L&L Hawaiian Barbecue. With a lucky 13 of these in the valley, you don't have to go far to go Hawaiian, but there's no location on the Strip. ⌧ *Sahara Square, 4030 S. Maryland Pkwy., University District.*

$$$$
ASIAN
✕**TAO Asian Bistro & Nightclub.** The tunneled vestibule of this nightclub-cum-bistro is lined with stone tubs filled with water and rose petals, leading patrons—including lots of celebrities, some of them hired to host—into the dim, lavishly decorated space. The pan-Asian menu is almost endless, with dishes from sushi to dim sum and everything in between, but you don't necessarily come for the food. **Known for:** celebrity-sighting hot spot; dramatic Asian decor; lots of offbeat dishes. ⑤ *Average main: $33* ⌧ *The Venetian, 3355 Las Vegas Blvd., North Strip* ☎ *702/388–8338* ⊕ *taolasvegas.com* ☉ *No lunch.*

$$$$
EUROPEAN
✕**Top of the World.** Reserve a window-side table at twilight to see sunset melt into sparkling night while savoring Continental cuisine à la carte or from the four-course tasting menu (with optional wine pairings). From 844 feet high, floor-to-ceiling windows display 360-degree views of the Vegas Valley as the entire 106th-floor dining room makes a complete revolution every 80 minutes. **Known for:** expansive, continually changing views; menu mix of classic and innovative; romantic atmosphere. ⑤ *Average main: $55* ⌧ *Stratosphere, 2000 Las Vegas Blvd. S, 106th fl., North Strip* ☎ *702/380–7711* ⊕ *www.topoftheworldlv.com.*

$$$$
CHINESE
Fodor's Choice
★
✕**Wing Lei.** With all the panache of an Asian royal palace, this fine-dining restaurant serves some of the choicest Chinese food on the Strip. Chefs present contemporary French-inspired cuisine that blends the Cantonese, Shanghai, and Sichuan traditions. **Known for:** fine Chinese food; Peking duck; elegant atmosphere. ⑤ *Average main: $38* ⌧ *Wynn Las Vegas, 3131 Las Vegas Blvd. S, North Strip* ☎ *702/248–3463* ⊕ *www.wynnlasvegas.com/restaurants* ☉ *No lunch.*

$$$
AMERICAN
FAMILY
✕**Yardbird.** A craft-ice program may seem a bit much, but that's indicative of Yardbird's attention to detail, as first evidenced at the Miami original. Go for the artisanal beverages but stay for Southern-leaning favorites. **Known for:** fare like chicken, watermelon, and waffles; upscale cocktails program with artisanal ice; fun, countrified decor. ⑤ *Average main: $30* ⌧ *The Venetian, 3355 Las Vegas Blvd. S, North Strip* ☎ *702/297–6541* ⊕ *runchickenrun.com.*

PARADISE ROAD AND THE EAST SIDE

PARADISE ROAD

$$$
AMERICAN

✗**Culinary Dropout.** Five-time James Beard Award finalist for Outstanding Restaurateur Sam Fox has put a unique stamp on this irreverent hangout inside the Hard Rock. The restaurant flaunts all the rules but turns out seriously reinvented pub food with sometimes whimsical names. **Known for:** fun, offbeat cuisine; servers that match the food; view overlooking resort pool. ⑤ *Average main: $25* ✉ *Hard Rock Hotel & Casino, 4455 Paradise Rd., Paradise Road* ☎ *702/522–8100* ⊕ *www.hardrockhotel.com.*

$$$$
STEAKHOUSE

✗**ENVY Steakhouse.** This hip restaurant at the elegant Renaissance Las Vegas offers an updated, clubby version of the Las Vegas steak house. The preparations are inventive but don't veer too far from the beaten path. **Known for:** modern steak-house vibe; steaks broiled at 1,400 degrees; indulgent desserts. ⑤ *Average main: $42* ✉ *Renaissance Las Vegas, 3400 Paradise Rd., Paradise Road* ☎ *702/784–5716* ⊕ *www.renaissancelasvegas.com* ⊗ *No lunch.*

$$$
MEDITERRANEAN
FAMILY

✗**Firefly Tapas Kitchen.** As the name suggests, this hip bistro focuses on small plates (few of which cost more than $10), reflecting most of the world's cuisines. Order several and you've got a meal, made even better with one of Firefly's signature sangrias or mojitos, available by the glass or pitcher. **Known for:** tapas from multiple cuisines; quick, friendly service; funky decor. ⑤ *Average main: $24* ✉ *3824 Paradise Rd., Paradise Road* ☎ *702/369–3971* ⊕ *www.fireflylv.com.*

$$$
GERMAN

✗**Hofbräuhaus Las Vegas.** Enjoy a heavy dose of kitsch at this gargantuan offshoot of Munich's most famous brewery. The interior beer garden is the perfect spot to down a brew in those notorious liter mugs, especially on too-hot Vegas evenings. **Known for:** raucous beer hall front room; quieter indoor beer garden; menu of German classics. ⑤ *Average main: $25* ✉ *4510 Paradise Rd., Paradise Road* ☎ *702/853–2337* ⊕ *www.hofbrauhauslasvegas.com.*

$$$$
MOROCCAN

✗**Marrakech.** Sprawl out on soft floor cushions and feel like a pampered pasha as belly dancers shake it up in a cozy Middle Eastern–style "tent" with a fabric-covered ceiling and eye-catching mosaics. The prix-fixe feast is a six-course affair that you eat with your hands. **Known for:** exotic decor; fun atmosphere; great for groups. ⑤ *Average main: $50* ✉ *3900 Paradise Rd., Paradise Road* ☎ *702/737–5611* ⊕ *www.marrakechvegas.com* ⊗ *No lunch.*

$$
ECLECTIC
FAMILY

✗**Mr. Lucky's.** The hippest casino coffee shop in Las Vegas is still inside the Hard Rock Hotel, overlooking the main gaming area. Light-wood floors and vintage rock-and-roll posters highlight this bubbly, circular café. **Known for:** hip, trendy, and reliable; off-menu specials (you have to ask); open 24/7. ⑤ *Average main: $19* ✉ *Hard Rock Hotel & Casino, 4455 Paradise Rd., Paradise Road* ☎ *702/693–5000* ⊕ *www.hardrockhotel.com.*

$$$
MEXICAN

✗**Pink Taco.** Nothing inside the Hard Rock Hotel is boring, and that goes for this over-the-top take on a Mexican cantina, which evokes a playful, even rollicking, vibe. The Tex-Mex food, though good, takes a decided backseat to the party scene, which includes a huge four-sided bar, patio doors that open onto the hotel's elaborate pool area, and waitresses in low-cut tops. **Known for:** lively, party atmosphere;

all the Mexican standards; selection of street tacos. $ *Average main: $22* ⊠ *Hard Rock Hotel & Casino, 4455 Paradise Rd., Paradise Road* ☎ *702/693–5000* ⊕ *www.hardrockhotel.com.*

$$$$ ✕ **Roy's.** A popular import from Hawaii, Roy's is plush without feel-
HAWAIIAN ing pretentious or overdone—a good bet for a relaxed, elegant meal. Executive Chef Roy Yamaguchi has become synonymous with creative Hawaiian fusion fare, such as the ahi poke, tempura-crusted ahi roll, or macadamia-crusted mahimahi. **Known for:** Hawaiian-imbued menu; great Aloha Hour values; sleek, slightly tropical decor. $ *Average main: $41* ⊠ *620 E. Flamingo Rd., Paradise Road* ☎ *702/691–2053* ⊕ *www. roysrestaurant.com* ⊗ *No lunch.*

$$$ ✕ **Table 34.** Run by Wes Kendrick, a well-known local chef who's dedi-
AMERICAN cated to local sourcing, this intimate, modern restaurant with clean lines, blond-wood floors, and high ceilings looks like something you'd find in California wine country. Especially good among the reasonably priced, outstanding bistro creations are the fresh pastas and thin-crust pizzas (try the one topped with bacon, Gouda, wilted spinach, and mushrooms). **Known for:** fresh, farm-to-table creations; house-made pastas; contemporary decor. $ *Average main: $30* ⊠ *600 E. Warm Springs Rd., South Las Vegas* ☎ *702/263–0034* ⊗ *Closed Sun. No lunch Sat.*

UNIVERSITY DISTRICT

$$ ✕ **Blueberry Hill.** This local mini-chain feels a bit like Denny's but serves
DINER far superior food, including hearty Mexican specialties, fruit-topped
FAMILY pancakes and waffles, and a number of "diet delight"–type platters. Blueberry Hill has four locales within a short drive of the Strip, three of them open 24 hours. **Known for:** varied breakfast specialties; most meals available all day; casual, diner-esque atmosphere. $ *Average main: $12* ⊠ *1505 E. Flamingo Rd., University District* ☎ *702/696–9666* ⊕ *www.blueberryhillrestaurants.com.*

$$ ✕ **Crown & Anchor British Pub.** With 24-hour service and graveyard spe-
BRITISH cials, Crown & Anchor is uniquely Las Vegas (and a favorite haunt of
FAMILY students from nearby UNLV). Most of the food is British, including the steak-and-kidney pie, bangers and mash, and authentic fish-and-chips. **Known for:** classic English foods; live "football" from across the pond; open 24/7. $ *Average main: $20* ⊠ *1350 E. Tropicana Ave., University District* ☎ *702/739–8676* ⊕ *www.crownandanchorlv.com.*

EAST SIDE

$$ ✕ **Lindo Michoacán.** Javier Barajas, the congenial owner and host of this
MEXICAN colorful cantina group, named it for his home in Mexico. He presents
FAMILY outstanding specialties that he learned to cook while growing up in the culinary capital of Michoacán. **Known for:** specialties from Michoacán region; table-side guacamole; colorful, lively atmosphere. $ *Average main: $17* ⊠ *2655 E. Desert Inn Rd., East Side* ☎ *702/735–6828* ⊕ *www.lindomichoacan.com.*

$$$$ ✕ **Lotus of Siam.** This simple Thai restaurant has attained near-fanatical
THAI cult status, leaving some to wonder what all the fuss is about. It's just that
Fodor's Choice everything is so very good. **Known for:** spicy Issan Thai cuisine; garlic
★ prawns; cult following. $ *Average main: $33* ⊠ *953 E. Sahara Ave., East Side* ☎ *702/735–3033* ⊕ *www.saipinchutima.com* ⊗ *No lunch weekends.*

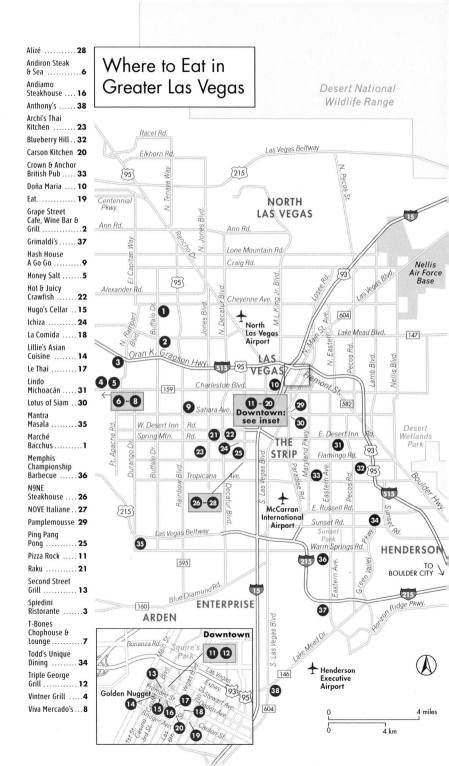

Where to Eat in Greater Las Vegas

Desert National
Wildlife Range

Racel Rd.

Elkhorn Rd.

Las Vegas Beltway

Centennial Pkwy.

Ann Rd.

Ann Rd.

NORTH
LAS VEGAS

Lone Mountain Rd.

Craig Rd.

Cheyenne Ave.

Nellis
Air Force
Base

Alexander Rd.

North
Las Vegas
Airport

Lake Mead Blvd.

Oran K. Gragson Hwy.

LAS
VEGAS

Fremont St.

Charleston Blvd.

Sahara Ave.

Downtown:
see inset

Desert
Wetlands
Park

W. Desert Inn Rd.

Spring Mtn. Rd.

E. Desert Inn Rd.

THE
STRIP

Flamingo Rd.

Tropicana Ave.

McCarran
International
Airport

E. Russell Rd.

Sunset Rd.

Sunset
Park

Warm Springs Rd.

Las Vegas Beltway

HENDERSON

TO
BOULDER CITY

Blue Diamond Rd.

ENTERPRISE

ARDEN

Horizon Ridge Pkwy.

0   4 miles

0   4 km

Downtown

Bonanza Rd.

Squire's
Park

Golden Nugget

Fremont St.

Ogden Ave.

Carson St.

Henderson
Executive
Airport

$$ ✕**Memphis Championship Barbecue.** Barbecue the old-fashioned way:
BARBECUE that's what fans are looking for, and that's what Memphis Champion-
FAMILY ship Barbecue delivers. The owner–founder, a winner of numerous bar-
becue competitions, hails from Murphysboro, Illinois, which is between
St. Louis and Memphis, and his food has influences from each. **Known
for:** big barbecue platters; fried pickles; house-made sauce. $ *Average
main: $20* ✉ *2250 E. Warm Springs Rd., East Side* ☎ *702/260–6909*
⊕ *www.memphis-bbq.com.*

$$$$ ✕**Pamplemousse.** The name, which is French for "grapefruit," was
FRENCH chosen on a whim by the late singer—and restaurant regular—Bobby
Darin. The dominant color at this old-school restaurant notable for
its kitschy pink-glowing sign is burgundy, orchestral music is played
over the stereo system, and the food is classic French. **Known for:**
Old Vegas vibe; classic French food; prix-fixe available. $ *Average
main: $38* ✉ *400 E. Sahara Ave., East Side* ☎ *702/733–2066* ⊕ *www.
pamplemousserestaurant.com* ☾ *Closed Mon. No lunch.*

DOWNTOWN

Even during its heyday as the city's casino-gaming hot spot, Downtown
was never much of a haven for gourmets, but things have gotten better
with the influence of the Downtown Redevelopment Project. Down-
town's big revitalization over the past few years includes a budding
restaurant scene with a few places that are on par with the big Strip
properties, and some casual but very tasty spots in the Downtown
Container Park.

$$$$ ✕**Andiamo Steakhouse.** This offshoot of Joe Vicari's numerous restau-
ITALIAN rants in the Detroit area is right at home in the loosely Detroit-themed
STEAKHOUSE D Las Vegas. The menu is evenly split between steak-house classics and
Italian-American favorites. **Known for:** elegant, subdued atmosphere;
steaks aged 30 days; polished, dignified service. $ *Average main: $45*
✉ *The D Las Vegas, 301 Fremont St., Downtown* ☎ *702/388–2220*
⊕ *www.thed.com* ☾ *No lunch.*

$$ ✕**Carson Kitchen.** The late rock-and-roll chef Kerry Simon brought his
AMERICAN fun, contemporary cuisine to this restored hotel in the Downtown
redevelopment district, and his legacy continues. It's small and kind
of rustic, with an airy patio out back and one on the roof. **Known
for:** seasonal—and surprising—cuisine; counter seating with a view
of kitchen; rooftop patio. $ *Average main: $20* ✉ *John E. Carson
Bldg., 124 S. 6th St., Downtown* ☎ *702/473–9523* ⊕ *www.carson-
kitchen.com.*

$$ ✕**Doña Maria.** You'll forget you're in Las Vegas after a few minutes in
MEXICAN this relaxed and unpretentious Downtown cantina. All of the combina-
FAMILY tions and specials are good, but the best play here is to order tamales,
in particular, the enchilada-style tamale (with red or green sauce), for
which Doña Maria is justly renowned. **Known for:** four varieties of
tamales; well-prepared Mexican favorites; lively, colorful atmosphere.
$ *Average main: $20* ✉ *910 Las Vegas Blvd. S, Downtown* ☎ *702/382–
6538* ⊕ *www.donamariatamales.com.*

4

$$ ✕ **Eat.** Eat may serve only breakfast and lunch, but the food is so hearty
MODERN (and so uniquely appealing), you may not feel the need for dinner.
AMERICAN Among the specialties are cinnamon biscuits with warm strawberry
FAMILY compote, shrimp and grits with bacon, and the DWBLTA, thick toasted
sourdough bracketing thick-sliced bacon, tomato, lettuce, and avocado.
Known for: creative, indulgent fare; truly killer grilled cheese; tiny,
intimate spot. ⑤ *Average main: $20* ✉ *707 Carson St., Downtown*
☎ *702/534–1515* ⊕ *eatdtlv.com* ⊗ *No dinner.*

$$$$ ✕ **Hugo's Cellar.** This venerable restaurant dates to the Rat Pack era.
AMERICAN The "cellar" aspect (it's about a half flight below ground) gives it a
Fodor's Choice cozy feel, as do old Vegas touches like table-side salad preparation
★ with every dinner (you choose what you want from the cart), a red
rose for each woman, and formal, impeccable service. **Known for:** cozy,
semi-underground location; lots of table-side service; menu of old Las
Vegas classics. ⑤ *Average main: $55* ✉ *Four Queens, 202 Fremont St.,*
Downtown ☎ *702/385–4011* ⊕ *www.hugoscellar.com* ⊗ *No lunch.*

$$$ ✕ **La Comida.** This Baja-rustic restaurant and lounge is brought to you
MEXICAN by Michael and Jenna Morton, late of the N9NE Group. The menu
FAMILY focuses on updated Mexican food served on what looks like Abuelita's
old china with mismatched furniture and plenty of depictions of the
Virgin of Guadalupe. **Known for:** updated versions of Mexican classics;
creative margaritas; rustic, fun atmosphere. ⑤ *Average main: $25* ✉ *100*
6th St., Downtown ☎ *702/463–9900* ⊕ *lacomidalv.com.*

$$ ✕ **Le Thai.** Noodles are the house specialty at this intimate restaurant in
THAI the Fremont East district of Downtown. Although most of the dishes are
FAMILY Thai (try the Awesome Noodles; the name isn't hyperbole), others lean
more toward Chinese and Japanese influences. **Known for:** tiny spot
with expansive patio; some other Asian influences; Awesome Noodles
really are. ⑤ *Average main: $15* ✉ *523 Fremont St. E, Downtown*
☎ *702/778–0888* ⊕ *www.lethaivegas.com* ⊗ *No lunch Sun.*

$$ ✕ **Lillie's Asian Cuisine.** This longtime Golden Nugget favorite specializes
ASIAN in Cantonese and Szechuan dishes, but its menu is really Pan-Asian.
FAMILY You'll also find chicken satay, pad Thai, and sushi beside old favorites
like beef chow-fun, General Tso's chicken, and sweet-and-sour pork.
Known for: pan-Asian menu; Golden Nugget landmark; subdued
decor. ⑤ *Average main: $20* ✉ *Golden Nugget Hotel & Casino, 129*
E. Fremont St., Downtown ☎ *702/386–8131* ⊕ *www.goldennugget.*
com ⊗ *No lunch.*

$$ ✕ **Pizza Rock.** Eleven-time world pizza champion Tony Gemignani
PIZZA installed four ovens in this heavily renovated, industrial-chic space in
FAMILY the Downtown Third district so he could produce all styles of pizza.
And he does: Neapolitan, Romano, American, New York, classic Ital-
ian, Californian, New York/New Haven, Sicilian, and Chicago. **Known**
for: all styles of pizzas; don't-miss appetizers; hipsterish quasi-industrial
vibe. ⑤ *Average main: $20* ✉ *201 N. 3rd St., Downtown* ☎ *702/385–*
0838 ⊕ *www.pizzarocklasvegas.com.*

$$$$ ✕ **Second Street Grill.** The art deco–style dining room in this vener-
SEAFOOD able Downtown casino restaurant is dark and intimate, with over-
sized chairs and elegant wood paneling. The menu is much more new
Vegas than old, with a Pacific Rim emphasis. **Known for:** Downtown

standard; Pacific Rim–flavored menu; contemporary interior. $ *Average main: $32* ✉ *Fremont Hotel and Casino, 200 E. Fremont St., Downtown* ☎ *702/385–6277* ⊕ *www.fremontcasino.com* ☺ *Closed Tues. and Wed.*

$$$
AMERICAN
FAMILY
✕**Triple George Grill.** You won't find too much in the way of nouvelle flourishes or ultramod decor at this San Francisco–style restaurant, and that's just how both visitors and locals prefer it—the elegant dining room is a favorite haunt for power-lunching and hobnobbing. Triple George is known for its commendably prepared traditional American fare such as oysters on the half shell, classic "wedge" salad, oh-so-tender pot roast, and truly stellar sourdough. **Known for:** eclectic menu, including vegan choices; San Francisco food and decor; intimate, semi-enclosed booths. $ *Average main: $30* ✉ *201 N. 3rd St., Downtown* ☎ *702/384–2761* ⊕ *www.triplegeorgegrill.com* ☺ *No lunch Sun.*

HENDERSON AND LAKE LAS VEGAS

$$
PIZZA
FAMILY
✕**Grimaldi's.** A branch of the legendary coal-fired pizza-baker nestled beneath the Brooklyn Bridge, this casual little joint in Henderson doesn't quite conjure up the atmosphere of the original, despite exposed-brick walls and red-checked tablecloths, but it does have a wine list and a martini menu. What counts, of course, is the pizza, and in this regard, Grimaldi's deserves high praise. **Known for:** coal-fired pizza; specialty white pizza; monthly specials. $ *Average main: $18* ✉ *9595 S. Eastern Ave., Henderson* ☎ *702/657–9400* ⊕ *www.grimaldispizzeria.com.*

$$$$
AMERICAN
✕**Todd's Unique Dining.** What's really unique (for Vegas) about this intimate spot a short drive southeast of the airport is that artful, creative contemporary cuisine is served in an easygoing space with an unpretentious vibe. This place, from a former Strip executive chef, used to be something of a sleeper, but it's becoming better known. **Known for:** innovative dishes; former Strip chef; cozy suburban spot. $ *Average main: $35* ✉ *4350 E. Sunset Rd., Henderson* ☎ *702/259–8633* ⊕ *www. toddsunique.com* ☺ *Closed Sun. No lunch.*

WEST SIDE

$$$$
FRENCH
Fodor's Choice
★
✕**Alizé.** This fine French restaurant with soaring glass walls set high atop the Palms Resort offers one of the best views of the city, including the Strip. At the helm is André Rochat, a French expatriate who's been in Las Vegas long enough to have earned the title of homegrown celebrity chef. **Known for:** expansive view of city; French-imbued menu; seasonal specialties. $ *Average main: $50* ✉ *The Palms, 4321 W. Flamingo Rd., West Side* ☎ *702/951–7000* ⊕ *www.palms.com* ☺ *No lunch.*

$$
THAI
FAMILY
✕**Archi's Thai Kitchen.** Fans of Thai food flock here for spot-on exceptional chow with few surprises—just expertly prepared curries, tom yum soups, fish cakes, and pad thais. In particular, the shrimp "ginger ginger ginger" (or you can choose it with meat or tofu) has drawn raves; yes, it really is that gingery. **Known for:** carefully executed Thai classics; Thai iced tea; lovely interiors. $ *Average main: $20* ✉ *6360 W. Flamingo Rd., West Side* ☎ *702/880–5550* ⊕ *www.archithai.com* ☺ *Closed Mon.*

$$$ ✕ **Hash House A Go Go.** Hearty appetites and a dash of patience will be
AMERICAN richly rewarded at this quirky purveyor of so-called twisted farm food.
FAMILY Heaps of savory comfort food are cooked to order in this spacious
restaurant done up in industrial, urban-farmhouse decor. **Known for:**
oversized servings; "twisted farm food"; lively atmosphere. $ *Average
main: $25* ⊠ *6800 W. Sahara Ave., West Side* ☎ *702/804–4646* ⊕ *www.
hashhouseagogo.com.*

$$$ ✕ **Honey Salt.** Frequented by local professionals and ladies-who-lunch,
ECLECTIC this spacious suburban spot serves farm-to-table–inspired dishes. Expect
FAMILY to see a lot of free-range poultry, whole grains, and seasonal produce on
your plate. **Known for:** farm-to-table food; brown-bag apple pie; con-
vivial atmosphere. $ *Average main: $28* ⊠ *Rampart Commons, 1031
S. Rampart Blvd., West Side* ☎ *702/445–6100* ⊕ *www.honeysalt.com.*

$$ ✕ **Hot & Juicy Crawfish.** This busy eatery has developed a loyal follow-
SEAFOOD ing for its delicious, fresh seafood, where crawfish from Louisiana is
FAMILY delivered regularly and available with five seasoning choices at five
heat levels. But other shellfish can be just as good. **Known for:** craw-
fish and other seafood; messy, pound-it self-service; lively atmosphere.
$ *Average main: $15* ⊠ *4810 Spring Mountain Rd., Suite C, West Side*
☎ *702/891–8889* ⊕ *www.hotnjuicycrawfish.com.*

$$ ✕ **Ichiza.** Modest little Ichiza has developed a cult following for serving
JAPANESE sublimely delicious, authentic Japanese food and drink in a casual social
Fodor's Choice environment that borders on controlled chaos. Located on the second
★ floor of a shopping center in the city's Chinatown section, this boisterous pub is crammed with tourists, students, and local hipsters who
love a good value and the chance to chow down on a variety of tasty
small-plate offerings (aka "Japa tapas") until the wee hours. **Known
for:** pub-style Japanese food; daily specials; service into the wee hours.
$ *Average main: $19* ⊠ *4355 Spring Mountain Rd., Suite 205, West
Side* ☎ *702/367–3151* ⊗ *No lunch.*

$$ ✕ **Mantra Masala.** Indian-food purists insist it's no big deal to drive 15
INDIAN minutes from the Strip to the back of a bland strip mall for exception-
FAMILY ally authentic cuisine. While meat and fish make notable appearances, a
dozen vegetarian dishes are on the menu as well. **Known for:** authentic
Indian food; healthy emphasis; soothing environment. $ *Average main:
$19* ⊠ *Durango Springs Plaza, 8530 W. Warm Springs Rd., West Side*
☎ *702/598–3663* ⊕ *www.mantramasala.com* ⊗ *Closed Mon.*

$$$$ ✕ **Marché Bacchus.** The list of wines at this French bistro-cum-wineshop
FRENCH in a quiet northwest neighborhood is nearly 1,000 deep, and tastings
FAMILY and wine dinners are held regularly. You can buy a bottle at retail prices
in the store and then drink it on the premises ($10 corkage fee). **Known
for:** serene view of lake and swans; updated French classics; nearly
1,000 wines. $ *Average main: $31* ⊠ *2620 Regatta Dr., Suite 106, West
Side* ☎ *702/804–8008* ⊕ *www.marchebacchus.com.*

$$$$ ✕ **N9NE Steakhouse.** A trendy, attractive clientele often populates this
STEAKHOUSE sleek and upscale-but-unstuffy restaurant. Keep your eyes wide open for
the occasional celebrity sweeping in for face time, champagne, and cav-
iar. **Known for:** celebrity hot spot; prime aged steaks; tabletop s'mores.
$ *Average main: $55* ⊠ *The Palms, 4321 W. Flamingo Rd., West Side*
☎ *702/933–9900* ⊕ *www.n9nesteak.com* ⊗ *No lunch.*

$$$$
ITALIAN
✕**NOVE Italiano.** Head to the Palms's opulent Fantasy Tower to try out this see-and-be-seen Italian restaurant with an excellent view of the Strip, vaulted ceilings, classical statuary, and ornately upholstered armchairs. There's an intentionally gaudy look about the place, and that's part of its allure among high rollers and poseurs. **Known for:** well-prepared Italian food; opulent decor; scenic views. $ *Average main: $40* ✉ *The Palms Fantasy Tower, 4321 W. Flamingo Rd., 51st fl., West Side* ☎ *702/942–6800* ⊕ *www.palms.com* ⊗ *Closed Sun. and Mon. No lunch.*

$$
CHINESE
FAMILY
✕**Ping Pang Pong.** Delicious regional (mostly Cantonese) fare includes marvelous dim sum made fresh daily (and available until 3 pm). The great food often compels discerning diners—many of whom hail from Vegas's large Asian community—to brave the smoky, low-rollers gaming area of the Gold Coast. **Known for:** dim sum plentiful and varied; authentic Chinese specialties; lots of Chinese expats. $ *Average main: $19* ✉ *Gold Coast Hotel and Casino, 4000 W. Flamingo Rd., West Side* ☎ *702/247–8136* ⊕ *www.goldcoastcasino.com/dine.*

$$
JAPANESE
FAMILY
Fodor's Choice
★
✕**Raku.** Seating is at a premium in this softly lighted strip-mall *robata*, a favorite of almost every chef in town. At 6 pm sharp every day but Sunday, doors open for small-plate offerings of creamy house-made tofu, fresh sashimi (no sushi), and savory grilled meats, fish, and veggies (cooked over charcoal imported from Japan) that reflect the culinary mastery of its Tokyo-born owner-chef. **Known for:** agedashi tofu, robata foods; daily specials; cozy atmosphere. $ *Average main: $15* ✉ *5030 W. Spring Mountain Rd., Suite 2, West Side* ☎ *702/367–3511* ⊕ *www.raku-grill.com* ⊗ *Closed Sun. No lunch.*

$$
MEXICAN
✕**Viva Mercado's.** Locals rejoiced when Bobby Mercado opened a new restaurant after a recession-prompted absence of a few years, and no wonder. This colorful, comfortable spot (with patio dining when the weather's pleasant) features 10 house-made salsas and a well-executed seafood-heavy menu. **Known for:** 10 house-made salsas; seafood-heavy menu; friendly, efficient service. $ *Average main: $18* ✉ *9440 W. Sahara Ave., West Side* ☎ *702/454–8482* ⊕ *vivamercadoslv.com.*

SUMMERLIN AND RED ROCK CANYON

$$$$
AMERICAN
FAMILY
✕**Andiron Steak & Sea.** The husband-and-wife team of restaurant developer Elizabeth Blau and chef Kim Canteenwalla, who also own Honey Salt, opened this nearby restaurant in downtown Summerlin. The menu is more eclectic than the name might indicate. **Known for:** eclectic menu; light, airy interior; weekend brunch. $ *Average main: $33* ✉ *1720 Festival Plaza Dr., Summerlin South* ☎ *702/685–8002* ⊕ *andironsteak.com.*

$$$
MEDITERRANEAN
✕**Grape Street Cafe, Wine Bar & Grill.** This smart neighborhood restaurant that has relocated to the downtown Summerlin shopping district serves food intended to coordinate nicely with the restaurant's interesting, affordable, and plentiful (as in, 30 selections by the glass) wine list. The menu features salads, sandwiches, pizzas, pasta, and seafood, as well as traditional dishes such as short ribs and chicken Parmesan or marsala. **Known for:** wine-complementing menu; wines by the glass; varied offerings. $ *Average main: $30* ✉ *Downtown Summerlin, 2120 Festival Plaza Dr., Summerlin South* ☎ *702/478–5030* ⊕ *www.grapestreetdowntownsummerlin.com.*

$$$ ✕ **Spiedini Ristorante.** Longtime local chef Gustav Mauler serves tradi-
ITALIAN tional favorites including his signature osso buco, shrimp fra diavolo,
FAMILY and chicken saltimbocca—along with house-made pastas, risotti, and
gnocchi. Starters like Tuscan hummus and beef carpaccio make way
for chicken involtini and wild Alaskan halibut. **Known for:** signature
Italian favorites; monthly wine dinners; sophisticated decor. $ *Av-
erage main: $30* ⊠ *JW Marriott Las Vegas Resort & Spa, 221 N.
Rampart Blvd., Summerlin South* ☎ *702/869–7790* ⊕ *www.spiedini.
com* ⊘ *No lunch.*

$$$$ ✕ **T-Bones Chophouse & Lounge.** Well-dressed local professionals are
STEAKHOUSE drawn in by the striking slabs of dragon onyx guarding the entrance to
this upscale steak house. It's the perfect spot for a romantic or celebra-
tory meal, especially since live music enhances the ambience after 5 on
weekends (6 on Friday and Saturday). **Known for:** dry-aged steaks;
"Seafood Jumbo Jackpot" cold platter with lobster, crab, and more;
elegant atmosphere. $ *Average main: $50* ⊠ *Red Rock Casino Resort
Spa, 11011 W. Charleston Blvd., Summerlin South* ☎ *702/797–7576*
⊕ *redrock.sclv.com* ⊘ *No lunch.*

$$$ ✕ **Vintner Grill.** Once you get past the bland office-park setting, you'll
MEDITERRANEAN find that this sumptuously decorated spot near Red Rock Resort has
plenty to recommend in the way of contemporary Mediterranean fare.
A Spanish- and Italian-influenced menu is enhanced by a large selection
of wines by the glass. **Known for:** broad cheese selection; varied menu;
outdoor dining area. $ *Average main: $30* ⊠ *Summerlin Centre, 10100
W. Charleston Blvd., Suite 100, Summerlin South* ☎ *702/214–5590*
⊕ *www.vglasvegas.com* ⊘ *No lunch Sun.*

ELSEWHERE IN LAS VEGAS

SOUTH SIDE

$$$$ ✕ **Anthony's.** Anthony's is The M Resort's version of the steak house
STEAKHOUSE that's de rigueur in every casino. The atmosphere is sleek and sophisticated, with the feel, food, and service of a Strip spot without the steep
Strip prices. **Known for:** beef from family's Montana ranch; oysters
Rockefeller; quiet elegance. $ *Average main: $44* ⊠ *The M Resort,
12300 Las Vegas Blvd. S, South Las Vegas* ☎ *702/797–1000* ⊕ *www.
themresort.com* ⊘ *No lunch.*

WHERE TO STAY

TOP LAS VEGAS POOLS

You, a lounge chair, a tropical drink, and a gorgeous pool. Sound like your kind of vacation? Then plant yourself poolside in Sin City. Las Vegas might just be America's best landlocked beach resort.

Vegas swimming pools can be quite extravagant: fringed with lush landscaping and tricked out with wave machines, swim-up bars, ultraquiet misting machines, and wild waterslides. Or they can be snazzy affairs with private cabanas (including satellite TV, Wi-Fi, and private misting machines) that range in price from about $40 a day for a basic one at Excalibur to $825 a day for a 145-square-foot cabana at Mandalay Bay's Moorea Beach Club, which offers European-style (i.e., topless) sunbathing for guests 21 and older.

Alas, unless you're a guest of the resort, many resorts don't allow you to use their pool facilities. If swimming and sunning are important to you, then choose from any of the following resorts with pools that are guaranteed to be the perfect oases in the desert.

TOP PICKS

Caesars Palace. The ancient Romans revered water for its healing powers, and they built sumptuous public baths amid fragrant gardens, exercise areas, and playing fields. Caesars Palace has re-created those glorious havens with its 4½-acre Garden of the Gods Pool Oasis, which comprises seven pools and two whirlpool spas. Surrounding each pool are posh rental cabanas and ample room for sunbathing. A poolside bar serves up cold treats as well as a full food menu. There's also swim-up blackjack.

Encore. Building off the success of the opulent pool next door at Wynn Las Vegas, Encore boasts the Encore Beach Club, a two-tier pool and dayclub. The complex is open to hotel guests and the general public (generally beautiful public, that is). Inside, the semicircular spectacle revolves around a main pool with daybed-style cushions that appear to float like lily pads. Twenty-six cabanas ring the perimeter and eight two-story bungalows offer the most indulgent accommodations (private hot tubs and bathrooms and individual air-conditioning). There's a gaming pavilion with craps and blackjack. In summer, premier DJs spin house every Sunday. The dayclub, naturally, becomes a happening nightclub after dark when the pool complex becomes an extension of Surrender Nightclub.

Hard Rock. The Hard Rock throws fabulous pool parties and bears an uncanny resemblance to that Polynesian beach hideaway you've always dreamed about. Its lushly landscaped Rehab Beach Club has truckloads of soft, white sand. There's even a high-quality underwater sound system. Grab a colorful cocktail at Palapa Lounge, with its Indonesian vibe and tropical waterfalls. Feeling lucky? Hit the swim-up blackjack bar. The cabanas resemble Tahitian huts, with thatch roofs and rattan chairs. Predictably, the Hard Rock caters to a young-adult crowd of hipsters and bon

vivants in their twenties and thirties. If you're outside this demographic, you may feel a bit like a fish out of water.

Mandalay Bay. The mother of all Vegas pools. The experience includes an 11-acre beach spread with a huge wave pool, a Euro-inspired topless pool club with plush daybeds, a meandering river, and some of the cushiest cabanas in town. The beach is piled high with a couple thousand tons of California-imported golden sand, which feels just perfect between the toes. You can raft along the river, admiring the verdant foliage. After the sun sets, the beach becomes one of the city's hottest nightspots. There are also two casual restaurants. A huge soundstage overlooks the wave pool, hosting concerts by a wide range of rock and pop acts all summer long.

HONORABLE MENTIONS

The Flamingo. The Flamingo may have lost its luster, but its main pool still is one of the best around. Take a ride down a waterslide, play swim-up blackjack, explore waterfalls in the lagoon pool, or swim beneath stone grottoes not unlike those at the Playboy Mansion (sorry, no naked women here). Throughout the entire pool area, real penguins, swans, and pink flamingos roam free. Average pool furniture is on the cheap side, but it's Vegas—you can always pay to upgrade.

The Mirage. If you prefer a shaded, tropical spread, check out the verdant pool area at the classy Mirage. The two main pools are connected through a series of dramatic lagoons and waterfalls. The Mirage won't wow you with nonstop activities or goofy gimmicks—it's just a handsome, well-maintained pool that's ideal whether you're a serious aficionado or a toe-dipping dabbler. Lounge chairs are outfitted with comfy mesh sailcloth. Oh, and if you want to commune with other mammals, you always can pay to swim with the dolphins in Siegfried & Roy's Secret Garden and Dolphin Habitat.

The Palms. This 3-acre complex at the Palms is open to the public (weekdays 9–6). It has three separate pools, all of which are fed by waterfalls and have colorful underwater lighting. The best feature is the triangular Glass Bar, set cleverly under a glass-bottom pool deck. If you want to go all out, book one of the 27 cabanas or bungalows, which are outfitted with high-end sound systems, plasma TVs, and swank furnishings. Some bungalows have their own lap pools, double-sided fireplaces, bedrooms, and lawns.

Red Rock Resort has a beautiful swimming complex with a giant circular pool. The best of the Downtown pools is at the **Golden Nugget.** Be sure to try the waterslide that tunnels through the middle of the 200,000-gallon aquarium. At the posh **M Resort** in Henderson, the entire pool complex offers sweeping views of desert mountains and the entire Strip.

Updated by
Matt Villano

5

Since the late 2000s, Vegas has had a construction boom, with major resorts rising on the Strip from the south to the north. And whereas the early 2000s saw a short-lived (ill-advised) attempt to brand Vegas as family-friendly, now the focus is rightfully back on decadence and indulgence.

Just about every property now has a special pool for topless (they call it "European-style") sunbathing. Many resorts also have expanded their cocktail programs (the fancy word for this is now "mixology").

Some of these efforts have been more successful than others. The posh Encore Beach Club, at Encore, is an exemplary model of the "dayclub" in that it creates a nightclub vibe during the day. Developments at The Cosmopolitan Las Vegas have had a similar impact; the property has three on-staff mixology gurus and a special kitchen where these cocktail whizzes whip up recipes all day long.

Other properties have established new benchmarks in amenities. When CityCenter opened in 2010, the $8.5-billion complex included Crystals, a new-era shopping mall with flagship stores of Prada, Tiffany & Co, and some of the spendiest boutiques in America. Also in 2010, The Palazzo launched a new club level dubbed "Prestige," which grants guests access to a special lounge that includes daily snack service, drink service, and a business center.

Despite competition from these up-and-comers, the established properties still pack 'em in. Bellagio's rooms still carry cachet, and The Mirage—the hotel that started the megaresort trend more than 20 years ago—continues to sell out. At Wynn Las Vegas and The Venetian, guests rave about everything from comfy beds to exquisite restaurants and great shopping. Qua Baths & Spa at Caesars Palace might be one of the top spas in town. And for overall experience, the Four Seasons Las Vegas, which occupies top floors of the tower at Mandalay Bay, is still one of the best.

LAS VEGAS LODGING PLANNER

TIMING YOUR TRIP

Especially on weekends, accommodations in Las Vegas fill up fast. When it's time for a big convention—or a big sporting event—it's not unusual for all of the Las Vegas area's roughly 150,000 hotel rooms to sell out completely. Combine those with three-day holidays, and you can see why it's wise to make lodging arrangements for busy weekends as far ahead as possible.

The age of the last-minute deal seems to be coming to an end. There was a time when many hotels, eager to fill rooms, offered rock-bottom prices and tempting packages for as low as $79 per night (most offered these deals on their Twitter accounts). These type of deals still exist, but with Vegas enjoying high-occupancy rates year-round now, they're increasingly more difficult to find. However, if you're not traveling during a busy weekend and have the luxury of waiting until the last minute, you can still find some discounted rates.

GETTING THE BEST ROOM

There's no surefire way to ensure that you'll get the room you want, when you want it, and for the lowest price possible. But here are a few tips for increasing your chances:

Book early. This town's almost always busy, so book as early as possible. Generally, if you book a room for $125 and later find out that the hotel is offering the same category of room for $99, the hotel will match the lower price, so keep checking back to see if the rates have dropped. Of course, this won't work if you prepay for a room on Expedia, Kayak, or Priceline. It also won't work if you buy in for a prepaid package deal. Once you go this route, you either can't get out of the reservation or you may have to pay a hefty cancellation fee.

Getting the room you want. Actual room assignments aren't determined at most Vegas hotels until the day before, or the day of, arrival. If you're hoping for a particular room (for example, a room with a view of the Strip), phone the hotel a day before you arrive and speak with somebody at the front desk. This applies whether you booked originally through the hotel or some other website. Don't be pushy or presumptuous. Just explain that although you realize the hotel can't guarantee a specific room, you'd appreciate it if they'd honor your preference.

Your second-best bet. Simply check in as early as possible on the day of arrival—even if no rooms are yet available (and you have to wait in the casino), you're likely to get first preference on the type of room you're seeking when it opens up.

What about upgrades? It's virtually never inappropriate to request a nicer room than the one you've booked. At the same time, it's virtually always inappropriate to expect that you'll receive the upgrade. The front-desk clerk has all the power and discretion when it comes to upgrades, and is unlikely to help you out if you act pushy or haughty. Gracious humility, smiles, and warmth go a long way.

WHERE SHOULD I STAY?

	Vibe	Pros	Cons
South Strip	Fun! Resorts here are glamorous, but not as serious as Center and North Strip properties. With roller coasters, arcades, shows, and beaches, properties are also the most kid-friendly.	Close to airport; plenty of diversions for the whole family; bargains at top Strip properties can be found here.	Need to take a taxi or monorail to hit Center Strip. Fewer shopping options than Center and North Strip.
Center Strip	Happening, hip section of Strip has the newest resorts with all of the latest and greatest amenities. Shopping in this part of town also is second to none.	Many rooms are new or recently renovated; spas are among the largest and most popular in town.	Traffic congestion, both on sidewalks and off; rooms generally pricier than they are elsewhere in town.
North Strip	Glitz and glamour rule. Rooms are among the largest and most ornate, and on-property amenities are all top-of-the-line.	Most (but not all) rooms are suites; incredible restaurant options.	Highest prices on-site; long (and pricey) cab ride from the airport.
Downtown	Vegas as it used to be—back when rooms were an afterthought and everything was about the casino downstairs.	Affordable lodging; classic casinos; proximity to other diversions in the area.	Rooms are bare-bones; streets aren't entirely safe after dark; expensive taxi ride to big resorts on the Strip.
West Side and Summerlin	Smaller, more amenity-heavy resorts sit west of the Strip, with the most lavish of the bunch offering glamorous pools and golf courses nearby. Many resorts appeal to locals.	Quieter and away from the hustle of the Strip; lower room rates; incredible views of the Spring Mountains and the Strip.	Summerlin is a half hour from the Strip.
East Side and Henderson	Resorts here (and along Paradise Road) are functional. Instead of offering the latest and greatest in amenities, rooms are on the small side.	Lower prices than the Strip; on-site diversions such as bowling; proximity to local services.	Long taxi ride to the Strip (half hour from Henderson); doesn't have the excitement of the Strip.

Do I tip for an upgrade? It's not customary to tip hotel clerks for upgrades, especially at nicer properties. If you wave some cash around discreetly, it might not hurt, but it won't necessarily help either.

THE LOWDOWN ON RATES

In general, at an average of about $120 per night (per the Las Vegas Convention and Visitors' Authority), rates for Las Vegas accommodations are lower than those in most other American resort and vacation cities. Still,

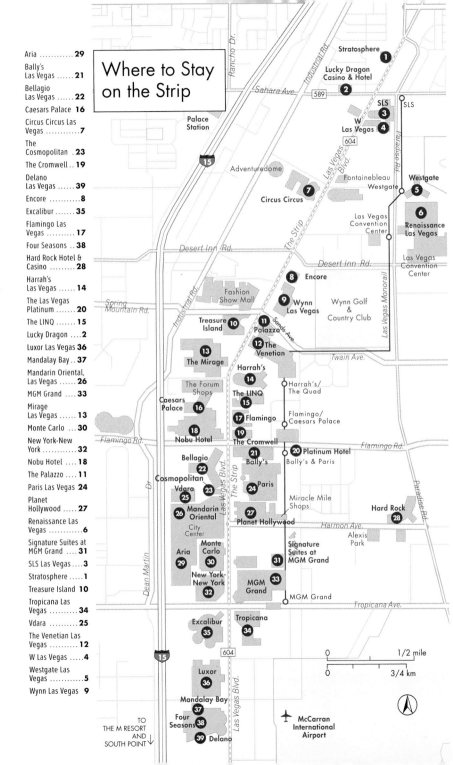

Where to Stay on the Strip

the situation is changing; though rack rates for fancy properties are higher than ever, many hotels still offer fantastic deals. There are about a hundred variables that impact price, depending on who's selling the rooms (reservations, marketing, casino, conventions, wholesalers, packagers), what rooms you're talking about (standard, deluxe, minisuites, standard suites, deluxe suites, high-roller suites, penthouses, bungalows), and demand (weekday, weekend, holiday, conventions or sporting events in town).

When business is slow, many hotels reduce rates on rooms in their least desirable sections, sometimes with a buffet breakfast or even a show included. Most "sales" occur from early December to mid-February and in July and August, the coldest and hottest times of the year, and you can often find rooms for 50% to 75% less midweek than on weekends. Members of casino players clubs often get offers of discounted or even free rooms, and they can almost always reserve a room even when the rest of the hotel is "sold out."

Over the last few years, most Strip hotels have clustered "amenities" such as Wi-Fi, fitness center access, and morning newspapers into mandatory resort fees. These fees vary from property to property, and generally range from $12.99 to $29. In addition to the resort fees, starting in 2016, most Las Vegas resorts began to charge for parking. ■ TIP→ If you book a room through a casino host, request that he or she eliminate resort and parking fees from your folio.

WHAT IT COSTS			
$	**$$**	**$$$**	**$$$$**
Hotels under $150	$150–$230	$231–$330	over $330

Prices in the hotel-resort reviews are the lowest cost of a standard double room in high season.

HOTEL REVIEWS

Hotel reviews have been shortened. For full information, visit Fodors.com.

SOUTH STRIP

With an Oz-like structure that stretches forever, a pyramid with a light you can see from space, and a replica of the New York City skyline, the southern third of the Strip between CityCenter and the iconic "Welcome to Fabulous Las Vegas" sign could be considered the entertainment hub of Vegas.

Major resorts in this area include the Tropicana, Mandalay Bay, Luxor, Excalibur, MGM Grand, New York–New York, and Monte Carlo. Rooms here are generally within 10 to 15 minutes of the airport and are slightly more affordable than their Center and North Strip counterparts. After the addition of The Park and T-Mobile Arena, the South Strip has reestablished itself as the most popular section of Sin City's most famous street.

This part of town has a small claim on Strip history as well; the Tropicana dates back 50 years, and the MGM, Mandalay Bay, and the Luxor were early entrants in the megaresort race of the 1990s. And in November 2017, when the puck drops for the first time at T-Mobile Arena, the city will welcome its first-ever major professional sports franchise in the National Hockey League's Las Vegas Golden Knights.

Another trend here: ultra-exclusive hotels within the ordinary hotels. Mandalay has Delano Las Vegas and the Four Seasons; MGM has Skylofts; Monte Carlo has Hotel 32 (though the name was expected to change by early 2018). You don't have to splurge to have a great time on the South Strip, but enjoying sumptuous linens, exclusive amenities, and unparalleled service every once in a while sure is special.

$$$
RESORT
Fodor's Choice
★

Delano Las Vegas. South Beach meets desert Zen at this all-suites tower inside Mandalay Bay. Elaborate wet bars, giant 42-inch plasma TVs, plush carpeting, and floor-to-ceiling windows make the all-white guest rooms oases in the Nevada desert. **Pros:** lavish suites; great views; separate and swanky entrance. **Cons:** long walk to main casino; hard-to-find entrance; white can get monotonous. $ *Rooms from: $299* ⊠ *3950 Las Vegas Blvd. S, South Strip* ☎ *877/632–7800, 702/632–7777* ⊕ *www.delanolasvegas.com* ⤳ *1,117 suites* ⦿ *No meals.*

$
RESORT
FAMILY

Excalibur Hotel and Casino. The giant castle is popular with families— child-oriented attractions include the basement arcade (dubbed the Fun Dungeon) and the medieval-theme *Tournament of Kings* dinner show—but recent makeovers in all of the property's rooms make much of it look more grown-up (though still nondescript). **Pros:** low table minimums make for more accessible gambling; easy access to Luxor and Mandalay Bay; lively casino atmosphere. **Cons:** low table minimums also attract huge crowds; most on-site dining options are mediocre; few legitimately cool attractions. $ *Rooms from: $139* ⊠ *3850 Las Vegas Blvd. S, South Strip* ☎ *702/597–7777, 800/937–7777* ⊕ *www.excalibur.com* ⤳ *3,981 rooms* ⦿ *No meals.*

$$$$
RESORT
FAMILY
Fodor's Choice
★

Four Seasons Hotel Las Vegas. If peace and quiet are what you're after, this is your spot; with its own ground-level lobby and separate floors, the Four Seasons is cushioned from the general casino ruckus. **Pros:** kid-friendly; ultraposh; access to the elaborate resort facilities at Mandalay Bay. **Cons:** pricey; far from rest of Vegas action; stuffy at times. $ *Rooms from: $429* ⊠ *Mandalay Bay Resort, 3960 Las Vegas Blvd. S, South Strip* ☎ *702/632–5000* ⊕ *www.fourseasons.com/lasvegas* ⤳ *424 rooms* ⦿ *No meals.*

$$
RESORT

Luxor Las Vegas. Unlike other hotels on the Strip, this one has no elevators—at least in the main pyramid; instead, in order to reach rooms, guests must climb the slanted walls in one of four "inclinators." On each floor, open-air hallways overlook the world's largest atrium. **Pros:** decent value; hip casino; expansive pool. **Cons:** slanted room walls; removed from main Strip action; cheesy decor. $ *Rooms from: $199* ⊠ *3900 Las Vegas Blvd. S, South Strip* ☎ *702/262–4000, 877/386–4658* ⊕ *www.luxor.com* ⤳ *4,400 rooms* ⦿ *No meals.*

$$$
RESORT
FAMILY

Mandalay Bay. Mandalay is decked out like a South Seas beach resort, complete with cavernous rooms and one of the best pool areas on the Strip. **Pros:** large rooms; ample options for everything; the beach. **Cons:** concerts can be loud; so large it's easy to get lost. $ *Rooms from: $279*

⊠ *3950 Las Vegas Blvd. S, South Strip* ☎ *702/632–7777, 877/632–7800* ⊕ *www.mandalaybay.com* ⋘ *3,211 rooms* ⦿ *No meals.*

$$ ▦ **MGM Grand Hotel & Casino.** The MGM Grand is one of the largest
RESORT hotels in the world, with five 30-story towers with rooms in nine differ-
ent categories. **Pros:** something for everyone; StayWell rooms; fantastic
restaurants. **Cons:** easy to get lost; schlep to parking lot; check-in can
have very long lines. ⑤ *Rooms from: $229* ⊠ *3799 Las Vegas Blvd. S,
South Strip* ☎ *702/891–1111, 877/880–0880* ⊕ *www.mgmgrand.com*
⋘ *5,044 rooms* ⦿ *No meals.*

$ ▦ **Monte Carlo Resort and Casino.** The Strip could use more places like
RESORT this—handsome but not ostentatious, elegant rooms outfitted with
FAMILY cherrywood furnishings. **Pros:** low-key way to have a fabulous Strip
experience; exceptional rooms; proximity to T-Mobile Arena. **Cons:**
taxi entrance not close to main entrance; uncertain future; small-ish
casino. ⑤ *Rooms from: $149* ⊠ *3770 Las Vegas Blvd. S, South Strip*
☎ *702/730–7777, 888/529–4828* ⊕ *www.montecarlo.com* ⋘ *2,768
rooms, 224 suites* ⦿ *No meals.*

$$ ▦ **New York–New York Resort & Casino.** The mini-Manhattan skyline is
RESORT one of our favorite parts of the Strip—there are third-size to half-
size re-creations of the Empire State Building, the Statue of Liberty,
and the Chrysler Building, as well as the New York Public Library,
Grand Central Terminal, and the Brooklyn Bridge. **Pros:** authentic New York experience; art deco lobby; casino floor center bar.
Cons: layout is somewhat confusing; cramped sports book; mediocre pool. ⑤ *Rooms from: $169* ⊠ *3790 Las Vegas Blvd. S, South
Strip* ☎ *702/740–6969, 800/689–1797* ⊕ *www.newyorknewyork.
com* ⋘ *2,024 rooms* ⦿ *No meals.*

$$ ▦ **Signature Suites at MGM Grand.** The three towers that comprise this
RESORT spacious and well-appointed luxury resort adjacent to the MGM Grand
are perhaps most notable for what they lack: a casino. **Pros:** relatively
inexpensive room rates; spacious suites; en-suite kitchens to save money
on food. **Cons:** inconvenient off-Strip entrance; a trek to nearest casino
(at MGM Grand); views of TopGolf. ⑤ *Rooms from: $189* ⊠ *145 E.
Harmon Ave., South Strip* ☎ *702/797–6000, 877/612–2121* ⊕ *www.
signaturemgmgrand.com* ⋘ *1,728 suites* ⦿ *No meals.*

$$ ▦ **Tropicana Las Vegas.** Today's "Trop" (as it's been known for more than
RESORT 50 years) features some of the most spacious rooms in town with a pleas-
ant (and whitewashed) South Beach/Miami style. **Pros:** views from the new
Sky Villa Suites; breezy style; pool still has pizzazz. **Cons:** small casino;
interior layout can be confusing; restaurants better at other casino resorts.
⑤ *Rooms from: $169* ⊠ *3801 Las Vegas Blvd. S, South Strip* ☎ *702/739–
2222, 800/462–8767* ⊕ *www.troplv.com* ⋘ *1,454 rooms* ⦿ *No meals.*

CENTER STRIP

Things tend to be larger than life in the heart of the Strip. Consider the
scale replica of the Eiffel Tower—half the size of the original. Or wander
into CityCenter, the $8.5-billion city-within-a-city.

This part of the Strip stretches from CityCenter and Planet Hollywood
to the Mirage, including Mandarin Oriental, The Cosmopolitan, Paris,

Bally's, The Cromwell, Caesars Palace (and the Nobu Hotel), the Flamingo, and Harrah's along the way. Taken as a group, these properties represent some of the most storied on the Strip (Caesars Palace and the Flamingo) and the newest (The Cromwell).

The Center Strip also can be characterized by shopping. Lots and lots of shopping. The highest of the high-end stores are inside Crystals, the gateway to CityCenter. At Planet Hollywood, reputable brands dominate the Miracle Mile. Stores inside the astonishing Forum Shops, next to Caesars, fall somewhere in between. Outside Bally's, the Grand Bazaar Shops replicates an open-air mall. The Center Strip even is home to one of the largest Walgreens in the world. Another commonality among hotels here: great spas. Treatment options at Mandarin Oriental, Aria, the Cosmopolitan, and Caesars Palace could keep visitors busy (or is it relaxed?) for months. Some spas also offer hammams.

Rooms themselves in this area are all over the lot; some, like standard rooms at Bally's, are affordable and bare-bones; others, such as those inside The Cosmopolitan, with balconies, make all others appear plebeian. It pays to shop around.

$$$ | 🛏 **Aria.** Unlike most casino hotels, Aria has an abundance of light, even in standard guest rooms, and their modern style makes this one of the Strip's most contemporary-feeling options. **Pros:** high-tech rooms; natural light; excellent restaurants. **Cons:** shower setup soaks the tub; long walk to Strip; end rooms are a very long walk to the single elevator bank. $ *Rooms from: $289* ✉ *3730 Las Vegas Blvd. S, Center Strip* ☎ *702/590–7757, 866/359–7757, 877/580–2742 SkySuites* ⊕ *www. aria.com* ↻ *4,004 rooms* ❌ *No meals.*

RESORT
Fodor's Choice
★

$$ | 🛏 **Bally's Las Vegas.** An old-school property with contemporary rooms in its Jubilee Tower make the reasonably priced Bally's Resort, in the heart of the Strip, an underrated choice for a Vegas vacation. **Pros:** affordable rooms with a perfect Center-Strip location; tennis courts. **Cons:** rooms in Indigo tower could use an upgrade; casino floor can get smoky. $ *Rooms from: $169* ✉ *3645 Las Vegas Blvd. S, Center Strip* ☎ *702/967–4111, 877/603–4390* ⊕ *www.ballyslasvegas.com* ↻ *2,814 rooms* ❌ *No meals.*

RESORT

$$$ | 🛏 **Bellagio Las Vegas.** The Grand Dame of Strip resorts is still as exquisite as ever, with snazzy rooms full of Italian marble and luxurious fabrics. **Pros:** centrally located; posh suites; classy amenities. **Cons:** pricey; can be difficult to grab a quick bite because of crowds; a very long walk out to the Strip. $ *Rooms from: $269* ✉ *3600 Las Vegas Blvd. S, Center Strip* ☎ *702/693–7111, 888/987–6667* ⊕ *www.bellagio.com* ↻ *3,933 rooms* ❌ *No meals.*

RESORT
Fodor's Choice
★

$$$ | 🛏 **Caesars Palace.** Caesars was one of the first properties in town to create rooms so lavish that guests might actually want to spend time in them, and all come standard with marble bathrooms and sumptuous beds. **Pros:** Arctic ice rooms at Qua; Garden of the Gods pool oasis; storied property. **Cons:** floorplan is difficult to navigate; small casino; limited on-site parking. $ *Rooms from: $279* ✉ *3570 Las Vegas Blvd. S, Center Strip* ☎ *702/731–7110, 866/227–5938* ⊕ *www.caesarspalace. com* ↻ *3,992 rooms* ❌ *No meals.*

RESORT

$$$
RESORT
Fodor's Choice
★

🎨 **The Cosmopolitan of Las Vegas.** Balconies make The Cosmopolitan's rooms stand apart: the vast majority have balconies or terraces, the only ones on the Strip. **Pros:** terraces; in-room technology; Yoo-hoo in minibar. **Cons:** kitchenettes seem random; walls paper-thin; queues for Marquee can get annoying. ⑤ *Rooms from: $299* ✉ *3708 Las Vegas Blvd. S, Center Strip* ☎ *702/698–7000* ⊕ *www.cosmopolitanlasvegas. com* ✈ *2,995 rooms* ⦿ *No meals.*

$$
HOTEL

🎨 **The Cromwell.** Caesars has transformed Bill's Gambling Hall into the only small boutique hotel on the Las Vegas Strip. **Pros:** intimate, exclusive vibe; steam showers; stellar Giada restaurant. **Cons:** limited dining and entertainment options; thumping bass from Drai's upstairs; cramped rooms. ⑤ *Rooms from: $189* ✉ *3595 Las Vegas Blvd. S, Center Strip* ☎ *702/777–3777, 844/426–2766* ⊕ *www.caesars.com/cromwell* ✈ *188 rooms* ⦿ *No meals.*

$
RESORT

🎨 **Flamingo Las Vegas.** This elaborately landscaped, pink, classic-era resort with a 15-acre pool complex is still one of the best choices in town, and "Go" rooms (which run about $50 to $100 more per night than standard rooms), with MP3 docking stations and 42-inch flat-screen TVs, are downright stylish. **Pros:** Margaritaville is a laid-back place for drinks and live music; heart-of-the Strip location; terrific pool. **Cons:** entrance is difficult to navigate by car or taxi; standard rooms are pretty old; crowds near LINQ Promenade entrance. ⑤ *Rooms from: $119* ✉ *3555 Las Vegas Blvd. S, Center Strip* ☎ *702/733–3111, 888/902–9929* ⊕ *www. flamingolasvegas.com* ✈ *3,460 rooms* ⦿ *No meals.*

$
RESORT

🎨 **Harrah's Las Vegas.** Old-school Vegas is alive and well at this affordable Center-Strip property. **Pros:** throwback vibe with some modern touches thrown in; affordable, reliable rooms; ideal location. **Cons:** zero wow factor; small pool; lots and lots of mirrors. ⑤ *Rooms from: $119* ✉ *3475 Las Vegas Blvd. S, Center Strip* ☎ *800/214–9110* ⊕ *www. harrahslasvegas.com* ✈ *2,530 rooms* ⦿ *No meals.*

$
RESORT

🎨 **The LINQ Hotel & Casino.** Rooms in The LINQ (which was briefly known as The Quad after a long stint as Imperial Palace) are small but have been recently renovated with a modern, clean design. **Pros:** Center-Strip location; car collection; Hash House a Go Go is a great dining option. **Cons:** no-frills; many have complained that check-in can be very slow. ⑤ *Rooms from: $119* ✉ *3535 Las Vegas Blvd. S, Center Strip* ☎ *800/634–6441* ⊕ *www.caesars.com/linq* ▭ *No credit cards* ✈ *2,253 rooms* ⦿ *No meals.*

$$$$
RESORT
Fodor's Choice
★

🎨 **Mandarin Oriental, Las Vegas.** As a brand, Mandarin Oriental pledges to provide everything for the business traveler, and the Vegas property certainly delivers on that promise. **Pros:** a peaceful retreat on the Strip; valet closet; foot spa. **Cons:** smallish rooms; almost overly formal for a leisure vacation; no casino downstairs. ⑤ *Rooms from: $419* ✉ *3752 Las Vegas Blvd. S, Center Strip* ☎ *702/590–8888, 888/881–9578* ⊕ *www. mandarinoriental.com/lasvegas* ✈ *392 rooms* ⦿ *No meals.*

$$
RESORT

🎨 **Mirage Las Vegas.** After a comprehensive makeover throughout the decade, rooms at The Mirage are decorated in a cosmopolitan style, with blacks, dark browns, and deep reds. **Pros:** classic Vegas; dolphins!; one of the best pools in town. **Cons:** smoky casino; rooms hard to get to. ⑤ *Rooms from: $219* ✉ *3400 Las Vegas Blvd. S, Center Strip* ☎ *702/791–7111, 800/374–9000* ⊕ *www.mirage.com* ✈ *3,044 rooms* ⦿ *No meals.*

5

$$$
HOTEL
Fodor's Choice
★

🍴 **Nobu Hotel.** The hotel from celebrity chef Nobu Matsuhisa and partner Robert DeNiro is a sleek foodie haven tucked inside the Centurion Tower of the Caesars Palace complex. **Pros:** foodie paradise; insider access and VIP treatment; quiet haven in central Vegas. **Cons:** view of air-conditioning units atop Caesars casino; hard to locate entrance; almost too much technology. $ *Rooms from: $279* ✉ *3570 Las Vegas Blvd. S, Center Strip* ☎ *702/785–6677* ⊕ *www.nobucaesarspalace.com* ⤴ *181 rooms* ⊖ *No meals.*

$$
RESORT

🍴 **Paris Las Vegas.** Life is *magnifique* at this French-themed hotel, but some find the heavy-handed decor a little busy. **Pros:** campy decor; spacious rooms; views. **Cons:** some rooms are tired; lack of standout restaurants; big crowds and long lines. $ *Rooms from: $199* ✉ *3655 Las Vegas Blvd. S, Center Strip* ☎ *702/946–7000, 877/796–2096* ⊕ *www.parislasvegas.com* ⤴ *2,916 rooms* ⊖ *No meals.*

$$
RESORT

🍴 **Planet Hollywood Resort & Casino.** Everything at Planet Hollywood is designed to make ordinary people feel like stars, and the spacious rooms are no exception. **Pros:** classic Hollywood vibe; incredible views; posh suites. **Cons:** relatively small casino; in-room bath products are nothing special. $ *Rooms from: $189* ✉ *3667 Las Vegas Blvd. S, Center Strip* ☎ *702/785–5555, 866/919–7472* ⊕ *www.planethollywoodresort.com* ⤴ *2,496 rooms* ⊖ *No meals.*

$$
RESORT

🍴 **Vdara.** This low-key property is actually a hotel-condo, with beautiful, independently owned suites that have efficiency kitchens, pull-out sofas, and lots of extra space. **Pros:** quiet retreat right in the middle of the action; efficiency kitchens; nice spa. **Cons:** lacks the excitement of splashy resort properties; no casino; underwhelming pool. $ *Rooms from: $209* ✉ *2600 W. Harmon Ave., Center Strip* ☎ *702/590–2111, 866/745–7111* ⊕ *www.vdara.com* ⤴ *1,495 suites* ⊖ *No meals.*

NORTH STRIP

Luxury reigns supreme in the top third of the Las Vegas Strip. There aren't as many resorts here, but spacious rooms, exquisite details, and deep-sleep-inducing beds make four of them among the most luxurious in the world. This part of town is about a 30-minute ride from the airport and at least 20 minutes to the South Strip, so visitors often stay put once they're here. Then again, when you're staying at resorts that have just about everything, who wants to leave?

The cluster of hotels that make up this section include The Venetian, Palazzo, Treasure Island, Wynn, Encore, SLS Las Vegas, and Circus Circus. Of particular interest: pools. Swanky, ultra-exclusive day-lounge areas surround the pools at North Strip properties; The Palazzo's Azure Pool is one of the newest, and Encore Beach Club is by far the most popular. As with most pools in Vegas, these offer European-style sunbathing sections, too. Bikini tops optional.

Other amenities are worth raves as well. Wynn, for instance, has a men's barbershop. The Venetian's spa is operated by none other than the world-renowned Canyon Ranch. Factor in additional amenities such as high-end shopping, indoor gardens, and breathtaking design, and it's no wonder the North Strip is seen as the spot where Vegas meets high fashion, year after year.

$ ▦ **Circus Circus Las Vegas Hotel and Casino.** The hotel at the "Big Top" has
RESORT renovated all of its rooms in the last decade, giving some much-needed
FAMILY TLC to some of the oldest rooms on the Strip (the resort opened in 1968).
Pros: Adventure Dome Theme Park; pet-friendly; old-school. **Cons:** gaming atmosphere isn't nearly as elegant as most Strip properties'; not close
to any other casinos; no good restaurants. $ *Rooms from: $79* ⊠ *2880*
Las Vegas Blvd. S, North Strip ☎ *702/734–0410, 800/634–3450* ⊕ *www.*
circuscircus.com ↪ *3,632 rooms* ⫿⊙⫿ *No meals.*

$$$$ ▦ **Encore.** As far as luxury is concerned, Las Vegas simply doesn't get
RESORT much better than Encore. **Pros:** huge suites; glorious pools; casino is
Fodor's Choice fun and intimate. **Cons:** cab ride to South Strip; pricey rates; check-in
★ can be very slow. $ *Rooms from: $349* ⊠ *3131 Las Vegas Blvd. S,*
North Strip ☎ *702/770–7000, 888/320–7123* ⊕ *www.encorelasvegas.*
com ↪ *2,034 suites* ⫿⊙⫿ *No meals.*

$$$ ▦ **Lucky Dragon Casino & Hotel.** The sparsely decorated rooms at this
RESORT hotel, much like the casino itself, are geared toward Asian travelers.
Pros: attention to detail; tea service; genuine Asian vibe. **Cons:** few frills
in rooms; limited restaurant options; very small pool area. $ *Rooms*
from: $249 ⊠ *300 W. Sahara Ave., North Strip* ☎ *702/889–8018*
⊕ *www.luckydragonlv.com* ↪ *203 rooms* ⫿⊙⫿ *No meals.*

$$$ ▦ **The Palazzo Resort Hotel Casino.** The $1.8-billion, all-suites Palazzo
RESORT offers downright huge suites, almost exactly the same as those of the
Fodor's Choice nearby Venetian. **Pros:** state-of-the-art amenities; spacious suites; sumptu-
★ ous linens. **Cons:** thin walls; deserted on weekdays; long walk to Venetian.
$ *Rooms from: $239* ⊠ *3325 Las Vegas Blvd. S, North Strip* ☎ *702/607–*
7777, 866/263–3001 ⊕ *www.palazzo.com* ↪ *3,064 suites* ⫿⊙⫿ *No meals.*

$ ▦ **SLS Las Vegas Hotel & Casino.** SLS delivers a premium Vegas stay with
HOTEL just a bit of attitude, which is not a surprise considering that the property
was designed by a nightclub company. **Pros:** hipster haven; great restaurants; happening pool. **Cons:** the not-quite-Downtown, not-quite-North-
Strip location; terrible table rules; loud music from pool area. $ *Rooms*
from: $149 ⊠ *2535 Las Vegas Blvd. S, North Strip* ☎ *702/761–7000,*
855/761–7757 ⊕ *www.slslasvegas.com* ↪ *1,324 rooms* ⫿⊙⫿ *No meals.*

$ ▦ **Stratosphere Casino Hotel & Tower.** The Stratosphere's 1,149-foot obser-
RESORT vation tower soars over every other building in town, and it's an iconic
part of the Las Vegas skyline. **Pros:** Top of the World restaurant and
observation deck; Radius Pool; value for the rooms. **Cons:** surrounding
neighborhood sketchy; nondescript casino; rides and Tower cost more
than a movie. $ *Rooms from: $139* ⊠ *2000 Las Vegas Blvd. S, North*
Strip ☎ *702/380–7777* ⊕ *www.stratospherehotel.com* ↪ *2,427 rooms*
⫿⊙⫿ *No meals.*

$$ ▦ **Treasure Island (T.I.).** Whether you call it Treasure Island or T.I., what
RESORT sets this resort apart is a dash of elegance mixed with a decidedly unpre-
FAMILY tentious vibe. Whereas other properties boast of a branch of Tiffany,
this one features a jewelry store that specializes in cubic zirconia. **Pros:**
fairly modest price point; convenient location; giant CVS on-site. **Cons:**
no real nightlife or stand-out amenities; tiny poker room; Sirens show
now too risque for young kids. $ *Rooms from: $179* ⊠ *3300 Las Vegas*
Blvd. S, North Strip ☎ *702/894–7111, 800/944–7444* ⊕ *www.treasu-*
reisland.com ↪ *2,885 rooms* ⫿⊙⫿ *No meals.*

$$$ 🖵 **The Venetian Las Vegas.** It's no secret that this themed hotel re-creates
RESORT Italy's most romantic city with meticulous reproductions of Venetian
Fodor'sChoice landmarks, and the large suites aren't too shabby, either. **Pros:** excellent
★ re-creations of Italian sights; modern amenities; tremendous rooms.
Cons: sometimes difficult to navigate to rooms; poker room action can
be aggressive. $ *Rooms from: $239* ⊠ *3355 Las Vegas Blvd. S, North
Strip* ☎ *702/414–1000, 866/659–9643* ⊕ *www.venetian.com* ⤳ *4,028
suites* ⍨ *No meals.*

$$$ 🖵 **W Las Vegas.** For years Las Vegas was one of the few major markets in
RESORT the United States without a W hotel, but that all changed in early 2017,
when Starwood took control of the Lux Tower at SLS Las Vegas and
re-branded it as a W. The new hotel-within-a-hotel has its own lobby
(dubbed the Living Room, like all W lobbies), porte cochere, spa, pool
deck, and conference space. **Pros:** swanky design; expansive suites; self-
contained conference space. **Cons:** more expensive than SLS; some taxi
drivers can't find entrance; pool isn't as fun as the one at SLS. $ *Rooms
from: $299* ⊠ *2535 Las Vegas Blvd. S, North Strip* ☎ *701/761–8700*
⊕ *www.wlasvegas.com* ⤳ *289 suites* ⍨ *No meals.*

$$$$ 🖵 **Wynn Las Vegas.** Decked out with replicas of Steve Wynn's acclaimed
RESORT art collection, the princely rooms here, averaging a whopping 650
Fodor'sChoice square feet, offer spectacular views through wall-to-wall, floor-to-ceil-
★ ing windows. **Pros:** signature Desert Bambu bath products; access to
gorgeous pool; on-site golf course. **Cons:** cramped casino walkways;
slow elevators. $ *Rooms from: $389* ⊠ *3131 Las Vegas Blvd. S, North
Strip* ☎ *702/770–7000, 888/320–7123* ⊕ *www.wynnlasvegas.com*
⤳ *2,716 rooms* ⍨ *No meals.*

PARADISE ROAD AND THE EAST SIDE

PARADISE ROAD

$$ 🖵 **Hard Rock Hotel & Casino.** This sprawling resort is a shrine to rock and
RESORT roll—with rock tributes, exhibits, and authentic memorabilia everywhere,
and many rooms in the Casino Tower received upgrades at the end of
2016 as part of a major $13-million renovation. **Pros:** party central; pool
party haven; lively casino. **Cons:** rowdy crowd; close but not quite close
enough to the Strip; long walks between buildings. $ *Rooms from: $189*
⊠ *4455 Paradise Rd., Paradise Road* ☎ *702/693–5000, 800/473–7625*
⊕ *www.hardrockhotel.com* ⤳ *1,500 rooms* ⍨ *No meals.*

$$ 🖵 **The Platinum Hotel and Spa.** This swank, nongaming, and LGBT-
RESORT friendly condo-hotel has become a fashionable hideaway for Vegas
Fodor'sChoice regulars who prefer top-notch amenities but don't need to stay on the
★ Strip. **Pros:** cocktail menu at STIR Lounge; lavish rooms with comfy
sofas and beds; popularity with LGBTQ community. **Cons:** no casino;
off-Strip location; quieter than Strip hotels. $ *Rooms from: $189* ⊠ *211
E. Flamingo Rd., Paradise Road* ☎ *702/365–5000, 877/211–9211*
⊕ *www.theplatinumhotel.com* ⤳ *255 suites* ⍨ *No meals.*

$ 🖵 **Renaissance Las Vegas Hotel.** Everything is intimate at this nongam-
HOTEL ing Rat Pack–inspired hotel off the Strip on Paradise Road. **Pros:**
ENVY steak house; fresh, stylish rooms; no casino. **Cons:** rooms a bit
small; pool can get overcrowded; geared more to business travelers

than vacationers. $ *Rooms from: $149* ✉ *3400 Paradise Rd., Paradise Road* 🕾 *702/784–5700, 800/750–0980* ⊕ *www.renaissancelasvegas. com* ⇌ *578 rooms* ❧ *No meals.*

$ **Westgate Las Vegas Resort & Casino.** Despite the fairly basic rooms, con-
RESORT vention attendees have loved the convenience of this hotel for decades; it's connected to the Las Vegas Convention Center. **Pros:** great location for convention goers; classic sports book; world's largest Benihana. **Cons:** no poker room; outdated rooms; horrible name. $ *Rooms from: $129* ✉ *3000 Paradise Rd., Paradise Road* 🕾 *702/732–5111, 888/732–7117* ⊕ *www.westgatedestinations.com* ⇌ *3,000 rooms* ❧ *No meals.*

DOWNTOWN

$ **Four Queens Resort and Casino.** Named after former owner Ben Goffs-
HOTEL tein's four daughters, the circa-1966 Four Queens is what Vegas regulars would consider an "oldie but goodie," one of the most iconic casinos on Fremont Street. **Pros:** no resort fees; kitsch factor; Hugo's Cellar steak house. **Cons:** rooms need a remodel; pool off-site; outdated gaming floor. $ *Rooms from: $69* ✉ *202 Fremont St., Downtown* 🕾 *702/385–4011, 800/634–6045* ⊕ *www.fourqueens.com* ⇌ *694 rooms* ❧ *No meals.*

$ **Golden Nugget Hotel & Casino.** The Golden Nugget has reigned as
RESORT Downtown's top property since the mid-1970s, evolving with the times but maintaining classic appeal. **Pros:** legendary Vegas property; one-of-a-kind pool; great poker room. **Cons:** small sports book; table games change frequently; too many room options. $ *Rooms from: $129* ✉ *129 E. Fremont St., Downtown* 🕾 *702/385–7111, 800/634–3454* ⊕ *www.goldennugget.com* ⇌ *2,345 rooms* ❧ *No meals.*

$ **Main Street Station Casino Brewery & Hotel.** It's worth a visit to this
HOTEL pint-size property for the Victorian-era aesthetics alone, displaying stained glass, marble, and an antiques collection that includes Buffalo Bill Cody's private railcar, a fireplace from Scotland's Preswick Castle, and lamps that graced the streets of 18th-century Brussels. **Pros:** decor and quirky antiques; great value; few restaurant options. **Cons:** no pool; no gym; no Internet in rooms (only Wi-Fi in lobby). $ *Rooms from: $59* ✉ *200 N. Main St., Downtown* 🕾 *702/387–1896* ⊕ *www. mainstreetcasino.com* ⇌ *406 rooms* ❧ *No meals.*

HENDERSON AND LAKE LAS VEGAS

$ **Green Valley Ranch Resort & Spa.** Locals have long known that Green
RESORT Valley is a low-key, refined resort for the high-end crowd that prefers
Fodor'sChoice style over bustle (the Strip is a 25-minute drive away). **Pros:** sophisti-
★ cated casino; proximity to malls that offer great shopping; newer sports book. **Cons:** 25 minutes from the Strip; not much in the immediate area; can be overrun with locals. $ *Rooms from: $129* ✉ *2300 Paseo Verde Pkwy., Henderson* 🕾 *702/617–7777, 866/782–9487* ⊕ *greenvalleyranch.sclv.com* ⇌ *496 rooms* ❧ *No meals.*

$$ **Hilton Lake Las Vegas Resort & Spa.** After previous lives as the Ritz-
RESORT Carlton Lake Las Vegas and Ravella, this property was re-branded yet
FAMILY again in 2013, retaining its Mediterranean vibe and resplendent pool complex. **Pros:** relaxing ambience; complimentary shuttle; golf nearby.

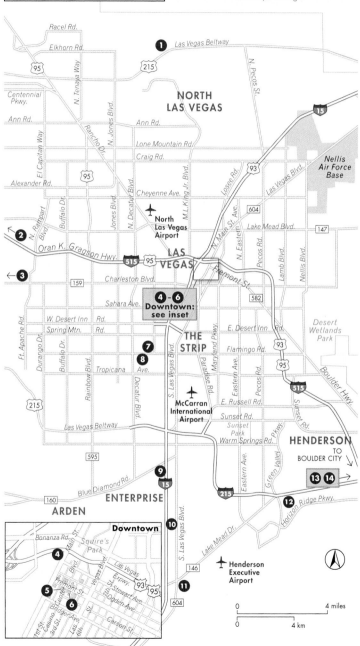

Where to Stay in Greater Las Vegas

Desert National
Wildlife Range

NORTH
LAS VEGAS

Nellis
Air Force
Base

LAS
VEGAS

Downtown;
see inset

THE
STRIP

McCarran
International
Airport

Desert
Wetlands
Park

HENDERSON
TO
BOULDER CITY

ENTERPRISE

ARDEN

Downtown

Squire's
Park

Henderson
Executive
Airport

0   4 miles

0   4 km

Cons: still has a lack of identity; far from Strip; disappointing restaurants. ⑤ *Rooms from: $209* ✉ *1610 Lake Las Vegas Pkwy., Henderson* ☎ *702/567–4700* ⊕ *www3.hilton.com* ⟿ *349 rooms* ⑩ *No meals.*

$ 🖼 **The M Resort.** Built by the Marnells, the same family that created the
RESORT   Rio, this resort is 6 miles south of McCarran Airport and is a destination unto itself. **Pros:** huge rooms; convenient yet removed from hubbub; views of Strip. **Cons:** cab ride to other casinos; planes roaring overhead; location in the middle of nowhere. ⑤ *Rooms from: $109* ✉ *12300 Las Vegas Blvd. S, Henderson* ☎ *702/797–1000, 877/673–7678* ⊕ *www.themresort.com* ⟿ *390 rooms* ⑩ *No meals.*

$$ 🖼 **Westin Lake Las Vegas Resort & Spa.** This lavish resort with a Moroc-
RESORT   can vibe sits on the shore of Lake Las Vegas and has richly appointed rooms with arched windows that offer sweeping views of the glittering lake and desert. **Pros:** lake vistas; Marssa restaurant; activity center on beach rents kayaks and paddleboats. **Cons:** nearby casino is not for avid gamblers; manic design; 30 minutes from Strip. ⑤ *Rooms from: $219* ✉ *101 Montelago Blvd., Lake Las Vegas, Henderson* ☎ *702/567–6000* ⊕ *www.westinlakelasvegas.com* ⟿ *447 rooms, 46 suites* ⑩ *No meals.*

WEST SIDE

$ 🖼 **Palms Casino Resort.** Rooms at the Palms are large, opulent, and mod-
RESORT   ern, with some unusual amenities for Las Vegas, such as beds with ultrafirm mattresses, duvets, and ample minibars. **Pros:** renowned, three-story spa; excellent coin games; low table-game minimums. **Cons:** it's taxi-distance from the Strip; doesn't quite have the of-the-moment hipness it had in the early 2010s; food and beverage stumbling. ⑤ *Rooms from: $149* ✉ *4321 W. Flamingo Rd., West Side* ☎ *702/942–7777, 866/942–7770* ⊕ *www.palms.com* ⟿ *1,312 rooms.*

$ 🖼 **Rio All-Suite Hotel & Casino.** In Brazil, Rio is party central, and in Las
HOTEL   Vegas so is this sprawling resort with spacious rooms just west of the Strip. **Pros:** mecca for poker fans; festive atmosphere; VooDoo ZipLine. **Cons:** just off-Strip enough to be inconvenient; terrible house advantage for gaming; rooms need a refresh. ⑤ *Rooms from: $129* ✉ *3700 W. Flamingo Rd., West Side* ☎ *702/777–7777, 866/746–7671* ⊕ *www.riolasvegas.com* ⟿ *2,522 suites* ⑩ *No meals.*

SUMMERLIN AND RED ROCK CANYON

$$ 🖼 **JW Marriott Las Vegas Resort & Spa.** If you have a penchant for pam-
RESORT   pering and personal service—or if your plans include golfing or hiking—this stunner in Summerlin is for you. **Pros:** proximity to golf and Red Rock National Conservation Area; terrific spa; large, nice rooms. **Cons:** a bit pricey for a Marriott; casino can fill up quickly during big conferences; far from the Strip. ⑤ *Rooms from: $209* ✉ *221 N. Rampart Blvd., Summerlin South* ☎ *702/869–7777* ⊕ *www.jwmarriottlv.com* ⟿ *548 rooms* ⑩ *No meals.*

$ 🖼 **Red Rock Casino Resort & Spa.** Way out on the western edge of the Las
RESORT   Vegas suburbs, this swanky golden-age Vegas property looks out on the ocher-red Spring Mountains, just a stone's throw from Red Rock National Conservation Area. **Pros:** bowling alley and movie theater

on-site; nice, expansive pool area; proximity to Red Rock canyon. **Cons:** waitress service in gaming areas can be slow; long distance from Strip; summertime concerts by pool bring crowds. ⑤ *Rooms from: $119* ✉ *11011 W. Charleston Blvd., Summerlin South* ☎ *702/797–7777, 866/767–7773* ⊕ *redrock.sclv.com* ⤳ *813 rooms* ⑩ *No meals.*

ELSEWHERE IN LAS VEGAS

NORTH SIDE

$ 🎰 **Aliante Casino + Hotel.** Nestled in the beautiful Aliante planned com-
HOTEL munity, this offering is a place as much for locals as for visitors looking to escape from the hubbub of the Strip. **Pros:** intimate vibe; swanky rooms; sexy pool. **Cons:** off the beaten path; casino a bit small; scene is locals only. ⑤ *Rooms from: $69* ✉ *7300 Aliante Pkwy., North Las Vegas* ☎ *702/692–7777* ⊕ *www.aliantegaming.com* ⤳ *200 rooms* ⑩ *No meals.*

SOUTH SIDE

$ 🎰 **Silverton Casino Hotel.** Don't overlook this Rocky Mountain lodge–
HOTEL theme hotel with popular attractions such as a huge Bass Pro Shop, a
FAMILY 117,000-gallon saltwater aquarium (complete with mermaid shows), and the Shady Grove Lounge, which has plasma-screen televisions and a mini–bowling alley. **Pros:** Bass Pro Shop is a fisherman's heaven; mermaid shows are one-of-a-kind; great value not too far from Strip. **Cons:** casino underwhelms; mediocre dining options; rooms are small and have absolutely no frills. ⑤ *Rooms from: $79* ✉ *3333 Blue Diamond Rd., South Las Vegas* ☎ *702/263–7777, 866/722–4608* ⊕ *www.silvertoncasino.com* ⤳ *300 rooms* ⑩ *No meals.*

$ 🎰 **South Point Hotel Casino & Spa.** Perk or quirk—the South Point is
HOTEL the only resort in the Las Vegas area to house an equestrian cen-
ter, a venue that frequently hosts rodeos and other horse-oriented shows. **Pros:** pool area; equestrian center; lively sports book. **Cons:** proximity to airport; distance from Strip hotels; rooms could use a refresh. ⑤ *Rooms from: $79* ✉ *9777 Las Vegas Blvd. S, South Las Vegas* ☎ *702/796–7111, 866/796–7111* ⊕ *www.southpointcasino.com* ⤳ *2,163 rooms* ⑩ *No meals.*

6

SHOPS AND SPAS

Updated by Susan Stapleton

Vegas is an international shopping destination. The square footage in The Forum Shops at Caesars alone makes it some of the most valuable retail real estate in the country; bankrolls are dropped there as readily as on the gaming tables. It's the variety that has pushed Las Vegas near the ranks of New York City, London, and Rome: you could send home a vintage slot machine or tote back a classic Hermès handbag.

Most Strip hotels offer designer dresses, swimsuits, jewelry, and menswear; almost all have shops offering logo merchandise for the hotel or its latest show. Inside the casinos the gifts are often elegant and exquisite. Outside, all the Elvis clocks and gambling-chip toilet seats you never wanted to see are available in the tacky gift shops. Beyond the Strip, shopping in Vegas can encompass such extremes as finding a couture ball gown in a vintage store and, in a Western store, a fine pair of Tony Lama boots left over from the town's cowboy days. Shoppers looking for more practical items can head for neighborhood malls, supermarkets, shopping centers, and specialty stores. Bargain-hunters seeking to avoid the stratospheric prices on the Strip, and not averse to traveling a bit, can usually find the same high-ticket items at discounted prices in the local or nearby factory outlet malls.

SHOPPING PLANNER

GETTING AROUND

Shopping in Las Vegas—so demanding, yet so rewarding. With malls encompassing millions of square feet of retail space, you won't have any trouble finding ways to part with your cash. But to make the most of your time and money, you should map out your shopping safaris. Distances are deceiving because of the scale of the resort casinos. What looks like a quick walk might take a half hour, or more. Because of crowd-control measures, you'll find yourself squeezing around barriers and leaping over bridges instead of just crossing a street. Grab a cab or ride the monorail ($5 a trip) and save the time for shopping. Buses, which are $8 for 24 hours along the Strip, are a cheaper option, but crowded at all hours.

Got a car? Unfortunately, very few resorts still offer free parking and/or free valet service. Mandalay Bay, Luxor, Excalibur, MGM Grand, New York–New York, Monte Carlo, Aria, Bellagio, Cosmopolitan, Caesars Palace, and The LINQ now charge for self-parking and valet. Rates vary depending on the amount of time parked.

SEND THEM PACKING
Who wants to lug packages from store to store? Most stores are happy to send your purchases back to your hotel or even ship them back home for you.

HOURS OF OPERATION
Although Las Vegas may be up all night, the people who work in the retail establishments need a little rest. Many places are open from 10 am to 11 pm during the week, and stay open an hour later on weekends. And the shopping, like the gambling, goes on every day.

The city's daily newspaper, the *Las Vegas Review-Journal* (⊕ *www. reviewjournal.com*), and weekly publications *Las Vegas Weekly* (⊕ *www.lasvegasweekly.com*) and *Vegas Seven* (⊕ *www.vegasseven. com*) offer guides to local malls and discount coupons. Many malls supply their own coupon booklets at on-site customer service or information desks as well. Some will discount even further when you present a student ID or AAA member card. Social networking sites, such as Twitter, Foursquare, and Facebook, are also excellent resources for on-the-spot discounts and freebies, detailed product information, and exclusive product previews and offerings.

SHOPS

SOUTH STRIP

FOOD AND DRINK
FAMILY **Hershey's Chocolate World.** At 13,000 square feet and spanning two levels, with a 74-foot-high-by-24-foot-wide replica of a Hershey's Milk Chocolate Bar on the façade, it's easy to spot Hershey's Chocolate World. The 18-foot Reese's Peanut Butter Cup that lights up and the 38-foot-wide, 10-foot-tall Hershey's Milk Chocolate Bar sign made of LED bulbs may also light your way. Inside find 800 different candies and chocolates, a Hershey's Kisses Chocolates Flavor Wall, and a photo booth for prints to wrap your own Vegas souvenir. ⊠ *New York–New York, 3790 Las Vegas Blvd. S, South Strip* ☏ *702/437–7439* ⊕ *hersheyschocolateworldlasvegas.com.*

FAMILY **M&M's World.** Every day till midnight, all manner of M&M merchandise is sold here—a slot machine that dispenses M&M jackpots is a best seller—and the popular candy may be purchased by the pound. Four air-conditioned levels of colorful, milk-chocolate goodies attract crowds

DID YOU KNOW?

St. Mark's Square, inside the Grand Canal Shoppes, is full of little gift-shop carts and street performers. Shoppers may experience one or more of the approximately 30 "street" performances that go on each day.

of families with children (and strollers). Those who use the personalized printing machine can create and print custom messages on M&M's, or select from unique Las Vegas images (the "Welcome to Las Vegas" sign or a deck of cards). NASCAR champion Kyle Busch hails from Las Vegas, and a full-size reproduction of his M&M's-sponsored #18 racing Toyota Camry is on display (floor 4) along with racing merchandise. About every half hour, the short 3-D movie *I Lost My M in Vegas* (G-rated, free), starring spokescandies Red and Yellow, is screened on floor 3 until 6 pm. ⊠ *Showcase Mall, 3785 Las Vegas Blvd. S, next to MGM Grand, South Strip* ☎ *702/736–7611* ⊕ *www.mymms.com.*

GIFTS AND SOUVENIRS

Guinness Store. The only Guinness Store in the United States features all things that go with the dark Irish beer. Have etched Guinness glasses personalized while you restock your bar with coasters, bar mats, and an essential authentic pouring spoon for making a perfect black and tan. Learn the six steps to pouring the perfect pint at the bar for $20. ⊠ *Shoppes at Mandalay Place, 3930 Las Vegas Blvd. S, South Strip* ☎ *702/632–7773* ⊕ *www.guinness.com/en-us/home.html.*

House of Blues. Blues music is an original American art form. Buy music, books, hot sauce, and T-shirts at the souvenir shop in the popular bar–restaurant at Mandalay Bay, where an expansive, remarkable collection of colorful folk art decorates the walls. ■**TIP→ Show your restaurant receipt to save an additional 10%.** ⊠ *Mandalay Bay, 3950 Las Vegas Blvd. S, South Strip* ☎ *702/632–7600* ⊕ *www.houseofblues. com/lasvegas.*

Vom Fass. This gourmet store, designed for those who enjoy the finer things in life, offers a variety of vinegars and oils on tap (*vom Fass* is German for "on tap"), including extra-virgin olive, nut, and seed; as well as scotches, cognacs, whiskeys, brandies, grappas, and absinthes. In addition to the retail offerings, Vom Fass offers tastings for a $5.99 fee. ⊠ *Grand Canal Shoppes, 3377 Las Vegas Blvd. S, South Strip* ☎ *702/388–2022* ⊕ *www.vomfassusa.com.*

MALLS

The Shoppes at Mandalay Place. Request the savings booklet at the north end of this sky-bridge mall, which spans the gap between Mandalay Bay and the Luxor, to receive immediate discounts at 40 shops and eateries, including Slide of Vegas, Hussong's Cantina, and the budget fashion store Fashion 101, Elton's Men's Store, or Nora Blue's. You can practice your golf swing with Nike irons and drivers at the first-ever Nike Golf store, or pick up sterling-silver razors at the Art of Shaving, a high-roller "barber spa" and grooming emporium. Beauty fans will love the all-natural Lush with its "cosmetic deli." You can also buy new sandals at Flip Flop Shops or surf gear at Ron Jon Surf Shop. ⊠ *Mandalay Bay, 3930 Las Vegas Blvd. S, South Strip* ☎ *702/632–9333* ⊕ *www.mandalaybay.com.*

FAMILY **Showcase Mall.** "Mall" is a bit of a misnomer here, where stores are more like highly evolved interactive marketing concepts. First off, there's M&M's World, the four-story homage to the popular candy, where huge dispensers with every color and type line one wall. More

Where to Refuel

If you're on a shopping mission, keep your strength up at one of these delicious pit stops.

MALLS ON THE STRIP
Bellagio: Olives

Caesars Palace: Mesa Grill

Fashion Show: Stripburger

The Forum Shops at Caesars: Border Grill, Il Mulino New York, Sushi Roku, the Palm, or Spago

Paris Las Vegas: Mon Ami Gabi

Planet Hollywood Resort & Casino: Pink's Hot Dogs or Gordon Ramsay BURGR

The Shoppes at Mandalay Place: Burger Bar

The Venetian: Sushisamba

OUTLET MALLS
Fashion Outlets of Las Vegas: Kelly's Cajun Grill

Las Vegas Premium Outlets—North: The Cheesecake Factory

Town Square: California Pizza Kitchen or Capriotti's Sandwich Shop

sugar awaits you at Everything Coca-Cola, where $8 buys either the Around the World sampler of 16 colorful, international soda flavors or eight flavors of floats. Be sure to get a photo of the 100-foot bottle of Coca-Cola outside. Branded apparel, accessories, and interesting collectibles are also for sale. Post–sugar buzz, you can head to the Hard Rock Cafe to browse the interactive video Rock Wall or buy T-shirts, Las Vegas–branded clothing, and souvenirs. An inexpensive place to buy souvenirs, snacks, water, and booze is in the Grand Canyon Experience, with its faux rocks and wooden rope bridge. The Showcase Mall's parking structure ($3) is right next to MGM Grand; the best access is from the 5th floor, where a pedestrian bridge crosses into the mall. A less hectic option is to park at any of the surrounding hotels (MGM, NY–NY, Monte Carlo) and walk here. ⊠ *3785 Las Vegas Blvd. S, near corner of Tropicana Ave., South Strip* ☎ *702/597–3122.*

MEN'S CLOTHING

Suitsupply. Suits, blazers, shirts, shoes, and accessories can be purchased and fitted on the spot at the tailoring bar situated front and center. ⊠ *Grand Canal Shoppes, 3327 Las Vegas Blvd. S, South Strip* ☎ *702/359–6100* ⊕ *us.suitsupply.com.*

WOMEN'S CLOTHING

Givenchy. No longer in the Holly Golightly style of Audrey Hepburn, Givenchy's whimsical looks have nevertheless made it a fashion forerunner. The brand's first U.S. boutique brings its entire collection of men's and women's lines to a store that looks like one of its coveted boxes. ⊠ *Wynn Las Vegas, 3131 Las Vegas Blvd. S, South Strip* ☎ *702/737–1091* ⊕ *givenchy.com.*

CENTER STRIP

CHILDREN'S CLOTHING

Though the casino-hotel malls and area shopping centers have the usual children's clothing stores such as Gap Kids and Gymboree, you can find some great gifts for kids at the shops below.

FAMILY **Kids Kastle.** For the fashionistas-in-training, Marc Jacobs, Lipstick, and Sister Sam ensembles await you. The boys can dress themselves in equally impressive duds from True Religion and Diesel. ⊠ *Forum Shops at Caesars, 3500 Las Vegas Blvd. S, Center Strip* ☎ *702/369–5437.*

FAMILY **Vilebrequin.** If there's a daddy's boy in the family, this is the place to shop for him. Vilebrequin specializes in matching father-son swim trunks with a stylish aesthetic and speedy drying technology. A second location is at Fashion Show mall and a discount store is at the Las Vegas Premium Outlets—North. ⊠ *Forum Shops at Caesars, 3500 Las Vegas Blvd. S, Center Strip* ☎ *702/894–9460* ⊕ *us.vilebrequin.com.*

FOOD AND DRINK

La Cave. Take your pick of decadent delights and gifts for the gourmand such as French-imported wines and Godiva chocolate. ⊠ *Paris, 3655 Las Vegas Blvd. S, Center Strip* ☎ *702/946–4339.*

GIFTS AND SOUVENIRS

Curios. This little gem of a store carries more than just alcohol, snacks, and everything you may have left at home. Gifts for him and her with a British theme pepper the shelves here. Snap up a top hat from Christy's (made for the royals, so why not you?), clever men's products, including shaving brushes and mustache wax, Union Jack–emblazoned knick-knacks, and even decorative pieces for your bathroom at home. ⊠ *The Cromwell, 3595 Las Vegas Blvd. S, Center Strip* ☎ *702/777–3777* ⊕ *www.caesars.com/cromwell.*

JEWELRY

Cartier. There are three outposts of this venerable jeweler in Las Vegas: at The Forum Shops, Wynn Las Vegas, and The Shops at Crystals. You'll find a fine collection of jewelry, watches, leather goods, accessories, and fragrances. ⊠ *Forum Shops at Caesars, 3500 Las Vegas Blvd. S, Center Strip* ☎ *702/418–3904* ⊕ *www.cartier.us.*

Harry Winston. Celebrities continually turn to this exclusive jeweler for red-carpet-worthy diamonds and rare gemstones. There are locations at Via Bellagio and The Shops at Crystals. ⊠ *The Shops at Crystals, 3720 Las Vegas Blvd. S, Level 2, Center Strip* ☎ *702/262–0001* ⊕ *www.harrywinston.com.*

Richard Mille. Make like tennis star Rafael Nadal and shop for high-end Swiss watches that can reach six figures. Chichi surroundings swaddled in macassar wood, steel, and leather help soften the sticker shock, but the museumlike setting makes Richard Mille worth at least a walk-through. ⊠ *The Shops at Crystals, 3720 Las Vegas Blvd. S, Center Strip* ☎ *702/588–7272* ⊕ *www.richardmille.com.*

Tiffany & Co. Browse through a full selection of Tiffany's timeless merchandise as well as the exclusive jewelry designs of Elsa Peretti, Paloma

Picasso, and Jean Schlumberger. Cleaning and repair services are also offered. Additional store locations include The Forum Shops at Caesars, The Shops at Crystals, and Fashion Show mall. ⊠ *Via Bellagio, 3600 Las Vegas Blvd. S, Center Strip* ☎ *702/697–5400* ⊕ *www.tiffany.com.*

Van Cleef & Arpels. French jewelry, watches, and perfume find a home at this boutique founded in 1896. Even royalty turn to this jewelry maker; Prince Rainier of Monaco gave Grace Kelly a Van Cleef & Arpels pearl and diamond necklace and earrings. ⊠ *The Shops at Crystals, 3720 Las Vegas Blvd. S, Center Strip* ☎ *702/560–6556* ⊕ *www.vancleefarpels.com.*

MALLS

Appian Way Shops. A majestic replica of Michelangelo's *David* in Carrara marble marks the entrance to the Appian Way Shops, where a dozen stores sell wares such as luggage, home goods, gifts, eyewear, skin-care products, cigars, condiments, and apparel. King Baby has a wealth of rock-and-roll handcrafted sterling silver pieces with elements of precious stones. Take home olive oils and vinegars from around the world at Olive & Beauty. Carina can spiff up your wardrobe with brands such as Joseph Ribkoff, True Religion, Betsey Johnson, Jessica Simpson, and Vince Camuto. Martin & MacArthur, from Hawaii, specialize in accessories for both men and women, but especially Koa wood furnishings and wooden watches, while Roberto Coin, an Italian jeweler, focuses on sleek designs, each of which contains a signature hidden ruby. ⊠ *Caesars Palace, 3570 Las Vegas Blvd. S, Casino floor near Forum Tower elevators, Center Strip* ☎ *866/227–5938* ⊕ *www. caesars.com/caesars-palace.*

Fodor's Choice ★ **The Forum Shops at Caesars.** Amazing ambience, architecture, and design means visitors won't have to drop a single dime to enjoy touring this highly accessible mid-Strip mall. Leave the high heels at home to better roam three levels of restaurants and retail—some paths cobblestoned—that resemble an ancient Roman streetscape, with scattered statuary, immense columns and arches, two central piazzas with ornate fountains, and a cloud-filled ceiling-sky that changes from sunrise to sunset over the course of three hours (to subconsciously spur shoppers to step up their pace of acquisition, perhaps?). ■TIP→ The Mitsubishi-designed freestanding Spiral Escalator is a must-ride for the view.

Of course, shopaholics will rejoice at the selection of designer shops and traditional standbys, from high-end heavy hitters such as Elie Tahari, Brooks Brothers, Gucci, Fendi, Michael Kors, Christian Louboutin, Jimmy Choo, Salvatore Ferragamo, Louis Vuitton, Marc Jacobs, and Balenciaga, to more casual labels like Abercrombie & Fitch, Bebe, Diesel, Nike, Guess, and Gap/Gap Kids. Armani fans will find an Emporio *and* Exchange for menswear, along with John Varvatos, Valentino Red, Hugo Boss, and Canali. Gaze at stunning jewelry, watches, and crystal works at Baccarat, Cartier, Hearts on Fire, Tourneau, Tiffany & Co., Pandora, Swarovski, and David Yurman. Apple offers a whole host of electronics, too. Cosmetics queens will keep themselves busy at Chanel Beauty, NARS, Dior Beauty, Kiehl's, and MAC Pro Store. And don't miss the flagship Victoria's Secret for lingerie and swimwear, or Agent Provocateur and La Perla, for that matter.

6

When all this walking/shopping brings on the inevitable hunger, head to the renovated The Palm or Wolfgang Puck's Spago. The Cheesecake Factory is popular, as are Border Grill and Joe's Seafood, Steak & Stone Crab. ⊠ *Caesars Palace, 3500 Las Vegas Blvd. S, Center Strip* ☎ *702/893–4800* ⊕ *www.simon.com.*

Grand Bazaar Shops. In front of Bally's Las Vegas, a "21st-century bazaar" inspired by the world's great outdoor markets showcases 150 shops over 2 acres. A giant crystal starburst by Swarovski re-creates Times Square, New York's New Year's Eve nightly while the booths feature glowing, mosaic, undulating rooftops over a broad selection of retail covering apparel, footwear, accessories, electronics, jewelry, and beauty. Swarovski, Alex & Ani, Superdry, Lush, and Havaianas take up the front of the market, and smaller boutiques line four alleys stretching back to the resort along with Wahlburgers from the Wahlberg brothers and Giordano's deep-dish pizza. ⊠ *Bally's Las Vegas, 3645 Las Vegas Blvd. S, Center Strip* ☎ *702/967–4111* ⊕ *www. grandbazaarshops.com.*

Le Boulevard. Petite by Vegas standards, this Parisian-style shopping lane is chock-full of Gallic delights. Le Journal stocks sundries and that jaunty French beret you know you're longing for. La Cave offers Godiva chocolates and wines. Premium cigars and international cigarettes are sold at Davidoff Boutique (until 2 am). Les Elèments keeps a stock of nice gifts and children's toys. ⊠ *Paris Las Vegas, 3655 Las Vegas Blvd. S, Center Strip* ☎ *702/946–7000* ⊕ *caesars.com/paris-las-vegas.*

The LINQ Promenade. The focal point of Caesars Entertainment's 300,000-square-foot entertainment district is the High Roller, the world's tallest observation wheel at 550 feet, but there's also shopping. A boutique specializing in urban wear and sneakers from rapper Nas is called 12 A.M. Run. Polaroid Fotobar lets you turn your own photographs into a variet of keepsakes. Chilli Beans brings sunglasses and Brazil's largest eyewear brand. Goorin Bros. fulfills all your headgear needs. Pick up some sweets at Ghirardelli, Sprinkles, or Honolulu Cookie Co. ⊠ *3475 Las Vegas Blvd. S, Center Strip* ☎ *702/322–0560* ⊕ *www.caesars.com/linq/things-to-do.*

Miracle Mile Shops. The shops here line an indoor sidewalk built around the circular theater called The Axis, where Britney Spears and Jennifer Lopez have their resident shows. Along the way, you'll find such notable and diverse fashion names as Herve Leger, Bebe, Urban Outfitters, H&M, and Tatyana. Beauty lovers will enjoy Bath & Body Works and Sephora, the authority in beauty retail stores, which are well worth the walk on the cobblestone flooring. Miracle Mile does an admirable job of balancing fashion designer boutiques with modestly priced shops. Many of the stores are at your local mall, but you still may discover a treasure here. ⊠ *Planet Hollywood Resort & Casino, 3663 Las Vegas Blvd. S, Center Strip* ☎ *702/866–0703, 888/800–8284* ⊕ *www.miraclemileshopslv.com.*

Fodor'sChoice
★   **The Shops at Crystals.** Two levels of opulent boutiques, restaurants, and artistic flourishes are housed within the dramatic steel-and-glass structure that envelops The Shops at Crystals shopping venue at

CityCenter. True to its gleaming facade, scads of swanky designer apparel and accessories from fashion's crème de la crème line the clean, minimalist confines within. Touch-screen directories guide you to brands such as Pucci, Prada, Bulgari, Lanvin, Balenciaga, Bottega Veneta, Stella McCartney, Bally, and Tom Ford. Come dressed to impress if you intend to do anything more than ogle the latest and greatest offerings; some of the salespeople here can be more haughty than the couture.

Roberto Cavalli has a two-story boutique that sells everything Cavalli—even the pet line—and features a built-in catwalk. One of Louis Vuitton's largest locations in North America is here, with two levels that extend beyond leather goods to include men and women's ready-to-wear, shoes, jewelry, textiles, ties, and more.

Among the places to dine are Bobby Flay's Bobby's Burger Palace; Mastro's Ocean Club sitting inside a tree house; and Cucina by Wolfgang Puck. Afterward, stroll outdoors to cross the CityCenter Sky Bridge to Gallery Row (near the Mandarin Oriental and giant, 4-ton sculpture of a blue-and-red typewriter eraser by Claes Oldenburg and Coosje van Bruggen), where three galleries feature the work of Seattle glass master Dale Chihuly, bronze sculptures by Richard MacDonald, and wilderness photography by Rodney Lough Jr.

■TIP➔ For a fun way to access The Shops at Crystals, ride the sleek and silent Aria Express, CityCenter's free electric tram with a fantastic elevated view of the complex. ⊠ *CityCenter, 3720 Las Vegas Blvd. S, adjacent to Aria, Center Strip* ✛ *By car: cross Las Vegas Blvd. via E. Harmon Ave. to enter Aria's South Parking garage. Park on its southwestern side for closest elevator access to Monte Carlo's casino level. Once inside, turn right on Monte Carlo's shopping walkway, Street of Dreams, for short walk to tram's boarding platform. Board and travel one stop to Crystals Station; downward escalator deposits you onto level 2 of Crystals* ☎ *866/754–2489* ⊕ *www.simon.com.*

Via Bellagio. Steve Wynn spared no expense to create the Bellagio, so be prepared to spare no expense shopping at its exclusive boutiques. Elegant luxury stores, such as Prada, Chanel, Giorgio Armani, Gucci, Harry Winston, and Tiffany & Co., line a long passage. When you're ready to cool your heels, dine on the balcony at Olives, right in the promenade, to snag the best patio seat (first come, first served) for watching the Fountains of Bellagio (aka dancing waters). Children, with few exceptions (such as those of hotel guests), aren't allowed anywhere in the Bellagio casino areas. ⊠ *Bellagio, 3600 Las Vegas Blvd. S, Center Strip* ☎ *702/693–7111, 888/987–6667* ⊕ *www.bellagio.com.*

MEN'S CLOTHING

You can't walk into the shopping areas of Strip hotels without encountering high-end men's clothing stores. If the price tags on the Strip are too out of reach, the outlet malls have brand names for less, such as Tommy Hilfiger, Perry Ellis, Hugo Boss, Van Heusen, Polo Ralph Lauren, and DKNY. Streetwear and high-end sneaker stores also abound; you just have to know where to find the boutiques.

Berluti. Parisian luxury brand Berluti brings luxe shoes and leather accessories for men. Find oxfords, derbies, and loafers in alligator skin, kangaroo leather, and calfskin, as well as business portfolios, wallets, belts, and bags. ⊠ *The Shops at Crystals, 3720 Las Vegas Blvd. S, Center Strip* ☎ *702/795–1542* ⊕ *store.berluti.com.*

Ermenegildo Zegna. You'll find the finest in Italian men's suits on this store's racks. High-quality craftsmanship, superior fit, and impeccable style dominate here. Made-to-measure service, small leather goods and accessories, and a selection of apparel from fashion lines Z Zegna and Zegna Sport are also available. There's an additional location at The Shops at Crystals. ⊠ *Forum Shops at Caesars, 3500 Las Vegas Blvd. S, Center Strip* ☎ *702/369–5458* ⊕ *www.zegna.com.*

Giorgio Armani. Italian designer Armani cuts a cloth like nobody's business. Clean lines, high-quality fabrics, expert stitching—all are evident in the luxury formalwear displayed throughout this elegant store. The maestro's signature spiffy sportswear, shoes, handbags, and accessories are sold here, too, as well as fragrances and cosmetics. ⊠ *Via Bellagio, 3600 Las Vegas Blvd. S, Center Strip* ☎ *702/893–8327* ⊕ *www.armani. com/giorgioarmani.*

Hugo Boss. Browse men's fashions straight from European and New York runways, also at two additional local branches (The Venetian and Fashion Show mall), plus three factory store outlets. ⊠ *Forum Shops at Caesars, 3500 Las Vegas Blvd. S, Center Strip* ☎ *702/696–9444* ⊕ *www.hugoboss.com.*

John Varvatos. Casual-chic men's clothes and a slew of shoes, belts, and messenger bags make up the offerings here. The Forum Shops location also carries formalwear. The version at the Hard Rock Hotel is a boutique store modeled after their New York City Bowery location (former site of the iconic rock club CBGB). ⊠ *Forum Shops at Caesars, 3500 Las Vegas Blvd. S, Center Strip* ☎ *702/939–0922* ⊕ *www.johnvarvatos.com.*

Paul Smith. The designer hails from England, and his British-inspired menswear makes that quite clear. Emphasizing understated patterns and colors, Paul Smith's designs have a cool, relaxed quirkiness to them. Some call it geek chic. In addition to accessories and shoes, this Daniel Libeskind–designed store also carries women's wear. Books, art, vintage furniture, and other curios are also for sale. ⊠ *The Shops at Crystals, 3720 Las Vegas Blvd. S, Level 1, Center Strip* ☎ *702/796–2640* ⊕ *www. paulsmith.co.uk/us-en/shop.*

Stitched. Men who want the best of the latest and greatest fashions will be right at home here. Jacks & Jokers, Zachary Prell shirts, and the XXXX Stitched collection of suits and sports coats are carried here. An on-site tailor can personalize garments. Made-to-measure suits are a specialty. Hang out in the Scotch lounge while you pick out your new wardrobe. ⊠ *The Cosmopolitan of Las Vegas, 3708 Las Vegas Blvd. S, Center Strip* ☎ *702/698–7630* ⊕ *www.stitchedlifestyle.com.*

Tom Ford. The designer put his stamp on the fashion world when he brought Gucci back from the dead. Since then the outstanding craftsmanship of his modern menswear line has suited Brad Pitt, George Clooney, and Jay-Z on the red carpet. Men's eyewear, accessories, and fragrances are offered, as well as women's ready-to-wear. Nei-man Marcus in Fashion Show has an impressive counter of Tom Ford Beauty products for both men and women. ⊠ *The Shops at Crystals, 3720 Las Vegas Blvd. S, Level 1, Center Strip* ☎ *702/740–2940* ⊕ *www.tomford.com.*

12 A.M. Run. This sneaker boutique with backing from rapper NAS features brands such as The Hundreds, Billionaire Boys Club, Young & Reckless, Primitive, Stance, Adidas, Puma, Stüssy, Asics, and exclusive sneaker collaborations. ⊠ *The LINQ Promenade, 3545 Las Vegas Blvd. S, Center Strip* ☎ *702/912–5968* ⊕ *www.12amrun.com.*

SPORTING GOODS AND CLOTHING

Niketown. This multilevel Nike theme park features attractive displays, inspirational slogans, and giant swoosh symbols amid the latest cool technology in athletic shoes. Flashy and crowded, it's full of "Nike athletes" yelling into two-way radios. ⊠ *Forum Shops at Caesars, 3500 Las Vegas Blvd. S, Center Strip* ☎ *702/650–8888* ⊕ *www.nike.com.*

WOMEN'S CLOTHING

AllSaints Spitalfields. The British brand uses vintage themes as its inspiration for graphic tees and embellished dresses that cater to a youthful demographic. Celebrities like Vanessa Hudgens, Jessica Alba, and Dakota Fanning have been known to wear the edgy styles here. The flagship location at The Forum Shops features two levels of shopping for men and women. Also located at The Cosmopolitan. ⊠ *Forum Shops at Caesars, 3500 Las Vegas Blvd. S, Center Strip* ☎ *702/893–4800* ⊕ *www.us.allsaints.com.*

Balenciaga. The highly stylish Italian fashion house brings an architectural approach to men's and women's ready-to-wear fashions, handbags, and accessories. Additional location at The Shops at Crystals. ⊠ *Forum Shops at Caesars, 3500 Las Vegas Blvd. S, Center Strip* ☎ *702/732–1660* ⊕ *www.balenciaga.com.*

Bottega Veneta. Renowned for its modern, sophisticated take on the classics, this Italian fashion house melds elegant style with leather fabrics. The line appeals to the woman with a taste for timelessness. Additional locations at Via Bellagio and the Grand Canal Shoppes. ⊠ *The Shops at Crystals, 3320 Las Vegas Blvd. S, Center Strip* ☎ *702/369–0747* ⊕ *www.bottegaveneta.com.*

CH Carolina Herrera. Chic sophistication is the name of the game at this fashion boutique where you can find the acclaimed designer's bridge collection. ⊠ *Forum Shops at Caesars, 3500 Las Vegas Blvd. S, Level 2, Center Strip* ☎ *702/894–5242.*

DNA 2050. Shopping for jeans has never been so easy. This 2,305-square-foot branch specializes in denim, carrying all the old faithfuls such as True Religion, Hudson, and J Brand as well as the latest trendsetters such as Nudie, G-Star, Current Elliott, and Fidelity. Don't overlook the handbag collection here. ⊠ *The Cosmopolitan of Las Vegas, 3708 Las Vegas Blvd. S, Center Strip* ☎ *702/698–7610* ⊕ *www.emporiumdna.com.*

6

Fendi. The Italian designer offers elegant garments, furs, shoes, and handbags that transcend trends. The boutique at The Shops at Crystals features a replica of Rome's Trevi Fountain inside, and The Forum Shops at Caesars boutique features a jewel box of a glass-enclosed store with its handbags and shoes as well as a traditional shop across the aisle. There are additional locations at the Grand Canal Shoppes and Via Bellagio. ⊠ *Forum Shops at Caesars, 3500 Las Vegas Blvd. S, Center Strip* ☎ *702/732–9040* ⊕ *www.fendi.com.*

Gucci. The Italian luxury designer features the men's and women's clothing and shoe collections as well as leather goods, luggage, jewelry, timepieces, silks, and eyewear. Additional locations at Via Bellagio and The Shops at Crystals. ⊠ *Forum Shops at Caesars, 3500 Las Vegas Blvd. S, Center Strip* ☎ *702/369–7333* ⊕ *www.gucci.com.*

H&M. The crème de la crème of fast fashion, this Swedish retailer features affordable apparel and accessories that rival what you'll see on high-profile runways. Diffusion lines from acclaimed designers are also prevalent here, and generally make an appearance only at this location. The store contains three floors, three checkout stations, an elevator, and a cut-open facade. ■TIP➜ **The location at The Forum Shops is the second-biggest H&M in the country.** Find men's and children's attire as well. There's an additional location at the Miracle Mile Shops. ⊠ *Forum Shops at Caesars, 3500 Las Vegas Blvd. S, Center Strip* ☎ *702/207–0167* ⊕ *www.hm.com.*

Lanvin. The creative decor in the windows alone is reason enough to check out this boutique that carries men's and women's fashions and accessories. Inside you'll be dazzled by the bold, sophisticated fashions. ⊠ *The Shops at Crystals, 3720 Las Vegas Blvd. S, Center Strip* ☎ *702/982–0425* ⊕ *www.lanvin.com.*

Louis Vuitton. Stash your winnings in a designer bag from one of five Vegas branches of this famous French accessories maker. Hot-stamping services are offered at all branches. The store at The Shops at Crystals is the largest in North America and houses James Turrell's *Akhob*, a walk-in light installation, the artist's largest Ganzfeld exhibit to date; it's accessible by reservation only, so call ahead. There are additional locations at Wynn Esplanade, The Forum Shops at Caesars, Via Bellagio, and Fashion Show. ⊠ *The Shops at Crystals, 3720 Las Vegas Blvd. S, Center Strip* ☎ *702/262–6262* ⊕ *www.louisvuitton.com.*

Mulberry. Make like the Duchess of Cambridge at British handbag designer Mulberry with its line of leather handbags and shoes. Paper patterns of the brand's popular Bayswater handbag greet guests as they walk in. Find Vegas-only fashions worthy of a night on the town here, too. ⊠ *Forum Shops at Caesars, 3500 Las Vegas Blvd. S, Center Strip* ☎ *702/382–0496* ⊕ *www.mulberry.com.*

Rent the Runway. In a pinch and need a dress? Try on designer gowns in sizes 0 to 22, rent them for the night (or the weekend), and return them before you head home, leaving more room in your wallet and space in your suitcase. Hats, scarves, jewelry, handbags, and more are also available. ⊠ *The Cosmopolitan of Las Vegas, 3708 Las Vegas Blvd. S, Center Strip* ☎ *702/698–2500* ⊕ *www.renttherunway.com.*

Stella McCartney. Sharp tailoring and feminine lines mark Stella McCartney's clothing. The lifelong vegetarian does not use any leather or fur in her collections for women and children. The centerpiece of this flagship store is a horse sculpture made from 8,000 Swarovski crystals dubbed *Lucky Spot.* McCartney commissioned the sculpture in 2004 and named it for a horse once owned by her late mother. ☒ *The Shops at Crystals, 3720 Las Vegas Blvd. S, City Center* ☏ *702/798–5102* ⊕ *www.stellamccartney.com/us.*

Tory Burch. Rich textures, zippy colors, perky prints, and Bohemian spirit infuse the stylish, wearable clothing and accessories at Tory Burch. The handbags, pumps, and ballet flats are staples here. Additional locations are at the Grand Canal Shoppes and Fashion Show Mall. ■TIP➔ **The Forum Shops branch is the largest and carries a wider selection.** ☒ *Forum Shops at Caesars, 3500 Las Vegas Blvd. S, Center Strip* ☏ *702/369–3459* ⊕ *www.toryburch.com.*

Versace. This boutique features a body-conscious, seductive line of ready-to-wear clothes that speak to a confident woman. Additional location at The Shops at Crystals. ☒ *Forum Shops at Caesars, 3500 Las Vegas Blvd. S, Center Strip* ☏ *702/932–5757* ⊕ *www.versace.com.*

NORTH STRIP

BOOKS

Bookstores aren't exactly as ubiquitous in Las Vegas as video-poker machines, but if you venture out into the greater metro area, you inevitably find them. They're stashed among the many strip malls and neighborhood shopping centers. The more rarified, albeit pricier, offerings are found on the Strip.

Bauman Rare Books. Housing an exquisite collection of first-edition titles in pristine condition, this antiquarian bookstore carries such classics as Dr. Seuss's *The Cat in the Hat,* Truman Capote's *Breakfast at Tiffany's,* and *A Farewell to Arms,* inscribed by Hemingway himself. A large-folio 1679 edition of the King James Bible contains meticulous engraved-plate illustrations, as does Ellen Willmott's rare first-edition printing of *The Genus Rosa,* with its full-page color pages of roses. Historical documents showcase the original signatures of Jung, Edison, and presidents Lincoln and FDR, among other notables. Special binding services are also offered. You may have seen this bookshop on the History Channel's *Pawn Stars.* ☒ *Grand Canal Shoppes, 3377 Las Vegas Blvd. S, North Strip* ☏ *702/948–1617, 888/982–2862* ⊕ *www.baumanrarebooks.com.*

GIFTS AND SOUVENIRS

Bonanza "World's Largest Gift Shop". Okay, so it may not, in fact, be the world's largest, but at more than 40,000 square feet, it's Vegas's largest souvenir store. And although it carries most of the usual junk, this peddler of pop-culture kitsch also stocks some most unusual junk. A pair of fuzzy pink dice? Check. Blinking "Welcome to Fabulous Las Vegas" sign? Check. Elvis aviator sunglasses complete with black sideburns? Check. How about a battery-operated parrot with a potty mouth or a

3-inch plastic slot machine that squirts water? They're all here, seven days a week, open until 9 pm. Check out an area of the store that contains Elvis and Marilyn Monroe gifts. As the store likes to say, "If it's in stock, we have it." ⊠ *2440 Las Vegas Blvd. S, North Strip* ☎ *702/385–7359* ⊕ *www.worldslargestgiftshop.com.*

JEWELRY

Ca'd'Oro. Fittingly named after a Venetian palace, this exclusive boutique specializes in European jewelry and carries collections from Baume & Mercier, Gucci, Hearts on Fire, Longines, Movado, and Tag Heuer. ⊠ *Grand Canal Shoppes, 3377 Las Vegas Blvd. S, Venetian, North Strip* ☎ *702/650–0225* ⊕ *www.cadorojewelers.com.*

Chopard. This Swiss watchmaker is known particularly for its ladies' timepieces but creates an astonishing collection of diamond pieces of jewelry as well. ⊠ *Wynn Esplanade, 3131 Las Vegas Blvd. S, North Strip* ☎ *702/862–4522* ⊕ *www.chopard.com.*

Rolex. Many other authorized stores sell Rolex, but the standalone boutique at Wynn showcases the entire line from the Swiss luxury watchmaker. ⊠ *Wynn Esplanade, 3131 Las Vegas Blvd. S, North Strip* ☎ *702/770–3560* ⊕ *www.rolex.com.*

MALLS

Fashion Show. The frontage of this fashion-devoted mall is dominated by The Cloud—a giant, oblong disc that looms high above the entrance. Ads and footage of the mall's own fashion events are continuously projected across the expanse of this ovoid screen. Inside, the mall is sleek, spacious, and airy—a nice change from some of the claustrophobic casino malls. The mall delivers on its name: fashion shows are staged in the Great Hall on an 80-foot-long catwalk that rises from the floor, Friday through Sunday, every hour noon–6 pm.

Although you can find many of the same stores in the casino malls, there's a smattering of different fare, such as bareMinerals, which carries many different types and shades of natural, mineral-based cosmetics, and the yoga-inspired Lululemon Athletica. Topshop and neighboring TopMan bring British fashions to the desert. Neiman Marcus, Saks Fifth Avenue, Nordstrom, Forever 21, and Dillard's serve as the mall's anchors. ⊠ *3200 Las Vegas Blvd. S, next to Trump Hotel, North Strip* ☎ *702/369–8382* ⊕ *www.thefashionshow.com* ☞ *Free valet and self-parking.*

Fodor's Choice ★ **Grand Canal Shoppes.** This is one of the most unforgettable shopping experiences on the Strip. Duck into shops like Dooney & Bourke, Sephora, and the Art of Shaving, or Peter Lik's rustic gallery of fine-art photography. Amble under blue-sky ceilings alongside the Grand Canal. All roads, balustraded bridges, and waterways lead to St. Mark's Square, an enormous open space filled with Italian opera singers and costumed performers. Watch for the living statues, who will intrigue and amuse. If you need to take a load off, hail a gondola ($29 per person)! The mall is open late (until 11 pm Sunday through Thursday, until midnight Friday and Saturday).

On The Palazzo side, find powerhouse names such as Diane von Furstenberg, Michael Kors, Bottega Veneta, and Tory Burch. Shoe lovers will swoon over the Christian Louboutin and Jimmy Choo boutiques, and jewelry aficionados will delight in Piaget and Cartier. The main attraction for many, though, is the mall's anchor, Barneys New York. The reputable department store brings in up-and-coming, cutting-edge designers as well as established, exclusive ones such as Balenciaga and Lanvin. ⊠ *The Venetian, 3377 Las Vegas Blvd. S, North Strip* ☏ *702/414–4500* ⊕ *www.grandcanalshoppes.com.*

MEN'S CLOTHING

Brioni. High rollers can have an impeccably tailored suit made to order for a cool six grand. Or splurge on a crocodile watch case for $11,000. ⊠ *Wynn Esplanade, 3131 Las Vegas Blvd. S, North Strip* ☏ *702/770–3440* ⊕ *www.brioni.com.*

Elton's. Exclusive men's designers, both high profile (Hugo Boss, Diesel, D. J. Pliner) and obscure (Cult of Individuality, George Roth L.A., Great China Wall) come together in this premium men's boutique. Additional location at The Shoppes at Mandalay Place. ⊠ *Grand Canal Shoppes, 3377 Las Vegas Blvd. S, North Strip* ☏ *702/853–0571.*

WOMEN'S CLOTHING

Alexander McQueen. The British designer's store on the Wynn Esplanade features men's and women's attire as well as shoes and handbags, including the coveted brass knuckle clutches. ⊠ *Wynn Esplanade, 3131 Las Vegas Blvd. S, North Strip* ☏ *702/369–0510* ⊕ *www.alexandermcqueen.com.*

Burberry. The luxury British brand features its famous trench coats and rain gear as well as hot fashion accessories. Additional location at The Forum Shops at Caesars. ⊠ *Grand Canal Shoppes, 3377 Las Vegas Blvd. S, North Strip* ☏ *702/382–1911* ⊕ *us.burberry.com.*

Chanel. The boutiques for this fine French couturier at Bellagio and Wynn stock the latest women's ready-to-wear fashions, accessories, sunglasses, leather goods, shoes, jewelry, cosmetics, and fragrances. The boutique at Encore carries a smaller, ultralux selection and is home to Chanel's Fine Jewelry Collection. Additional locations at Encore Esplanade and Via Bellagio. The Forum Shops at Caesars now has the first Chanel boutique dedicated to beauty and fragrances only. ⊠ *Wynn Esplanade, 3131 Las Vegas Blvd. S, North Strip* ☏ *702/765–5055* ⊕ *www.chanel.com.*

Chloé. This high-end French fashion house sports a large selection of women's ready-to-wear collections, as well as gorgeous handbags, shoes, and accessories for the bohemian in every woman. ⊠ *Wynn Esplanade, 3131 Las Vegas Blvd. S, North Strip* ☏ *702/675–9998* ⊕ *www.chloe.com.*

Diane von Furstenberg. Head here for something figure-flattering, comfortable, and high on the style scale. Diane von Furstenberg, or DVF as she's known to longtime followers, first made her fashion presence known in 1972 with her iconic wrap dress, which is still a staple in her collections to this day. There's an additional location at The Forum Shops at Caesars. ⊠ *Grand Canal Shoppes, 3377 Las Vegas Blvd. S, North Strip* ☏ *702/818–2294* ⊕ *www.dvf.com.*

6

Dior. Clothes from this storied fashion house appeal to the sophisticated woman who still wants to stand out in a crowd. The Wynn and The Shops at Crystals locations also carry the collection of Dior Homme menswear. There's an additional location at Via Bellagio. ⊠ *Wynn Esplanade, 3131 Las Vegas Blvd. S, North Strip* ☏ *702/735–1345* ⊕ *www.dior.com.*

Forever 21. This two-level store-worthy location features all the fast fashion you can imagine for young women, men, and children. Shoes, jewelry, and even games make an appearance here. ⊠ *Fashion Show Mall, 3200 Las Vegas Blvd. S, North Strip* ☏ *702/735–1014* ⊕ *www.forever21.com.*

Hermès. The Parisian brand's iconic Birkin bags are so exclusive, you could be on a waiting list for several years—yes, years—before securing one. The fine silk scarves and well-crafted clothes carry the same prestige without the waiting game. Additional locations at Via Bellagio and The Shops at Crystals. ⊠ *Encore Esplanade, 3121 Las Vegas Blvd. S, North Strip* ☏ *702/650–3116* ⊕ *hermes.com.*

Herve Leger. Expect to find the famous, sexy, strappy bandage dresses that put this brand on the map and in the nightclubs of Las Vegas. The clothes aren't modest and neither are the price tags. ⊠ *Grand Canal Shoppes, 3377 Las Vegas Blvd. S, North Strip* ☏ *702/893–4723* ⊕ *www.herveleger.com.*

Pinto Ranch. Boot scoot on over to this Western store that carries brands such as Lucchese, Old Gringo, Stetson, and a collection of 5,000 handmade cowboy boots in stock. ⊠ *Fashion Show Mall, 3200 Las Vegas Blvd. S, North Strip* ☏ *702/228–3400* ⊕ *www.pintoranch.com.*

Topshop. Eclectic British style meets high fashion at this London clothier's U.S. outposts. Men's fashions also find a home inside neighboring Top-Man. The stores carry limited-edition items for Vegas. ⊠ *Fashion Show, 3200 Las Vegas Blvd. S, North Strip* ☏ *702/866–0646* ⊕ *us.topshop.com.*

DOWNTOWN

BOOKS

Gamblers General Store. This independent bookstore specializes in books about blackjack, craps, poker, roulette, and all the other games of chance. With more than 3,000 titles in stock, the place dubs itself the "World's Largest Gambling Bookstore." You'll also find novels about casinos, biographies of crime figures, and other topics that relate to Las Vegas history and gambling. Time your visit right and you might even score autographed copies of some of your favorite tomes. ⊠ *800 S. Main St., Downtown* ☏ *702/382–7555, 800/522–1777* ⊕ *www.gamblersbookclub.com.*

FOOD AND DRINK

The Beef Jerky Store. A few steps from Fremont Street find every conceivable form of jerky, including bacon, ostrich, alligator, salmon, and even tofu, and adds hot and spicy choices to boot. Take home the Las Vegas specialty jerky shaped like all four suits in a deck of cards. It's not all jerky; there's candy as well. ⊠ *112 N. 3rd St., Downtown* ☏ *702/388–0073* ⊕ *www.beefjerkystore.com.*

MALLS

Fodor's Choice
★
Las Vegas Premium Outlet—North. The upscale mix at this racetrack-shaped Downtown outlet mall includes names you can find at your own mall, such as Nine West, Charlotte Russe, and Quiksilver, but with better discounts; and rarely seen outlets of fashion heavyweights such as Dolce & Gabbana, St. John Company Store, Brooks Brothers Factory Store, Kate Spade New York, Ted Baker London, Tory Burch, and Salvatore Ferragamo. Fashion jeweler David Yurman and coveted handbag designer Coach are also here. Neiman Marcus Last Call and Saks Off Fifth anchor the mall. This is one of the few outdoor malls in town, and plenty of shade as well as misting towers help keep you cool in the Vegas heat. Take a taxi or ride a regional bus: purchase tickets aboard for $6 (2-hour Access Pass), or $8 (24-hour Access Pass), with pickup/drop-off at several Strip locations. Call RTC for more information. Three parking garages afford easy access to the mall but tend to fill up quickly; valet parking is available in the main garage. ⊠ *875 Grand Central Pkwy. S, Downtown* ☎ *702/474–7500, 702/228–7433 RTC* ⊕ *www.premiumoutlets.com.*

ONLY IN LAS VEGAS

Fodor's Choice
★
Gold and Silver Pawn Shop. Home to the History Channel's *Pawn Stars*, Gold and Silver Pawn Shop has a little bit of everything. Shop for rare coins, first-edition books, and jewelry and watches galore, including Super Bowl rings or that special piece of history you saw on the show. With ever-changing stock, you never know what you will see. Lines to get in can get long, and the store is open 24/7. The neighboring Pawn Plaza—a two-story shopping center made from shipping containers—features Rick's Rollin Smoke BBQ from Gold and Silver Pawn Shop co-owner Rick Harrison, along with other small stores. ⊠ *713 Las Vegas Blvd. S, Downtown* ☎ *702/385–7912* ⊕ *gspawn.com.*

VINTAGE CLOTHING

Buffalo Exchange. This is a thrift store must-stop for the terminally hip. The chain's extensive collection of trendy vintage and used clothing at reasonable prices makes for satisfying shopping. You also can find great recycled discards and, since we all could use the help, lots of suggestions from the staff. ⊠ *1209 S. Main St., Downtown* ☎ *702/791–3960* ⊕ *www.buffaloexchange.com.*

PARADISE ROAD AND THE EAST SIDE

MEN'S CLOTHING

Fruition. Kanye West heads to this off-the-Strip locale when he's in Vegas. Why? The owners have a great eye for the next big thing. That's why they've styled videos for Lil' Kim and M.I.A. The look here is accomplished by fusing the old with the new. Men's and women's vintage Yves Saint Laurent, Christian Dior, Alexander McQueen, and more can be found here. You'll also uncover up-and-comers just making their mark at this urban-meets-tribal-meets-geek-meets-hipster store. ⊠ *4139 S. Maryland Pkwy., East Side* ☎ *702/796–4139* ⊕ *shop. fruitionlv.com.*

Undefeated. This store is the authority on premium sneakers and street wear. Look for classic brands sitting next to limited-edition pieces as well as UNDFTD, their own label, which collaborates with the big boys to create lustful objects such as the Air Jordan IV Retro and Nike Dunk Hi Ballistic. ⊠ *Paradise Esplanade, 4480 Paradise Rd., Suite 400, Paradise Road* ☎ *702/732–0019* ⊕ *undefeated.com.*

MUSIC

Zia Records. This store is for the music lover who enjoys shopping for tunes the old-fashioned way—thumbing through title after title, hoping to get that lucky break. The vinyl selection at Zia is diverse and vast, but the real gems here are in the pop and rock genres. That goes for CDs, too, which can be found at rates as low as four for $10. Whether it's Wilson Phillips, Fleetwood Mac, Elvis, or a little Richard Marx, you'll find what you didn't know you were looking for in this store that feels like the basement where the ol' band once practiced. In fact, you might get lucky on your visit and enjoy local talent performing live. Take advantage of the knowledgeable staff, who can test your music trivia or offer recommendations based on your current collection. There's an additional location in west Las Vegas on Sahara Avenue. ⊠ *4225 S. Eastern Ave., East Side* ☎ *702/735–4942* ⊕ *www.ziarecords.com.*

HENDERSON AND LAKE LAS VEGAS

FOOD AND DRINK

FAMILY   **Ethel M Chocolates Factory and Cactus Garden.** The *M* stands for Mars, the name of the family (headed by Ethel in the early days) that brings you Snickers, Milky Way, Three Musketeers, and M&Ms. Come here for two special reasons: one, to watch the candy making, and two (more important), to taste four free samples in the adjoining shop that was recently renovated. As for the other half of this place's name, yes, there is, indeed, a cactus garden—Nevada's largest—with more than 300 species of succulents and desert plants. It's at its peak during spring flowering but also takes on a holiday spirit when it's lit up in November through December. ■TIP➔ **The factory tour and gardens are free, but if you forget to go, McCarran International Airport features branches at all gates after airport security.** ⊠ *2 Cactus Garden Dr., Henderson* ☎ *702/435–2655, 702/435–2608* ⊕ *www.ethelm.com.*

HOME FURNISHINGS

Williams-Sonoma Marketplace. Many of the cleverly designed and stylish cooking tools, gourmet goodies, and home-decor items at Williams-Sonoma are suitcase-friendly for the gourmand in your life. Of course, looking through the shelves upon shelves of cookbooks, dishes, and utensils also makes a pleasant way to pass an hour before going to lunch. Call the branch for a rundown on its monthly cooking demos, hands-on workshops, or other technique classes. There's an additional location on the west side of Las Vegas. ⊠ *The District at Green Valley Ranch, 2255 Village Walk Dr., Suite 129, Henderson* ☎ *702/897–2346* ⊕ *www.williams-sonoma.com.*

MALLS

FAMILY **Galleria at Sunset.** This enclosed mall in northwest Henderson boasts dozens of stores and boutiques, restaurants such as Larsen's Grill and Bravo! Cucina Italiana, and seasonal carnivals. There's also a Funset Kids Club for kids 12 and under that provides sitting services for parents who wish to be child-free while they shop. ✉ *1300 W. Sunset Rd., Henderson* ☎ *702/434–0202* ⊕ *www.galleriaatsunset.com.*

WEST SIDE

BOOKS

Amber Unicorn Books. Food lovers will enjoy this used-book store with its catalog of cookbooks from Thomas Keller, Wolfgang Puck, and other chefs. Find the rare and the antique. ✉ *2101 S. Decatur Blvd., Suite 14, West Side* ☎ *702/648–9303* ⊕ *www.amberunicornbooks.com.*

Psychic Eye Book Shop. Behind the innocuous strip-mall façade are all sorts of esoteric books, lucky talismans, tarot cards, and candles. Get a psychic reading or an astrological chart on where to place your bets. Additional locations are in the McCarran International Airport area and Henderson. ✉ *6848 W. Charleston Blvd., West Side* ☎ *702/255–4477* ⊕ *www.pebooks.com.*

ONLY IN VEGAS

Serge's Wigs. If you've always wished for the sleek tresses of the stunning Vegas showgirls (or female impersonators), or if you want to try a daring new look for the clubs, head to this bright and spacious Vegas institution. You'll find an expansive selection of natural-hair and synthetic wigs and hairpieces available in many styles, lengths, and colors, as well as accoutrements such as Styrofoam heads, hair adhesives, shampoos, scarves/turbans, and eyelashes. ■TIP➔ **A hair covering must be worn (scarf, bandana, nylon stocking) or purchased ($2) before trying on wigs. Allow additional time for cutting, styling, and proper fitting of your hairpiece if you plan to wear it on the same day of purchase.** ✉ *4515 W. Sahara Ave., West Side* ☎ *702/207–7494* ⊕ *www.sergeswigs.com* ☾ *Closed Sun.*

SUMMERLIN AND RED ROCK CANYON

HOME FURNISHINGS

FAMILY **Ikea.** Billy bookcases, Swedish meatballs, Poang chairs, and Kallax shelving units now have a home in Las Vegas at the mammoth warehouse store. The two floors of shopping feature 50 inspirational room settings along with a convenience store with frozen meats and Nordic-inspired desserts, a 450-seat restaurant, and a bistro with cinnamon buns, hot dogs, and pizza. ✉ *600 Ikea Way, Summerlin South* ☎ *888/888–4532* ⊕ *www.ikea.com.*

MALLS

Downtown Summerlin. This 1.6-million-square-foot open-air shopping mall just south of Red Rock Resort features 125 restaurants and retailers anchored by Macy's, Dillard's, and a to-die-for Nordstrom Rack. Apple, Michael Kors, Sephora, Fabletics, Chico's, and J. Jill are just some of the stores there. Try Wolfgang Puck Bar & Grill or MTO Cafe when shopping wears you out, or head to Dave & Busters for some games with your food and drink. ⊠ *1980 Festival Plaza Dr., I–215 at W. Sahara Ave., Summerlin South* ☎ *702/832–1000* ⊕ *downtownsummerlin.com.*

ELSEWHERE IN LAS VEGAS

SOUTH SIDE

MALLS

FAMILY **Las Vegas Premium Outlets—South.** Like its northern sister outlet, this branch has a vast selection of popular brands such as Bose, Fossil, Easy Spirit, Lucky Brand, Ann Taylor, Brooks Brothers, Calvin Klein, DKNY, Kenneth Cole, Nautica, Nike, Skechers, Wet Seal, Wilsons Leather, and Zales at 65% off. But these shops, 2.5 miles south of the Strip, are indoors and air-conditioned, with plenty of free on-site parking. ■TIP➜ **Stop at the Information Center for a layout and listings brochure, which includes coupons and daily specials. Moreover, AAA card members receive a free discount card for additional savings.** Some stores offer student discounts as well. The Disney store, Carter's, and Gymboree stock stuff for kids, and there's a carousel ride, too. Regional buses will pick up or drop off shoppers at Silverton and South Point hotel-casinos, as well as from several on-Strip locations. (Call RTC at *702/228–7433* for information.) ⊠ *7400 Las Vegas Blvd. S, Airport* ☎ *702/896–5599* ⊕ *www.premiumoutlets.com.*

FAMILY **Town Square.** Constructed to resemble Main Street America with open-air shopping and dining, this 100-acre complex contains more than 150 shops, including MAC and Sephora cosmetics, H&M, Apple, Saks Off Fifth, and Banana Republic. When you tire of shopping (or the kids do, anyway), there's also a children's play area, multiplex cinema, and rides on the Town Square train. Lazy Dog lets you bring Fido on the patio, while Yard House brings pub fare. There's also a Capriotti's, Tommy Bahama's, and several other on-site eateries, including a Whole Foods Market. Stoney's Rockin' Country dance and live-music venue fires up the country tunes Thursday through Saturday. ■TIP➜ **Need to make a quick stop? Town Square offers curbside parking so you don't have to schlep all the way from one of three parking garages to your shopping destination.** ⊠ *6605 Las Vegas Blvd. S, at junction of I–15 and I–215 Beltway, Airport* ☎ *702/269–5000* ⊕ *www.mytownsquarelasvegas.com.*

ONLY IN VEGAS

FAMILY **Houdini's Magic Shop.** Magicians are hot tickets in Vegas, so it's no surprise that Houdini's corporate headquarters are in town. Find replicas of some of Harry Houdini's favorite illusions as well as volumes of books on how to perform magic, complete with costumes. Smaller branches can be found in the Grand Canal Shoppes at The Venetian, Miracle Mile Shops at Planet Hollywood Resort, Circus-Circus, and New York–New York. ⊠ *Peterson Center, 6455 Dean Martin Dr., Suite L, Airport* ☎ *702/798–4789* ⊕ *www.houdini.com* ☉ *Closed weekends* ☞ *Free parking.*

SPAS

SOUTH STRIP

Bathhouse Spa. Dark slate and suede-covered walls wrap this modern and sexy boutique spa at the Delano. The 16,000-square-foot spa features a nightclub-like scene, but with the thump, thump, thumping music replaced with the serene melody of water trickling. Baths are a specialty here with treatments such as the Moor mud bath that beautifies and soothes arthritis, respiratory issues, and more, and the signature fizz bath, which bubbles with fragrances that turn into essential oils. ⊠ *Delano, 3940 Las Vegas Blvd. S, South Strip* ☎ *877/632–9636* ⊕ *www.delanolasvegas.com.*

Grand Spa & Fitness Center. Though this well-managed spa lacks the stunning architecture of other Strip spas, it makes up for it with accommodating attendants and a serene, feng shui–designed atmosphere. The World Therapies menu features creative treatments, including the Dreaming Ritual inspired by Aborigines in Australia, and the Moroccan Hydration Ritual that combines exfoliation with a moisture treatment applied with hot stones. Too adventurous? Detox your hangover with the Morning Latte, an exfoliating scrub with coffee, or the Citrus Splash with salt grains. ■TIP→ **Spa services are available to nonguests Monday through Thursday only.** ⊠ *MGM Grand, 3799 Las Vegas Blvd. S, South Strip* ☎ *702/891–3077* ⊕ *www.mgmgrand.com.*

Nurture Spa. Perhaps one of the most accessible spas on the Strip, Nurture Spa features a bright and airy setting giving it an inviting, earthy feel. Try one of the signature treatments such as the peppermint foot and leg therapy to recuperate from a long day of walking the Strip or the sugar scrub, a 20- or 50-minute treatment that nourishes skin all over your body. ⊠ *Luxor Las Vegas, 3900 Las Vegas Blvd. S, South Strip* ☎ *800/258–9308* ⊕ *www.luxor.com.*

Spa Mandalay. Modeled after Turkish-style baths, the hot, warm, and cold plunges at this spa are surrounded by marble, fountains, and plenty of places to lounge. Try the Aromatherapy Massage, which uses essentials oils and Swedish massage techniques, or the Foot Focus that uses reflexology on legs and tired feet. The spa offers what may be the only hot-stone pedicure in town. ⊠ *Mandalay Bay, 3950 Las Vegas Blvd. S, South Strip* ☎ *877/632–7300* ⊕ *www.mandalaybay.com.*

CENTER STRIP

ESPA at Vdara. British skin-care line ESPA brings a slice of tranquillity to the clamorous Strip. With it comes a line of products with natural ingredients that ties in with Vdara's commitment to organic and natural spa treatments and skin-care products. Try the Desert Rose, a 110-minute body treatment that includes a welcoming foot bath, body scrub, shower, and massage with body butter. On the Rocks uses a body brush followed by a massage using hot stones. ESPA takes care of the men with treatments such as a purifying facial and a fitness massage. ⊠ *Vdara, 2600 Harmon Ave., Center Strip* ☎ *702/590–2474* ⊕ *www.vdara.com.*

6

Qua Baths & Spa. This behemoth of a spa at Caesars Palace bases its philosophy on the calming properties of water. Many of the treatments and special features here draw heavily on this element, beginning with the Roman Baths. Qua's social spa-ing concept of encouraging guests to verbally interact comes naturally when indulging in these three soothing baths. For guests suffering from heat exhaustion, the Arctic Room offers the perfect solution: snow falling from a glass sky. If traditional treatments bore you, consider visiting the Crystal Body Art Room. Qua also has Men's Zone, a salon for men, and the Tea Lounge, where an in-house tea sommelier blends you a cup. Color, a phenomenal hair salon from colorist to the stars Michael Boychuck, is right next door. ■TIP➡ The Nobu Hotel flexes its influence with a whole series of treatments including the Nagomi Ritual with a welcoming foot bath, aroma nectars, and massage. ✉ *Caesars Palace, 3570 Las Vegas Blvd. S, Center Strip* ☎ *866/782–0655* ⊕ *www.caesars.com/ caesars-palace/things-to-do/qua.*

Sahra Spa and Hammam. Omnipresent slot machines and neon lights can make you forget that you're in the desert, but Sahra Spa is designed to return you to the peace and solitude of the Southwest. It starts with the Space Between, the serenity lounge that makes you feel transported to the peak of a canyon, and stretches all the way to the metallic ceilings that twinkle like only a nighttime desert sky can. Highlights here include the extensive skin-care treatments, special baths, and hammam, one of only three in Las Vegas. Two of the "transformations," the Sahra Journey and the Sahra Select, incorporate the heat-infused hammam to address the body's needs and all its senses. At the center of the hammam is a heated slab of stone that feels like it's been sitting in the warm sun for hours. Follow this up with the Red Flower Bathing Ritual, which exfoliates and moisturizes your desert-dried skin. ✉ *The Cosmopolitan of Las Vegas, 3708 Las Vegas Blvd. S, Center Strip* ☎ *855/724–7258* ⊕ *www.cosmopolitanlasvegas.com.*

The Spa at Aria. Aria provides a contemporary way to spa, starting with the design, which is all about clean lines and modern furniture. Some of the furniture is even functional to your pampering, like the Japanese *gabanyoku* beds. Made up of warm stones, the beds are designed to balance metabolism, circulation, and muscle movement. The services are just as innovative, like the ashiatsu massage that has therapists using ceiling bars to balance as they walk on your back. The Shio Salt Room uses lamps and a brick wall to emit salt to improve breathing as guests lounge. A customized men's menu includes the Man Tan and extensive barber services. A Vichy rain bar enhances certain body treatments, and facial add-ons include a firming system for décolletage, an eye mask, and hand and feet massages. ✉ *Aria, 3730 Las Vegas Blvd. S, Center Strip* ☎ *702/590–9600* ⊕ *www.aria.com.*

The Spa at Mandarin Oriental. It's luxury all the way at this spa, where every imaginable form of pampering is offered. Upon entering the two-story space, guests take in the art deco style of 1930s Shanghai and prepare to be catered to hand and foot, emphasis on foot. One of the optional add-ons for treatments here is the foot spa, where guests can have those long walks on the Strip forgiven through a cleansing ritual and foot and leg massage while sitting in a chair overlooking the Las Vegas Strip. Other features include a hammam with showers for cooling off, a vitality pool, and a women's rhassoul that combines mud, heat, and steam for exfoliation and toxin-purging. Treatments here, many of which start with a consultation, are tailored to individual needs. Journeys combine treatments for a full body experience, and the Time Rituals vary from two to three hours. Topping off the experience here is the beautiful view of the Strip from the relaxation room. ☒ *Mandarin Oriental, 3752 Las Vegas Blvd. S, Center Strip* ☎ *702/590–8886* ⊕ *www.mandarinoriental.com/lasvegas.*

Spa Bellagio. Besides the calming reflecting pools and the Reflexology Pebble Walk, this swank Zen sanctuary has treatments such as Thai yoga massage and a hydrotherapy bath. The 6,000-square-foot fitness center has a gorgeous view of the Mediterranean gardens and the pool. There's even a candlelit meditation room with fountain walls. If overindulging and the dry climate have gotten to you, try the Thermal Seaweed Body Wrap for a seaweed- and water-based detoxifying and hydrating treatment. Water-based treatments such as the Watsu Massage, which combines Zen shiatsu and stretching while gently floating in a private 94-degree pool, and the Aquastretch, which increases flexibility and releases tension, are specialties here. The massages can even be done poolside or in a hotel room. ■TIP➔ Spa services are exclusive to Bellagio guests Friday through Sunday. ☒ *Bellagio, 3600 Las Vegas Blvd. S, Center Strip* ☎ *702/693–7472* ⊕ *www.bellagio.com.*

NORTH STRIP

Fodor's Choice ★ **Canyon Ranch SpaClub at The Venetian and The Palazzo.** Vegas's largest spa—one of the best day spas in the country—is this outpost of Tucson's famed Canyon Ranch connected to The Venetian and The Palazzo. The extensive treatment menu here covers any desire, including Vibrational Therapy and an ayurvedic herbal rejuvenating treatment. The real treat here is the Aquavana, a European-inspired space that offers a host of water-related experiences. The Wave Room simulates ocean waves under a domed canopy; the Finnish sauna infuses colored light into a dry heat sauna; and the Igloo cools guests off with three arctic mist experiences and sparkling fiber optics. Weekend warriors love the health club, the Strip's largest, with its 40-foot climbing wall and frequent fitness and yoga classes. The nutrition, wellness, and exercise physiology departments also offer free lectures, Lifetime Nutrition Consultation, and acupuncture. An adjoining café serves healthy cuisine and smoothies. ☒ *The Venetian, 3355 Las Vegas Blvd. S, North Strip* ☎ *877/220–2688* ⊕ *www.canyonranch.com.*

The Spa at Encore. The opulent Spa at Encore feels like a splendid outdoor retreat, with natural sunlight, limestone, and water features. Try the Nalu Body Ritual with its relaxing Polynesian fusion massage, full-body exfoliation, and scalp treatment with coconut oil, or the Encore Escape, a massage that incorporates a multitude of techniques. Claude

Baruk provides the hair services, including Kérastase treatments. Perhaps the only drawback is the spa's exorbitant prices. ⊠ *Encore Las Vegas, 3121 Las Vegas Blvd. S, North Strip* ☎ *702/770–4772* ⊕ *www. wynnlasvegas.com.*

The Spa at Wynn Las Vegas. Designed according to feng-shui principles and set away from the bells and jangles of the Strip, this spa exudes an elegant Zen calm while remaining very cozy. There's a fireplace and flat-screen TV in the lounge areas, and the hot and cool plunge area is naturally lighted and lush with thriving palms and orchids. Treatments, such as the Thai oil fusion massage, are Asian-inspired. The Good Luck Ritual is based on the five elements of feng shui, and includes a fusion massage, an ultramoisturizing hand therapy, and a wild lime botanical scalp treatment. For the ultimate in combating the drying desert clime, try the Hydrating Collagen Booster Therapy facial, which infuses phytonutrients, ceramides, and plant-based minerals. Claude Baruk Salon provides the latest styles and techniques, including Kérastase treatments. ⊠ *Wynn Las Vegas, 3131 Las Vegas Blvd. S, North Strip* ☎ *702/770–3900* ⊕ *www.wynnlasvegas.com.*

NIGHTLIFE

Updated
by Susan
Stapleton

Inspired by the "What happens in Vegas, stays in Vegas" attitude, and that it usually happens after dark, nightlife impresarios keep dipping into their vast pockets to create over-the-top experiences where party-mad Visigoths—plus, well, you and me—can live out some wild fantasies. The number of high-profile nightclubs, trendy lounges, and sizzling strip bars continues to grow, each attempting to trump the other to attract not just high rollers, but A-list celebrities and the publicity that surrounds them.

Many of the newest clubs even have gambling. Though, we ask, Why bother when you can lounge beside the pool by day and bellow at the moon by night while dancing half clad at a club until noon the following day (when it's back into the pool you go)?

In the late 1990s, once the Vegas mandarins decided that the "family experience" just wasn't happening, Sin City nightlife got truly sinful again, drawing raves from clubbers worldwide. A wave of large dance clubs, such as the Luxor's (now-defunct) Ra, opened their doors, followed by a trendy batch of cozier ultralounges—lounges with dance floors and high-tech amenities.

The game of one-upmanship has continued—recent additions that have kept the city hopping include the massive Omnia at Caesars Palace and more intimate Intrigue Nightclub at Wynn Las Vegas. What's more, bawdy 1950s-era burlesque lounges are continuing their comeback with a gaggle of clubs now dedicated to the art of striptease.

Few cities on Earth match Vegas in its dedication to upping the nightlife ante. So with all these choices, no one—not even the Visigoths—has an excuse for not having fun, however you define the "f" word.

NIGHTLIFE PLANNER

FIND OUT WHAT'S GOING ON

With the number of nightlife options in Las Vegas, it's easy to get overwhelmed. Several local publications can steer you in the right direction and help you plan your ultimate Vegas night out. Remember that party schedules—as well as the popularity of any one spot—can change overnight, so the best way to keep current is to consult these publications.

Eater Vegas (⊕ *www.vegas.eater.com*) provides invaluable information on dining and nightlife, many times long before the newspapers.

Anthony Curtis's *Las Vegas Advisor* (☎ *702/252–0655* ⊕ *www.lasvegasadvisor.com*) is a monthly newsletter that's invaluable for its information on Las Vegas dining, entertainment, gambling promotions, comps, and news. If you're here for a short visit, pick up free copies of *Where Las Vegas* and *Las Vegas Magazine* at hotels and gift shops.

The *Las Vegas Review-Journal*, the city's daily newspaper, publishes a tabloid pull-out section each Friday. It provides entertainment features and reviews, and showroom and lounge listings with complete time and price information. The *Review-Journal* maintains a website (⊕ *www.reviewjournal.com*) where show listings are updated each week. The *Las Vegas Sun*, once a competing daily, is now a section inside the *Review-Journal* but maintains its own editorial staff and website (⊕ *www.lasvegassun.com*).

Two excellent alternative weekly newspapers are distributed at retail stores and coffee shops around town and maintain comprehensive websites. *Las Vegas Weekly* (⊕ *www.lasvegasweekly.com*) and *Vegas Seven* (⊕ *www.vegasseven.com*) offer some timely and incisive reflections on the nightclub scene and music outside the realm of the casinos.

HOW TO GET IN

Nobody comes to Las Vegas to wait in line. So how exactly do you get past those velvet ropes? Short of personally knowing the no-nonsense bouncers and serious-looking women holding clipboards who guard the doors, here are a few pointers.

First, know that even though this is a 24-hour town, lines start forming around 10 pm (or earlier). If you're not on a list, get there after dinner and dress the part—which is to say, don't expect to go straight from the pool to the club. Vegas bars and clubs have pretty strict dress codes, so leave those T-shirts, baseball caps, and ripped jeans in your hotel room (unless you're headed to the Griffin Lounge or some other hipster haven). Arguing that your sneakers were made by Alexander McQueen probably won't help, either. At most of the trendier spots, at least for women, skin is in—this *is* Sin City, after all. And needless to say, the universal rule of big-city nightlife also applies in Vegas: groups of guys almost always have a harder time getting in without a few women in the mix. If your group is gender impaired, consider politely asking some unaccompanied women to temporarily join you, perhaps in exchange for some drinks once you're all inside. Too shy, you say? If there was ever a place to check your shyness at the airport, it's this town.

Out at 4 am

Vegas is a 24-hour town, and when the party starts to wind down in some places, the doors to others are just opening. The following are our picks for after-hours hot spots. Remember, even after 4 am, expect lines—sometimes very long ones—to get in. And bring your sunglasses to protect those bleary eyes from the morning rays when you finally stumble out.

The revamped **Drai's After Hours** is most definitely the after-hours king,

with killer DJs and cocktail specials that keep the party going until the sun comes up and later.

For those seeking a different kind of decadence, go to Sin City's best strip joint, the gloomy yet glorious **Spearmint Rhino.**

Finally, if you're looking for a chill atmosphere rather than a club or strip joint, check out The Cosmopolitan's **Chandelier** for three levels of cocktail splendor, or hang at Aria's lounge, **Alibi Cocktail Lounge.**

Most spots have two lines: a VIP line (for those on the guest list or who have a table with bottle service reserved) and a regular line. You can either ask your hotel concierge for help contacting a club to get on a guest list, or contact the club directly. Some websites such as ⊕ *www.vegas.com* sell passes they guarantee will get you past the crush, but save your money for the door—better to slip the bouncer $20 per person than hope they'll acknowledge the Internet ticket you've bought for the same amount. If you have a few people in your group, it might be worth it to splurge on a table reservation: without one, a group of five could easily spend $20 each getting in good with the bouncers, plus $20 each for the cover charge, and then there's always the expensive drinks.

A further note on going deluxe: If you're getting a table with bottle service, note that your VIP host will expect something from you, as will the busboy who actually lugs over your booze. On holiday weekends and New Year's Eve, expect to multiply what you plan to give them by at least two.

NIGHTLIFE REVIEWS

SOUTH STRIP

BARS AND LOUNGES

The lounges of the Las Vegas casino-hotels were once places where such headliners as Frank, Dean, and the gang would go after their shows, taking a seat in the audience to laugh at the comedy antics of Shecky Greene or Don Rickles. For a while lounges were mostly reduced to small bars within the casino where bands played Top 40 hits in front of people pie-eyed from the slots. The turn of the 21st century, however, brought an explosion of hybrid nightspots—the so-called ultralounges—that aimed for the middle ground between dance club and conventional lounge. Some of the best of them—Skyfall

Lounge at the Delano, Bellagio's Hyde Lounge, and the Mandarin Oriental's Mandarin Bar—are worth a separate trip, given how much of a pleasure-jolt they offer.

Fodor's Choice ★ **The Chandelier.** True to its name, this swanky lounge sits in a chandelier with 2 million crystal beads, making it the largest chandelier in town (and, perhaps, the world). The bar is separated into three separate levels, and each has a different theme. The ground floor—dubbed "Bottom of the Chandelier," for those of you scoring at home—is dedicated to intricate specialty drinks, the kinds of cocktails you'll find only here. The second floor (non-smoking!) pays homage to molecular gastronomy in cocktail form; spiked sorbets and dehydrated fruits are common in drinks here. Finally, at the top of the Chandelier, everything's coming up floral, with rose and lavender syrups and violet sugar. If you're particularly adventuresome (and you can get a seat on the first floor), try the off-menu Verbena cocktail with a "Szechuan button." This desiccated flower from Africa numbs your mouth to make flavors more potent; it also prompts you to down your cocktail in mere seconds. All three levels offer excellent people-watching opportunities. ⊠ *The Cosmopolitan, 3708 Las Vegas Blvd. S, South Strip* ☎ *702/698–7000* ⊕ *www.cosmopolitanlasvegas.com/experience.*

Eyecandy Sound Lounge. High technology hits the Strip at this vast "interactive" ultralounge in the center of Mandalay Bay's casino floor. For "future shock" freaks, there are tented "touch tables" on which you can draw messages, words, and images projected onto video screens above the dance floor, and "sound stations" that let you send music of your choice to the DJ. More important than the technology here, though, is the cocktail menu; crafted by master mixologist Tony Abou-Ganim, drinks are so scrumptious they could call the place "mouthcandy," too. Best of all, there's no cover charge. ⊠ *Mandalay Bay, 3950 Las Vegas Blvd. S, South Strip* ☎ *702/632–4760* ⊕ *www.mandalaybay.com.*

Foundation Room. Ancient statues, tapestry-covered walls, pirated Mississippi road signs—the Foundation Room gets high marks for aesthetic appeal. Though it used to be open to members only, this secluded subsidiary of the House of Blues is now open to everyone seven nights a week—provided you're willing to wait in line. The venue itself is a series of different rooms, each with its own set of design themes and type of music that could range from Top 40 hits to house, depending on the night. ■TIP→ **A main attraction is the view of the Strip; because the club is on the 43rd floor, it provides some of the best panoramic vistas of the entire town, but the views come with a hefty cover charge.** ⊠ *Mandalay Bay, 3950 Las Vegas Blvd. S, South Strip* ☎ *702/632–7601* ⊕ *www.mandalaybay.com.*

INDUSTRY NIGHTS

Although most bars, clubs, and strip bars rely primarily on out-of-towners for their income, locals—especially those who work in the nightlife biz—bring much welcome spirit, sex appeal, and insider-hipness to the mix, so many hot spots feature special (always nonweekend) nights in which these folks get free admission, free drinks, and so on. Don't be put off by "Industry" or "Locals" parties—they tend to be even cooler than "regular" evenings.

7

Franklin. The Delano gives its classy lobby lounge a moniker that goes with its theme: the 32nd president. Bourbons, whiskeys, and barrel-aged drinks are specialties here, so belly up, let the DJs help you relax, and ask the bartender to prep you a little something. They can recommend a drink if you just don't know what to order. Since it's a lobby lounge, there's no cover. ⊠ *Delano Las Vegas, 3940 Las Vegas Blvd. S, South Strip* ☎ *702/632–7888* ⊕ *www.delanolasvegas.com.*

Minus5 Ice Bar. Did you ever think you'd be wearing a winter parka in the Las Vegas desert? If not, then you've underestimated just how gimmicky these 21st-century bars can be. Don the parka provided by Minus5, pay attention to your orientation speech, buy those drink tickets, and step into the Ice Bar, where the temperature is always 5 below zero Celsius (23 Fahrenheit). This frosty clime ensures that you'll have a "cool" time here, but it also keeps the walls, bar, cocktail glasses, chairs, couches, and decorative sculpture in their frozen-solid state. Expensive fun for the sheer weirdness of it? Definitely! The drinks are tasty, too. Additional location at the Monte Carlo. ⊠ *The Shoppes at Mandalay Place, 3930 Las Vegas Blvd. S, South Strip* ☎ *702/632–7714* ⊕ *www.minus5experience.com.*

Press. The very swanky but very inviting Press features fire pits with seating overlooking the private pool at the Four Seasons, cooled off by misters in the hotter months. Like everything at the upscale resort, the libations and accompanying bites are near perfection. Free high-speed Internet, 12 charging docks, and access to 2,000 digital newspapers and magazines from 100 countries in 56 languages highlight the complimentary services at this lobby bar that doubles as a coffee shop by day. ⊠ *Four Seasons Hotel Las Vegas, 3960 Las Vegas Blvd. S, South Strip* ☎ *702/632–5000* ⊕ *www.fourseasons.com.*

Skyfall Lounge. Head up to the 64th floor of the Delano for the 180-degree views of the city inside Skyfall Lounge. Proprietors LLC heads up the cocktail program that divides drinks into four types: refreshing, complex, boozy, and martinis. Order up punch bowls that serve six to eight people for a cool $150. Do step into the bathrooms for a different view of the city while you relieve yourself. ⊠ *Delano Las Vegas, 3940 Las Vegas Blvd. S, South Strip* ☎ *702/632–7575* ⊕ *www.delanolasvegas.com.*

COMEDY CLUBS

Even when Las Vegas wasn't the hippest place to catch a musical act, it was always up-to-the-minute in the comedy department. From Shecky Greene to Daniel Tosh, virtually every famous comedian has worked a Las Vegas showroom or lounge. The Strip still has a handful of dependable comedy rooms that copy the nightclub multiple-act format featuring top names on the circuit. Cover charges are in the $40 range, but two-for-one coupons are easy to come by in freebie magazines and various coupon packages.

Brad Garrett's Comedy Club. Brad Garrett has returned to his stand-up roots in a classic comedy-club setting—a bar with plenty of photos of…Brad Garrett on the walls. He handpicks the comedians and headlines almost monthly himself: "It was either this or *Jews on Ice* at the

Stratosphere," he likes to tell audiences. There's a hefty cover charge of at least $75. ⊠ *MGM Grand, 3799 Las Vegas Blvd. S, South Strip* ☎ *866/740–7711* ⊕ *www.mgmgrand.com.*

DANCE CLUBS AND NIGHTCLUBS

Vegas dance clubs come in three basic flavors—up-to-the-moment trendy (such as Marquee, Omnia, Jewel, and XS), established classic (Tao and The Bank), and fun for the great unwashed masses (LAX and Chateau). The usual Catch-22 of nightlife applies: the more "in" the place, the harder it is to get in and the more oppressively crowded and noisy it'll be once you do. Cover charges have crept into the $20 to $30 or $40 range—and don't be surprised to find that, even in these enlightened times, men pay higher cover charges than women. Although the level of capital investment gives these clubs a longevity their New York counterparts don't enjoy, dance clubs are still by nature a fickle, fleeting enterprise, so check with more frequently updated sources (such as the Fodor's website as well as local periodicals) to ensure they're still hot.

Fodor's Choice ★ **Hakkasan.** The 80,000-square-foot Vegas haunt is one of the latest iterations of the nightclub brand that started in London. The space is one part nightclub, one part modern Cantonese restaurant—five floors in all with three dedicated to nightlife. To fill this space, the venue has booked some of the biggest DJs in the world, including Calvin Harris, Steve Aoki, and Tiësto. For a more casual experience, head to the third-level Ling Ling Club. Hakkasan is open Wednesday through Sunday nights. ⊠ *MGM Grand Hotel & Casino, 3799 Las Vegas Blvd. S, South Strip* ☎ *702/891–3838* ⊕ *www.hakkasanlv.com* ⊗ *Closed Mon.–Wed.*

LAX. At one point in recent Vegas history (circa 2007/08), this tremendous club was the hottest ticket in town. And although no single club in Vegas reigns supreme for too long, LAX still shines: crazy flashing lights, deafening music, and shaking sweaty bodies. Preferred spots to dance here are the anarchically crowded stage or the less frenetic wraparound balcony, which offers a delightful bird's-eye view of all the heaving, writhing behavior down below. Throwback Thursdays bring some of the hottest acts from the 1980s into a present-day setting. It's generally open Thursday through Saturday nights. ⊠ *Luxor Las Vegas, 3900 Las Vegas Blvd. S, South Strip* ☎ *702/262–5279* ⊕ *www.luxor.com.*

Light Nightclub. Combining the acrobatics of co-creators Cirque du Soleil with a nightclub environment gives this hot spot an element of theatrics. State-of-the-art lighting, sound, and special effects give this DJ-driven nightclub the upper hand. The aerialists floating over the masses tip it over the edge. Even if you're not ordering bottle service, the video screens behind the DJ booth will wow. ⊠ *Mandalay Bay, 3950 Las Vegas Blvd. S, South Strip* ☎ *702/693–8300* ⊕ *thelightvegas.com.*

Marquee. This cavernous joint boasts three different rooms spread across two levels, as well as 50-foot ceilings. In the main area, stadium-style seating surrounds the dance floor, and four-story LED screens and projection walls display light and image shows customized for every performer. For a more intimate experience, check out the Boom Box, a smaller room (usually featuring something other than house music) with windows overlooking the Strip. On the top level, the Library provides a respite from the thumping downstairs with dark wood, books (actual books!), and billiard tables. In spring and summer, the hot spot opens Marquee Dayclub, which features two pools, several bars, a gaming area, and DJs all day long. A dome even permits the pool party to rage on in colder months. It's usually open Friday, Saturday, and Monday nights. ✉ *The Cosmopolitan, 3708 Las Vegas Blvd. S, South Strip* ☎ *702/333–9000* ⊕ *marqueelasvegas.com.*

IRISH PUBS

Nine Fine Irishmen. Don't be surprised to see patrons break into impromptu bouts of step-dancing at this authentic Irish pub inside New York–New York. It's so authentic that the place was built in Ireland, shipped over, and reassembled in Vegas. Today, barkeeps pour all sorts of Irish whiskeys, and cooks crank out Irish food and traditional Irish breakfast all day long. Live Irish music rounds out the toe-tapping sing-along entertainment here. ✉ *New York–New York, 3790 Las Vegas Blvd. S, South Strip* ☎ *866/815–4365* ⊕ *www.newyorknewyork.com.*

Rí Rá Irish Pub. Like the Statue of Liberty, this pub was constructed in Europe, then shipped over piecemeal and reassembled in The Shoppes at Mandalay Place (yes, Lady Liberty is in New York; you know what we mean). Highlights include the music—which regularly comprises Irish sessions—and the menu, which boasts enough sausage rolls and fish-and-chips to make you feel like you've flown to Dublin. ✉ *The Shoppes at Mandalay Place, 3930 Las Vegas Blvd. S, South Strip* ☎ *702/632–7771* ⊕ *www.rira.com.*

LIVE MUSIC

Small, medium, or large? From bohemian indie-band showcases (the Beauty Bar) and kooky kitschy lounges (the Rocks Lounge) to big concert halls (the House of Blues, the Joint, and Pearl)—and *then* on to truly *gargantuan* venues like the new T-Mobile Arena, The Smith Center for the Performing Arts, and the MGM Grand Garden Arena—Vegas is a world capital of live music. The trick, as always with local nightlife, is to check current news listings for performers, showtimes, and locations. (Why locations? Because even certain hot spots not ordinarily given over to live music—Drai's Nightclub, for example—will host concerts when you least expect it.) And, of course, the Vegas lounge act has come a long way. Nearly every big Strip resort features a high-energy dance band that expertly performs hits from the '60s to today's hottest tunes.

House of Blues. This nightclub–concert hall hybrid at Mandalay Bay was the seventh entry in this chain of successful, intimate music clubs. As if the electric roster of performers taking the stage almost nightly wasn't enough (past acts include Carlos Santana, Billy Idol, Social Distortion, Joe Walsh, Slash, the Dropkick Murphys, and Seal), the decor is lusciously imaginative. (Our favorite decoration isn't inside, though—it's the Voodoo Mama statue greeting you outside.) The Gospel Brunch on Sunday has great live music and is worth a visit. ✉ *Mandalay Bay, 3950 Las Vegas Blvd. S, South Strip* ☎ *702/632–7600* ⊕ *www.houseofblues.com.*

CENTER STRIP

BARS AND LOUNGES

Alibi Cocktail Lounge. Who knew you could have an alibi 24 hours a day in Las Vegas? This cocktail lounge offers up that along with bottle service, but you don't have to go all out. Get creative libations as well. Alibi is perhaps best suited for those who want a VIP experience without waiting in line for the club or shelling out extravagant prices. ⊠ *Aria, 3730 Las Vegas Blvd. S, Center Strip* ☏ *702/590–9777* ⊕ *alibiloungelv.com.*

Bound. Salvatore Calabrese created the inventive cocktails at this hidden gem tucked away at the back of the Cromwell. Try a breakfast martini with orange marmalade and espresso drinks served in frozen traditional Italian moka pots, a concoction Calabrese created when his wife wanted him to eat breakfast. ■ **TIP→ The bar even serves bites from Giada de Laurentiis's restaurant upstairs, and because that's such a tough ticket to nab, take advantage of the little-known fact.** ⊠ *The Cromwell, 3595 Las Vegas Blvd. S, Center Strip* ☏ *702/777–3777* ⊕ *www.caesars.com/cromwell.*

Fodor'sChoice ★ **Drai's After Hours.** All hail Victor Drai, classiest of Vegas nightlife sultans. The wild scene inside this after-hours titan is closer to a dance club or a rave than to a lounge, even though its four rooms with two music formats are as gorgeous as any lounge in town. The vibe of decadence can reach an extraordinary pitch, but this, of course, is exactly how an after-hours club *should* be, right? Besides, you'll be hard-pressed to find a more beautiful insider crowd anywhere within the city limits. ⊠ *The Cromwell, 3595 Las Vegas Blvd. S, Center Strip* ☏ *702/777–3800* ⊕ *www.caesars.com/cromwell.*

Drai's Beach Club and Nightclub. The innovations continue in Las Vegas, and this incarnation includes full concerts from hip-hop stars such as Nelly, Future, Fat Joe, Trey Songz, Jeremih, G-Eazy, and even Chris Brown. The 70,000-square-foot venue sits on top of the resort replete with a pool with some pretty amazing views of the Strip. ⊠ *The Cromwell, 3595 Las Vegas Blvd. S, Center Strip* ☏ *702/737–0555* ⊕ *www.draislv.com.*

Fizz Las Vegas. Drink like Sir Elton John and his husband, David Furnish, at this chichi and very private champagne bar decked out with more than 50 provocative photos from the famous couple's private collection. Champagne obviously is the name of the game at this bubblicious lounge replete with lighting under the sofas to highlight the ladies' high, high heels. Furnish, the creative director for the lounge, and Sir Elton lent their own private chef to create a small-bites menu of caviar (natch), gourmet paninis, and more. The cocktail menu even includes a $2,500 libation for those inclined to drop some Benjamins. ■ **TIP→ Everyone's a celebrity here, including you, so no photos are allowed inside.** ⊠ *Caesars Palace, 3570 Las Vegas Blvd. S, Center Strip* ☏ *702/776–3200* ⊕ *fizzlv.com.*

7

Hit Bar & Lounge. Located next to the high-limit area on Monte Carlo's main casino floor, the swanky and intimate Hit Lounge doubles as the classroom where members of MGM's M Life Rewards Club can experience a hands-on mixology class. The two-hour tutorial, available for the member and up to nine friends, is essentially a private session with the director of beverage, who'll teach the secrets behind mastering the perfect cocktail. Students don't only learn how to make cocktails; they also drink them. Otherwise grab one of the leather-bound menus and peruse cocktails of yore complete with stories about the inspirations behind them. This lounge is probably one of the best-kept secrets on the Strip. ⊠ *Monte Carlo Resort and Casino, 3770 Las Vegas Blvd. S, Center Strip* ☏ *702/730–7000* ⊕ *www.montecarlo.com.*

Fodor'sChoice
★
Hyde Bellagio. This posh ultralounge is famous for its front-and-center view overlooking the Bellagio fountains. Inside, the theme is library chic—there are actual books on the walls. Outside, a small patio harbors what some deem the most romantic table in Vegas—a two-top that looks out on the water show. The real star at this swanky lounge, however, is the cocktail program, complete with roving Bellini carts. Later at night, the space converts into a happening nightclub, and there's a cover. ⊠ *Bellagio, 3600 Las Vegas Blvd. S, Center Strip* ☏ *702/693–8700* ⊕ *www.bellagio.com.*

Lily Bar & Lounge. This colorful (hence the name) ultralounge is quite literally at the center of the action in Bellagio; it's smack-dab in the middle of the casino floor, which you can view through windows on two sides. Community-style ottomans lend themselves to conversation. At the bar, expert mixologists pour cocktails made with seasonally fresh ingredients. DJs spin most nights until the venue closes around 4. ⊠ *Bellagio, 3600 Las Vegas Blvd. S, Center Strip* ☏ *702/693–8384* ⊕ *lilylasvegas.com.*

Fodor'sChoice
★
Mandarin Bar. Few views of the Strip are as breathtaking as the one you'll get from this über-chic lounge on the 23rd floor of the Mandarin Oriental at CityCenter. The room is wrapped with floor-to-ceiling windows, meaning just about every one of the plush banquettes is a winning seat. Mixologists concoct cocktails based on individual preferences, though Dom Perignon is always on hand. There's a small menu of bite-size appetizers and hip live music on weekends. Business-casual dress is recommended. ⊠ *Mandarin Oriental, 3752 Las Vegas Blvd. S, Center Strip* ☏ *888/881–9367* ⊕ *www.mandarinoriental.com/lasvegas.*

Parlor Lounge. Be serenaded by a piano while imbibing creative cocktails at this little lounge on the casino floor. The Typhoon is a tropical drink that comes in a custom, limited-edition, Mirage souvenir tiki mug. ⊠ *Mirage, 3400 Las Vegas Blvd. S, Center Strip* ☏ *702/791–7111* ⊕ *www.mirage.com* ⊡ *Free.*

Fodor'sChoice
★
Petrossian Bar. Leave your designer handbags on the bar; this is a place to see and be seen. Sophisticated clientele frequent this piano lounge with experts tickling the ivories of a one-of-a-kind, art deco–styled Steinway grand while patrons sup on three refined versions of the gin and tonic. Whether you're catching your breath or going for full

elegance at this 24-hour lounge overlooking the grandiose entrance to Bellagio, you can sip on sublime cocktails such as the Beluga vodka martini with a cube of namesake Petrossian caviar at the bottom of the glass or pair up your vodkas with caviar in a tasting of three of each. ✉ *Bellagio, 3600 Las Vegas Blvd. S, Center Strip* ☎ *702/693–7111* ⊕ *www.bellagio.com.*

Vesper Bar. The Chandelier Bar may be Cosmopolitan's bar of the moment, but you shouldn't overlook the sleek Vesper Bar, the true mixologist space here. Name an ingredient, any ingredient, and the talented staff behind the bar can come up with a drink for you. Long-forgotten cocktail recipes are a specialty at this very modern square bar sitting alongside hotel registration. ✉ *Cosmopolitan, 3708 Las Vegas Blvd. S, Center Strip* ☎ *702/698–7969* ⊕ *www.cosmopolitan-lasvegas.com.*

Vista Cocktail Lounge. Different cityscapes ranging from sunset in Hong Kong to night in Dubai to evening in New York City change on huge screens that make up the background at this lounge. ✉ *Caesars Palace, 3570 Las Vegas Blvd. S, Center Strip* ☎ *702/731–7852* ⊕ *www.caesars.com.*

CIGAR BARS

Casa Fuente. This full-service cigar shop reproduces the decor and atmosphere of El Floridita, Ernest Hemingway's favorite Havana watering hole. Its sophisticated lounge, which obviously specializes in rum drinks, is a great place to enjoy your smoke. ✉ *Forum Shops, 3500 Las Vegas Blvd. S, Center Strip* ☎ *702/731–5051* ⊕ *www.casafuente.com* Ⓜ *Center Strip.*

Montecristo Cigar Bar. Cigars team up with whiskeys and small bites at this respite in the center of the resort. Find more than 1,000 cigars housed in a climate-controlled humidor, one of the largest in the city. Head to the library, out on the courtyard, or to the bar. ✉ *Caesars Palace, 3570 Las Vegas Blvd. S, Center Strip* ☎ *866/733–5827* ⊕ *www.caesars.com.*

DANCE CLUBS AND NIGHTCLUBS

The Bank. "Status is everything!" goes the motto at this white-hot, megadance club. The Bank sets itself apart with etched-glass walls, avant-garde chandeliers, and an entrance foyer lined floor to ceiling with illuminated Cristal bottles. Weekends generally draw the biggest crowds, but other nights boast special parties, promo events, and live performances (by, say, Sean Paul or Common, among others). In fact, the only thing really wrong about The Bank is its motto, because status isn't *everything*. Or is it? ✉ *Bellagio, 3600 Las Vegas Blvd. S, Center Strip* ☎ *702/693–8383* ⊕ *thebanklasvegas.com.*

Chateau Nightclub and Rooftop. A staircase leads revelers straight from the Paris casino floor up to this French-inspired nightclub. The space itself offers three distinct experiences: a main dance room, a bar, or the open-air terrace, for the rooftop portion of the name ready for Instagram-worthy photos. In the main room, house DJs spin from a booth atop a 10-foot-high fireplace, and go-go dancers in French maid costumes abound. If you're looking for something different, don't miss the chandeliers made of globes near the bar; with LED screens in every nightclub these days, the handmade fixtures are wonderfully unique. It's generally open Wednesday, Friday, and Saturday nights. ⊠ *Paris Las Vegas, 3655 Las Vegas Blvd. S, Center Strip* ☏ *702/776–7777* ⊕ *www.chateaunights.com.*

Drai's. Victor Drai wants your business day and night, and he nabs it with his multiuse space 11 stories up at The Cromwell. Drai's boasts the only rooftop day- and nightclub on the Strip with pools and cabanas for basking in the sun or dancing to the beats under the moon. It's huge, too, clocking in at 70,000 square feet with a monster-size 7,000-square-foot LED screen and every imaginable seating option. Go ultraswanky at one of 150 VIP tables. ⊠ *The Cromwell, 3595 Las Vegas Blvd. S, Center Strip* ☏ *702/777–3800* ⊕ *draislv.com.*

Omnia. Las Vegas nightlife is always looking for the next big thing, and in the case of Omnia, that means a 75,000-square-foot behemoth of a club with an ultralounge dubbed Heart of Omnia tucked to the side. This monster features liquid-crystal display portals embedded in black one-way mirrors on all four sides as you walk in and a 65-foot-tall ceiling dome anchored by a 22,000-pound chandelier with eight rings that dance with light to the music. The lines to enter stretch through the casino floor with gaggles of trendy girls and dapper guys hoping to attract the ladies. ⊠ *Caesars Palace, 3570 Las Vegas Blvd. S, Center Strip* ☏ *702/785–6200* ⊕ *omnianightclub.com.*

1 OAK. The "OAK" in this nightclub's name is an acronym for "Of A Kind," and, indeed, it's darker and louder than just about any other dance club in Vegas. And on a good night, sexy revelers are packed in and pumping like you wouldn't believe. Two separate rooms each have a bar and DJ (music styles change weekly). An animal theme is prevalent throughout, with zebra stripes, jaguar spots, and other patterns visible from just about every angle. The influence is subtle, but don't be surprised if your inner beast bursts out. ⊠ *Mirage, 3400 Las Vegas Blvd. S, Center Strip* ☏ *702/792–7900* ⊕ *www.1oaklasvegas.com.*

LIVE MUSIC

Cleopatra's Barge. This kitschy lounge, which features a replica of the floating boats that once carried Egyptian royalty down the Nile, has been transformed in recent years into a short-term room for Blues Traveler and Plain White Ts. When not rocking out to name-brand bands, the space is thumping with beats from local bands. "The Barge," as it's known, isn't exactly cool or hip, but that's part of its appeal. Besides, where else can you dance around on a makeshift boat inside a casino with a man-made lake, all in the middle of the desert? ⊠ *Caesars Palace, 3570 Las Vegas Blvd. S, Center Strip* ☏ *702/731–7333* ⊕ *www.caesars.com* ☾ *Closed Sun.*

PIANO BARS

Napoleon's Dueling Pianos. This baroque Paris piano bar can get loud, but it's all good fun. Free performances nightly at 9 pm. Tip the dueling piano players even more if you really want to hear your favorite song. ⊠ *Paris Las Vegas, 3655 Las Vegas Blvd. S, Center Strip* ☏ *702/946–7000* ⊕ *www.caesars.com/paris-las-vegas.*

NORTH STRIP

BARS AND LOUNGES

Encore Players Lounge. Blackjack, roulette, and craps mingle with a Las Vegas nightlife vibe in an effort to capture the elusive millennial dollar across from Surrender Nightclub. Play pool or shuffleboard, hang out at interactive tables, or watch the sports on one of 23 56-inch HDTVs. A live DJ keeps the beats going. ⊠ *Encore Las Vegas, 3121 Las Vegas Blvd. S, North Strip* ☏ *702/770–7300* ⊕ *wynnsocial.com.*

Lavo Casino Club. From the people who brought us the titanic Tao comes this restaurant-lounge with a vaguely—though attractive— Middle Eastern vibe. Ascend past cisterns and ceramics to the top floor's dome-roofed lounge, where a modern gaming experience fuses blackjack and craps table games with craft cocktails, bottle service, and Lavo's Italian menu. ■TIP➜ **During the cooler months, Lavo hosts its Party Brunch, an excuse to drink and party by day, on Saturday.** Check ahead for hours; this places closes for private events frequently. ⊠ *Palazzo, 3325 Las Vegas Blvd. S, North Strip* ☏ *702/791–1800* ⊕ *www.lavolv.com.*

107 SkyLounge. The Stratosphere might be downscale compared with other Vegas hotels, but there ain't nothing "down" about the high-in-the-sky experience to be had here. From this sleek, attractive room, the view of Sin City is truly amazing (if slightly remote). For an even bigger thrill, head upstairs and outside (to level 108, of course) to AirBar. The signature drink: something called Jet Fuel served in a souvenir cup. Consider yourself warned. ⊠ *Stratosphere, 2000 Las Vegas Blvd. S, North Strip* ☏ *702/380–7777* ⊕ *www.stratospherehotel.com.*

Fodor's Choice ★ **Parasol Up.** Not to be confused with sister lounge "Parasol Down," this exquisite-looking—and exquisitely tranquil—setting near the entrance of Wynn Las Vegas ensures you can indulge in that most endangered of all pleasures: a good conversation. Tufted leather chairs and an extensive menu of house martinis certainly contribute to the vibe. Best of all, the menu features a handful of snacks, and the place stays open all night. ⊠ *Wynn Las Vegas, 3131 Las Vegas Blvd. S, North Strip* ☏ *702/770–7000* ⊕ *www.wynnlasvegas.com.*

Fodor's Choice ★ **Peppermill's Fireside Lounge.** Pining for a genuine taste of retro Las Vegas? This kitschy and shagadelic lounge remains one of the town's truly essential nightspots. Just north of Encore, this evergreen romantic getaway serves food, but what you're really here for is the prismatic fire pit and signature cocktails such as the Key Lime Pie Martini and the lethal, 64-ounce Scorpion. ⊠ *2985 Las Vegas Blvd. S, North Strip* ☏ *702/735–4177* ⊕ *www.peppermilllasvegas.com.*

DANCE CLUBS AND NIGHTCLUBS

Intrigue Nightclub. Leave your cell phones in the room and head to this nightclub that colors itself a bit different than the rest. Inside, a private club-within-a-club is designated as a social media–free zone so revelers can concentrate on the here and now. ⊠ *Wynn Las Vegas, 3131 Las Vegas Blvd. S, North Strip* ☏ *702/770–7300* ⊕ *intriguevegas.com.*

Fodor'sChoice
★
Surrender. Steve Wynn and nightclub impresario Sean Cristie came together in 2010 to create an indoor/outdoor lounge unlike anything else on the Strip. The experience begins indoors, in a giant living room designed by Roger Thomas, the same aesthetic genius behind Encore itself. At the back, the space transitions into the Encore Beach Club, an intimate, open-air dayclub that is transformed into a nightclub after dark. Some of the private cabanas out here feature balconies that overlook Las Vegas Boulevard. There's also an open-air gaming pit. Perhaps the highlight of the entire facility is the 120-foot-long silver snake over the bar inside; this artwork, much like Surrender itself, glistens all night long. ⊠ *Encore Las Vegas, 3121 Las Vegas Blvd. S, North Strip* ☎ *702/770–7300* ⊕ *www.surrendernightclub.com.*

Fodor'sChoice
★
Tao. Nowhere else in Vegas furnishes you with the four Ds—dining, drinking, dancing, and drooling—in quite as alluring a mix as this multilevel (and multimillion-dollar) playground. The ground floor and mezzanine levels are exquisite enough (you almost tumble into rosewater baths with women bathing inside before you're in the door), but once you get off the elevator at the top floor, where an army of dramatically lighted stone deities greets you, the party truly begins. Chinese antiques, crimson chandeliers, and a so-called Opium Room set the mood. It's still one of the best dance clubs in Vegas, and its Thursday locals' "Worship" night is one of the most popular theme parties in town. In spring and summer, Tao Beach opens with daytime pool parties. ⊠ *Venetian, 3355 Las Vegas Blvd. S, North Strip* ☎ *702/388–8588* ⊕ *taolasvegas.com.*

Fodor'sChoice
★
XS. This club backs up onto a pool that converts into one of the most spacious open-air dance floors in town. Wynn's signature attention to detail shines through with touches such as a chandelier that doubles as a psychedelic disco ball, light fixtures that turn into stripper poles, and walls imprinted with golden body casts (the waitresses modeled for them). At the pool are cabanas, another bar, and outdoor gaming, where the sexiest croupiers in town ply their trade. *Excess* is a pretty good word for all of this. ⊠ *Encore, 3121 Las Vegas Blvd. S, North Strip* ☎ *702/770–0097* ⊕ *www.xslasvegas.com.*

SPORTS BARS

Fodor'sChoice
★
Lagasse's Stadium. Jumbo video screens on the walls, more than 100 high-def TVs, stadium seating, and delicious down-home cooking (from celebrity chef Emeril Lagasse!) are all found at Lagasse's Stadium. Add in mobile sports betting devices from The Palazzo's sports book (next door) and there's no better place to enjoy a game. ⊠ *Palazzo, 3325 Las Vegas Blvd. S, North Strip* ☎ *702/607–2665* ⊕ *www.emerilsrestaurants.com.*

DOWNTOWN

LIVE MUSIC

JAZZ AND CLASSICAL

Fodor'sChoice ★ **The Smith Center for the Performing Arts.** Las Vegas got its very own ($150-million) world-class performing arts center in 2012, and what a spot it is. The multibuilding complex (complete with a bell tower) was designed to invoke 1930s-era art deco construction, the same motif you'll find at the Hoover Dam. Here, this elegance graces the main concert hall, which hosts everything from rock bands and Broadway hits to musical theater and traveling orchestras. ■TIP➔ Caberet Jazz across the breezeway hosts live jazz every weekend. ⊠ *361 Symphony Park Ave., Downtown* ☎ *702/749–2012* ⊕ *www.thesmithcenter.com.*

ROCK

Bunkhouse Saloon. Offering raucous rock in a raucous Downtown saloon, this is where the most clued-in locals go to shake, rattle, head-bang, and roll. Brandon Flowers, Bob Mould, and Local H are some of the bigger names to play the tiny stage. ⊠ *124 S. 11th St., Downtown* ☎ *702/982–1764* ⊕ *www.bunkhousedowntown.com.*

LOCAL HANGOUTS

Outside the realm of the big casinos, the Las Vegas bar scene is dominated by so-called video-poker taverns, named after the 15 video-poker machines they're legally allowed to have. Most other Vegas bars are generic, but there are exceptions—in some cases, glorious exceptions—scattered about town and clustered in the Downtown area. Despite the touristy "Fremont Street Experience," Downtown is the gritty birthplace of Las Vegas. It can be quite dangerous if you stray from the tourist circuit at night, but visiting its nightspots is essential if you want to claim you've truly experienced Vegas.

Atomic Liquors. This Downtown bar owns the oldest liquor license in the state and used to be the place to watch atomic blasts. The Rat Pack and Barbra Streisand drank here. Fast-forward to now and it's become the place to hang out, with 20 microbrews on tap and an inventive menu that specializes in fancy beer cocktails. ⊠ *917 Fremont St., Downtown* ☎ *702/982–3000* ⊕ *atomic.vegas.*

Beauty Bar. This charming little Downtown joint, spun off from a popular Manhattan watering hole, is laid out like an old-fashioned hair salon, complete with hair-dryer chairs acquired from a defunct New Jersey salon. It's a kitschy spot to listen to local bands (primarily rockers), get entranced by the curve of the pink walls, and ogle the hipster crowd. On warm nights, a spacious patio with a bar and stage for live music is opened out back. ⊠ *517 Fremont St., Downtown* ☎ *702/598–3757* ⊕ *beautybarlv.com.*

Commonwealth. As urban renewal continues Downtown, the one-block stretch of Fremont east of Las Vegas Boulevard (dubbed Fremont East) remains the hottest of the hot spots, and Commonwealth arguably is the epicenter. Inside, wrought-iron railings, chandeliers, and a tin ceiling create a feeling of old-school opulence without being excessive.

7

Drink options range from handcrafted cocktails to microbrews; there's also good live music on most nights. For a change of scenery, venture upstairs to the rooftop bar, or try to secure an invite to the private Laundry Room speakeasy. ⊠ *525 Fremont St., Downtown* ☎ *702/445–6400* ⊕ *www.commonwealthlv.com* ⊘ *Closed Mon. and Tues.*

Downtown Cocktail Room. Hiding from your creditors? Seeking a good spot for a séance or a Spin-the-Bottle party? If so, then consider stepping—carefully—into the gorgeous gloom of this hipster hangout, which is just around the corner from the Griffin and the Beauty Bar. The modest-size, minimalist lounge glows from candle-filled tables and thumps with simmering house music, making the vibe mysterious and romantic. Weeknight happy hour from 4 to 8 pm is popular among locals, as are the seasonal cocktail menus. Just beware: the front door is hard to find. ⊠ *111 Las Vegas Blvd. S, Downtown* ☎ *702/880–3696* ⊕ *www.downtowncocktailroom.com* ⊘ *Closed Sun.*

Oak & Ivy. Should you happen to be Downtown, head over to the Downtown Container Park and sit inside a shipping container to sip barrel-aged cocktails and whiskeys galore. Although tiny—it's sometimes tough to nab a spot at the bar—this little railroad car of a drinking spot packs a punch with a well-crafted menu of drinks. Can't decide on a whiskey? Order a flight. ⊠ *Downtown Container Park, 707 Fremont St., Downtown* ☎ *702/945–6717* ⊕ *oakandivy.com.*

Fodor's Choice ★ **Velveteen Rabbit.** Nothing like a feel-good story in Las Vegas. Sisters Pamela and Christina Dylag saved and scrimped to open this great, velvet-lined cocktail lounge dotted with furniture they found at vintage shops and equipped with beer taps that look like hands. A great cocktail list with a vintage feel and punches are just some of the treasures behind the bar. ⊠ *1218 S. Main St., Downtown* ☎ *702/685–9645* ⊕ *velveteenrabbitlv.com.*

PARADISE ROAD AND THE EAST SIDE

BARS AND LOUNGES

Paymon's Mediterranean Cafe and Hookah Lounge. The hookah is an elaborate Middle Eastern water pipe that is used to smoke exotic tobaccos (and yes, we just mean *tobacco*). It also happens to be a trend popular at Vegas lounges and clubs these days. Thanks to a helpful "Hookah Man" and some available samples, no prior experience with water pipes is required. But the hookah is only one part of the appeal here: designed by local entrepreneur Paymon Raouf for the ultimate chill-out experience, this red velvet–laden, exquisitely carpeted, incense-filled environment redefines Vegas plush, and its young, somewhat bohemian crowd and those sexy paintings on the wall don't hurt the romance, either. ⊠ *4717 S. Maryland Pkwy., University District* ☎ *702/731–6030* ⊕ *paymons.com.*

GAY AND LESBIAN

Las Vegas was never really known for gay tourism, but things have changed rapidly in the past few years. Now a number of bars and nightclubs cater to different segments of the community.

Most gay and lesbian nightlife is concentrated in two areas of town. The most prominent is the so-called "Fruit Loop"—which wins our award for best nickname for a North American gay neighborhood—which you enter near the intersection of Naples Drive and Paradise Road, just north of the airport and close to the Hard Rock Hotel. The other is the area in and around Commercial Center, one of the city's oldest shopping centers, on East Sahara Avenue, just west of Maryland Parkway. If there are cover charges at all, expect them to be around $10 for dance clubs on weekends.

Unfortunately, there are no all-out lesbian bars in Vegas, although many of the gay bars (most prominently FreeZone) host special nights for their sapphic sisters. These parties, like so much in Sin City, change frequently, so it's best to consult a copy of *Q Vegas* (⊕ *gay.vegas*), the city's gay monthly.

Badlands Saloon. Consider the Badlands a 24-hour haven for local gay cowboys. It's decorated with a mock-log-cabin façade and offers cubbyholes in which regulars can store their beer steins. There's also a jukebox crammed to the coin slot with country-and-western hits. Plus, the Nevada Gay Rodeo Association hosts its fund-raisers here. Perhaps the only downside is the smoke. ⊠ *Commercial Center, 953 E. Sahara Ave., East Side* ☎ *702/792–9262.*

Fodor's Choice
★ **FreeZone.** An egalitarian mix of (straight and gay) men and women congregates at this 24-hour bar with a dance floor, pool tables, karaoke, and video-poker machines. Each night brings a different theme: Ladies' Night is Sunday (lesbians, unite!), male go-gos "come out" on Thursday, and Drag Madness with lovely drag queens is held Friday and Saturday. ⊠ *610 E. Naples Dr., University District* ☎ *702/794–2300* ⊕ *www.freezonelv.com.*

Piranha Nightclub—8½ Ultra Lounge. Revelers pack this gorgeous spot every night of the week. Although the dance floor at Piranha is legendary, the best spot in the house is the spacious, fireplace-ringed open-air patio out back. Head here for a Latin night on Sundays and partake in the fun. ⊠ *4633 Paradise Rd., Paradise Road* ☎ *702/379–9500* ⊕ *www.piranhavegas.com.*

LIVE MUSIC
ROCK

The Joint. From Tim McGraw to Bon Iver to R. Kelly, this music venue inside the Hard Rock Hotel hosts some of the best touring acts in the nation. Not only does The Joint have some of the best acoustics in town, but short of the big arenas, it's also one of the largest venues around. Big-name acts like Journey and Rascal Flatts take residency at The Joint, playing for monthlong and longer stretches. Past acts have included Guns N' Roses, KISS, Def Leppard, and Mötley Crüe. ⊠ *Hard Rock Hotel, 4455 Paradise Rd., Paradise Road* ☎ *702/693–5000* ⊕ *www.hardrockhotel.com.*

LOCAL HANGOUTS

Double Down Saloon. The grand poo-bah of Vegas dive bars, the Double D is a short walk from the Hard Rock Hotel and a long, long way from Paradise—although a sign above the door has proclaimed it "The

Happiest Place on Earth." Delicious decadence prevails here 24 hours a day; no wonder it's a fave of world traveler and chef Anthony Bourdain. For the boho crowd, this deliberately downscale bar has everything from great local bands to a satisfying jukebox with truly eclectic selections. Our advice: Go late, wear black, and try the (fabled) Ass Juice cocktail. Also, don't miss the clever, mostly obscene graffiti; it'll have you guffawing in minutes. ⊠ *4640 Paradise Rd., Paradise Road* ☎ *702/791–5775* ⊕ *www.doubledownsaloon.com.*

STRIP CLUBS

It's not called Sin City for nothing. "Exotic dancing" clubs are a major industry here, but they do have some quirks. Zoning laws restrict most clubs to industrial areas not far off the Strip. Fully nude clubs are available in Vegas but such venues can't carry liquor licenses. (The Palomino Club, in North Las Vegas, is the one exception.) Joints with liquor licenses have the sharper designs, the bigger spaces, the more savory customers, and the more glamorous gals. Some, depending on how loosely you define the term, can be pretty classy.

Wherever you go, be prepared to shell out some serious cash. Most places have instituted cover charges of $20 or more, but that's just the beginning. The real money's made on the table dances continuously solicited inside, with most going for $20 per song (and four VIP dances often for a C-note).

Centerfolds Cabaret. This club was one of the first in town to embrace the "gentlemen's club" boom of the 1990s. Be sure to ask about the facility's cigar menu. Book one of the club's packages and get free limo service and admission to boot. ⊠ *4416 Paradise Rd., Paradise Road* ☎ *702/767–8757* ⊕ *centerfoldscabaretlv.com.*

HENDERSON AND LAKE LAS VEGAS

WINE BARS

Fodor'sChoice **Hostile Grape.** Despite what the name implies, there's nothing hostile
★ about this upscale wine bar in The M Resort downstairs, away from the casino floor. Instead, with 160 wines by the glass, the place offers visitors a welcoming and intimate environment in which to sample some new vino. The collection includes fine American, Italian, and French wines, as well as selections from Spain, South Africa, and Germany (to name a few). Visitors can taste as much as they like, thanks to the venue's innovative dispensing system that doles out prepaid tasting cards to allow guests to enjoy pours of 1, 3, or 5 ounces at a time. ⊠ *The M Resort, 12300 Las Vegas Blvd. S, Henderson* ☎ *702/797–1000* ⊕ *www. themresort.com* ☾ *Closed Sun.–Tues.*

WEST SIDE

BARS AND LOUNGES

Fodor'sChoice **The Artisan Lounge.** This not-yet-well-known favorite of ours is in the
★ slightly out-of-the-way Artisan Hotel and is sort of an upscale version of the Peppermill. The vibe is relatively chill even on weekends, so it can serve as a tonic to the usual Vegas lunacy. The interior is filled with

gilt-framed paintings (and sometimes frames without the paintings), which are even on the ceiling. Ordinarily, a crazy ceiling stunt like this one would seem silly, but the muted romantic ambience here (candlelight, soft music, dark wood, comfy leather couches) makes it work. On Friday and Saturday nights DJs spin electro, house, and techno from 10 pm until dawn, but you can party 24 hours a day here. ⊠ *The Artisan Hotel, 1501 W. Sahara Ave., West Side* ☎ *702/214–4000* ⊕ *artisanhotel.com.*

Ghostbar. Perched atop The Palms, this apex of ultralounges has rock music, glamorous patrons, glowing lights, and a glassed-in view of the city. Step outside and you'll find that the outdoor "Ghostdeck" is cantilevered over the side of the building, with a Plexiglas platform that allows revelers to look down 450 feet below. Because of the laughably complicated process to get in the door, some might find this spot frustrating (although, with the right blend of patience and good humor, getting inside can be highly entertaining). Still, for the views of the Strip skyline from the 55th floor alone, it's worth the effort. During the cooler months, Ghostbar Dayclub takes over the venue with a rollicking party on Saturdays. ⊠ *The Palms, 4321 W. Flamingo Rd., West Side* ☎ *702/942–6832* ⊕ *www.palms.com.*

VooDoo Rooftop Nightclub. Take in great views of the city at this indoor/outdoor club 51 floors atop the Rio. DJs, great dance bands, and well-trained flair bartenders, serving concoctions such as the rum-packed Witch Doctor with dry ice, keep things lively. Faux-primitive voodoo paintings on the walls of the dance rooms maintain a tenuous thematic connection. The crowd tends to be slightly older and less, shall we say, sophisticated than at similar clubs. The party starts at 8 pm daily. ⊠ *Rio, 3700 W. Flamingo Rd., West Side* ☎ *702/777–7800* ⊕ *www.caesars.com.*

GAY AND LESBIAN

Flex Cocktail Lounge. A small, neighborhood-oriented club for men, this 24-hour dive bar sometimes has floor shows, banana-eating contests, and entertainment (think male strippers, folks, sometimes in drag). Of course, we like the strong and inexpensive drinks. ⊠ *4371 W. Charleston Ave., West Side* ☎ *702/385–3539* ⊕ *flexlasvegas.com.*

LIVE MUSIC
ROCK

Fodor's Choice
★

The Pearl. Not only does The Palms have its own studio where the likes of Lady Gaga, Mary J. Blige, and The Killers recorded, but it's got this gorgeous, state-of-the-art concert venue, which boasts a stream of big-name rock, country, and hip-hop acts year-round. ⊠ *Palms, 4321 W. Flamingo Rd., West Side* ☎ *702/942–3200* ⊕ *www.palms.com.*

LOCAL HANGOUTS

Frankie's Tiki Room. You want Polynesian tiki-bar culture, Vegas-style? You want grass huts, carved wooden furniture, and cocktails such as the Green Gasser, the Thurston Howl, the Lava Letch, and the Bearded Clam? You'll get it all here, and more, 24 hours a day. On Friday, if you wear a Hawaiian shirt, your first drink is half price from 4 to 8 pm. Better still: If you love your mug (and trust us, you will), there's a gift shop where you can buy one to bring the spirit of aloha home with you. ⊠ *1712 W. Charleston Blvd., West Side* ☎ *702/385–3110* ⊕ *www.frankiestikiroom.com.*

The Golden Tiki. This classic mid-century tiki bar might remind you of Don the Beachcomber and Trader Vic's. It's tucked inside a strip mall in Chinatown with a cocktail menu spilling over with nostalgic classics. Order up a traditional Martinique tea service and a special treasure chest VIP experience. The decor here can keep you busy for hours, finding treasures such as an animatronic skeleton of the mythical privateer and legend behind The Golden Tiki, William Tobias Faulkner. It's open 24 hours a day. ⊠ *3939 Spring Mountain Rd., West Side* ☎ *702/222–3196* ⊕ *www.thegoldentiki.com.*

Fodor's Choice
★
Herbs & Rye. Classic cocktails are the name of the game at this bar off the Strip and worth the cab ride. Each cocktail comes with a story and quite a show while it's being made. Crack open the menu to learn the history behind each libation from the Prohibition era. This is the place to rub elbows with bartenders from other joints who often visit when finished with their shifts on the Strip. ⊠ *3713 W. Sahara Ave., West Side* ☎ *702/982–8036* ⊕ *www.herbsandrye.com.*

STRIP CLUBS

Cheetah's. This gentleman's club is no stranger to headlines. It has been featured in that pinnacle of late-20th-century cinematic excellence *Showgirls*, and also was a favorite hangout of famous Vegas casino scion and murder victim Ted Binion. The place ain't the Rhino, but it does have plenty of hotter-than-average dancers, plus a free shuttle from the Strip, and more than 500 girls dancing topless every 24 hours. ⊠ *2112 Western Ave., West Side* ☎ *702/384–0074* ⊕ *www.cheetahslasvegas.com* ⟳ *Open 24 hrs.*

Crazy Horse III. Rising from the ashes of two previous strip clubs (Sin and the Penthouse Club) on the same site is this mammoth tribute to flesh and hedonism. Unlike many other strip clubs in town, this one offers a number of promotions throughout the week, including free limo rides. Private cabanas off the main room require a one-drink minimum, one of the best "deals" in town. Carmen Electra, Snoop Dogg, Joanna Krupa, Tiesto, Skrillex, and Lil Jon are just some of the celebrities who have dropped some bills here. ⊠ *3525 W. Russell Rd., West Side* ☎ *702/673–1700* ⊕ *www.crazyhorse3.com.*

Déjà Vu Showgirls. No city in the free world can boast of more breast implants per capita than Las Vegas, and few all-nude clubs in Vegas can boast of *less* artificial pulchritude than this lovable little joint (that's part of a national chain). There's lots of "natural beauty" here amid the silicone and saline, not to mention red velvet curtains, tasteful PLPs (that's private lap-dance pods for the uninitiated), a special bachelor-party area, and a shower show in which two naked women demonstrate inventive ways to lather up. All drinks on Tuesday are $2. ⊠ *3247 Industrial Rd., West Side* ☎ *702/308–4605* ⊕ *dejavuvegas.com.*

Sapphire. The owners claim to have spent $26 million for the bragging rights of proclaiming their club the "largest adult entertainment complex in the world," which means that what it loses in intimacy it makes up for in excess. Formerly a gym, this place provides 70,000 square feet of topless dancing, complete with 10 second-floor "skyboxes" and a phalanx of dancers who rank among Vegas's most talented. Sapphire

Pool & Dayclub opens during the warmer months on weekends with an $8-million, three-level party mecca with cabanas and daybeds. El Dorado Cantina, Island Sushi, and Sysco—all part of the complex—dish to the club and pool party 24 hours a day. ⊠ *3025 Sammy Davis Jr Dr., West Side* ☎ *702/869–0003* ⊕ *www.sapphirelasvegas.com.*

Fodors Choice ★ **Spearmint Rhino.** At the Rhino, as everyone calls it, you can expect a veritable onslaught of gorgeous half-clad women: possibly the best-looking dancers west of the Mississippi. The place got a late start in Vegas, but it grew fast, expanding its original space to more than 20,000 square feet. It's also the rare topless club that offers lunch, including steak sandwiches, not to mention an adjoining shop for lingerie, sex toys, and various other implements of physical naughtiness. Of course, it's always crowded, but tipping the staff lavishly will get you a table, not to mention anything else that's not too illegal, immoral, or fattening. (Further tipping might even snag you some of that immoral and fattening stuff.) Our only gripe: The lighting here is usually so low that you can't get a good enough gander at all the wonders worth gandering at. Still, that's a small price to pay for American beauty in all its grandeur. ⊠ *3340 S. Highland Dr., West Side* ☎ *702/796–3600* ⊕ *www.spearmintrhinolv.com.*

SUMMERLIN AND RED ROCK CANYON

BARS AND LOUNGES

Lucky Bar. This circular bar's casual, lively atmosphere, comfy couchlike seats, sexy staff, and giant chandelier make it one of the best in town, and worth the trip to the impressive Red Rock Resort complex. What's more, the bar is steps away from Rocks Lounge, another hip spot that features live performers (like Zowie Bowie!) most nights of the week. ⊠ *Red Rock Casino, Resort & Spa, 11011 W. Charleston Blvd., Summerlin South* ☎ *702/797–7777* ⊕ *redrock.sclv.com.*

ELSEWHERE IN LAS VEGAS

NORTH SIDE
STRIP CLUBS
Palomino Club. This is one of the oldest strip clubs in the area (the Rat Pack used to hang out here), as well as the most notorious; two separate owners have been accused of murders, and it was also owned briefly by a noted heart surgeon. Because the "Pal" was grandfathered into the North Las Vegas zoning codes, it's allowed to have both a full bar *and* full nudity. There's also a burlesque stage and an all-male revue dubbed Club Lacy's next door. ⊠ *1848 Las Vegas Blvd. N, North Las Vegas* ☎ *702/642–2984* ⊕ *www.palominolv.com.*

SOUTH SIDE
DANCE CLUBS
Stoney's Rockin' Country. What do you get when you fill a country-theme Texas saloon with slick dance-music-crazed nightclubbers? Madness—10-gallon-hat madness. Behind the Texas-shaped neon sign, Stoney's Rockin' Country has all the glam hot-spot fixings: one of the largest

dance floors in Nevada, private tables, a VIP lounge, bottle service, and music that can segue from Merle Haggard to Jay Z. With all-you-can-drink draft beer specials on Thursday and free dance lessons daily, you can't beat the prices either. The location in Town Square makes the club convenient to visit from casinos on the Strip. ⊠ *Town Square, 6611 Las Vegas Blvd. S, South Las Vegas* ☎ *702/435–2855* ⊕ *stoneysrockincountry.com* ⊗ *Closed Sun.–Wed.*

LOCAL HANGOUTS

Blue Martini Lounge. It's in a shopping mall eight minutes from the Strip (by taxi), but we won't hold that against the Blue Martini, because it's still pretty cool. The cream of local bands plays here nightly, an attractive blue interior curves from room to room, and the cocktail menu is impressive (the signature martinis are served in the shaker). Also, there's a legendary happy hour from 4 to 8 pm daily. Best of all, hordes of the kind of people you'll want to meet (that is, sexy nontourists of both genders) keep pouring in. ⊠ *Town Square, 6593 Las Vegas Blvd. S, South Las Vegas* ☎ *702/949–2583* ⊕ *lasvegas. bluemartinilounge.com.*

8

SHOWS

Updated
by Mike
Weatherford

The very name *Las Vegas* has been synonymous with a certain style of showbiz ever since Jimmy Durante first headlined at Bugsy Siegel's Flamingo Hotel in 1946. Through the years this entertainment mecca has redefined itself a number of times, but one thing has remained consistent: doing things big.

The star power that made the old "supper club" days glitter with names like Frank Sinatra and Dean Martin is making a latter-day comeback in recurring concert showcases, or "residencies," by everyone from Rod Stewart to the Backstreet Boys. Nationally known performers such as Penn & Teller and Boyz II Men have come to roost on the Strip after years of living out of a suitcase. Cirque du Soleil still dominates the Strip with its technologically advanced shows presenting little or no language barrier to the city's large numbers of international tourists. But concert acts join younger-skewing production shows (such as the break-dancing Jabbawockeez) to lure younger audiences that nightclubs have skimmed from the ticketed shows.

In the not-so-olden days, shows were loss leaders intended to draw patrons who would eventually wind up in the casino. Nowadays the accounting's separate, and it can cost you more than $100 to see name performers such as Donny and Marie Osmond and $250 for Celine Dion. Meanwhile, the lesser names and production shows that run year-round have become a confusing, "never pay face value" circus of discount outlets and offers.

The new generation of resident headliners ranges from ventriloquist Terry Fator to "mindfreak" Criss Angel to pop star Ricky Martin. There's still no other place in the world to find such a concentration of female impersonators, "dirty" dancers, magicians, and comedians—all continuing the razzle-dazzle tradition Las Vegas has popularized for the world.

SHOWS PLANNER

RESERVED-SEAT TICKETING

Most hotels offer reserved-seat show tickets, and nearly all the Las Vegas shows are available through ticketing networks such as Ticketmaster, AXS, and Vegas.com. If you don't buy in advance, an old-fashioned visit to the show's box office is still your best bet for minimizing add-on charges. It's advisable to purchase tickets to concerts or the hotter shows, such as the Colosseum at Caesars Palace headliners, ahead of a visit. For smaller shows or spontaneous decisions, visit the various discount kiosks along the Strip; most producers "mark 'em up to mark 'em down" at these outlets anyway. Pay full face value only for a headliner name or a show you really want to see. Remember, too, that for the ongoing shows under their roofs, casinos make sure their big players are always taken care of. If advance tickets are no longer available, check for last-minute cancellations. Your chances of getting a seat are usually better when you're staying—and gambling—at the hotel.

If you plan on spending a fair amount of time at the tables or slots, call VIP Services or a slot host to find out what their requirements are for getting a comp, paid tickets that have been withheld for last-minute release, or perks such as premium seating or a line pass (it allows you to go straight to the VIP entrance without having to wait in line with the hoi polloi).

CONTACTS AND RESOURCES

AXS. AXS is the exclusive agency for some headliners in Las Vegas, including Celine Dion. ☎ *888/929–7849* ⊕ *www.axs.com.*

Ticketmaster. As most of the venues in town are part of Ticketmaster, you can buy tickets at any Ticketmaster outlet or on the website. More and more, even if you begin your purchase on a hotel or show's dedicated website, you will be routed to Ticketmaster to complete the purchase. ☎ *800/745–3000* ⊕ *www.ticketmaster.com.*

Tickets & Tours. Tickets & Tours, operated by Entertainment Benefits Group, sells tickets online and in 45 booths or kiosks around town, including the airport, The Venetian, Planet Hollywood, and the Golden Nugget. See their website for all locations. They also sell tickets for tours, including backstage peeks at some of the shows. ✉ *Las Vegas* ☎ *702/617–5595* ⊕ *www.ticketsandtours.com.*

Tix4tonight. With 10 locations, Tix4tonight is the place to visit for most ongoing shows (but not the hot concert acts or headliners). There's a service charge for each ticket, and the majority of business is for same-day walk-up sales. Strip locations include the Grand Bazaar Shops in front of Bally's, Circus-Circus, Slots-A-Fun, the Fashion Show mall, the Showcase Mall (look for the giant Coke bottle), Planet Hollywood, and the Casino Royale. The Downtown location is inside the Four Queens casino. Another outlet is on Las Vegas Boulevard, way south of the pedestrian part of the Strip, in the popular Town Square shopping center. Originally, prices were half-price across the board and only for that day's performance. But discounting is now so widespread that some titles are available in advance or via phone reservations. ☎ *877/849–4868* ⊕ *www.tix4tonight.com.*

RAVES AND FAVES

Splashiest opening: The beginning of *O* gets things off to an astonishing start when a regal curtain is whooshed away into the backstage recesses as though sucked into a giant vacuum cleaner. Not to be outdone, Celine Dion's intro drops and then whisks away a 2,000-pound white scrim to reveal the orchestra.

Best finale: The climactic scene of *LOVE* just had to be "A Day in the Life." Cirque du Soleil rises to the challenge of the famous orchestral buildup with a symbolic, moving scene featuring an angelic, floating mother figure. (Remember that both John Lennon and Paul McCartney's mothers died young.)

Best band in town: The blue baldies in the *Blue Man Group* never talk, so it's even more important that their silent antics be backed by a rocking sound track. The seven-piece band keeps the sound percussive and otherworldly.

Most words per minute: Penn & Teller discuss everything from "ocular hygiene" to "petroleum by-products" (meaning Solo cups), conveniently overlooking the fact that most Vegas shows push spectacle over words. What's even more amazing? Only one of them (Penn) talks.

Most deliberately provocative: There was much speculation about whether a man-to-man kiss would stay in Cirque du Soleil's *Zumanity*. It did, although now it's later in the show and placed in a more comedic context.

Best guilty pleasure: The title says it all: *Zombie Burlesque*. The unlikely fusion of two hot trends is a smartly silly twist on *Cabaret*. As an opening video explains, a truce between zombies and humankind results in the undead entertaining us with original songs and a live band in a place called Club Z.

Vegas.com. This major sales outlet for full-priced tickets and discount offers spells out "convenience" and "processing" fees clearly before you hit the final button to place your order. ☎ *866/983–4279* ⊕ *www.vegas.com.*

FIND OUT WHAT'S GOING ON

Information on shows, including their reservation and seating policies, prices, and suitability for children (or age restrictions), is available by calling or visiting box offices. It's also listed in several local publications or websites.

The **Las Vegas Advisor** (✉ *3665 S. Procyon Ave., West Side* ☎ *800/244–2224* ⊕ *www.lasvegasadvisor.com*) is available as a monthly printed newsletter at its office for $5 per issue or $50 per year. An online membership is $37, and the website has become a font of free news and coupons. It's a bargain-focused consumer's guide to Las Vegas dining, entertainment, gambling promotions, comps, and news.

The *Las Vegas Review-Journal,* the city's morning daily newspaper, publishes a pull-out section each Friday called *Neon.* It provides entertainment features, reviews, and showroom and lounge listings with complete time and price information. In the tourist corridor, the daily *Review-Journal* is wrapped inside a Daily Visitor's Guide that includes show listings. The newspaper also maintains a website (⊕ *www.reviewjournal.com*).

Two weekly newspapers—*Vegas Seven* (⊕ *www.vegasseven.com*) and *Las Vegas Weekly* (⊕ *www.lasvegasweekly.com*)—are distributed at retail stores and coffee shops around town and maintain comprehensive websites. They tend to be the best source for nightclub ads and star DJ schedules, plus live music beyond the realm of the casinos.

WHAT'S NEW?

Three sports arenas on the Strip and six concert venues seating 2,500 or more reflect the Strip's collective shift to concerts and special events. Both the 6,000-capacity Park Theater and the 20,000-seat T-Mobile Arena opened in 2016 in the area between New York–New York and the Monte Carlo, booking Las Vegas exclusives for George Strait, Cher, and Bruno Mars. Las Vegas got in on the outdoor festival action, too, with fairground sites at both ends of the Strip. Perhaps not coincidentally, the Strip said goodbye to several long-running shows in 2016, including the 40-year showgirl spectacular *Jubilee* and the eight-year Broadway transplant *Jersey Boys*.

"Residency" continues to be the casino buzzword for big-name concert headliners playing a stretch of shows and/or returning several times per year. The combined forces of **Reba McEntire** with a reunited **Brooks & Dunn** joined the star rotation that still includes **Elton John** and **Rod Stewart** in the 4,300-seat Colosseum at Caesars Palace (aka "The House that Celine Built" thanks to Celine Dion's 1,000-plus performances there). Planet Hollywood's bet on **Britney Spears** and her dance-oriented *Piece of Me* paid off handsomely; and she paved the way for younger-skewing stars such as Pitbull and Jennifer Lopez. Limited runs by the likes of **Rascal Flatts** and **Journey** at the Hard Rock Hotel continue to promote that venue as a place to see customized, only-in-Vegas showcases as well as major tours.

The Park is the new outdoor restaurant and retail plaza connecting the T-Mobile with the namesake theater. Like the pedestrian-friendly LINQ on the other side of the Strip, these new diversions are both enhancements and indirect competition for the traditional Las Vegas shows, which had already been challenged by nightclubs and celebrity-chef eateries. But depending on how you count comedy clubs and short-haul headliners such as Bruno Mars or the Backstreet Boys, the number of shows can still get close to the 100 mark. It seems the city isn't ready to surrender its self-appointed status of "The Entertainment Capital of the World" just yet.

AFTERNOON SHOWS

Las Vegas has become a wider-reaching and more family-friendly destination. But at the same time, evening show prices can be in the triple digits. These factors are sometimes at odds with one another and help explain a few afternoon shows that hold their ticket prices down or discount heavily with promotional coupons. The following are the most proven and popular.

Legends in Concert. The durable *Legends* is one of the longest-running shows in Las Vegas and inspired many imitators. But its production values seemed more modest as the big shows got bigger. In 2013 it moved to the Flamingo and became the rare show to split its schedule between afternoons and evenings, with the matinees avoiding competition from the big-budget spectacles. It's still the same basic formula of "mini-concerts" by a rotating lineup of celebrity impersonators, and can still attract the best in the profession. The Elvis Presley finale used to be the only constant, but occasionally a rousing Michael Jackson tribute is the dramatic closer. There's no lip-syncing, and there's always a band. ⊠ *Flamingo Las Vegas, 3555 Las Vegas Blvd. S, Center Strip* ☎ *702/777–2782* ⊕ *legendsinconcert.com* ✉ *$52–$81* ☞ *Dark Fri.*

FAMILY
Fodor's Choice
★

Mac King. The reigning king of Las Vegas afternoons—he celebrated 15 years at Harrah's Las Vegas in 2015—seems more like a ragtime-era court jester with his plaid suit and folksy "Howdy!" King stands apart from the other magic shows on the Strip with a one-man hour of low-key, self-deprecating humor and the kind of close-up magic that's baffling but doesn't take the focus away from the running banter. ⊠ *Harrah's Las Vegas, 3475 Las Vegas Blvd. S, Center Strip* ☎ *702/777–2782* ⊕ *mackingshow.com* ✉ *$38–$49* ☞ *Dark Sun. and Mon.*

FAMILY

Nathan Burton Comedy Magic. The likable magician whom many came to know on *America's Got Talent* puts a fun spin on familiar illusions—behold! The "Microwave of Death"—and is family-friendly for those with older children. ⊠ *Saxe Theater, 3667 Las Vegas Blvd. S, Miracle Mile Shops, Planet Hollywood, Center Strip* ☎ *866/932–1818* ⊕ *www.nathanburton.com* ✉ *$50–$60; $25 for ages 3–12* ☞ *Dark Mon.*

EVENING REVUES

Absinthe. Sometimes it's not the elements but how they are combined. *Absinthe* takes circus acrobatics, raunchy comedy, and a couple of saucy burlesque numbers and puts them all under a cozy tent in front of Caesars Palace. (At least it's a tentlike structure; once it was decided the show would stick around, fire inspectors insisted on a sturdy, semipermanent pavilion.) The audience surrounds the performances on a small, 9-foot stage. The festive, low-tech atmosphere is furthered along by the host, a shifty insult comic known as the Gazillionaire. This is cheap raunch for a discerning audience. And, like Penn & Teller's show, it's a winking salute to the show-business tradition itself. ⊠ *Caesars Palace, 3570 Las Vegas Blvd. S, Center Strip* ☎ *800/745–3000* ⊕ *www.absinthevegas.com* ✉ *$120–$147* ☞ *Dark Mon. and Tues.*

FAMILY
Fodor's Choice
★

Blue Man Group. The three bald, blue, and silent characters in utilitarian uniforms have become part of the Las Vegas landscape. The satire of technology and information-overload merges with classic physical comedy and the Blue Man's unique brand of interstellar rock and roll. The group's latest home, a cozy theater at Luxor, is downsized from a Las Vegas–sized spectacle to bring the Blue dudes closer to their more humble off-Broadway origins: paint splattering,

Blue Man Group is a show for the whole family.

mouth-catching marshmallows, and rollicking percussion jam sessions on PVC pipe contraptions. ⊠ *Luxor, 3900 Las Vegas Blvd. S, Center Strip* ☎ *800/258–3626* ⊕ *www.blueman.com* ✆ *$75–$136* ☞ *Usually plays nightly.*

Chippendales: The Show. Score one for the ladies: The Rio builds a theater dedicated to the men of Chippendales, surrounds it with a lounge and gift shop, and makes "girls night out" an identified (and coveted) Las Vegas target demographic. The show has fancier staging than any G-string revue traveling on the nightclub circuit, and the bowtied hunks keep it respectable enough to let Mom tag along with the bachelorette party. Tyson Beckford signed on to be a long-term guest host in 2017. ⊠ *Rio All-Suite Hotel & Casino, 3700 W. Flamingo Rd., West Side* ☎ *702/777–2782* ⊕ *www.riolasvegas.com* ✆ *$61–$90* ☞ *Plays nightly.*

Crazy Girls. *Crazy Girls* is the second-longest-running show on the Strip, surviving even the demolition of its longtime home, the Riviera. Now ensconced in a cabaret-sized venue at Planet Hollywood, it's the most retro of the Las Vegas topless shows, with a European feel to the topless dance numbers spelled by a comedian or magician. ⊠ *Planet Hollywood Resort, 3667 Las Vegas Blvd. S, South Strip* ☎ *702/777–2782* ⊕ *www.caesars.com* ✆ *$55–$99* ☞ *Dark Tues.*

Criss Angel—Mindfreak Live. Criss Angel lives up to his Goth-rock image with the loudest magic show in town, full of blistering music and pyrotechnics. He rebooted his long-running showcase in mid-2016, and the fast-paced barrage of illusions unfold with a schizophrenic tone that shifts from heavy-metal sinister to rave-up dance party. Even more than most magic shows, this one really depends on whether you like the magician. Though Cirque du Soleil serves as a presenter (and coproducer), the company has minimal creative input. ✉ *Luxor Las Vegas, 3900 Las Vegas Blvd. S, South Strip* ☎ *702/262–4400* ⊕ *crissangel.com* ✆ *$64–$142* ☞ *Dark Mon. and Tues.*

Defending the Caveman. Comedian/author Rob Becker's anthropological take on the battle of the sexes brought something new to Las Vegas: theatrical long-form comedy, delivered by a lone actor mixing jokes with real anthropological insight. It's an extended monologue by one likable schlub (enhanced with lighting and sound cues) that preaches greater understanding. ✉ *The D, 301 Fremont St., Downtown* ☎ *702/388–2111* ⊕ *www.defendingthecaveman.com* ✆ *$51–$79* ☞ *Plays nightly.*

Fantasy. Fantasy is a topless show (un)dressed up as a variety show, with power-pop singing by its female host and, most nights, impressions and clowning from Sean Cooper. It's the least strip club–like of the Las Vegas topless revues, so it's not uncommon to see couples in the audience at this durable show that's been around since 1999. ✉ *Luxor Las Vegas, 3900 Las Vegas Blvd. S, South Strip* ☎ *702/262–4400* ⊕ *www. fantasyluxor.com* ✆ *$46–$68* ☞ *Plays nightly.*

Human Nature: Jukebox. Human Nature is a vocal quartet that enjoyed 1990s fame as an Australian "boy band" and then reinvented itself as keepers of the Motown sound. These friends from childhood sing together almost instinctively in a flashy showcase, which folds in their own curious history as they cover classic pop hits from the Temptations to the Backstreet Boys. The four aren't famous outside Australia, but they've filled a niche for an old-school musical group with a year-round presence on the Strip. ✉ *The Venetian, 3355 Las Vegas Blvd. S, Center Strip* ☎ *702/414–9000* ⊕ *www.humannaturelive.com* ✆ *$66–$120* ☞ *Dark Sun. and Mon.*

FAMILY   **Jabbawockeez JREAMZ.** The only Las Vegas performers who don't show their faces speak with their feet in the rare Las Vegas show that is designed to appeal to the younger nightclub demographic. The masked hip-hop dance collective has steadily improved its showmanship since it settled on the Strip in 2010. There's plenty of break dancing but also lots of comedy and warm-hearted themes of brotherhood and inclusiveness. Their latest home in a 300-seat theater only lets four to six of the dancers onstage at the same time, but video projections expand the sense of space in the down-the-rabbit-hole tale of a suburban "zombie" gradually shaken to life. ✉ *MGM Grand Hotel, 3799 Las Vegas Blvd. S, South Strip* ☎ *866/740–7711* ⊕ *www.jbwkz.com* ✆ *$79–$120* ☞ *Dark Tues. and Wed.*

KÀ. *KÀ* is Cirque du Soleil's bold interpretation of live martial-arts period fantasies like *Crouching Tiger, Hidden Dragon* in the adventures of two separated twins. The $165-million opus includes huge puppets and a battle on a vertical wall. A fixed stage is replaced by an 80,000-pound deck that's maneuvered by a giant gantry arm into all sorts of positions, including vertical. Though no other Cirque in Las Vegas rivals it for sheer spectacle, those not sitting close enough to see faces can be confused by the story, which is told without dialogue. Still, it

Discount Tickets Vegas Style

CLOSE UP

Just as you learn not to ask people in your airline row what they paid for their plane tickets, don't bring up the question at a Las Vegas show. The answer might ruin your fun.

Internet discounting and "half-price" ticket booths on the Strip have made the standing Las Vegas shows a game of "mark 'em up to mark 'em down." While you will still pay face value (or more) for the big touring concerts, it pays to shop around for most of the titles here week in and week out. When the first Tix4Tonight discount booths arrived on the Strip, they functioned more like their counterparts on Broadway, selling remaining seats at half-price once it appeared full-price sales had peaked for the day.

But with 10 outlets in prominent locations—and now, online vendors such as Groupon as well—a middle-tier show such as *Fantasy* lists at $46 to $68 in order to get roughly half that. Any budget-minded person is almost forced to seek out the discount outlets for all but a handful of shows that still sell run close to

capacity: Cirque du Soleil's *O*, usually, or headliners such as Elton John, who offers a limited number of performance dates.

Discount vendors also changed what once used to be a simple, across-the-board pricing scheme—all seats half-price, plus a service charge—to offer discounts of less than 50% and some shows available a day in advance or by telephone. "Half-price outlets are like crack," noted one veteran of the ticket wars. "You start with a few and get that easy sale, so you start doing more and more."

The walk-up outlets still make it deliberately inconvenient with no Internet sales. But when you do start shopping online vendors such as Vegas.com or Travelzoo—even the casinos themselves, who often offer room-and-show packages—it can get bewildering. The *Las Vegas Advisor* experimented to see how many options for Britney Spears tickets it could find, and came up with 37 different prices.

—Mike Weatherford

8

stands as an amazing monument to the sky's-the-limit mentality that fueled Vegas in the go-go 2000s. ⊠ *MGM Grand Hotel & Casino, 3805 Las Vegas Blvd. S, South Strip* ☎ *866/740–7711* ⊕ *cirquedusoleil.com* 🎫 *$75–$196* ☞ *Dark Thurs. and Fri.*

Le Rêve. *Le Rêve* has lived up to the surreal dream implied in its title, ever shifting and evolving but always bizarre and beautiful. What started as a knockoff of Cirque's *O* from the same director, Franco Dragone, has come into its own with a sketch of a story about a dreamer on a romantic journey through a sexy world of bald men and women in high heels and dripping-wet cocktail dresses. The circular seating configuration gets everyone close to the water-based stunts, 80-foot dives, and aerial acrobatics, and there's an upgraded seating area with easy chairs and champagne service. ⊠ *Wynn Las Vegas, 3131 Las Vegas Blvd. S, North Strip* ☎ *702/770–9966* ⊕ *www.wynnlasvegas.com/entertainment/lereve* 🎫 *$125–$223* ☞ *Dark Wed. and Thurs.*

SAVE OR SPLURGE

SAVE

Carnaval Court. Balmy nights bring a bit of Fremont Street's crazy scene to the heart of the Strip, with this outdoor stage as well as "flair" bartenders, both right off the south door of Harrah's Las Vegas. If the band isn't your favorite, head a few yards in either direction for more free live music in the O'Sheas section of The LINQ Hotel, or in the Jimmy Buffet–themed Margaritaville mini-casino inside the Flamingo.

Fremont Street Experience. Dazzling video shows on Fremont Street's overhead canopy aren't the only thing happening in Glitter Gulch. The street itself has become a midway, from sidewalk musicians and artists to bar-top go-go dancers and of course, Slotzilla, an overhead zip line. Every weekend live performers play free gigs on two stages on 1st and 3rd Streets. ☎ 702/678–5777.

Mac King. The comedy magic of Mac King is worth every penny of the full $38 ticket price, and full-price tickets send you to the front of the line. But if you look for coupon-dispensing showgirls within Harrah's or check in at a players club booth, you can often get in for as little as $10.

SPLURGE

Le Rêve. Wynn Las Vegas experimented with an "upsell" ticket for its water show in-the-round, adding a "VIP Indulgence" section of seating that's been so successful, the producers say they wish there was room for more seats. The top $223 ticket includes champagne, chocolate-covered strawberries, and video monitors offering backstage and underwater views of the action.

Axis VIP section. Sure you can get a conventional theater seat for a fair price to see Axis theater headliners such as Backstreet Boys and Jennifer Lopez. But if you want to go big, try to score a VIP booth in the crescent-shaped row that runs right along the stage extension. You might be paying $329 for a ticket, but the booth comes with bottle service from Drai's nightclub, and you can't get any closer to the star without being in the show.

O. Cirque's big water show has been around since 1998, but you won't ever see it go on tour. Pony up the $196 and save on your water bill when you get home.

Fodor's Choice
★ **LOVE.** Meet the Beatles again—well, sort of—in a certified home run for Cirque du Soleil. Before he died, George Harrison persuaded the surviving Beatles (and Yoko Ono) to license the group's music to Cirque. The remixed music by Beatles producer George Martin and his son Giles is revelatory on 7,000 speakers, often like hearing the songs for the first time. Coming up with visuals to match was more of a challenge. In the summer of 2016, Cirque tweaked the show for its 10th anniversary, dialing down the elegiac version of postwar Liverpool, and punching up the dance elements to emphasize the youth culture of Beatlemania. Cirque also added literal depictions of the Fab Four in videos and projection mapping. It's still a great marriage of sensibilities that explodes with joy. ✉ *Mirage Las Vegas, 3400 Las Vegas Blvd. S, Center Strip* ☎ *702/792–7777* ⊕ *www.cirquedusoleil.com* ✍ *$87–$196* ☞ *Dark Tues. and Wed.*

FAMILY **Michael Jackson ONE.** After traveling the world as *The Immortal*, Cirque du Soleil's salute to Michael Jackson took on its second iteration in a remodeled Mandalay Bay theater. Cirque artistic directors wanted the permanent installation to be more theatrical than the arena spectacle, so they added a few "small" moments amid the bombardment of dancers and video imagery. Instead of a live band, the show opts to remix Jackson's actual recordings in earth-shaking sound delivered by more than 7,000 speakers. The story follows the journey of four misfits who discover Jackson's "agility, courage, playfulness, and love." It appeals to casual fans by ignoring the creepier aspects of the legacy and capturing Jackson in his 1980s heyday, when he appears on video now and then as the quartet's spirit guide. ⊠ *Mandalay Bay, 3950 Las Vegas Blvd. S, South Strip* ☎ 877/632–7400 ⊕ *www.cirquedusoleil. com* ☑ *$75–$196* ☞ *Dark Wed. and Thurs.*

FAMILY **Mystère.** Since 1993, Cirque du Soleil's new-age circus has been the town's most consistent family show. The Strip's first permanent Cirque show most purely preserves the original Montreal company's innovative reinvention of the circus and has held up to the increased spectacle of its sister shows by being the funniest of the bunch—and by keeping the spectators close to the action and the human acrobatics in the spotlight. You're intimately involved with this surreal wonderland and the comic characters, who interact with the audience. If you're not careful, you could even end up onstage. ⊠ *Treasure Island, 3300 Las Vegas Blvd. S, North Strip* ☎ 800/392–1999 ⊕ *cirquedusoleil.com* ☑ *$75–$136* ☞ *Dark Thurs. and Fri.*

FAMILY

Fodor's Choice
★

O. More than $70 million was spent on Cirque du Soleil's theater at Bellagio back in 1998, and its liquid stage is the centerpiece of a one-of-a-kind show. It was money well spent: O remains one of the best-attended shows on the Strip. The title is taken from the French word for water (*eau*), and water is everywhere—1.5 million gallons of it, 12 million pounds of it, contained by a "stage" that, thanks to hydraulic lifts, can change shape and turn into dry land in no time. The intense and nonstop action by the show's acrobats, aerial gymnasts, trapeze artists, synchronized swimmers, divers, and contortionists make for a stylish spectacle that manages to have a vague theme about the wellspring of theater and imagination. ⊠ *Bellagio Las Vegas, 3600 Las Vegas Blvd. S, Center Strip* ☎ 702/693–8866 ⊕ *www.cirquedusoleil. com* ☑ *$107–$196* ☞ *Dark Mon. and Tues.*

FAMILY **Tournament of Kings.** One of the last vestiges of Las Vegas's "family" phase is 25-plus years of this Arthurian stunt show in a dirt-floor arena, with the audience eating a Cornish hen dinner (warning: no utensils) and cheering on fast horses, jousting, and swordplay. Those familiar with Medieval Times around the country will know the drill. The show remains a great family gathering—especially for preadolescents, who get to make a lot of noise—and the realistic stunts speak to the commitment of the cast. ⊠ *Excalibur, 3850 Las Vegas Blvd. S, South Strip* ☎ 702/597–7600 ⊕ *www.excalibur.com* ☑ *$75* ☞ *Dark Tues.*

FAMILY **V — The Ultimate Variety Show.** This mid-priced variety show has held its own against the splashier Cirque-type productions for more than 10 years. The lineup varies, but it usually has magic, juggling, and acrobatics such as hand balancing. Perhaps the real secret is the "front of curtain" atmosphere with likable performers making direct contact with the audience. ⊠ *Miracle Mile Shops at Planet Hollywood, 3667 Las Vegas Blvd. S, Center Strip* ☎ *866/932–1818* ⊕ *www.vtheaterbox-office.com* ✉ *$80–$100* ☞ *Plays nightly.*

X Burlesque. This is no old-timey burlesque. Instead, an edgy attitude permeates this dance-intensive topless revue with impressive video and lighting effects. A comedian doing a 10-minute set is the only spoken contact with the audience. It's much closer to a strip-club vibe than the more theatrical *Fantasy* at Luxor, which should serve as a recommendation to some and a warning to others. But even the more intense gyrations are leavened with a winking humor . ⊠ *Flamingo Las Vegas, 3555 Las Vegas Blvd. S, Center Strip* ☎ *702/777–2782* ⊕ *www.xburlesque.com* ✉ *$59–$90* ☞ *Plays nightly.*

Zombie Burlesque. The zombie craze meets retro burlesque and camp humor for a ribald spoof of *Cabaret* that has the undead entertaining us with raunchy songs and a live band in a place called Club Z. *Zombie Burlesque* has found an audience for daring to think small and try something original—and for being more like something you'd find at a fringe festival than on the Strip. ⊠ *V Theater at Planet Hollywood Resort, 3667 Las Vegas Blvd. S, South Strip* ☎ *866/932–1818* ⊕ *zombieburlesqueshow.com* ✉ *$60–$80* ☞ *Dark Sun.*

Zumanity. *Zumanity* is the Strip's "R-rated" Cirque, one that deliberately shuns the family market to indulge in an erotic, near-naked exploration of sexuality. The end product still fuses Cirque acrobatics with European cabaret and English music-hall tradition. And the show has changed a lot over the years, in search of the right blend of song, comedy, and omnisexual titillation. The familiar Cirque acrobatics literalize metaphors for love and sex: taking flight, soaring, and so on. The challenge is trying to play to both the easily shocked and the jaded. But if you approach it with the winking, accepting tone of drag host Edie, it's easy to be seduced. ⊠ *New York–New York, 3790 Las Vegas Blvd. S, South Strip* ☎ *702/740–6815* ⊕ *www.cirquedusoleil.com* ✉ *$75–$136* ☞ *Dark Wed. and Thurs.*

RESIDENT HEADLINERS

The turn of the 21st century took Las Vegas back to one of the traditions from its past. The explosion of new room volume on the Strip combined with the hassles of modern air travel opened the doors to a wave of resident headliners, those who live in Las Vegas and perform on a year-round schedule comparable to the revues. Donny and Marie Osmond, Louie Anderson, and Carrot Top all bet that audiences were ready to embrace the down-front performing tradition (not letting anything get between the performer and the audience) that put Las Vegas on the map.

Now Las Vegas is returning to its 1960s and 1970s-era concept of stars who don't live here, but come in several times a year for extended stretches. Rod Stewart and Elton John assembled custom showcases. Plenty of other stars seem willing to get in line, with Pitbull, John Fogerty, Lionel Richie, and the Backstreet Boys the latest to test the waters. With nonstar production shows having hit a creative wall outside of Cirque, count on this star-plus-spectacle formula to continue for some time.

Carrot Top. After years on the college circuit, the prop comic moved his trunks full of tricks into the Luxor, where he became one of the Strip's longest-running year-round names. The Florida native known offstage as Scott Thompson still is most unique when wielding his visual gags, but he sells them with a manic energy, a tourist's street-level view of Vegas, and a running commentary on the act itself, perhaps a sly nod to his eternal lack of respect. ⊠ *Luxor Las Vegas, 3900 Las Vegas Blvd. S, South Strip* ☎ *702/262–4400* ⊕ *www.luxor.com/entertainment* 🎟 *$60–$71* 🎭 *Dark Tues.*

Fodor's Choice
★

Celine Dion. Celine Dion transcended her divisive 1990s pop stardom to become a Las Vegas perennial with a loyal, international following. Those willing to approach with an open mind will be treated to a lavish and universally entertaining showcase which goes beyond her expected hits to embrace a James Bond movie medley and tributes to Ella Fitzgerald and Michael Jackson. A 33-piece orchestra puts the focus squarely on the music, trading the large ensemble of dancers from the five-year run of *A New Day* for impressive video and a few production surprises. ⊠ *Caesars Palace, 3570 Las Vegas Blvd. S, Center Strip* ☎ *877/423–5463* ⊕ *www.celineinvegas.com* 🎟 *$55–$250* 🎭 *Select dates in Sept.–Jan. and Mar.–June, but dark Mon.*

8

FAMILY **David Copperfield.** The master magician has made Las Vegas a part of his career since the 1980s and now roosts at the MGM Grand for more than 40 weeks per year. At this point, Copperfield is sort of the Rolling Stones of magic; you sense his authority and submit to it from the minute the show opens, and trust him to wow you with illusions such as a recent one involving a T. rex, which take years to perfect. He varies the pace with illusions that can be touching or funny, but most of all they still genuinely fool you. ⊠ *MGM Grand Hotel & Casino, 3799 Las Vegas Blvd. S, South Strip* ☎ *800/745–3000* ⊕ *www.davidcopperfield.com* 🎟 *$86–$119* 🎭 *Select dates almost year-round.*

FAMILY **Donny and Marie Osmond.** The Mormon siblings who grew up in front of America still look and sound great, and their variety training on the Strip back in the 1970s allows them to work this old-school showroom setting with ease. The two are quick to split into lengthy solo sets that let Marie sing opera and rock out to Aerosmith and Donny give the old Osmonds pop ditty "Yo-Yo" a Justin Bieber treatment. You still sense a serious sibling rivalry, but the time apart just makes their time together more valuable. The production numbers with a campy squad of badly costumed dancers will rekindle memories of their toothier, bad-hair days on variety TV. ⊠ *Flamingo Las Vegas, 3555 Las Vegas Blvd. S, Center Strip* ☎ *702/777–2782* ⊕ *www.caesars.com* 🎟 *$116–$306* 🎭 *Dark Sun. and Mon.*

Elton John. The pop and rock legend's Caesars Palace showcase is called *The Million Dollar Piano*, based on embedded video panels that display everything from Versace design patterns to old videos. But the show as a whole is longer and more subdued than his previous *Red Piano* run at Caesars. The focus is more on his early 1970s classics, with even a few rarities to please serious fans. Check the schedule at the Colosseum at Caesars Palace, as John rotates dates with Rod Stewart and others. ⊠ *Caesars Palace, 3570 Las Vegas Blvd. S, Center Strip* ☎ *888/929–7849* ⊕ *www.caesarspalace.com or www.eltonjohn.com* ✉ *$55–$500* ☞ *Select dates.*

Jennifer Lopez "All I Have". Lopez is so well known beyond her fading pop career that her long-promised, long-delayed Las Vegas showcase was wise to focus more on her magnetic personality than her music. *All I Have* turns out to be a full-blown variety show in the old-Vegas tradition of amazing dancers and lavish costumes, divided into colorful segments that include a tribute to roaring 1950s Havana and a burlesque strip-tease number by the star. The singing is in fact the least of it, although the energetic, personable star tries to branch out here as well, covering some pop classics along with her own hits. ⊠ *Planet Hollywood, 3667 Las Vegas Blvd. S, South Strip* ☎ *855/234–7469* ⊕ *caesars.com/planet-hollywood/shows/jennifer-lopez* ✉ *$79–$417* ☞ *Select dates; dark Mon., Tues., and Thurs.*

FAMILY **Mat Franco.** A winning smile (and winning *America's Got Talent*) turned out to be a formidable combination for a young magician who settled on the Strip after the TV talent show fast-tracked his fame in 2014. Franco's charm and likable attitude compensate for a streamlined production still rooted in his light-traveling days on the college circuit. But he makes the classics seem new to a younger audience, and a couple of routines will surprise even the magic-jaded. ⊠ *Harrah's Las Vegas, 3475 Las Vegas Blvd. S, Center Strip* ☎ *702/777–2782* ⊕ *matfranco. com* ✉ *$52–$100* ☞ *Dark Wed.*

Fodor's Choice **Penn & Teller.** Eccentric comic magicians Penn & Teller once seemed an
★ unlikely fit for Las Vegas, but they're more popular now than when they came to town more than a decade ago. The two have spread into mainstream culture beyond the Strip, and they turn up almost everywhere, from Penn (the big loud one to Teller's short mime) as a cable news pundit to the duo judging the TV magic contest *Fool Us*. Their off-kilter humor now seems less jarring as they age gracefully at the Rio. Their magic in a gorgeous 1,500-seat theater is topical and genuinely baffling, the only show in town to push the form into new creative directions. And their comedy is satiric, provocative, and thoughtful. ⊠ *The Rio, 3700 W. Flamingo Rd., West Side* ☎ *702/777–7776* ⊕ *www.pennandteller.com* ✉ *$82–$104* ☞ *Dark Thurs. and Fri.*

Piff the Magic Dragon. Billing himself as "The Loser of *America's Got Talent*" fits the droll humor of the British comedy-magician, whose goal of competing on the TV show was to get a berth in Las Vegas. It worked. The magician who stands out for his satin dragon suit, bad attitude and stoic chihuahua sidekick, Mr. Piffles, keeps the jokes coming as fast as the card tricks in a cozy cabaret venue that allows plenty of audience interaction. ⊠ *Flamingo Las Vegas, 3555 Las Vegas Blvd. S, Center Strip* ☎ *702/777–2782* ⊕ *piffthemagicdragon.com* ⊠ *$41–$61* ☞ *Dark Fri.–Sun.*

Rod Stewart. Wearing his age as comfortably as a mop of sandy hair, Rod Stewart breezes through a gentle-rocking showcase of his hits. You can almost see him winking as he agitates the ladies with a bit of the soft shoe on "Tonight's the Night" or kicks soccer balls to the balcony. And yet, in some of his shows, Stewart buckles down in a few places to remind audiences of the more serious moments of his past. ■ TIP→ **Fans will want to plan in advance a Las Vegas visit around Stewart's blocks of shows at the Colosseum; he's there only a few times per year.** ⊠ *Caesars Palace, 3570 Las Vegas Blvd. S, Center Strip* ☎ *888/929–7849* ⊕ *www. rodstewart.com* ⊠ *$55–$250* ☞ *Select dates.*

Terry Fator. Las Vegas has long been a haven for impressionists, only this one lets his puppets do the talking. Fator is the likable second-season winner of *America's Got Talent* who does singing impressions as well as ventriloquism. During his run at the Mirage he's added new puppets to the act, including Vicki the Cougar (on the prowl for younger men) and a beetle who sings the Beatles. Fator may not be as popular as new Las Vegas neighbor (and fellow Texan) Jeff Dunham, but his show is more family-friendly. ■ TIP→ **Fator's Christmas show, during the holiday stretch when many titles go on vacation, is even more charming.** ⊠ *Mirage, 3400 Las Vegas Blvd. S, Center Strip* ☎ *702/792–7777* ⊕ *terryfator.com* ⊠ *$65–$163* ☞ *Dark Fri.–Sun.*

Vinnie Favorito. The late Don Rickles has an heir apparent in this insult comic, who devotes all but the first five minutes of his set to working the crowd, singling out victims for all sorts of racial profiling and raunchy interrogation. The politically correct should stay far away or try to hide in the back of the room, but it usually doesn't help. He will find you. And most people end up not minding so much, or forgetting they should know better. ⊠ *Westgate Las Vegas, 3000 Paradise Rd., East Side* ☎ *800/222–5361* ⊕ *www.westgateresorts.com* ⊠ *$49–$125* ☞ *Dark Mon. and Tues.*

PERFORMING ARTS

Although it's known more for theatrical spectacles than serious theater, Las Vegas does have a lively cultural scene. The arrival of the Smith Center for the Performing Arts Downtown in 2012 was a game-changer, giving new prominence to the city's ballet and philharmonic, which offer full seasons of productions each year. And although some Broadway musicals are still viable on the Strip, the Smith Center also filled the previously missing niche of touring Broadway musicals that drop in for a week or so, and hosts multi-week bookings of extra-commercial musicals such as *Book of Mormon* or *Hamilton*.

8

BALLET

Nevada Ballet Theatre. The city's longest-running fine-arts organization (this being Las Vegas, it only dates from 1973) stages five productions each year, anchored by an annual December presentation of *The Nutcracker.* The company performs at the Smith Center for the Performing Arts Downtown. ✉ *1651 Inner Circle Dr., Summerlin South* ☎ *702/804–0365 offices and group sales, 702/749–2000 tickets* ⊕ *www.nevadaballet.org.*

CLASSICAL MUSIC

Las Vegas Philharmonic. Formed in 1998, the Philharmonic performs a nine-show season, offering monthly concerts during the school year, with occasional added pops concerts. The orchestra performs at the Smith Center for the Performing Arts Downtown. ✉ *361 Symphony Park A, Downtown* ☎ *702/258–5438 schedule information, 702/249–2000 tickets* ⊕ *www.lvphil.org.*

THEATER

Away from the Strip, a booming community theater scene caters to the area's many new residents, from retirees to hipsters, who are looking for a low-cost alternative to the pricey shows. With the exception of Las Vegas Little Theatre, most don't have their own performance spaces and instead rent municipal auditoriums or storefront venues for their productions.

Las Vegas Little Theatre. Las Vegas's oldest community theater has branched out beyond the Neil Simon basics. Its main-stage season is augmented by a black-box season of smaller, more adventurous works, and it usually hosts summer festivals of "fringe" comedy or new works. Productions are staged in a cozy, comfortable theater in a strip mall that borders Las Vegas's Chinatown. ✉ *3920 Schiff Dr., West Side* ☎ *702/362–7996* ⊕ *www.lvlt.org.*

University of Nevada–Las Vegas Theater Department. UNLV's Nevada Conservatory Theatre brings in outside professionals and holds community-wide auditions for a full season of five productions each academic year, one of them a musical. Most performances are held in the Judy Bayley Theatre on campus. ✉ *4505 S. Maryland Pkwy., University District* ☎ *702/895–3663 tickets* ⊕ *www.unlv.edu/nct.*

SPORTS AND
THE OUTDOORS

Updated by
Matt Villano

Yes, the Las Vegas Valley sits smack in the middle of a desert that maintains triple-digit temperatures in mid-June, July, and August. But nearly all other times of year, the Las Vegas climate is perfect for enjoying the great outdoors. Ironic, but a town that was built on indoor casinos has plentiful options for outdoor recreation. Because many visitors rarely venture beyond their resort pools for outdoor recreation, those who choose to explore the surroundings often have hiking trails and open spaces all to themselves.

Beyond the green felt, you can discover many additional activities to get your heart rate up in this town. You can explore the region by bicycle, on foot, on horseback, and more. Other activities include bird-watching, rock climbing, golf, and skiing. And when the desert heat is too much, you can chill out in one of Vegas's many bowling alleys. Perhaps the four most popular places to get out and about are Lake Mead National Recreation Area (boating), Lake Las Vegas (fishing, boating), Red Rock National Conservation Area (hiking, biking, rock climbing), and Spring Mountain National Recreation Area (skiing! snowshoeing! sledding!). Another huge draw: the 36-mile River Mountains Trail, a paved loop that's perfect for bicycling or running. New in 2017 are the Las Vegas Golden Knights, the latest expansion franchise for the National Hockey League, and Sin City's first professional sports team, who will play in the new T-Mobile Arena. It also looks like the National Football League's Raiders will make the move to Vegas by 2020, if not before.

AUTO RACING

Fodor's Choice **Las Vegas Motor Speedway.** Although the Las Vegas Motor Speedway
★ is home to NASCAR and NHRA events throughout the year, it also is a mecca for racing fans of all kinds, with a variety of experiences available year-round. The Neon Garage, for instance, is in the center

of the infield; from there, fans can watch drivers and crews of the NASCAR Sprint Cup Series work magic on their cars. For zealots who want to be more hands-on, the Richard Petty Driving Experience puts laypeople behind the wheels of real-live (600 horsepower) race cars and gives them the chance to run the track (for 3, 8, 18, 30 or 40 laps) at speeds of more than 100 mph. Of course visitors can always opt for track tours as well. Reservations are required for all experiences. Adult diapers are optional. ⊠ *7000 Las Vegas Blvd. N, North Las Vegas* ☎ *800/644–4444* ⊕ *www.lvms.com* ✉ *Prices vary by experience.*

BASEBALL

FAMILY **Las Vegas 51s.** There's nothing like minor league baseball to bring fans close to the action, and the Class-AAA affiliate of the New York Mets certainly are fun to watch, especially from one of the berms in the outfield. Because Class-AAA is one step from the majors, lucky fans might see some big-leaguers down with the minor league ball club to rehab injuries. The team plays at Cashman Field, which celebrates its 35th anniversary during the 2017–2018 season. The mascot of the team is an alien, a reference to the litany of purported UFO sightings that occurred in the nearby desert during the 1950s. ⊠ *Cashman Field, 850 Las Vegas Blvd. N, Downtown* ☎ *702/943–7200* ⊕ *www.lv51. com* ✉ *Tickets from $11.*

BIKING

One of the best ways to explore the Las Vegas Valley is by bike. Outside of the urban area, roads are flat with spacious shoulders, providing great opportunities for serious road biking (early in the day, of course, before the desert sun has a chance to set the region to broil). Local conservation land offers epic options for mountain biking, too; in addition to hundreds of miles of mixed-use trails in the Red Rock National Conservation Area, the bike-specific trails of Bootleg Canyon, near Boulder City, are internationally renowned as challenging and fun. Perhaps the crown jewel of the local bicycling scene is the River Mountains Trail, a 36-mile trail that winds past Lake Mead National Recreation Area, Lake Las Vegas, Henderson, and Boulder City.

All-Mountain Cyclery. This full-service bike shop sits just outside downtown Boulder City, down the hill from the entrance to Bootleg Canyon and the River Mountains Trail. The rental program includes a variety of top-of-the-line road and mountain bikes; the shop also has a host of gear for visitors who come unprepared. Most of the employees are avid cyclists who are happy to offer up tips and suggestions about can't-miss trails or viable strategies for exploring on pedal power. Guided tours also are available. ⊠ *1404 Nevada Hwy., Suite C, Boulder City* ☎ *702/453–2453* ⊕ *www.allmountaincyclery.com.*

FAMILY **McGhie's Bike Outpost.** One of the largest outfitters in the Las Vegas Valley, McGhie's rents equipment for skiing, bicycling, and sandboarding. This location, in downtown Blue Diamond, which is just west of the city in Red Rock Canyon National Conservation Area (there are others in Henderson and on South Fort Apache in Las Vegas), specializes in bikes—convenient, since it's right on the doorstep of 125 miles of hard-core mountain biking. The company rents bikes individually, and also offers a host of guided tours around Red Rock and beyond. Unlike other outfitters in the area, McGhie's also rents bikes specifically for kids. ✉ *16 Cottonwood Dr., Suite B, Blue Diamond* ☎ *702/875–4820* ⊕ *www.mcghies.com.*

BIRD-WATCHING

FAMILY **Henderson Bird Viewing Preserve.** More than 200 bird species have been spotted among the system of nine ponds at the 140-acre Henderson Bird Viewing Preserve. The preserve's ponds, at the Kurt R. Segler Water Reclamation Facility, are a stop along the Pacific flyway for migratory waterbirds, and the best viewing times are winter and early spring. The earlier you get there, the better if you want to fill your bird checklist. The ponds also harbor hummingbirds, raptors, peregrine falcons, tundra swans, cormorants, ducks, hawks, and herons. The office will lend out a pair of binoculars if you ask. Keep the bags of bread crumbs at home; the preserve doesn't allow the feeding of wildlife, and bikes and domestic pets are not allowed. ✉ *350 E. Galleria Dr., Henderson* ☎ *702/267–4180* ⊕ *www.cityofhenderson.com* ✉ *Free.*

BOWLING

Bowling in Vegas incorporates elements of casinos, bars, and nightclubs, with lively crowds to match. Locals take their leagues seriously, so "spare" yourself some heartache and call ahead to make a lane reservation.

Brooklyn Bowl. This 32-lane bowling alley on The LINQ Promenade doubles as a live music venue, sometimes simultaneously. Bowlers can lounge on Chesterfield sofas and enjoy food from New York City's Blue Ribbon between frames. If you'd rather just watch, there's an elevated bowler's lounge from where you can observe the action. The biggest downside to this spot is the acoustics; oddly, for a music venue, they're incredibly poor. Be prepared to lose your voice if you want to converse with your pals. ✉ *LINQ Promenade, 3545 Las Vegas Blvd. S, Center Strip* ☎ *702/862–2695* ⊕ *www.brooklynbowl.com* ✉ *Bowling from $20; shoe rental $4.95.*

The Orleans Bowling Center. Tucked inside the Orleans Resort and Casino, this 70-lane bowling center is in a working-class neighborhood just off the Strip. Be sure to check out the pro shop, as well as the video arcade, which can get rocking on weekend nights. ✉ *4500 W. Tropicana Rd., West Side* ☎ *702/365–7400* ⊕ *www.orleanscasino.com* ✉ *From $3; shoe rental $3.50.*

Red Rock Lanes is one of the largest luxury bowling centers in Las Vegas.

Red Rock Lanes. This 72-lane bowling alley has all the amenities, including Cosmic Bowling—glow-in-the-dark bowling with a DJ—until 2 am on Friday and Saturday nights. Roll on through until morning—it's open 24 hours a day. If you've got the bankroll, you can live the full nightclub-plus-bowling dream with bottle service at your own VIP lanes. ✉ *Red Rock Casino Resort, 11011 W. Charleston Blvd., Summerlin South* 🕿 *702/797–7467, 866/767–7773* ⊕ *redrock.sclv.com* ✆ *From $3; shoe rental $3.50.*

Sam's Town Bowling Center. This is a 56-lane locals' alley where leagues and tournaments are taken seriously. Tourists come for the cocktail lounge, connecting casino, and "Xtreme Bowling Experience" starting at 9 pm on Friday and Saturday nights that will allow you to "strike out" in a nightclub like never before. Be sure to check for deals on Tuesday and Thursday nights, as well as Sunday mornings. ✉ *5111 Boulder Hwy., Boulder Strip* 🕿 *702/456–7777, 800/897–8696* ⊕ *www.samstownlv.com* ✆ *From $2.75; shoe rental $3.50.*

Santa Fe Station Bowling Center. This 60-lane facility at Santa Fe Station Casino is a traditional bowling center, with video arcade, bar, and top-of-the-line Brunswick electronic scoring system. Cosmic Bowling with a DJ is held every Friday and Saturday 1 pm–1 am. ✉ *4949 N. Rancho Dr., West Side* 🕿 *702/658–4988* ⊕ *www.stationcasinoslanes.com* ✆ *From $3.25; shoe rental $4.*

Silver Nugget Bowling Center. This alley has 24 lanes, a pro shop, and a modern automatic scoring system. Its version of Cosmic Bowling, which includes fancy lights and a booming sound system, goes 7 pm–2 am on Friday and Saturday. On weekend days you can rent lanes by the hour instead of paying per person per game. ⊠ *Silver Nugget Casino, 2140 Las Vegas Blvd. N, North Las Vegas* ☎ *702/399–1111* ⊕ *silvernuggetlv. com* ✉ *From $1; shoe rental $2.75.*

Suncoast Bowling Center. Reflecting its upscale Summerlin neighborhood, the bowling center at the Suncoast, with 64 lanes, is designed to provide every high-tech toy for bowlers. The alley has Cosmic Bowling on Saturdays 9 pm–2 am and hosts a number of different leagues throughout the week. ⊠ *Suncoast Hotel & Casino, 9090 Alta Dr., Summerlin South* ☎ *702/636–7111, 877/677–7111* ⊕ *www.suncoastcasino.com* ✉ *From $2.50; shoe rental $2.75.*

GOLF

With an average of 315 days of sunshine a year and year-round access, Las Vegas's top sport is golf. The peak season on the greens is any nonsummer month; only mad dogs and Englishmen are out on the courses in the noonday summer sun. However, most of the courses in Las Vegas offer reduced greens fees during the summer months, sometimes as much as 50%–70% lower than peak-season fees. If you want to golf a course on a weekend, call before you get into town, as the 8–11 am time slots fill up quickly. Starting times for same-day play are possible (especially during the week), but if you're picky about when and where you play, plan ahead. Some of the big Strip resorts have a dedicated golf concierge who can advise you on a course that fits your tastes. In some cases, these people can get you access to private courses.

Fodor's Choice
★
Bali Hai Golf Club. This island-theme course is dotted with palm trees, volcanic outcroppings, and small lagoons. The entrance is a mere 10-minute walk from Mandalay Bay. The clubhouse includes a pro shop and restaurant. Online specials can cut rates in half. ⊠ *5160 Las Vegas Blvd. S, South Strip* ☎ *888/427–6678, 702/450–8191* ⊕ *www. balihaigolfclub.com* ✉ *From $199 for nonresidents* ⌦ *18 holes, 7002 yards, par 71.*

Bear's Best Las Vegas. Jack Nicklaus created this course by placing replicas of his 18 favorite holes (from the 270 courses he's designed worldwide) into a single course. There's also a short course that measures just over 5,000 yards. If all of these on-greens options don't make you reach for your ugly pants, then consider that the clubhouse has enough Nicklaus memorabilia to fill a small museum. A huge dining area doubles as a banquet hall, and an even bigger pavilion provides beautiful views of the mountains and the Strip. Midday tee times are available online for less than half-price. ⊠ *11111 W. Flamingo Rd., Summerlin South* ☎ *702/804–8500* ⊕ *www.clubcorp.com/clubs/ bear-s-best-las-vegas* ✉ *From $149 for nonresidents* ⌦ *18 holes, 7194 yards, par 74.*

Las Vegas National Golf Club. Built in 1961, this historic course has played host to Vegas royalty and golf's superstars over the years. Tiger shot 70 on the final round of his first PGA Tour win during the 1996 Las Vegas Invitational, and Mickey Wright won two of her four LPGA Championships here. You'll find five difficult par-3s and a killer 550-yard par-5 at the 18th. "Las Vegas National," as it's known, was one of the first courses in the Valley to rent players the Golfboard, a mash-up between a golf cart and a long skateboard. The course is about a $15 cab ride from most properties on the Strip. ⊠ *1911 E. Desert Inn Rd., East Side* ☎ *702/889–1000* ⊕ *www.lasvegasnational.com* ✉ *$39–$109 for nonresidents* ⅄ *18 holes, 6721 yards, par 73.*

Las Vegas Paiute Golf Resort. You can play three Pete Dye–designed courses here: Wolf, Snow Mountain, and Sun Mountain. Snow Mountain fits most skill levels and has been ranked by *Golf Digest* as Las Vegas's best public-access course. Sun Mountain is a player-friendly course, but its difficult par-4s make it marginally more challenging than Snow. Six of those holes measure longer than 400 yards, but the best is the fourth hole, which is 206 yards over water. Wolf, with its island hole at No. 15, is the toughest of the three and the longest course in Nevada. If you want to play last-minute, all courses offer great twilight 9-hole rates. ⊠ *10325 Nu-Wav Kaiv Blvd., Summerlin South* ☎ *702/658–1400, 800/711–2833* ⊕ *www.lvpaiutegolf.com* ✉ *$129–$199 for nonresidents* ⅄ *Snow Mountain: 18 holes, 7164 yards, par 72; Sun Mountain: 18 holes, 7112 yards, par 72; Wolf: 18 holes, 7604 yards, par 72.*

Rhodes Ranch Golf Club. One of the better courses in the Las Vegas Valley, the Rhodes Ranch course was designed by renowned architect Ted Robinson to provide enough challenges for any skill level—numerous water hazards, difficult bunkers, and less-than-even fairways. Twilight rates can drop to $55 or lower. ⊠ *20 Rhodes Ranch Pkwy., West Side* ☎ *702/740–4114, 888/311–8337* ⊕ *www.rhodesranchgolf.com* ✉ *$79–$99 for nonresidents* ⅄ *18 holes, 6909 yards, par 72.*

Royal Links Golf Club. Similar in concept to Bear's Best, Royal Links is a greatest-hits course, replicating popular holes from 11 courses in the British Open rotation. You can play the Road Hole from the famed St. Andrews, and the Postage Stamp from Royal Troon. If you're feeling lonely, sign up to golf with one of the course's "Par Mates," a group of buxom beauties who are masters with the clubs. Also on-site is Stymie's Pub. Online specials can be as low as $95. ⊠ *5995 E. Vegas Valley Dr., East Side* ☎ *702/765–0484, 888/427–6678* ⊕ *www. royallinksgolfclub.com* ✉ *$125–$229 for nonresidents* ⅄ *18 holes, 7029 yards, par 72.*

SouthShore Lake Las Vegas. Technically, the Jack Nicklaus–designed Signature Course at this Lake Las Vegas golf club is members-only, but a relatively new change in the bylaws allows guests at some of the local resorts to play with limited access. Hard-core enthusiasts say the layout is challenging; there are nearly 90 bunkers in all. Still, with views of Lake Las Vegas and the surrounding River Mountains, the experience is second to few others in the Las Vegas Valley. ⊠ *100 Strada di Circolo, Lake Las Vegas* ☎ *702/856–8402* ⊕ *www.pacificlinks.com/southshore* ✉ *$150–$175 for nonmembers* ⅄ *18 holes, 6917 yards, par 71.*

9

Fodor's Choice
★ **Top Golf Las Vegas.** Sin City's newest driving range takes golf to another level. Situated on the back side of the MGM Grand, this three-story outpost of the national chain has 108 climate-controlled bays, all of which offer food and beverage service and TVs, just like a sports bar. State-of-the-art technology tracks each ball and gives an immediate distance reading on monitors so you can compare with your friends. Five bars make the vibe lively even when nobody's golfing. There also are two pools, in case you decide you want to take a dip after whacking your balls. ⌧ *MGM Grand, 4627 Koval La., South Strip* ☎ *702/933–8458* ⊕ *www.topgolf.com* ✉ *From $30 per hr (up to 6 players).*

TPC Las Vegas. The PGA manages this championship layout next to the JW Marriott Las Vegas Resort & Spa. The course, designed by Bobby Weed and Raymond Floyd, features a number of elevation changes, steep ravines, and a lake. It's also one of the venues for the Las Vegas Invitational, a stop on the PGA Tour. ⌧ *9851 Canyon Run Dr., Summerlin South* ☎ *702/256–2500, 888/321–5725* ⊕ *www.tpc.com/tpc-las-vegas* ✉ *$160–$250 for nonresidents* ⚑ *18 holes, 7104 yards, par 71.*

HIKING

Sweeping vistas. Ocher-color rocks. Desert flora and fauna. These are just some of the reasons to love hiking in and around Las Vegas. Most pedestrian trails in the area are mixed-use, meaning they double as bicycle and equestrian trails. All of the trails offer respite from the bustle of the resorts. The very best trails in the region are in Red Rock National Conservation Area. Here, the Ice Box Canyon trail heads 2.6 difficult miles from the exposed desert up into a shady box canyon, where waterfalls appear after rainstorms, and La Madre Springs trail stretches 3.3 miles up an old fire road to a spectacular vista point. What's more, the Willow Springs Loop, which is only 1.5 miles, takes hikers past some pictographs that have adorned the rocks for hundreds of years. (⇨ *For more information about Red Rock National Conservation Area, see Exploring.*)

Trails on the other side of the Spring Mountains, in the Spring Mountain National Recreation Area, are breathtaking in a different way; in winter, there's snow all over the place, and the shade of the canyon keeps temperatures about 15 degrees cooler than they are on the Valley floor. Popular tromps there include the 3-mile round-trip to Mary Jane Falls (a waterfall at the back of a pristine mountain bowl) and Bristlecone Trail, a strenuous 6-mile loop at the end of Lee Canyon that hugs the ridgeline and offers some of the most incredible vistas in the entire Las Vegas Valley. For more information about hikes in the Spring Mountains, check out the Spring Mountains Visitor Gateway on Kyle Canyon Road, about an hour outside of Downtown Las Vegas.

Before you lace up those hiking shoes, remember that trails at all the region's top spots dot the landscape across a variety of sites, and you'll need a car to get from one trailhead to the next. And, of course, this is the desert, so you'll need to bring plenty of water, especially if you plan to spend at least part of your hike in the heat of the day.

HOCKEY

Las Vegas Golden Knights. Generations of Las Vegans have dreamed about getting a professional sports franchise in town. For years, however, critics said the market was too small (and too overrun with gambling) to do it right. That all changed in the middle of this decade, when the National Hockey League granted Vegas an expansion team, the Las Vegas Golden Knights. MGM Resorts teamed with a number of outside companies to build the team a home at T-Mobile Arena, a state-of-the-art facility at the west end of The Park between New York–New York and Monte Carlo. The team is slated to drop the puck on its inaugural season in October 2017. ⊠ *T-Mobile Arena, 3780 Las Vegas Blvd. S, South Strip* ☎ *702/692–1600* ⊕ *www.nhl. com/goldenknights.*

HORSEBACK RIDING

Fodor'sChoice ★ **Cowboy Trail Rides.** The best way to explore the mountains of Red Rock National Conservation Area is by horseback, and Cowboy Trail Rides has it covered. The outfitter runs one-hour, half-, and full-day trips from a location just east of the Red Rock Visitor Center. Some of the trips include lunch or dinner. Scenic packages include the Sunset BBQ Ride (1 hour 45 minutes) and the WOW ride (5 hours). Beautiful views of the Strip give way to desert wilderness. Keep your eyes peeled for jackrabbits, Joshua trees, and other notable desert life. The view of the Strip isn't too shabby either. ⊠ *Red Rock Canyon Stables, Red Rock Canyon National Conservation Area, 4053 Fossil Ridge Rd., Las Vegas* ☎ *702/387–2457* ⊕ *www.cowboytrailrides.com* 🎫 *From $169.*

SKIING AND SNOWBOARDING

Hard to believe, but fewer than 50 miles from Downtown Las Vegas there are good skiing and snowboarding trails at the Las Vegas Ski and Snowboard Resort, with a half-pipe, a ski shop, rental equipment, and a day lodge.

FAMILY Fodor'sChoice ★ **Lee Canyon.** Southern Nevada's skiing headquarters is a mere 47 miles northwest of Downtown Las Vegas. Depending on traffic and weather conditions, it can take less than two hours to go from a 70°F February afternoon on the Strip to the top of a chairlift at an elevation of 9,370 feet. Lee Canyon is equipped with three chairlifts—two quads and a triple—plus a tubing lift (Las Vegas's only one!). The ski resort also offers complimentary coaching for beginners to intermediates, and has a terrain park, a ski shop, rental equipment, and a day lodge with a quick-serve restaurant and full-service bar. Clothing rentals are available. There are 195 acres of slopes: 20% of the trails are for beginners, 60% are intermediate, and 20% are advanced runs. The longest run is 3,000 feet, and there's a vertical drop of nearly 1,000 feet. You know you're at the closest ski resort to Las Vegas when you see the slope names: Blackjack, High Roller, Keno, the Strip, Bimbo 1 and 2, and

Slot Alley. The lifts are open from about late November to early April. Lift tickets are best purchased online and in advance at ⊕ *skilasvegas. com*. Information on transportation and lodging partners in Las Vegas is also found on the website. A telephone call can get you an update on either snow conditions or driving conditions in Nevada. ⊠ *6725 Lee Canyon Rd., Mt. Charleston* ⟷ *Take U.S. 95 north to Lee Canyon exit (Hwy. 156), and head up mountain* ☎ *702/385–2754, 702/593–9500 Nevada snow conditions, 877/687–6237 Nevada Road Conditions (out of state)* ⊕ *www.skilasvegas.com.*

SIDE TRIPS FROM LAS VEGAS

WELCOME TO SIDE TRIPS FROM LAS VEGAS

TOP REASONS TO GO

★ **Experiencing geologic history:** The breathtaking 277-mile Grand Canyon was created by the Colorado River over the course of 6 million years, yet it never gets old.

★ **Enjoying the outdoors:** With expansive views and acres upon acres of open space, Lake Mead National Recreation Area, and Death Valley are great places to reconnect with nature. Death Valley, although prohibitive in summer, is one of the most fascinating national parks in the United States.

★ **Alien encounters:** If you're interested in exploring some government secrets, Area 51 is within a few hours' drive of Las Vegas.

★ **Celebrating engineering:** It's hard to find a monument to man's ingenuity more impressive than the 1,244-foot concrete span of Hoover Dam.

1 Lake Mead Area. Lake Mead, the largest reservoir in the United States, and Hoover Dam are about 34 miles from Las Vegas. Nearby, Valley of Fire is a seemingly infinite landscape of sandstone outcroppings, petrified logs, and miles of hiking trails.

2 Grand Canyon. Only about four hours' drive from Las Vegas to the South Rim—less if you head to the West Rim—much of the canyon is a national park. The South Rim is where all the action is, although the North Rim is more for the adventurous. The Skywalk, a relatively new attraction in the West Rim, provides jaw-dropping views straight down.

3 Area 51. You may not find any aliens, but if it's on your bucket list, the so-called "Area 51" is out in the Nevada desert north of Las Vegas.

4 Death Valley. This is a vast, lonely, beautiful place with breathtaking vistas, blasting 120-degree heat in the summer, and mysterious moving rocks. The desert landscape is surrounded by majestic mountains, dry lake beds, spring wildflowers, and Wild West ghost towns.

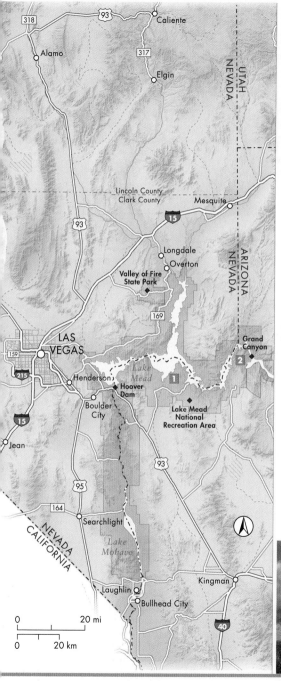

NEVADA

GETTING ORIENTED

In many ways, the expanse of Nevada to the west, south, and east of Las Vegas is a living museum. The breathtaking Grand Canyon offers a glimpse at 6 million years of erosion, and the Hoover Dam is an incredible exhibit of early-20th-century modern engineering. Beyond these attractions, untrammeled places like Lake Mead National Recreation Area provide a perfect counterpoint to the hubbub of Sin City.

10

Updated by
Joan Patterson

Nevada takes its name from a Spanish word meaning "snow-covered." So why, you might ask, is the southeastern corner of the state covered in scorching sands and desert landscapes that blend seamlessly with neighboring Arizona? Probably because before Nevada became a state, most of the land in what's now Clark County belonged to Arizona's "lost county of Pah-Ute."

At that time Las Vegas was a tiny settlement situated at the crossroads of the Old Spanish Trail and the Mormon Road. The Mormon town of Callville, later drowned beneath the waters of Lake Mead, was the Pah-Ute county seat. A smattering of agricultural communities sat on the banks of the Colorado River, and steamboats plied the river's waters.

Today the vast majority of the state's population resides in Clark County, and the nearby lakes, state parks, and geological wonders entertain even the most jaded city dwellers. Those pressed for time can take a short drive from Vegas to go hiking in Valley of Fire, or rock climbing in Red Rock Canyon. Those with a little more time can explore the wonderland of nearby waterways, stunning rock formations, and laid-back ranching communities. Water enthusiasts head to Lakes Mead. Nature lovers find prime wildlife-watching along the Colorado River. And those looking for the grandest spectacle in the region can take the longer drive to the Grand Canyon.

SIDE TRIPS PLANNER

WHEN TO GO

There's no bad time to visit the Grand Canyon, though summer and spring break are the busiest times. Visiting during these peak seasons, as well as holidays, requires patience and a tolerance for crowds. Weather changes on a whim in this exposed high-desert region. The more remote North Rim is off-limits for much of the winter. There are no services, and snow sometimes closes Highway 67 south of Jacob Lake.

Be prepared for hot, exceptionally dry summers in southern Nevada; temperatures can easily hit 105°F. Water destinations such as Lake Mead appeal to sports enthusiasts during the summer and major holiday weekends, while the mild winters are known for attracting retirees. Late fall and early spring are among the most enjoyable times to visit, particularly if you plan on making the trek to destinations such as Death Valley.

As for Death Valley: it's aptly named for the summer months. Believe the hype; summer highs often average 115°F (a record 134°F was set in 1913).

PLANNING YOUR TIME

Plan ahead if you're going to explore Grand Canyon National Park. Reservations for everything fill up during the busy summer months; mule rides and lodging may be reserved up to 13 months in advance. Perhaps the easiest way to visit the West Rim from Vegas is with a tour. **Bighorn Wild West Tours** (☎ *702/385–4676, 888/385–4676* ⊕ *bighorn-wildwesttours.com*) will pick you up in a Hummer at your Vegas hotel for an all-day trip that includes the shuttle-bus package and lunch for $259. Day-trippers heading to the Lake Mead National Recreation Area can stop at the Alan Bible Visitor Center near Boulder Beach. Death Valley can be reached by car in less than three hours. Leave early in the morning if you go late spring or early fall—midday temperatures can still reach triple digits during this time.

WHAT TO DO AND WHERE TO DO IT

Looking to hook the big one? Head to Lake Mead for excellent year-round fishing. To explore ghost towns and the Old West, check out the eastern reaches of Nevada en route to Death Valley. Nature buffs will find excellent birding and wildlife-watching at nature preserves along the Colorado River, but the grandest natural spectacle's a few hours away at the Grand Canyon. The South and North rims offer outdoor adventure and multiple viewpoints. The privately operated Grand Canyon West, easily accessible from Las Vegas by a quick flight or a relaxed bus tour, adds a Native American perspective to the world's grandest gorge with three developed viewpoints, horseback and Hummer rides to the rim, and the Skywalk—a glass U-shape bridge 4,000 feet above the Colorado River. Another geological marvel that's a short drive from Las Vegas is the dramatic red sandstone formations and stark views of the Mojave Desert at Valley of Fire State Park.

DRIVE TIMES

Approximate drive times from the Center Strip to areas of interest are as follows:

Grand Canyon South Rim: 4½ hours

Grand Canyon North Rim: 6 hours

Valley of Fire: 1 hour

Hoover Dam: 50 minutes

Area 51: 2½ hours

Death Valley: 2½ hours

SAFETY TIPS

Services can be few and far between in the more remote regions of southern Nevada and northwestern Arizona. Play it safe by packing an emergency car kit with basic automotive repairs, plenty of water, and overnight supplies. To avoid being stranded, let someone know where you're going and which route you plan to take. It's also a good idea to check road conditions (*Nevada* ☎ 877/687–6237; *Arizona* ☎ 888/411–7623; *Utah* ☎ 866/511–8824; *Grand Canyon National Park* ☎ 928/638–7888) before you set out.

ABOUT THE RESTAURANTS

Dining's generally relaxed and casual in southern Nevada. For the most part you'll find home-cooked American favorites and "South of the Border" specialties.

Dining options in Grand Canyon National Park are limited to the lodge restaurants working under contract with the government. However, you'll find everything from cafeteria food to casual café fare to elegant evening specials. On the Hualapai and Havasupai reservations in Havasu Canyon and at Grand Canyon West, options are limited to tribe-run restaurants.

ABOUT THE HOTELS

Of the nearly 1,000 rooms, cabins, and suites in Grand Canyon National Park, only 203—all at the Grand Canyon Lodge—are at the North Rim. Outside of El Tovar Hotel at the South Rim, frills are hard to find. Rooms are basic but comfortable, and most guests would agree that the best in-room amenity is a view of the canyon. Reservations are a must, especially during the busy summer season.

Lodging options are even more limited on the West Rim. The Hualapai Lodge in Peach Springs and the Hualapai Ranch at Grand Canyon West are run by the Hualapai tribe. The Havasupai Lodge in Supai offers the only rooms in Havasu Canyon. At the South Rim, motel chains make up the most abundant and affordable options in Tusayan, just outside the park entrance (but about 15 minutes from the rim itself) and in Williams, about 50 minutes from the park entrance, and home of the historic railroad line into the park.

Hotel and restaurant reviews have been shortened. For full information, visit Fodors.com.

WHAT IT COSTS				
	$	$$	$$$	$$$$
Restaurants	under $15	$15–$22	$23–$30	over $30
Hotels	under $140	$140–$220	$221–$300	over $300

Restaurant prices are the average cost of a main course at dinner or, if dinner is not served, at lunch. Hotel prices are the lowest cost of a standard double room in high season.

LAKE MEAD AREA

Southeast of Las Vegas sits Boulder City, which is quaint, languid, and dotted with a small downtown historic district and neighborhoods, small businesses, and parks—without a single casino. Over the hill from town, enormous Hoover Dam blocks the Colorado River as it enters Black Canyon. Backed up behind the dam is incongruous, deep-blue Lake Mead, the focal point of water-based recreation for southern Nevada and northwestern Arizona, and the major water supplier to seven Southwestern states. The lake is ringed by miles of rugged desert country. The breathtaking wonderland known as Valley of Fire, with its red sandstone outcroppings, petrified logs, petroglyphs, and hiking trails, is along the northern reach of the lake. And all of this is an hour or less from Vegas.

BOULDER CITY

25 miles southeast of Las Vegas.

In the early 1930s Boulder City was built by the federal government to house 5,000 construction workers on the Hoover Dam project. A strict moral code was enforced to ensure timely completion of the dam, and to this day the model city is the only community in Nevada in which gambling is illegal. (Note that the two casinos at either end of Boulder City are just outside the city limits.) After the dam was completed, the town shrank but was kept alive by the management and maintenance crews of the dam and Lake Mead. Today it's a vibrant little Southwestern town.

GETTING HERE AND AROUND

It takes about 30 minutes via U.S. 93/Interstate 515 or Interstate 215/Interstate 515 to get from the Las Vegas tourist corridor to Boulder City.

ESSENTIALS

Visitor Information Boulder City Chamber of Commerce. ⊠ *465 Nevada Way* ☎ *702/293–2034* ⊕ *www.bouldercitychamberofcommerce.com.*

EXPLORING

FAMILY **Boulder City/Hoover Dam Museum.** For its size, this small museum inside the Boulder Dam Hotel is well done. It includes hands-on exhibits, oral histories, artifacts from the building of Hoover Dam, and a glimpse at what it was like for Great Depression–era families to pull up roots and settle in the rock and dust of the harsh Mojave Desert. And don't forget to ask museum staff about the city's new audio walking tour of 11 historical sites around town. ⊠ *1305 Arizona St.* ☎ *702/294–1988* ⊕ *www.bcmha.org* ⊟ *$2.*

Boulder Dam Hotel. Be sure to stop at the Dutch Colonial–style Boulder Dam Hotel, built in 1933. On the National Register of Historic Places, the 20-room bed-and-breakfast once was a favorite getaway for notables, including the man who became Pope Pius XII and actors Will Rogers, Bette Davis, and Shirley Temple. It's still a point of pride for Boulder City and the heart of downtown. The guest rooms have been remodeled to stay competitive but retain a historic feel. ⊠ *1305 Arizona St.* ☎ *702/293–3510* ⊕ *www.boulderdamhotel.com.*

10

Grandma Daisy's Candy & Ice Cream Parlor. Located in the heart of downtown, Grandma Daisy's candy and ice cream shop offers a trip back in time. Its shelves are filled with homemade sweets such as fudge, giant caramel apples, and buttery toffee, or you can scoop up a bag of retro candies you haven't seen in years. ⊠ *530 Nevada Hwy.* ☎ *702/294–6639* ⊕ *www.grandmadaisys.com.*

WHERE TO EAT

The old downtown area of Boulder City has become a fun zone for drinks, dining, and antiques shopping. The center of the action is the 500 block of Nevada Highway (aka Nevada Way).

$
AMERICAN
✕**Boulder Dam Brewing Company.** Across the street from the Boulder Dam Hotel, the Boulder Dam Brewing Company is a lively, family-run brewery decorated with historic Hoover Dam photos and memorabilia. The menu focuses on hearty pub fare and beers with names such as High Scaler Pale Ale and Powder Monkey Pilsner. **Known for:** craft beers; live music; outdoor patio. $ *Average main: $10* ⊠ *453 Nevada Hwy.* ☎ *702/243–2739* ⊕ *www.boulderdambrewing.com.*

$
DINER
✕**The Coffee Cup.** The Coffee Cup is a bustling breakfast-and-lunch diner that's been featured on the Food Network's *Diners, Drive-Ins, and Dives.* Tourists line up on weekends for the quintessential small-town diner experience, complete with newspaper-strewn counter seating and the owners' family photos and water-sports memorabilia on the walls. It delivers on the food front, too, with giant portions of favorites such as huevos rancheros, biscuits and gravy, and barbecue sandwiches. **Known for:** hearty breakfasts; large portions; lively atmosphere. $ *Average main: $8* ⊠ *512 Nevada Hwy.* ☎ *702/294–0517* ⊕ *www.world-famouscoffeecup.com* ▭ *No credit cards* ☉ *No dinner.*

$
CAFÉ
✕**Milo's Cellar.** Sure, you can sit inside, but what draws locals and tourists alike is the alfresco dining. A well-considered menu offers gourmet sandwiches, soups and salads, platters for wine pairings, and a wide selection of both vino and beer by the glass. **Known for:** generous wine selection; alfresco dining; nightly dinner specials. $ *Average main: $12* ⊠ *538 Nevada Hwy.* ☎ *702/293–9540* ⊕ *www.milosbouldercity.com* ▭ *No credit cards.*

10

HOOVER DAM

8 miles northeast from Boulder City.

In 1928 Congress authorized $175 million for construction of a dam on the Colorado River to control destructive floods, provide a steady water supply to seven Colorado River basin states, and generate electricity. Considered one of the seven wonders of the industrial world, the art deco Hoover Dam is 726 feet high (the equivalent of a 70-story building) and at the base it's 660 feet thick (more than the length of two football fields). Construction required 4.4 million cubic yards of concrete—enough to build a two-lane highway from San Francisco to New York.

GETTING HERE AND AROUND

Hoover Dam is about a 45-minute drive from Las Vegas via U.S. 93; it's about 15 minutes from Boulder City.

EXPLORING

FAMILY

Fodor's Choice

★

Hoover Dam. Originally referred to as Boulder Dam, this colossal structure, widely considered one of the greatest engineering achievements in history, was later officially named Hoover Dam in recognition of President Herbert Hoover's role in the project. Look for artist Oskar Hansen's plaza sculptures, which include the 30-foot-tall *Winged Figures of the Republic* (the statues and terrazzo floor patterns were copied at the new Smith Center for the Performing Arts in Downtown Las Vegas).

The tour itself is a tradition that dates back to 1937, and you can still see the old box office on top of the dam. But now the ticketed tours originate in the modern visitor center, with two options. The cheaper, more popular one is the **Powerplant Tour**, which starts every 15 minutes. It's a half-hour, guided tour that includes a short film and then a 537-foot elevator ride to two points of interest: the chance to stand on top of one of the 30-foot pipes where you can hear and feel the water rushing through to the generators, and the more impressive eight-story room housing still-functional power generators. Self-paced exhibits follow the guided portion, with good interactive museum exhibits and a great indoor/outdoor patio view of the dam from the river side. The more extensive **Hoover Dam Tour** includes everything on the Powerplant Tour but limits the group size to 20 and spends more time inside the dam, including a peek through the air vents. Tours run from 9 to 5 all year, with the last Power Plant daily tour leaving at 3:45 pm, and the last Hoover Dam Tour at 3:30. Visitors for both tours submit to security screening comparable to an airport. January and February are the slowest months, and mornings generally are less busy. The top of the dam is open to pedestrians and vehicles, but you have to remain in your vehicle after sundown. Visitors can still drive over the dam for sightseeing, but cannot continue into Arizona; you have to turn around and come back after the road dead-ends at a scenic lookout (with a snack bar and store) on the Arizona side. ■TIP→ The dam's High Scaler Café offers fare such as cold drinks, ice cream, and hamburgers. ⊠ *U.S. 93, east of Boulder City, Boulder City* ☎ *702/494–2517, 866/730–9097, 888/248–1259 Security, road, and Hoover Dam crossing information* ⊕ *www.usbr.gov/lc/hooverdam* ☎ *Powerplant Tour $15, Hoover Dam Tour $30, visitor center $10; garage parking $10 (free parking on Arizona-side surface lots).*

The Mike O'Callaghan–Pat Tillman bridge. The Hoover Dam now has sightseer competition from the spectacular bridge that was built to bypass it. The Mike O'Callaghan–Pat Tillman bridge (named for the popular Nevada governor and the Arizona football star who was killed in Afghanistan) is the western hemisphere's longest single-span concrete arch bridge. It runs 1,905 feet long, and towers nearly 900 feet above the river and 280 feet above Hoover Dam. You don't see much by driving over it—scarcely anything from a sedan—but walking it is quite a thrill. A pedestrian walkway is well separated from the driving lanes,

DID YOU KNOW?

Franklin D. Roosevelt dedicated Hoover Dam on September 30, 1935, and the date is still part of the celestial map found on the dam's terrazzo floor.

the access path to the bridge has informational signage, and ramps offer an alternative to the steps. There are restrooms in the parking lot (labeled "Memorial Bridge Plaza"), where it can be hard to find a parking space on weekends. (If you can't get a spot, drive a few yards past the parking lot entrance and turn left into the lot for a trailhead on the other side of the road.) Bring water and sunscreen for the walk, and be prepared for broiling summer temperatures; there is no shade. ■ TIP➔ Remember to take Exit 2 if you want to go to the dam instead of the bypass bridge, or you will have to drive across it and turn back to visit the dam. ⊠ *U.S. 93, Boulder City.*

SPORTS AND THE OUTDOORS

RAFTING

Black Canyon, just below Hoover Dam, is the place for river running near Las Vegas. Guided raft trips down the Colorado River are available year-round from the Hoover Dam to Willow Beach. It is the Southwest's only natural water trail and includes views of vertical canyon walls, bighorn sheep on the slopes, peregrine falcons, and feeder streams and waterfalls coming off the bluffs. Transportation to and from Las Vegas is available.

If you want to go paddling in Black Canyon on your own, you can start upriver at Willow Beach in Arizona, where paddlecraft are rented at the marina. The other option is to start at Hoover Dam by making arrangements with one of the registered outfitters (having permission is mandatory). They provide permits ($12) and the National Park Service entrance fee ($10) as well as launch and retrieval services (the road in and out is in a security zone for the dam). You can get a list of outfitters at ⊕ *www.nps.gov/lake/planyourvisit/black-canyon-water-trail.htm.*

FAMILY **Black Canyon/Willow Beach River Adventures.** If you're interested in seeing the canyon and Hoover Dam on large motor-assisted rafts, Black Canyon/Willow Beach River Adventures has group excursions launching from the base of the dam for both five-hour and 90-minute tours. The full-day excursion includes lunch; the shorter "postcard" tour lasts about 90 minutes but includes only 30 minutes on the raft. Round-trip Las Vegas transportation is available. All tours depart from Hoover Dam Lodge. ⊠ *Hoover Dam Lodge, 18000 U.S. Hwy. 93, Boulder City* ☎ *800/455–3490* ⊕ *www.blackcanyonadventures. com* 🎫 *From $33.*

Desert Adventures. For a more hands-on approach, try a guided kayak trip through Black Canyon with Desert Adventures. The daylong excursion, including a soak in hot springs, slot-canyon hike, and lunch, requires an additional $22 permit fee. They'll pick you up at the Hoover Dam Lodge (formerly the Hacienda Hotel and Casino) or from your hotel on the Strip. ⊠ *Hoover Dam Lodge, 18000 U.S. Hwy. 93, Boulder City* ☎ *702/293–5026* ⊕ *www.kayaklasvegas.com* 🎫 *From $199.*

LAKE MEAD

About 4 miles from Hoover Dam.

Lake Mead is actually the Colorado River backed up behind Hoover Dam, making it the nation's largest man-made reservoir: it covers 225 square miles, is 110 miles long, and has an irregular shoreline that extends for 550 miles.

GETTING HERE AND AROUND

From Hoover Dam, travel west on U.S. 93 to the intersection with Lakeshore Drive to reach Alan Bible Visitor Center, which reopened in 2013 with a new welcome film and exhibits after two years and nearly $3 million in renovations. It's open every day, 9 to 4:30. Call ☎ 702/293–8990 for more information.

VISITOR INFORMATION

Alan Bible Visitor Center. The main information center for Lake Mead National Recreation Area had a recent face-lift complete with a new high-def film about the park. Also here are a bookstore, nature exhibits, and a cactus garden. It's at the Lake Mead turnoff from U.S. 93, before you get to the pay booth for park entry. A second, smaller visitor center at the park headquarters is in downtown Boulder City at 601 Nevada Way. ✉ *10 Lakeshore Dr., Boulder City* ☎ *702/293–8990* ⊕ *www.nps.gov/lake.*

EXPLORING

Lake Mead. People come to Lake Mead primarily for boating and fishing. There are marinas that offer watercraft rentals, restaurants, and paddle-wheeler cruises. A few cultivated areas allow for swimming but they are not designated swim beaches, so no lifeguards are on duty. In fact, the National Park Service highly recommends wearing life jackets, as high winds come up fast on the lake making for potentially dangerous swimming conditions. The closest swimming area to Las Vegas is rocky Boulder Beach, about 2 miles past the visitor center. ⚠ A fishing license is required within the states of Nevada and Arizona, so if you plan on fishing Lake Mead, get one. ✉ *Alan Bible Visitor Center, 10 Lakeshore Dr., Boulder City* ☎ *702/293–8990* ⊕ *www.nps.gov/lake* 🖀*$20 per vehicle, good for 7 days; lake-use fee $16 for 1st vessel, good for 7 days. Annual pass is $40 per vehicle or $50 per vessel.*

SPORTS AND THE OUTDOORS

BOATING

Las Vegas Boat Harbor and Lake Mead Marina. These side-by-side marinas are just north of the Alan Bible Visitor Center near Boulder City and jointly operated, with combined slips of nearly 1,500. In addition to boater amenities, both have marina stores and casual restaurants. A variety of watercraft and boats can be rented by the day or hour, and the marinas provide the closest services to nearby Boulder Beach, a popular public swimming beach. ✉ *490 Horsepower Cove Rd., Boulder City* ☎ *702/451–2901* ⊕ *www.boatinglakemead.com.*

10

LAKE CRUISES

Lake Mead Cruises. At Lake Mead Cruises you can board the 300-passenger *Desert Princess,* an authentic Mississippi-style paddle wheeler that plies a portion of the lake, offering impressive views of Hoover Dam, the bypass bridge, and ancient rock formations such as an extinct volcano called Fortification Hill. Brunch and dinner cruises are available seasonally, while 90-minute sightseeing cruises are offered year-round. Advance tickets are offered online. ⊠ *490 Horsepower Cove Rd., Boulder City* ✛ *Just north of Alan Bible Visitor Center, look for signs to Hemenway Harbor* ☎ *866/292–9191* ⊕ *www.lakemeadcruises. com* ⊐ *From $26.*

VALLEY OF FIRE

50 miles northeast of Las Vegas.

The 56,000-acre Valley of Fire State Park was dedicated in 1935 as Nevada's first state park. Valley of Fire takes its name from distinctive coloration of its rocky landscape, which ranges from lavender to tangerine to bright red, giving the vistas along the park road an otherworldly appearance.

GETTING HERE AND AROUND

From Las Vegas, take Interstate 15 north about 35 miles to Exit 75–Route 169 and continue 15 miles. If you're coming from the northern Overton Arm of Lake Mead, look for the sign announcing the Valley of Fire and head west onto Valley of Fire Highway for a few miles to the park's visitor center. ■ **TIP→** It may also be possible to see some of the remnants of St. Thomas, a settlement within the park that was washed away by the Colorado River after completion of the Hoover Dam, as drought conditions have lowered lake levels dramatically. It's located off unpaved St. Thomas Road north of Overton Beach.

EXPLORING

FAMILY **Valley of Fire State Park.** Valley of Fire's jumbled rock formations are
Fodor'sChoice remnants of hardened sand dunes more than 150 million years old. You
★ find petrified trees and one of the park's most photographed features—Elephant Rock—just steps off the main road. Mysterious petroglyphs (carvings etched into the rocks) are believed to be the work of the Basketmaker and early Puebloan people, with their occupation in the area estimated from 300 BC to AD 1150. The easy, essential trail is Mouse's Tank, named for an outlaw who hid out here and managed to find water; so will you in cooler months (but not for drinking). It's a short walk with views of petroglyphs and shaded by steep canyon walls. Sci-fi fans also might recognize Fire Canyon as the alien planet in *Starship Troopers* and several other movies.

The **Valley of Fire Visitor Center** was remodeled in 2011 and has displays on the park's history, ecology, archaeology, and recreation, as well as slide shows and films, and information about the two campgrounds (72 campsites, 20 of them with power and water for RVs) within the park. Campsites at Atlatl Rock and Arch Rock Campgrounds are available on a first-come, first-served basis. The park is open year-round; the best times to visit, especially during the heat of summer, are sunrise and sunset, when the light is truly spectacular. ✉ *29450 Valley of Fire Rd., Overton* ⊹ *I–15 N to Exit 75. Merge onto Valley of Fire Hwy. Entrance to park is about 14 miles* ☎ *702/397–2088* ⊕ *www.valley-of-fire.com* ✍ *$10 per vehicle ($2 discount for Nevada residents).*

OFF THE BEATEN PATH

Lost City Museum. The Moapa Valley has one of the finest collections of ancestral Puebloan artifacts in the American Southwest. Lost City, officially known as Pueblo Grande de Nevada, was a major outpost of the ancient culture. The museum's artifacts include baskets, weapons, a restored Basketmaker pit house, reconstructed pueblo houses, and black-and-white photographs of the excavation of Lost City in the 1920s and '30s. To get to the Lost City Museum from Valley of Fire, pass the park's east entrance and head north onto Northshore Drive, which becomes state route 169, toward Overton. ✉ *721 S. Moapa Valley Blvd., Overton* ☎ *702/397–2193* ✍ *$5.*

AREA 51

148 miles north of Las Vegas.

It's a long way to drive just to buy a T-shirt and take some quirky photos, but for those with Area 51 on their bucket list it can be worth it. It wasn't until 2013 that the CIA, following a Freedom of Information Act request, acknowledged the existence of the restricted Air Force installation, but conspiracy theories have been swirling around the desert facility for years. It's been rumored to contain everything from scientists replicating crashed alien spacecraft to those creating time travel. What we actually do know is the Air Force does, in fact, test top-secret aircraft and related technology here, resulting in many of the strange sights and sounds that have been reported for years. But it's all the mystery and secrecy, wrapped up in a desolate enigma in a locale that looks like the set of a 1950s sci-fi flick. And it's kept folks from around the world driving to the edge of the landmark (also known as Groom Lake and Dreamland) and its closest neighbor, the tiny hamlet of Rachel, Nevada, population about 100.

Keep in mind, it's illegal to get too close to the installation, launch drones in the area, or take photographs in the nearby vicinity. Fines are high, and military police have the authority to use deadly force if necessary. Locals can fill you in on the particulars, or simply heed the posted signs.

To get to Rachel, head north from Las Vegas on Interstate 15, then take U.S. 93 north for about 85 miles; you'll pass Alamo and Ash Springs, then go left onto Highway 318 and stay on it for less than a mile before veering left onto Highway 375, Nevada's officially designated "Extraterrestrial Highway." Drive about 40 miles to reach Rachel and the famous Little A'Le'Inn. More than a simple roadside diner, is the main destination for most visitors since places to stop and eat are few and far between. Keep in mind gas stations are also limited in this area, so fuel up before the trip or in Alamo, and look out for cows grazing in the area as they tend to cross the E.T. Highway. The drive from Las Vegas can take 2½ hours.

10

TOURS

Adventure Photo Tours. This tour company provides daylong Area 51 photo tours in luxury SUVs, stopping in Rachel and taking in the Air Force installation's guarded perimeter as well as highlights along the way, including ancient petroglyphs and dry lakes associated with UFO lore. The tour includes lunch and pickup at your Las Vegas hotel. It operates regularly on Monday and Wednesday (or other days if you have a group of four or more). ☎ 702/889–8687 ⊕ *www.vegassightseeing.com* ✉ *From $205.*

EXPLORING

Pahranagat National Wildlife Refuge. If you're looking for a bookend to your trip to Area 51 that, well, is just more down-to-earth, drop by these spring-fed wetlands, which serve as a stopover for thousands of birds migrating along the Pacific Flyway. The 5,380-acre Pahranagat National Wildlife Refuge is a chain of lakes, marshes, and meadows that provides a convenient stop on the Pacific Flyway for ducks, herons, egrets, eagles, and other species. The Upper Lake is the most accessible, with campsites, picnic tables, and observation points. For a bird list, stop at the refuge headquarters located 4 miles south of Alamo, at milepost 32 off U.S. 93. The best times to see more than 230 species of birds are early morning and late evening during the spring and fall migrations. ☎ 775/725–3417 ⊕ *www.fws.gov/refuge/pahranagat* ✉ *Free.*

WHERE TO EAT

$ ✕ **Little A'Le'Inn.** Even if you aren't hungry for a tasty "alien burger," a
AMERICAN pilgrimage to this restaurant/bar is practically a requirement to earn those Area 51 bragging rights. While the food is typical diner fare such as chili and sandwiches, it's very reasonably priced, and the owners put some tender-loving care into keeping their iconic landmark shipshape. **Known for:** reasonably priced diner fare with pretty good burgers; colorful owners; alien-inspired gifts. $ *Average main: $7* ✉ *9631 Old Mill St., Alamo* ✛ *Hwy. 375, about 45 miles northwest of Ash Springs* ☎ 775/729–2515 ⊕ *www.littlealeinn.com.*

GRAND CANYON

If you take only one side trip from Las Vegas, make it to the Grand Canyon. The Colorado River has carved through colorful and often contorted layers of rock, in some places more than 1 mile down, to expose a geologic profile spanning a time between 1.7 billion and 2.5 billion years ago—one-third of the planet's life. There's nothing like standing on the rim and looking down and across at layers of distance, color, and shifting light. Add the music of a canyon wren's merry, descending call echoing off the cliffs and spring water tinkling from the rocks along a trail, and you may sink into a reverie as deep and beautiful as the canyon.

GETTING HERE AND AROUND

There are two main access points to the canyon: the **South Rim** and the **North Rim,** both within the national park and both about the same distance from Las Vegas by road. The canyon is doable on a very long day-trip, but because of the amount of driving and traffic you might encounter, an overnight is more desirable if you are going on your own. The hordes of visitors converge mostly on the South Rim in summer, for good reason. Grand Canyon Village and the gateway community of Tusayan are here, with most of the lodging and camping, restaurants and stores, and museums in the park, along with the airport and the most popular rim roads, scenic overlooks, and trailheads into the canyon. The South Rim can be accessed either from the main entrance near Tusayan or by the East entrance near the Desert View Watchtower.

Directions to the South Rim: The South Rim is 278 miles southeast of Las Vegas (about a four-hour drive from Hoover Dam). Take Highway 93 south to Interstate 40 heading east. At Highway 64 drive 60 miles north to the park's southern entrance. ■TIP➔ In summer, roads are congested, so park your car and take the free shuttle to visit popular sights along the South Rim. Traffic's lighter and parking is easier October through April.

The North Rim, by contrast, stands 1,000 feet higher than the South Rim and has a more alpine climate, with twice as much annual precipitation. Here, in the deep forests of the Kaibab Plateau, the crowds are thinner (only 10% of the park's total visitors), the facilities fewer, and the views, arguably, even more spectacular.

Directions to the North Rim: The North Rim is 275 miles northeast of Vegas. Drive 128 miles north on Interstate 15 to Route 9 and then travel east 10 miles to Route 59/Route 389. Continue east 65 miles to U.S. 89A and head 30 miles east to Route 67 which dead-ends at the North Rim entrance.

If you don't have time for the 4½- to 6-hour drive to the North or South Rim, the **West Rim**—about 2½ hours from Las Vegas—is a more manageable excursion, especially now that the once-pitted road up to the entrance is entirely paved. As an alternative to driving, you can look into a helicopter, Hummer, or coach tour. Many tours will transport you to and from your Vegas hotel; park fees and lunch are usually part of the package. At the West Rim, which isn't part of the Grand Canyon National Park and is run by the Hualapai tribe, you can view the canyon from the horseshoe-shaped Skywalk.

Directions to the West Rim: Grand Canyon West is 121 miles southeast of Las Vegas. Travel 72 miles south on Highway 93 to Pierce Ferry Road (about 30 minutes from Hoover Dam) and travel north 28 miles to Diamond Bar Road. Drive 21 miles on Diamond Bar Road to the entrance at Grand Canyon West Airport, where a shuttle takes visitors to the West Rim.

10

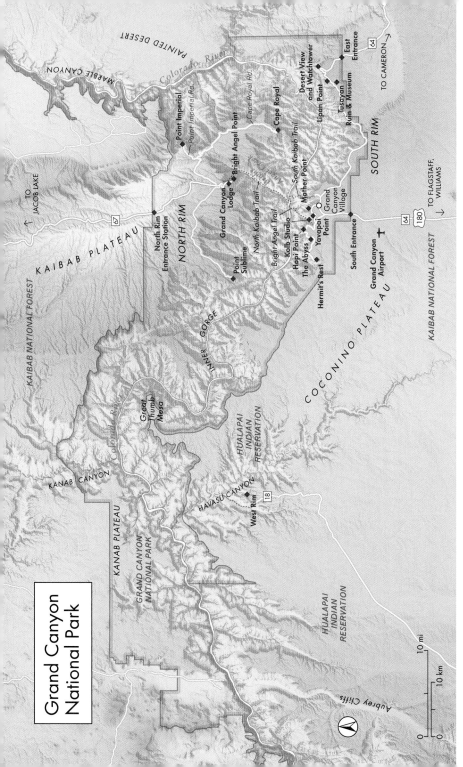

Grand Canyon
National Park

WHEN TO GO TO THE GRAND CANYON

Time of Year	Advantages	Disadvantages
Mar.–May	Cool temperatures and more elbow room than in summer.	Weather is unpredictable. Be prepared for chilly climate changes.
June–Sept.	Highs in the low to mid-80s but mostly pleasant.	High humidity from frequent afternoon thunderstorms.
Oct.–Feb.	You'll experience the South Rim in a different light, literally and figuratively.	Winter conditions can be extreme. The road to the North Rim is closed from mid-October (or the first heavy winter snow) until mid-May.

WHERE TO GO: SOUTH RIM VS. NORTH RIM

Grand Canyon National Park is located in the northeastern corner of Arizona. The Grand Canyon and the Colorado River physically separate the park's two distinct halves into the North Rim and the South Rim. The average distance from the North Rim to the South Rim is 10 miles, but to travel from rim to rim by car requires a journey of 200 miles. The action's in the South Rim: Grand Canyon Village has year-round lodging, dining, shopping, museums, and shuttle stops. Higher in elevation by 1,000 feet, the North Rim offers more solitude and higher, grander views, but it's only open part of the year.

	SOUTH RIM	NORTH RIM
Distance from Vegas	278 mi.	275 mi.
Distance from Phoenix	231 mi.	351 mi.
The experience	Fast action and a hurried pace, with plenty to see and do.	A leisurely look at the remote rim of this famous national park.
Why?	More amenities than the North Rim.	Geared for outdoor activities
Elevation	7,000 feet	8,000 feet
Timing	It's best to spend at least one night here. One day is good to see the main sites; two days are best for a leisurely exploration.	With the added driving distance, most people spend two days exploring this far-away corner.
Rim drives	Self-guided Desert View Drive and Hermit Road, accessible by shuttle only from March through November.	Self-guided driving tours to developed overlooks on Cape Royal Road and Point Imperial Road.
Trails	9-mile rim hike from Mather Point to Hermits Rest. 8 trails including the popular inner canyon South Kaibab and Bright Angel Trails.	10 trails including the popular inner canyon North Kaibab Trail; an extensive network of rim hikes.
Overlooks	18 developed viewpoints	7 developed viewpoints, one accessible by foot from the Grand Canyon Lodge. Folks with 4WD can take the 17-mi. dirt route to Point Sublime.
Other activities	Train travel; tours; mule and horse rides; camping; fine dining; guided hikes; ranger programs; shopping.	Biking, horseback riding, picnicking, camping, and ranger programs.

10

SAFETY AND PRECAUTIONS

To report a security problem, contact the Park Police stationed at all visitor centers. There are no pharmacies at the North or South Rim. Prescriptions can be delivered daily to the South Rim Clinic from Flagstaff. A health center is staffed by physicians from 8 am to 6 pm, seven days a week (reduced hours in winter). Emergency medical services are available 24 hours a day.

Contacts Emergency services. ☎ *911, 9–911 in park lodgings.* **North Country HealthCare Grand Canyon Clinic.** ☎ *928/638–2551.* **Park Police.** ☎ *928/638–7805.*

ADMISSION FEES AND PERMITS

A fee of $30 per vehicle or $15 per person for pedestrians and cyclists is good for one week's access at both rims.

The $60 Grand Canyon Pass gives unlimited access to the park for 12 months. The annual $80 America the Beautiful **National Parks and Recreational Land Pass** (☎ *888/275–8747* ⊕ *store.usgs.gov/pass*) provides unlimited access to all national parks and federal recreation areas for 12 months.

No permits are needed for day hikers, but **backcountry permits** (☎ *928/638–7875* ⊕ *www.nps.gov/grca* ✉ *$10, plus $8 per person per night*) are necessary for overnight hikers. Permits are limited, so make your reservation as far in advance as possible—they're taken up to four months ahead of arrival. **Camping** in the park is restricted to designated campgrounds (☎ *877/444–6777* ⊕ *www.recreation.gov*).

TOURS

You can take organized bus and air tours from Las Vegas to the Grand Canyon. Once you are in the park, transportation-services desks are maintained at El Tovar, Bright Angel, Maswik Lodge, and Yavapai Lodge (closed in winter) in Grand Canyon Village. The desks provide information and can handle bookings for sightseeing tours, taxi and shuttle services, and mule and horseback rides. On the North Rim, Grand Canyon Lodge has general information about local services.

AIR AND BUS TOURS

Ground tours to the Grand Canyon can be had from the Grand Canyon Tour Company, but if you're short on time (and can check your fear of heights at the bell desk), consider winging your way there in a small plane or helicopter. A host of air-tour companies will give you a bird's-eye view of the Strip, Hoover Dam, and Lake Mead on the way to the Grand Canyon rim and even down to the Colorado River bed itself on tours as brief as two hours and as inexpensive as $200 per person. Helicopter tours are usually more expensive than those in a small fixed-wing plane. All possible permutations of flight plans and amenities are available, from lunch to river rafting to overnight accommodations. Most tours include pickup and drop-off service from your hotel (sorry, Hotshot, you get picked up in a van or limo, not by a chopper). Weekday tours actually fill up faster than weekends; it can't hurt to book a few days in advance. The scenery is spectacular, but the ride can be bumpy and cold, even in summertime.

Grand Canyon Helicopters. If you are looking for an aerial day tour to the Grand Canyon, this company can provide you with a trip to either the South, North, or West Rim, by helicopter. You can also book overnight lodging through the company to extend your trip. Air tours leave from the company's terminal at McCarren Airport. ⊠ *McCarren International Airport, 275 E. Tropicana Ave., Las Vegas* ☎ *702/835–8477, 855/326–9617* ⊕ *www.grandcanyonhelicopter.com.*

Grand Canyon Tour Company. The largest company in Las Vegas offering day-trip bus tours to the Grand Canyon, this company offers several different alternatives, many of which are day-trips. But you can also book lodging at the Grand Canyon if you want to do an overnight. The company picks up at most major Las Vegas hotels. ☎ *702/655–6060, 800/222–6966* ⊕ *www.grandcanyontourcompany.com.*

Maverick Helicopter Tours. Travelers with more money than time will want to arrange an air tour with Maverick. The cheapest options take you over the canyon and back to Las Vegas. If you pay more, you'll get to land and do a tour in the canyon itself, either at the West or South Rim. ⊠ *Henderson Executive Airport, 1620 Jet Stream Dr., Henderson* ☎ *702/261–0007, 888/261–4414* ⊕ *www.maverickhelicopter.com.*

Papillon. Offering a bird's-eye view of either the West or North Rim, these aerial tours travel by either plane or helicopter. Helicopter tours leave from Las Vegas while airplane tours leave from Boulder City. The company offers pickup at all major hotels in Las Vegas. Papillon also offers bus tours of the canyon to the West Rim. ☎ *702/736–7243, 888/635–7272* ⊕ *www.papillon.com.*

Scenic Airlines. Flying out of Boulder City, Scenic offers either flyover tours of the canyon by airplane or tours that include a land component. Or you can simply take a bus tour to the South or West Rim. The company offers pickup and drop-off service from all major Las Vegas hotels. ☎ *702/638–3300, 800/634–6801* ⊕ *www.scenic.com.*

Sundance Helicopters. Take a luxury tour of the Grand Canyon by helicopter or bus. More expensive options drop you off at the bottom of the West Rim for a champagne picnic. Hotel pickups and drop-offs are made in a stretch limousine. ☎ *702/736–0606, 800/653–1881* ⊕ *www.sundancehelicopters.com.*

VISITOR INFORMATION

PARK CONTACT INFORMATION

Grand Canyon National Park. Before you go into the park, get the complimentary *Trip Planner,* updated regularly, from the Grand Canyon National Park. At the main visitor center, pick up a copy of the *Guide,* a weekly listing of ranger talks and other park activities. ☎ *928/638–7888* ⊕ *www.nps.gov/grca.*

VISITOR CENTERS

SOUTH RIM

Desert View Information Center. Near the watchtower, at Desert View Point, this nonprofit Grand Canyon Association store and information center has a nice selection of books, park pamphlets, gifts, and educational materials. It's also a handy place to pick up maps and info if you enter the park at the Eastern entrance. All sales from the Association stores go to support the park programs. ✉ *Eastern entrance, Grand Canyon National Park* ☎ *800/858–2808, 928/638–7888.*

Grand Canyon Verkamp's Visitor Center. This small visitor center is named for the Verkamp family, who operated a curios shop on the South Rim for more than a hundred years. The building serves as an official visitor center, ranger station (get your Junior Ranger badges here), bookstore, and museum, with compelling exhibits on the Verkamps and other pioneers in this region. ✉ *Desert View Dr. across from El Tovar Hotel, Grand Canyon Village* ☎ *928/638–7146.*

Grand Canyon Visitor Center. The park's main orientation center provides pamphlets and resources to help plan your visit. It also holds engaging interpretive exhibits on the park. Rangers are on hand to answer questions and aid in planning canyon excursions. A daily schedule of ranger-led hikes and evening lectures is available, and a 20-minute film about the history, geology, and wildlife of the canyon plays every 30 minutes in the theater. The bicycle rental office, a small café, and a huge gift store are also in this complex. It's a short walk from here to Mather Point, or a short ride on the shuttle bus, which can take you into Grand Canyon Village. The visitor center is also accessible via a leisurely 1-mile walk on the Greenway Trail, a paved pathway that meanders through the forest. ✉ *East side of Grand Canyon Village, 450 Hwy. 64* ☎ *928/638–7888* ⊕ *www.explorethecanyon.com.*

Yavapai Geology Museum. Learn about the geology of the canyon at this Grand Canyon Association museum and bookstore. You can also catch the park shuttle bus or pick up information for the Rim Trail here. The views of the canyon and Phantom Ranch from inside this historic building are stupendous. ✉ *1 mile east of Market Plaza, Grand Canyon Village* ☎ *928/638–7888.*

NORTH RIM

North Rim Visitor Center. View exhibits, peruse the bookstore, and pick up useful maps and brochures at this visitor center. Interpretive programs are often scheduled in summer. If you're craving refreshments, it's a short walk from here to the Roughrider Saloon at the Grand Canyon Lodge. ✉ *Near the Grand Canyon Lodge at the North Rim, Grand Canyon National Park* ☎ *928/638–7864* ⊕ *www.nps.gov/grca.*

SOUTH RIM

278 miles east of Las Vegas.

Visitors to the canyon converge mostly on the South Rim, and mostly during the summer. Believe it or not, the average stay in the park is a mere four hours, so those doing the canyon as a day-trip from Las Vegas aren't really being short-changed by the short stay. The 25-mile rim road (Desert View Drive) allows easy access to several highlights, including canyon viewpoints, the Tusayan Ruin, and the Yavapai Geology Museum with its incredible glassed-in views from the observation room. Day trekkers can also take a short hike down into the canyon to experience it close-up.

GETTING HERE AND AROUND

By car, travel south on U.S. 93 to Kingman, Arizona; Interstate 40 east from Kingman to Williams; then Route 64 and U.S. 180 to the edge of the abyss. The South Rim is open to car traffic year-round, though access to some of the overlooks west of Grand Canyon Village is limited to shuttle buses from March through November. Roads leading to the South Rim near Grand Canyon Village and the parking areas along the rim are congested in summer as well. If you visit from October through February, you can usually experience only light to moderate traffic and have no problem with parking.

When driving off major highways in low-lying areas, watch for rain clouds. Flash floods from sudden summer rains can be deadly.

There are also free shuttle routes. Hermits Rest Route operates from March through November between Grand Canyon Village and Hermits Rest; it runs every 15 to 30 minutes from as early as 5 am to 30 minutes after sunset, depending on the season. The Village Route operates year-round in the village area from one hour before sunrise until as late as 9 pm depending on the time of year; it's the easiest access to the Grand Canyon Visitor Center. The Kaibab Rim Route travels from Grand Canyon Visitor Center to viewpoints such as Yaki Point and the Yavapai Geology Museum.

TOURS

Narrated motor-coach tours on the South Rim cover Hermits Rest Road and Desert View Drive. Other options include sunrise and sunset tours. Prices range from around $22 to $65 per person.

SCENIC DRIVES

Desert View Drive. This heavily traveled 25-mile stretch of road follows the rim from the east entrance to Grand Canyon Village. Starting from the less-congested entry near Desert View, road warriors can get their first glimpse of the canyon from the 70-foot-tall watchtower, the top of which provides the highest viewpoint on the South Rim. Six developed canyon viewpoints in addition to unmarked pullouts, the remains of an Ancestral Puebloan dwelling at the Tusayan Ruin and Museum, and the secluded and lovely Buggeln picnic area make for great stops along the South Rim. The Kaibab Rim Route shuttle bus travels a short section of Desert View Drive and takes 50 minutes to ride round-trip without getting off at any of the stops: Grand Canyon Visitor Center, South Kaibab Trailhead, Yaki Point, Pipe Creek Vista, Mather Point, and Yavapai Geology Museum. ⊠ *Grand Canyon National Park.*

Hermit Road. The Santa Fe Company built Hermit Road, formerly known as West Rim Drive, in 1912 as a scenic tour route. Nine overlooks dot this 7-mile stretch, each worth a visit. The road is filled with hairpin turns, so make sure you adhere to posted speed limits. A 1.5-mile Greenway trail offers easy access to cyclists looking to enjoy the original 1912 Hermit Rim Road. From March through November, Hermit Road is closed to private auto traffic because of congestion; during this period, a free shuttle bus carries visitors to all the overlooks. Riding the bus round-trip without getting off at any of the viewpoints takes 80 minutes; the return trip stops only at Hermits Rest, Pima, Mohave, and Powell points. ⊠ *Grand Canyon National Park.*

10

Continued on page 280

EXPLORING THE
COLORADO RIVER

High in Colorado's Rocky Mountains, the Colorado River begins as a catch-all for the snowmelt off the mountains west of the Continental Divide. By the time it reaches the Grand Canyon, the Colorado has been joined by multiple tributaries to become a raging river, red with silt as it sculpts spectacular landscapes. A network of dams can only partially tame this mighty river.

Snaking its way through five states, the Colorado River is an essential water source to the arid Southwest. Its natural course runs 1,450 miles from its origin in Colorado's La Poudre Pass Lake in Rocky Mountain National Park to its final destination in the Gulf of California, also called the Sea of Cortez. In northern Arizona, the Colorado River has been a powerful force in shaping the Grand Canyon, where it flows 4,000 to 6,000 feet below the rim. Beyond the canyon, the red river takes a lazy turn at the Arizona–Nevada border, where Hoover Dam creates the reservoir at Lake Mead. The Colorado continues at a relaxed pace along the Arizona–California border, providing energy and irrigation in Arizona, California, and Nevada before draining into northwestern Mexico.

A RIVER RUNS THROUGH IT

Stretching along 277 miles of the Colorado River is one of the seven natural wonders of the world: the Grand Canyon ranges in width from 4 to 18 miles, while the walls around it soar up to a mile high. Nearly 2 billion years of geologic history and majesty are revealed in exposed tiers of rock cut deep in the Colorado Plateau. What caused this incredible marvel of nature? Erosion by water coupled with driving wind are most likely the major culprits: under the sculpting power of wind and water, the shale layers eroded into slopes and the harder sandstone and limestone layers created terraced cliffs. Other forces that may have helped shape the canyon include ice, volcanic activity, continental drift, and earthquakes.

WHO LIVES HERE
Native tribes have lived in the canyon for thousands of years and continue to do so, looking to the river for subsistence. The plateau-dwelling Hualapai ("people of the tall pines") live on a million acres along 108 miles of the Colorado River in the West Rim. The Havasupai ("people of the blue green water") live deep within the walls of the 12-mile-long Havasu Canyon—a major side canyon connected to the Grand Canyon.

ENVIRONMENTAL CONCERNS
When the Grand Canyon achieved national park status in 1919, only 44,173 people made the grueling overland trip to see it—quite a contrast from today's nearly 5 million annual visitors. The tremendous increase in visitation has greatly impacted the fragile ecosystems, as has Lake Powell's Glen Canyon Dam, which was constructed in the 1950s and '60s. The dam has changed the composition of the Colorado River, replacing warm water rich in sediments (nature's way of nourishing the riverbed and banks) with mostly cool, much clearer water. This has introduced nonnative plants and animals that threaten the extinction of several native species. Air pollution has also affected visibility and the constant buzz of aerial tours has disturbed the natural solitude.

Above and right, views of Colorado River in the Grand Canyon from Toroweap.

DID YOU KNOW?

The North Rim's isolated Toroweap overlook (also called Tuweep) is perched 3,000 feet above the canyon floor: a height equal to stacking the Sears Tower and Empire State Building on top of each other.

HOOVER DAM

HISTORY

Hoover Dam was built in 1935 and was the world's largest hydroelectric power plant and tallest dam. It has since lost these titles; however, it's still the tallest solid concrete arch-gravity dam in the western hemisphere. The dam was completed two full years ahead of the six year construction schedule during the Great Depression.

ENVIRONMENT VERSUS ECONOMY

Prior to the dam's construction, the river, swollen by snowmelt, flooded the lowlands along the California-Arizona border each spring before drying up so drastically that water levels were too low to divert for crops each summer. The dam tamed the mighty river and today provides a stable, year-round water supply for 18 million people and more than one million acres of farmland. However, the lack of flooding and the controlled waters have negatively affected the backwater riparian habitats bringing several native fish species to the brink of extinction.

WHAT'S IN A NAME?

Even though it was located in the Black Canyon, the Hoover Dam was originally referred to as the Boulder Dam Project. The dam was officially named

ARTISTIC LEANINGS

Hoover Dam is an engineering marvel *and* a work of art. The design features the flowing lines of Modernism and Art Deco used by architect Gordon B. Kaufmann, designer of the Los Angeles Times Building. Artist Allen True, whose murals are prominent in the Colorado State Capitol, used Native American geometric designs in the terrazzo floors. But it's the pair of 30-foot bronze statues—*Winged Figures of the Republic*—that dominate the dam. The striking figures were sculpted by Oskar J.W. Hansen, who also created the five bas-reliefs on the elevator towers and the bronze plaque memorial for the 96 workers who died during the construction.

after Herbert Hoover in 1931. When Hoover lost his bid for re-election to Franklin D. Roosevelt in 1932, Harold Ickes took the office of the Secretary of the Interior and immediately issued notice to the Bureau of Reclamation to refer to the structure as Boulder Dam. In 1947, Hoover was vindicated when the naming controversy was settled with a resolution signed by President Harry S. Truman, restoring the name to Hoover Dam—much to the retired Ickes' indignation.

DID YOU KNOW?

Hoover Dam was the biggest man-made masonry marvel to surpass the Great Pyramid of Giza. The dam is made of more than 5 million barrels of cement and 4.5 million cubic yards of aggregate—enough to pave a standard 16-foot-wide highway stretching from San Francisco to New York City.

LAKE MEAD

HISTORY

Prior to the construction of Hoover Dam, the canyon lands and river valleys along this western section of the Colorado River were home to settlements including the towns of St. Thomas and Kaolin as well as hundreds of Native American archaeological sites. After the dam was built, these towns and sites became submerged by Lake Mead.

ENVIRONMENT

The lakes's cool waters are surrounded by the stark drama of the Mojave Desert—North America's hottest and driest. Nearly 96% of its water comes from snowmelt in Colorado, New Mexico, Utah, and Wyoming. This means the water level is at its highest in early spring and late fall. Levels drop in summer when agricultural demands are at their highest and the surrounding desert heats up.

TODAY

Construction of Hoover Dam created Lake Mead's 100-mile long reservoir, which was named after Bureau of Reclamation Commissioner Elwood Mead. This enormous reservoir became the United States' first National Recreation Area in 1964. Today, more than 9 million people visit this wonderland each year.

TOMORROW

Over the last few years, Lake Mead's water levels have dropped drastically. As one of the largest reservoirs in the world, it provides water to residents and farmers in Arizona, California, Nevada and northern Mexico. An extended drought and the increased demand for this critical resource have exceeded the amount of water deposited into the lake by the Colorado River. Already the dramatic drop in the lake's water level has led to the exposure of parts of St. Thomas, as well as a series of islands in Boulder Basin. A recent study by the Scripps Institution of Oceanography shows that if the current conditions continue, there's a 50% chance that Lake Mead may be dry by 2021.

Above, Lake Mead. Opposite, sailing on the lake.

SPORTS IN THE AREA

Water recreation dominates the placid waters of Lake Mead. The dramatic scenery of the surrounding Mojave Desert just adds to the year-round draw. Some of the favorite sporting activities at this far-reaching reservoir include:

■ fishing for striped bass and rainbow trout
■ relaxing on a houseboat
■ exploring hidden coves by canoe or kayak
■ swimming at Boulder Beach
■ hitting the wakes on water skis
■ scuba diving at North Boulder Beach's Dive Park

HISTORIC SITES

Kolb Studio. The Kolb brothers began building their photographic work-shop and residence in 1904, a time when no pipeline meant Emery Kolb descended 3,000 feet each day to get water to develop his prints; he operated the studio until he died in 1976 at age 95. Today the building provides a view of Indian Garden and houses a gallery with paintings, photography, and crafts exhibitions. There's also a small Grand Canyon Association store here. In the winter, a ranger-led tour of the studio illus-trates the Kolb brothers' role in the development of the Grand Canyon. Call ahead to sign up for the tour. ⊠ *Grand Canyon Village near Bright Angel Lodge, Grand Canyon National Park* ☎ *928/638–2771* ⊕ *www. nps.gov/grca* ☜ *Free.*

Tusayan Ruin and Museum. This museum offers a quick orientation to the prehistoric and modern Indian populations of the Grand Canyon and the Colorado Plateau, including an excavation of an 800-year-old Pueblo Indian site. Of special interest are split-twig figurines dating back 2,000 to 4,000 years ago and other artifacts left behind by ancient cultures. A ranger leads daily interpretive tours of the Ancestral Puebloan village. ⊠ *Grand Canyon National Park* ⊹ *About 20 miles east of Grand Canyon Village on E. Rim Dr.* ☎ *928/638–7888* ☜ *Free.*

SCENIC STOPS

The Abyss. At an elevation of 6,720 feet, the Abyss is one of the most awesome stops on Hermit Road, revealing a sheer drop of 3,000 feet to the Tonto Platform, a wide terrace of Tapeats sandstone about two-thirds of the way down the canyon. From the Abyss you'll also see several isolated sandstone columns, the largest of which is called the Monument. ⊠ *Grand Canyon National Park* ⊹ *About 5 miles west of Hermit Rd. Junction on Hermit Rd.*

Desert View and Watchtower. From the top of the 70-foot stone-and-mor-tar watchtower with its 360-degree views, even the muted hues of the distant Painted Desert to the east and the Vermilion Cliffs rising from a high plateau near the Utah border are visible. In the chasm below, angling to the north toward Marble Canyon, an imposing stretch of the Colorado River reveals itself. Up several flights of stairs, the watchtower houses a glass-enclosed observatory with powerful telescopes ⊠ *Grand Canyon National Park* ⊹ *Just north of the East Entrance Station on Desert View Dr.* ☎ *928/638–7888* ⊕ *www.nps.gov/grca* ☉ *Check web-site for tower closing hrs as they fluctuate due to season.*

Hermits Rest. This westernmost viewpoint and Hermit Trail, which descends from it, were named for "hermit" Louis Boucher, a 19th-cen-tury French-Canadian prospector who had a number of mining claims and a roughly built home down in the canyon. The trail served as the original mule ride down to Hermit Camp beginning in 1914. Views from here include Hermit Rapids and the towering cliffs of the Supai and Redwall formations. You can buy curios and snacks in the stone building at Hermits Rest. ⊠ *Grand Canyon National Park* ⊹ *About 8 miles west of Hermit Rd. Junction on Hermit Rd.*

FodorsChoice ★ **Hopi Point.** From this elevation of 7,071 feet, you can see a large section of the Colorado River; although it appears as a thin line, the river is nearly 350 feet wide. The overlook extends farther into the canyon than any other point on Hermit Road. The incredible unobstructed views make this a popular place to watch the sunrise and sunset.

Across the canyon to the north is Shiva Temple. In 1937, Harold Anthony of the American Museum of Natural History led an expedition to the rock formation in the belief that it supported life that had been cut off from the rest of the canyon. Imagine the expedition members' surprise when they found an empty Kodak film box on top of the temple—it had been left behind by Emery Kolb, who felt slighted for not having been invited to join Anthony's tour.

Directly below Hopi Point lies Dana Butte, named for a prominent 19th-century geologist. In 1919, an entrepreneur proposed connecting Hopi Point, Dana Butte, and the Tower of Set across the river with an aerial tramway, a technically feasible plan that fortunately has not been realized. ⊠ *Grand Canyon National Park* ⊕ *About 4 miles west of Hermit Rd. Junction on Hermit Rd.*

FodorsChoice ★ **Mather Point.** You'll likely get your first glimpse of the canyon from this viewpoint, one of the most impressive and accessible (next to the main visitor center plaza) on the South Rim. Named for the National Park Service's first director, Stephen Mather, this spot yields extraordinary views of the Grand Canyon, including deep into the inner gorge and numerous buttes: Wotans Throne, Brahma Temple, and Zoroaster Temple, among others. The Grand Canyon Lodge, on the North Rim, is almost directly north from Mather Point and only 10 miles away—yet you have to drive 215 miles to get from one spot to the other. ⊠ *Near Grand Canyon Visitor Center, Grand Canyon National Park* ☎ *928/638–7888* ⊕ *www.nps.gov/grca.*

FodorsChoice ★ **Yavapai Point.** This is one of the best locations on the South Rim to watch the sunset. Dominated by the Yavapai Geology Museum and Observation Station, this point displays panoramic views of the mighty gorge through a wall of windows. Exhibits at the museum include videos of the canyon floor and the Colorado River, a scaled diorama of the canyon with national park boundaries, fossils and rock fragments used to re-create the complex layers of the canyon walls, and a display on the natural forces used to carve the chasm. Dig even deeper into Grand Canyon geology with free daily ranger programs. Check ahead for special events, guided walks, and program schedules. There's also a bookstore. ⊠ *Grand Canyon Village* ⊕ *1 mile east of Market Plaza.*

10

HIKING

Remember that the canyon has significant elevation changes and, in summer, extreme temperature ranges, which can pose problems for people who aren't in good shape or who have heart or respiratory problems. ■TIP➔ **Carry plenty of water and energy foods.** The majority of each year's 400 search-and-rescue incidents result from hikers underestimating the size of the canyon, hiking beyond their abilities, or not packing sufficient food and water.

⚠ It's not advised to attempt a day hike from the rim to the river and back. Canyon rangers will try to talk you out of the idea. It's legal, but only very fit, athletic people with proven hiking skills should attempt it. Remember that when it's 80°F on the South Rim, the temperature may be 105°F on the canyon floor.

EASY

Fodor's Choice ★ **Rim Trail.** The South Rim's most popular walking path is the 12-mile (one-way) Rim Trail, which runs along the edge of the canyon from Pipe Creek Vista (the first overlook on Desert View Drive) to Hermits Rest. This walk, which is paved to Maricopa Point and for the last 1.5 miles to Hermits Rest, visits several of the South Rim's historic landmarks. Allow anywhere from 15 minutes to a full day, depending on how much of the trail you want to cover; the Rim Trail is an ideal day hike, as it varies only a few hundred feet in elevation from Mather Point (7,120 feet) to the trailhead at Hermits Rest (6,650 feet). The trail also can be accessed from several spots in Grand Canyon Village and from the major viewpoints along Hermit Road, which are serviced by shuttle buses during the busy summer months. On the Rim Trail, water is only available in the Grand Canyon Village area and at Hermits Rest. *Easy.* ⊠ *Grand Canyon National Park.*

NEED A BREAK

If you've been driving too long and want some exercise, along with great views of the canyon, it's an easy 1.25-mile-long hike from the Information Plaza to El Tovar Hotel. The Greenway path runs through a quiet wooded area for about half a mile, and then along the rim for another three-quarters of a mile.

MODERATE

Bright Angel Trail. This well-maintained trail is one of the most scenic hiking paths from the South Rim to the bottom of the canyon (9.6 miles each way). Rest houses are equipped with water at the 1.5- and 3-mile points from May through September, and at Indian Garden (4 miles) year-round. Water is also available at Bright Angel Campground, 9¼ miles below the trailhead. Plateau Point, on a spur trail about 1.5 miles below Indian Garden, is as far as you should attempt to go on a day hike; the round-trip will take six to nine hours.

Bright Angel Trail is the easiest of all the footpaths into the canyon, but because the climb out from the bottom is an ascent of 5,510 feet, the trip should be attempted only by those in good physical condition and should be avoided in midsummer due to extreme heat. The top of the trail can be icy in winter. Originally a bighorn sheep path and later used by the Havasupai, the trail was widened late in the 19th century for prospectors and is now used for both mule and foot traffic. Also note that mule trains have the right-of-way—and sometimes leave unpleasant surprises in your path. *Moderate.* ⊠ *Grand Canyon National Park* ⊹ *Trailhead: Kolb Studio, Hermit Rd.*

DIFFICULT

South Kaibab Trail. This trail starts near Yaki Point, 4 miles east of Grand Canyon Village, and is accessible via the free shuttle bus.

Because the route is so steep (and sometimes icy in winter)—descending from the trailhead at 7,260 feet down to 2,480 feet at the Colorado River—and has no water, many hikers take this trail down, then ascend via the less-demanding Bright Angel Trail. Allow four to six hours to reach the Colorado River on this 6.4-mile trek. At the river, the trail crosses a suspension bridge and runs on to Phantom Ranch. Along the trail there is no water and little shade. There are no campgrounds, though there are portable toilets at Cedar Ridge (6,320 feet), 1.5 miles from the trailhead. An emergency phone is available at the Tipoff, 4.6 miles down the trail (3 miles past Cedar Ridge). The trail corkscrews down through some spectacular geology. Look for (but don't remove) fossils in the limestone when taking water breaks. Even though an immense network of trails winds through the Grand Canyon, the popular corridor trails (Bright Angel and South Kaibab) are recommended for hikers new to the region. *Difficult.* ⊠ *Grand Canyon National Park* ✚ *Trailhead: Yaki Point Rd., off Desert View Dr.*

MULE RIDES

Mule rides provide an intimate glimpse into the canyon for those who have the time, but not the stamina, to see the canyon on foot. ■TIP➔ **Reservations are essential and are accepted up to 13 months in advance.**

These trips have been conducted since the early 1900s. A comforting fact as you ride the narrow trail: no one's ever been killed while riding a mule that fell off a cliff. (Nevertheless, the treks aren't for the faint of heart or people in questionable health.)

OUTFITTERS

Fodor's Choice ★ **Xanterra Parks & Resorts Mule Rides.** These trips delve into the canyon from the South Rim to Phantom Ranch, or east along the canyon's edge (the Plateau Point rides were discontinued in 2009). Riders must be at least 55 inches tall, weigh less than 200 pounds (for the Phantom Ranch ride), and understand English. Children under 15 must be accompanied by an adult. Riders must be in fairly good physical condition, and pregnant women are advised not to take these trips.

The three-hour ride along the rim costs $118. An overnight with a stay at Phantom Ranch at the bottom of the canyon is $515 ($901 for two riders). Two nights at Phantom Ranch, an option available from November through March, will set you back $732 ($1,206 for two). Meals are included. Reservations (by phone), especially during the busy summer months, are a must, but you can check at the Bright Angel Transportation Desk to see if there's last-minute availability. ☎ *888/297–2757* ⊕ *www.grandcanyonlodges.com* ⌂ *Reservations essential.*

WHERE TO EAT

$$$ STEAKHOUSE ✕**Arizona Room.** The canyon views from this casual Southwestern-style steak house are the best of any restaurant at the South Rim. The dinner menu leans toward steak-house dishes while lunch is primarily salads and sandwiches with a Southwestern twist. **Known for:** views of the Grand Canyon; Southwest fare; local craft beers. ⑤ *Average main: $24* ⊠ *Bright Angel Lodge, Desert View Dr., Grand Canyon Village* ☎ *928/638–2631* ⊕ *www.grandcanyonlodges.com* ⊗ *Closed Jan.; limited service in Feb.*

10

White-water rafting is just one of the many activities you can experience in the Grand Canyon.

$$$
SOUTHWESTERN
Fodor's Choice
★

✕ **El Tovar Dining Room.** Even at the edge of the Grand Canyon it's possible to find gourmet dining, and this cozy room of dark wood beams and stone is nestled in the historic El Tovar Lodge which dates to 1905. Classics such as duck, veal chops, and salmon are on the menu, which focuses on locally sourced and organic ingredients. **Known for:** historic setting; gourmet fare; local and organic ingredients. $ *Average main: $28* ✉ *El Tovar Hotel, Desert View Dr., Grand Canyon Village* ☎ *928/638–2631* ⊕ *www.grandcanyonlodges.com.*

$
AMERICAN

✕ **Yavapai Lodge Restaurant.** If you don't have time for full-service, the restaurant in Yavapai Lodge offers cafeteria-style dining for breakfast, lunch, and dinner. Offerings include hot and cold sandwiches, pizza, and entrées such as barbecue ribs and rotisserie chicken. **Known for:** quick bites; convenience; beer and wine. $ *Average main: $14* ✉ *Yavapai Lodge, Desert View Dr., Grand Canyon Village* ☎ *928/638–4001* ⊕ *www.visitgrandcanyon.com.*

NORTH RIM

276 miles northeast of Las Vegas.

The North Rim stands 1,000 feet higher than the South Rim and has a more alpine climate, with twice as much annual precipitation. Here, in the deep forests of the Kaibab Plateau, the crowds are thinner, the facilities fewer, and the views even more spectacular. Because of snow, the North Rim is off-limits in winter. The park buildings are closed mid-October through mid-May. The road closes when the snow makes it impassable— usually by the end of November. Driving to the South Rim makes more sense if you are just going to the Grand Canyon for the day. Despite the

TOP PICNIC SPOTS

Bring your picnic basket and enjoy dining alfresco surrounded by some of the most beautiful backdrops in the country. Be sure to bring water, as it's unavailable at many of these spots, as are restrooms.

Buggeln, 15 miles east of Grand Canyon Village on Desert View Drive, has some secluded, shady spots. **Cape Royal,** 23 miles south of the North Rim Visitor Center, is the most popular designated picnic area on the North Rim because of its panoramic views. **Grandview Point** has, as the name implies, grand views; it is 12 miles east of the Village on Desert View Drive. **Point Imperial,** 11 miles northeast of the North Rim Visitor Center, has shade and some privacy.

fact that the mileage is similar to both North and South Rims from Las Vegas, the travel time to the North Rim is significantly more. If you head to the more remote North Rim it will take at least five hours one-way, and bus tours are lengthy. There is also more to see in a limited amount of time at the South Rim. If it's possible—and if your heart is set on the more secluded North Rim—look into an overnight stay, but remember a room at Grand Canyon Lodge means booking months in advance.

Lodgings are available but limited; the North Rim offers only one historic lodge and restaurant, and a single campground. The canyon's highest, most dramatic rim views can be enjoyed on two wheels (via primitive dirt access roads) and on four legs (courtesy of a trusty mule).

GETTING HERE AND AROUND

To get to the North Rim by car, take Interstate 15 east to Hurricane, Utah; Routes 59 and 389 to Fredonia; and U.S. 89 and Route 67 to the North Rim. Since it's so high in elevation (at 8,000 feet), the remote North Rim is closed to automobiles after the first heavy snowfall of the season (usually in late October or early November) through mid-May. All North Rim facilities close between October 15 and May 15. AZ 67 south of Jacob Lake is closed by the first heavy snowfall in November or December and remains closed until early to mid-May.

When driving off major highways in low-lying areas, watch for rain clouds. Flash floods from sudden summer rains can be deadly.

HISTORIC SITES

Grand Canyon Lodge. Built in 1937 by the Union Pacific Railroad (replacing the original 1928 building, which burned in a fire), this massive stone structure is listed on the National Register of Historic Places. Its huge sunroom has hardwood floors, high-beam ceilings, and a marvelous view of the canyon through plate-glass windows. On warm days, visitors sit in the sun and drink in the surrounding beauty on an outdoor viewing deck, where National Park Service employees deliver free lectures on geology and history. The dining room serves breakfast, lunch, and dinner; the Roughrider Saloon is a bar by night and a coffee shop in the morning. ⊠ *Grand Canyon National Park* ⊕ *Off Hwy. 67 near Bright Angel Point* ☎ *928/638–2611 May.–Oct., 928/645–6865 Nov.–Apr.* ⊕ *www.grandcanyonforever.com.*

SCENIC DRIVE

Fodor's Choice **Highway 67.** Open mid-May to roughly mid-November (or the first big
★ snowfall), this two-lane paved road climbs 1,400 feet in elevation as
it passes through the Kaibab National Forest. Also called the "North
Rim Parkway," this scenic route crosses the limestone-capped Kaibab
Plateau—passing broad meadows, sun-dappled forests, and small lakes
and springs—before abruptly falling away at the abyss of the Grand
Canyon. Wildlife abounds in the thick ponderosa pine forests and lush
mountain meadows. It's common to see deer, turkeys, and coyotes as
you drive through such a remote region. Point Imperial and Cape Royal
branch off this scenic drive, which runs from Jacob Lake to Bright Angel
Point. ⊠ *Hwy. 67, Grand Canyon National Park.*

SCENIC STOPS

Fodor's Choice **Bright Angel Point.** This trail, which leads to one of the most awe-inspir-
★ ing overlooks on either rim, starts on the grounds of the Grand Canyon
Lodge and runs along the crest of a point of rocks that juts into the
canyon for several hundred yards. The walk is only 0.5 mile round-trip,
but it's an exciting trek accented by sheer drops on each side of the trail.
In a few spots where the route is extremely narrow, metal railings ensure
visitors' safety. The temptation to clamber out on precarious perches to
have your picture taken should be resisted at all costs. ⊠ *North Rim Dr.,
Grand Canyon National Park* ✛ *Near Grand Canyon Lodge.*

Cape Royal. A popular sunset destination, Cape Royal showcases the canyon's jagged landscape; you'll also get a glimpse of the Colorado River,
framed by a natural stone arch called Angels Window. In autumn, the
aspens turn a beautiful gold, adding even more color to an already magnificent scene of the forested surroundings. The easy and rewarding 1-mile
round-trip hike along **Cliff Springs Trail** starts here; it takes you through a
forested ravine and terminates at Cliff Springs, where the forest opens to
another impressive view of the canyon walls. ⊠ *Cape Royal Scenic Dr., 23
miles southeast of Grand Canyon Lodge, Grand Canyon National Park.*

Point Imperial. At 8,803 feet, Point Imperial has the highest vista point at
either rim; it offers magnificent views of both the canyon and the distant country: the Vermilion Cliffs to the north, the 10,000-foot Navajo
Mountain to the northeast in Utah, the Painted Desert to the east, and
the Little Colorado River canyon to the southeast. Other prominent
points of interest include views of Mount Hayden, Saddle Mountain,
and Marble Canyon. ⊠ *Point Imperial Rd., 11 miles northeast of Grand
Canyon Lodge, Grand Canyon National Park.*

Fodor's Choice **Point Sublime.** You can camp within feet of the canyon's edge at this
★ awe-inspiring site. Sunrises and sunsets are spectacular. The winding
road, through gorgeous high country, is only 17 miles, but it will take
you at least two hours one-way. The road is intended only for vehicles
with high road clearance (pickups and four-wheel-drive vehicles). It
is also necessary to be properly equipped for wilderness road travel.
Check with a park ranger or at the information desk at Grand Canyon
Lodge before taking this journey. You may camp here only with a permit
from the Backcountry Information Center. ⊠ *North Rim Dr., about 20
miles west of North Rim Visitor Center, Grand Canyon National Park.*

HIKING
EASY

FAMILY **Transept Trail.** This 3-mile-round-trip, 1½-hour trail begins near the Grand Canyon Lodge at 8,255 feet. Well maintained and well marked, it has little elevation change, sticking near the rim before reaching a dramatic view of a large stream through Bright Angel Canyon. It leads to Transept Canyon, which geologist Clarence Dutton named in 1882, declaring it "far grander than Yosemite." Check the posted schedule to find a ranger talk along this trail; it's also a great place to view fall foliage. Flash floods can occur any time of the year, especially June through September when thunderstorms develop rapidly. *Easy.* ⊠ *Grand Canyon National Park* ⊹ *Trailhead near Grand Canyon Lodge east patio.*

MULE RIDES

FAMILY **Canyon Trail Rides.** This company leads mule rides on the easier trails of the North Rim. Options include one- to three-hour rides along the rim or three-hour rides down into the canyon (minimum age 7 for one-hour rides, 10 for three-hour rides) runs $45. Weight limits are 200 pounds for canyon rides and 220 pounds for the rim rides. Available daily from May 15 to October 15, these excursions are popular, so make reservations in advance. ☎ *435/679–8665* ⊕ *www.canyonrides. com* ✉ *From $45.*

WHERE TO EAT

$ ╳ **Deli in the Pines.** Dining choices are limited on the North Rim, but
AMERICAN this is your best bet for a meal on a budget or grabbing a premade sandwich on the go. Selections also include pizza, salads, custom-made sandwiches, and soft-serve ice cream. **Known for:** convenient location; sandwiches to take on the trail; outdoor seating. ⑤ *Average main: $6* ⊠ *Grand Canyon Lodge, Bright Angel Point, North Rim* ☎ *928/638–2611* ⊕ *www.grandcanyonforever.com* ☻ *Closed mid-Oct.–mid-May.*

$$ ╳ **Grand Canyon Lodge Dining Room.** The high wood-beam ceilings, stone
SOUTHWESTERN walls, and spectacular views in this spacious, historic room are perhaps
Fodor'sChoice the biggest draw for the lodge's main restaurant. Dinner includes South-
★ western steak-house fare that would make any cowboy feel at home, including selections such as bison and elk. **Known for:** incredible views; charming, historic room; some unique steak-house choices. ⑤ *Average main: $22* ⊠ *Grand Canyon Lodge, Bright Angel Point, North Rim* ☎ *928/638–2611* ⊕ *www.grandcanyonforever.com* ☻ *Closed mid-Oct.–mid-May.*

WHERE TO STAY

$ ⌂ **Grand Canyon Lodge.** This historic property, constructed mainly
HOTEL in the 1920s and '30s, is the premier lodging facility in the North
Fodor'sChoice Rim area. **Pros:** steps away from gorgeous North Rim views; close
★ to several easy hiking trails; historic lodge building a national landmark. **Cons:** fills up fast; limited amenities; most rooms in cabins that are far from main lodge building. ⑤ *Rooms from: $134* ⊠ *Hwy. 67, North Rim* ☎ *877/386–4383 reservations, 928/638–2611 May–Oct., 928/645–6865 Nov.–Apr.* ⊕ *www.grandcanyonforever.com* ☻ *Closed mid-Oct.–mid-May* ➾ *40 rooms, 178 cabins* ¦◯¦ *No meals.*

10

If you're driving to the Grand Canyon from Las Vegas, a detour in Kingman will lead you to Route 66—the longest remaining uninterrupted stretch of the "Main Street of America."

DEATH VALLEY

The desert is no Disneyland. With its scorching summer heat and vast, sparsely populated tracts of land, it's not often at the top of the list when most people plan their California vacations. But the natural riches of Death Valley—the largest national park outside Alaska—are overwhelming: rolling waves of sand dunes, black cinder cones thrusting up hundreds of feet from a blistered desert floor, riotous sheets of wildflowers, bizarrely shaped Joshua trees basking in the orange glow of a sunset, tiny pupfish that enthrall youngsters, and a silence that's both dramatic and startling.

WHEN TO GO

Most of the park's 1 million annual visitors come between late fall and early spring, taking advantage of moderate temperatures and the lack of rainfall. If you visit in summer, believe everything you've ever heard about desert heat—it can be brutal, with temperatures often topping 120°F (a record 134°F was set in 1913). The dry air wicks moisture from the body without causing a sweat, so drink plenty of water. Bring sunglasses, a hat, and sufficient clothing to block the sun's rays and the wind. Flash floods are fairly common; sections of roadway can be flooded or washed away, as they were after a major flood in 2015. The wettest month is February, when the park receives an average of 0.3 inches of rain.

GETTING HERE AND AROUND

It can take more than three hours to cross from one side of the park to another, so it's important to choose an entrance point that makes sense for what you want to see. From Las Vegas, enter from the north at Beatty, Nevada, or via the central entrance at Death Valley Junction.

Distances can be deceiving within the park: what seems close can be very far away. Much of the park can be viewed on regularly scheduled bus tours, but these often don't allow time for hikes to sites not seen from the road, such as Salt Creek, Golden Canyon, and Natural Bridge. The best option is to drive to a number of the sites, get out of the car, and walk.

When driving in Death Valley, reliable maps are important, as signage is often limited or, in a few places, nonexistent. Bring a phone but don't rely on cell coverage exclusively in every remote area, and pack plenty of food and water (3 gallons per person per day is recommended). Cars, especially in summer, should be prepared for the hot, dry weather, too. Some of the park's most spectacular canyons are only accessible via four-wheel-drive vehicles but if this is the way you want to travel, make sure the trip is well planned and use a backcountry map. Be aware of possible winter closures or driving restrictions because of snow. The National Park Service's website (⊕ *nps.gov/ deva*) stays up-to-date on road closures during the wet (and popular) months. ⚠ One of the park's signature landmarks, Scotty's Castle, and the 8-mile road connecting it to the park border may be closed until 2019 due to damage from a 2015 flood.

Driving Information California Highway Patrol. ☎ *800/427–7623 recorded info from CalTrans, 760/872–5900 live dispatcher at Bishop Communications Center* ⊕ *www.chp.ca.gov.*

VISITOR INFORMATION

PARK CONTACT INFORMATION

Death Valley National Park. ✉ *Death Valley National Park* ☎ *760/786– 3200* ⊕ *www.nps.gov/deva.*

PARK FEES AND PERMITS

The entrance fee is $25 per vehicle and $12 for those entering on foot or bike. The payment, valid for seven consecutive days, is collected at the park's ranger stations, self-serve fee stations, and the visitor center at Furnace Creek. Annual park passes, valid only at Death Valley, are $50.

PARK HOURS

Furnace Creek Visitor Center, open daily 8–5.

VISITOR CENTERS

The popular visitor center at Scotty's Castle is closed until at least 2019 as a result of a major flash flood in 2015 that damaged the structure and destroyed the access road.

Furnace Creek Visitor Center and Museum. The exhibits and artifacts here provide a broad overview of how Death Valley formed; you can pick up maps at the bookstore run by the Death Valley Natural History Association. This is also the place to sign up for ranger-led walks (available November through April) or check out a live presentation

"On my drive into Death Valley I was rewarded at Zabriskie Point with this amazing view." —photo by Rodney Ee, Fodors.com member

about the valley's cultural and natural history. The helpful center offers regular showings of a 20-minute film about the park and children can get their free Junior Ranger booklet here, packed with games and information about the park and its critters. ⊠ *Hwy. 190, Death Valley* ✛ *30 miles northwest of Death Valley Junction* ☎ *760/786–3200* ⊕ *www.nps.gov/deva.*

TOURS

Furnace Creek Visitor Center programs. This center has many programs, including ranger-led hikes that explore natural wonders such as Golden Canyon, nighttime star-gazing parties with telescopes, and evening ranger talks. There are also occasional programs at the Borax Museum at Furnace Creek Ranch and the historic Harmony Borax Works mining site, first established in 1883. Visit the website for a complete list. ⊠ *Furnace Creek Visitor Center, Rte. 190, 30 miles northwest of Death Valley Junction, Death Valley* ☎ *760/786–2331* ⊕ *www.nps.gov/deva/planyourvisit/tours.htm* ✉ *Free.*

Pink Jeep Tours Las Vegas. A 10-passenger luxury vehicle with oversized viewing windows will pick you up at most Strip hotels for visits to landmarks such as Dante's Peak, Furnace Creek, Devil's Golf Course, and Zabriskie Point. The tours run from about 7 am to 4 pm from September through May, are professionally narrated, and include lunch and bottled water. ⊠ *3629 W. Hacienda Ave., Las Vegas* ☎ *888/900–4480* ⊕ *pinkjeeptourslasvegas.com* ✉ *From $275.*

EXPLORING

Scotty's Castle, one of the most iconic sights in Death Valley is closed until further notice after a major flash flood in 2015 caused damage to both the sight and its access road.

SCENIC DRIVE

Artist's Drive. This 9-mile, one-way route skirts the foothills of the Black Mountains and provides intimate views of the changing landscape. Once inside the palette, the huge expanses of the valley are replaced by the small-scale natural beauty of pigments created by volcanic deposits or sedimentary layers. It's a quiet, lonely drive, and shouldn't be rushed. Reach Artist's Palette by heading south on Badwater Road from its intersection with Route 190. ⊠ *Death Valley National Park.*

SCENIC STOPS

Artist's Palette. So called for the contrasting colors of its volcanic deposits and sedimentary layers, this is one of the signature sights of Death Valley. Artist's Drive, the approach to the area, is one-way heading north off Badwater Road, so if you're visiting Badwater from Furnace Creek, come here on the way back. The drive winds through foothills of sedimentary and volcanic rocks. About 4 miles into the drive, a short side road veers right to a parking lot that's a few hundred feet before the "palette," whose natural colors include shades of green, gold, and pink. ⊠ *Off Badwater Rd., Death Valley ⊹ 11 miles south of Furnace Creek.*

Badwater. At 282 feet below sea level, Badwater is the lowest spot on land in North America—and also one of the hottest. Stairs and wheelchair ramps descend from the parking lot to a wooden platform that overlooks a sodium chloride pool, a small but remarkably persistent reminder that the valley floor used to contain a lake. You can continue past the platform on a broad, white path that peters out after a half mile or so. Badwater is one of the most popular and easily accessible sites within the park. From this lowest point, be sure to look across to Telescope Peak, which towers more than 2 miles above the valley floor. ⊠ *Badwater Rd., Death Valley ⊹ 19 miles south of Furnace Creek.*

Fodor's Choice ★ **Dante's View.** This lookout is 5,450 feet above sea level in the Black Mountains. In the dry desert air you can see across most of 160-mile-long Death Valley. The view is astounding. Take a 10-minute, mildly strenuous walk from the parking lot toward a series of rocky overlooks, where with binoculars you can spot some of Death Valley's signature sites. A few interpretive signs point out the highlights below in the valley and across, in the Sierra. Getting here from Furnace Creek takes about an hour—time well invested. ⊠ *Dante's View Rd., Death Valley ⊹ Off Hwy. 190, 35 miles from Badwater, 20 miles south of Twenty Mule Team Canyon.*

Devil's Golf Course. Thousands of miniature salt pinnacles carved into surreal shapes by the desert wind dot this wildly varied landscape. The salt was pushed up to the earth's surface by pressure created as underground salt- and water-bearing gravel crystallized. Get out of your vehicle and take a closer look; you'll see perfectly round holes descending into the ground. ⊠ *Badwater Rd., Death Valley ⊹ 13 miles south of Furnace Creek. Turn right onto dirt road and drive 1 mile.*

10

Sand Dunes at Mesquite Flat. These dunes, made up of minute pieces of quartz and other rock, are ever-changing products of the wind-rippled hills, with curving crests and a sun-bleached hue. The dunes are the most photographed destination in the park, and you can see them at their best at sunrise and sunset. Keep your eyes open for animal tracks—you may even spot a coyote or fox. Bring plenty of water, and note where you parked your car: It's easy to become disoriented in this ocean of sand. If you lose your bearings, climb to the top of a dune and scan the horizon for the parking lot. ⊠ *Death Valley* ✛ *19 miles north of Hwy. 190, northeast of Stovepipe Wells Village.*

Titus Canyon. This popular one-way, 27-mile drive starts at Nevada Highway 374 (Daylight Pass Road), 2 miles from the park's boundary. Along the way you'll see Leadville Ghost Town and finally the spectacular limestone and dolomite narrows. Toward the end, a two-way section of gravel road leads you into the mouth of the canyon from Scotty's Castle Road. This drive is steep, bumpy, and narrow. High-clearance vehicles are strongly recommended. ⊠ *Death Valley National Park* ✛ *Access road off Nevada Hwy. 374, 6 miles west of Beatty, NV.*

Zabriskie Point. Although only about 710 feet in elevation, this is one of Death Valley National Park's most scenic spots, overlooking a striking panorama of wrinkled, multicolor hills. It's a great place to watch the sunrise, but it can be bustling any time of day. Pair it with a drive out to magnificent Dante's View. ⊠ *Hwy. 190, Death Valley* ✛ *5 miles south of Furnace Creek.*

WHERE TO EAT

$$$$
AMERICAN
Fodor's Choice
★

✕ **Inn at Death Valley Dining Room.** Fireplaces, beamed ceilings, and spectacular views provide a visual feast to match this fine-dining restaurant's ambitious menu. Dinner entrées include fare such as salmon, free-range chicken, and filet mignon, and there's a seasonal menu of vegetarian dishes. **Known for:** views of surrounding desert; old-school charm; can be pricey. ⑤ *Average main: $38* ⊠ *Inn at Death Valley, Hwy. 190, Furnace Creek* ☎ *760/786–3385* ⊕ *www.furnacecreekresort.com* ⊘ *Closed mid-May–mid-Oct.*

TRAVEL SMART
LAS VEGAS

GETTING HERE AND AROUND

The sprawling city of Las Vegas is fairly easy to get around by car, as it's laid out largely in a grid, bisected by two Interstates, and mostly surrounded by a beltway. Traffic along the Strip, especially at its major intersections, as well as on parallel Interstates 15 and 515 (the latter of which is U.S. Highway 93/95 at most points), can be horrendous. It's particularly bad on weekend evenings and whenever there are conventions in town. Give yourself plenty of time when you're traveling to or from the Strip.

Outside the Strip, the city sprawls in all directions, and renting a car is the best way to get around, especially if you're staying in Lake Las Vegas, Summerlin, or similar areas more than a few miles away from the Strip. Las Vegas is also served by public buses; the one that travels up and down the Strip is particularly popular with visitors.

▌ AIR TRAVEL

Approximate flying times to Las Vegas: from New York, 5 hours; from Dallas, 2 hours; from Chicago, 4 hours; from Los Angeles, 1 hour; from San Francisco, 1½ hours.

If you're leaving Las Vegas on a Sunday, be sure to arrive at the airport at least two hours before your scheduled departure time. Though the TSA has improved its operation at McCarran International, security lines on busy days still seemingly stretch forever, and inevitably, travelers miss flights.

Airline Security Issues Transportation Security Administration. ☎ 866/289–9673 ⊕ www.tsa.gov.

AIRPORTS

The gateway to Las Vegas is McCarran International Airport (LAS), 5 miles south of the business district and immediately east of the southern end of the Strip. The airport, just a few minutes' drive from the Strip, is well served by nonstop and direct flights from all around the country and a handful of international destinations. The airport is consistently rated among the most passenger-friendly airports in the United States.

Also, McCarran is close enough to the Strip that, if you ever find yourself with a few hours to kill, you can easily catch a 15-minute cab ride to one of the South Strip casinos (Mandalay Bay and Luxor are closest) to while away some time. Additionally, as you might expect, McCarran has scads of slot machines to keep you busy.

Airport Information McCarran International Airport (LAS). ⊠ Paradise Rd., Airport ☎ 702/261–5211 ⊕ www.mccarran.com.

GROUND TRANSPORTATION

By bus: If you're heading Downtown or to the south end of the Strip, the public bus is the cheapest, and often quickest, way from the airport. The Westcliff Airport Express (WAX) travels south- and eastbound from McCarran Airport and includes stops along the Strip at Tropicana Avenue, the Las Vegas Premium Outlets, and Downtown at 4th and Carson, about a two-minute walk from Fremont Street Experience. The service operates seven days a week from approximately 5 am to midnight. The bus runs approximately every half hour during peak hours and every hour during non-peak hours. Just know that while the bus is clean and comfortable, it contains no racks for luggage. ■TIP➔ When boarding the bus, tell the driver where you're going before paying. When on board, alert him or her to your approaching stop by ringing the buzzer.

The Terminal 1 transit stop for WAX is on Level Zero, below baggage claim, at the south end of the bus plaza. Follow signs for Ground Transportation. Once outside, proceed across the pedestrian crosswalk, turn right toward the parking garage, and follow signs for the public bus stop. Exact change of $2 ($1 with a Medicare card, student ID [ages 6–17] or reduced-fare card from another system) is the fare for a single ride. The ticket vending machine accepts credit or debit cards to purchase a 2- or 24-hour pass, $3 and $5, respectively; passes also can be purchased aboard Deuce buses and SDX vehicles. The ride from the airport to the Strip will take 10 to 20 minutes, depending on ridership and traffic; to Downtown about 30 to 55 minutes. The transit stop for WAX in Terminal 3 is on the Departures Level. Follow signs for Ground Transportation and then for Public Transportation. ■ TIP→ Download a free Park & Ride Airport Guide at ⊕ rtcsnv.com.

By shuttle van: This is one of the cheapest ways to get from McCarran to your hotel if you don't take the public bus. Shuttle service is shared with other riders, and costs $9 to $13 per person to the Strip or Downtown, and about $25 to outlying casinos (excluding tips). If you have a large party, group rates are available. The vans wait for passengers outside the terminal in marked areas. Because the vans often make numerous stops at different hotels, it's not the best means of transportation if you're in a hurry. For round-trip service, save time and money by booking online and printing out your vouchers beforehand. ■ TIP→ Before you jump on a shuttle, check with your hotel, because several of them, such as Green Valley Ranch in Henderson and Red Rock Resort in Summerlin, offer customers free round-trip shuttle rides.

By taxi: The metered cabs awaiting your arrival at McCarran are one of the quickest ways to get to your destination (see Taxi Travel below for more information).

By town car: These rides are a bit more expensive than the average taxicab and must be reserved ahead of time, but they are cleaner and more convenient. A chauffeur from Las Vegas Limousines, for example, will meet and greet you at baggage claim, assist with luggage, and whisk you away in a luxury sedan, with seating for four, for $50 an hour.

Contacts Bell Trans. ☎ 800/274-7433 ⊕ www.airportshuttlelasvegas.com. **Las Vegas Limousines.** ☎ 702/888-4848 ⊕ www.lasvegaslimo.com. **Showtime Tours.** ☎ 702/895-9976 ⊕ www.showtimetourslv.com. **Westcliff Airport Express (WAX).** ☎ 800/228-3911 ⊕ www.rtcsnv.com.

FLIGHTS

The major airlines operate frequent service from their hub cities and, as a whole, offer one-stop connecting flights from virtually every city in the country. In addition to nonstop service from the usual hub cities (e.g., Atlanta, Chicago, Cincinnati, Dallas, Denver, Houston, Minneapolis, Newark, New York City, Phoenix, Salt Lake City, San Francisco), nonstop service is offered to many other destinations, sometimes by smaller airlines. Southwest remains a dominant airline, offering frequent flights to many cities in the south and west, including San Diego, Los Angeles, San Francisco, Oakland, Seattle, Salt Lake, Denver, Albuquerque, and Phoenix. Virgin America also has come on strong in recent years. Be sure to check the rates of the other airlines that serve Las Vegas, such as Delta, jetBlue, Frontier Airlines, United, and Alaska Airlines.

Airline Contacts Alaska Air. ☎ 800/426-0333 ⊕ www.alaskaair.com. **American Airlines.** ☎ 800/433-7300 ⊕ www.aa.com. **Delta Airlines.** ☎ 800/221-1212 ⊕ www.delta.com. **Frontier Airlines.** ☎ 800/432-1359 ⊕ www.flyfrontier.com. **jetBlue.** ☎ 800/538-2583 ⊕ www.jetblue.com. **Southwest Airlines.** ☎ 800/435-9792 ⊕ www.southwest.com. **United Airlines.** ☎ 800/864-8331 ⊕ www.united.com. **Virgin America.** ☎ 877/359-8474 ⊕ www.virginamerica.com.

▌ BUS TRAVEL

GREYHOUND

Greyhound provides regular Las Vegas service; the bus terminal is Downtown. Visit the website for fare, schedule, and baggage-allowance information. Cash and credit cards are accepted. Seating is on a first-come, first-served basis. The most frequent route out of Las Vegas is the one to Los Angeles, with departures several times a day; the trip takes five to eight hours, depending on stops. Fares begin at around $15 one-way, if you take advantage of the substantial discounts offered on the website. On Sunday evening and Monday morning, arriving an hour or more before departure is recommended.

RTC

The county-operated Regional Transportation Commission of Southern Nevada (RTC) runs local buses throughout the city and to most corners of sprawling Las Vegas Valley. The overall quality of bus service along the main thoroughfares is good. Nonlocals typically ride RTC buses only up and down the Strip, between Mandalay Bay and the Stratosphere. Some continue on to the Bonneville Transit Center. If you're heading to outlying areas, you may need to change buses Downtown. Mornings and afternoons the buses are frequently crowded, with standing room only. The fare for residential RTC buses is $2.

THE DEUCE

The Deuce is a special double-decker RTC bus that rides the Strip for $6 for two hours. All Deuce fares include transfers on residential routes as well. The Deuce, which began service in 2005, certainly is a unique way to explore new and old Vegas alike. Buses stop on the street in front of all the major hotels about every 15 minutes (in a perfect world) between 7 am and 2 am and every 20 minutes between 2 am and 7 am. Because traffic is quite heavy along the Strip, delays are frequent. Also, because the bus route has become popular among tourists, 24-hour

passes ($8), 3-day passes ($20), 15-day passes ($34), and 30-day passes ($65) are available. The 15- and 30-day passes are available only at sources listed on the RTC website.

Bus Information Greyhound. ☎ 800/231–2222 ⊕ www.greyhound.com. **Regional Transportation Commission of Southern Nevada.** ☎ 800/228–3911, 800/228–3911 ⊕ www.rtcsnv.com.

▌ CAR TRAVEL

Though you can get around central Las Vegas adequately without a car, the best way to experience the city can be to drive it. A car gives you easy access to all the casinos and attractions; lets you make excursions to Lake Mead, Hoover Dam, and elsewhere at your leisure; and gives you the chance to cruise the Strip and bask in its neon glow. If you plan to spend most of your time on the Strip, a car may not be worth the trouble, but otherwise, especially given the relatively high costs of taxis, renting or bringing a car is a good idea.

If you do choose to park at one of the casinos, you'll likely have to brave some rather immense parking structures. Valet parking is available but can take a while at busy times, and in most cases there is a fee in addition to your tip for the valets ($2 to $3 is expected). Self-parking on and around the Strip is, for the most part, no longer free. Still, it's usually less expensive to rent a car and drive around Vegas, or to use the monorail (or even—gasp!—to walk), than to cab it everywhere.

NAVIGATING THE CITY

The principal north–south artery is Las Vegas Boulevard (Interstate 15 runs roughly parallel to it, less than a mile to the west). A 4-mile stretch of Las Vegas Boulevard South is known as the Strip, where a majority of the city's hotels and casinos are clustered. Many major streets running east–west (Tropicana Avenue, Flamingo Road, Desert Inn Road, Sahara Avenue) are named for the casinos—past and present—built at their intersections with the Strip. Highway 215 circumnavigates the city, and the Interstate 515 freeway connects Henderson to Las Vegas; the Summerlin Parkway connects the city and that suburb. Because the capacity of the streets of Las Vegas hasn't kept pace with the city's incredible growth, traffic can be slow at virtually any time, especially on the Strip, and particularly in the late afternoon, in the evening, and on weekends. At those times drive the streets parallel to Las Vegas Boulevard: Koval Lane and Paradise Road to the east; Frank Sinatra Drive and Industrial Road/Dean Martin Drive/Sammy Davis Jr. Drive to the west. That last shortcut (from Tropicana Avenue almost all the way to Downtown) can save you an enormous amount of time. You can enter the parking lots at Fashion Show mall, Trump Las Vegas, and Circus Circus from Sammy Davis Jr. Drive. Exit Frank Sinatra Drive off Interstate 15 North, and you can access the hotels from Mandalay Bay to Caesars Palace (including CityCenter).

■ TIP➔ **Visitors from Southern California should at all costs try to avoid traveling to Las Vegas on a Friday afternoon and returning home on a Sunday afternoon. During these traditional weekend-visit hours, driving times (along Interstate 15) can be more than twice as long as during other, nonpeak periods.**

GASOLINE

It's easy to find gas stations, most of which are open 24 hours, all over town. There aren't any gas stations along the main stretch of the Strip, but you'll find them within a mile of the Strip in either direction, along the main east–west cross streets. Gas is relatively expensive in Las Vegas, generally 30¢ to 40¢ per gallon above the national average. There's no one part of town with especially cheap or pricey gas, although the stations nearest the airport tend to charge a few cents more per gallon—it's prudent to fill up your rental car a few miles away from the airport before returning it.

PARKING

You can't park anywhere on the Strip itself, and Fremont Street in the casino district Downtown is a pedestrian mall closed to traffic. Street parking regulations are strictly enforced in Las Vegas, and meters are continuously monitored, so whenever possible it's a good idea to leave your car in a parking lot or garage. Self-parking is available at most of the massive garages and lots of virtually every hotel, although you may have to hunt for a space and possibly wind up in the far reaches of immense facilities. It's also no longer free. You can avoid this challenge by opting for valet parking, but most hotels now charge for that as well. Parking in the high-rise structures Downtown is generally free or inexpensive, as long as you validate your parking ticket with the casino cashier or restaurant host.

The long tradition of free parking at all Strip resorts ended in mid-2016, when MGM Resorts International starting charging for both self-parking and valet at its resorts with the exception of Circus Circus, where it's still free. Caesars Entertainment Corporation followed suit, as did The Cosmopolitan of Las Vegas. Self-parking is still free at Wynn Las Vegas/Encore (although there's a fee for valet), The Venetian/Palazzo, the Hard Rock Hotel, Boyd Gaming properties, the Westgate Las Vegas, and non-gaming hotels in the tourism corridor. Also note that some players' card holders get free parking. (Most Downtown hotel-casinos charge, but you generally get a few hours of free parking if you gamble, dine, or otherwise patronize the property.) Parking rates can vary, even within the same company, so check with the property you'll be visiting.

RENTAL CARS

The airport's rental-car companies are off-site at McCarran Rent-a-Car Center, about 3 miles from the main airport complex, and visitors must take the Rental Car Shuttle buses from the center median, located just outside the baggage claim Ground Transportation exits from Level 1 (Terminal 1) and Level Zero (Terminal 3) to get there. The facility reduces congestion in and around the airport, and offers visitors the opportunity to check bags for flights on some airlines without setting foot in the main terminal. Still, the centralized location is far enough away from the airport that it can add anywhere from 15 to 25 minutes to your travel time. The bottom line: If you rent a car, be sure to leave yourself plenty of time to return the vehicle and catch your flight.

RENTAL CAR RATES

The Las Vegas average is anywhere from $20 to $70 a day for intermediate to full-size cars—usually you can find a car for less than $30 a day (and at very slow times for less than $20), but during very busy times expect sky-high rates, especially at the last minute. Las Vegas has among the highest car-rental taxes and surcharges in the country, however, so be sure to factor in the 8.5% (in Clark County) sales tax, a 2% county tax on rentals, 10% concession recovery fee, and a $1.90 per-day vehicle licensing fee. If you rent your car at the airport, an additional $3.75 per-day "customer facility charge" applies. Owing to the high demand for rental cars and significant competition, there are many deals to be had at the airport for car rentals. During special events and conventions, rates frequently go up as supply dwindles, but at other times you can find bargains. For the best deals, check with the various online services or your airline, or contact a representative of the hotel where you'll be staying, as many hotels have business relationships with car-rental companies.

Although there are several local car-rental companies along the Strip itself, they tend to be more expensive than those at the airport or elsewhere in the city.

RENTAL CAR REQUIREMENTS

In Nevada you must be 21 to rent a car, and some major car-rental agencies have a minimum age of 25. Those agencies that do rent to people under 25 often assess surcharges to those drivers. There's no upper age limit for renting a car. Non–U.S. residents will need a reservation voucher, a passport, a driver's license, and a travel policy that covers each driver when picking up a car.

Rental Center McCarran Airport Rent-A-Car Center. ☎ 702/261–6001 ⊕ www.mccarran.com.

ROAD CONDITIONS

It might seem as if every road in Las Vegas is in a continuous state of expansion or repair. Orange highway cones, road-building equipment, and detours are ubiquitous. But once the roads are widened and repaved, they're efficient and comfortable. The city's traffic-light system is state of the art, and you can often drive for miles on major thoroughfares, hitting green lights all the way. Signage is excellent. The local driving style is fast and can be less than courteous. Watch out for unsignaled lane changes and turns.

There are rarely weather problems in Las Vegas, but flash flooding can wreak havoc. For information about weather conditions, highway construction, traffic incidents, and road closures, visit the website of the Nevada Department of Transportation, or call its Travel Info system by dialing ☎ 511 in Nevada or ☎ 877/687–6237 if calling outside Nevada.

ROADSIDE EMERGENCIES

Call ☎ 911 to reach police, fire, or ambulance assistance. Dial ☎ *647 to reach the Nevada Highway Patrol.

RULES OF THE ROAD

Right turns are permitted on red lights after coming to a full stop. Nevada requires seat-belt use in the front and back seats of vehicles. Chains are required on Mt. Charleston and in other mountainous regions when snow is fresh and heavy; signs indicate conditions.

CHILDREN

Always strap children under age six or less than 60 pounds into approved child-safety seats. In Nevada children must wear seat belts regardless of where they're seated.

DWI

The Las Vegas police are extremely aggressive about catching drunk drivers—you're considered legally impaired if your blood-alcohol level is 0.08% or higher (this is also the law in neighboring states).

SPEED LIMITS

The speed limit on residential streets is 25 mph. On major thoroughfares it's 45 mph. On the interstate and other divided highways within the city the speed limit is 65 mph; outside the city the speed limit is 70 or 75 mph. Police officers are highly vigilant about speeding laws within Las Vegas, especially in school zones, but enforcement in rural areas is rare.

Information Nevada Department of Transportation. ☎ 775/888–7000 or call 511 locally for travel information ⊕ www.nevadadot.com. **Nevada Highway Patrol.** ☎ 702/486–4100, 775/687–5300 ⊕ nhp.nv.gov.

▌ MONORAIL TRAVEL

The Las Vegas Monorail stretches from MGM Grand, in the south, to Sahara Avenue Station, to the north, with five stops in between, including the Las Vegas Convention Center. All told, the trains make the 4-mile trip in about 14 minutes, arriving every 4 to 8 minutes. The monorail runs Monday 7 am–midnight; Tuesday–Thursday 7 am–2 am; and Friday–Sunday 7 am–3 am. Fares are $5 for a single-ride ticket, $12 for a one-day pass, $22 for a two-day pass, $28 for a three-day pass, and so forth. Unlimited Ride passes are also available. You can purchase tickets at the vending machines at the entrance to each station or in advance online, where special deals on passes are sometimes offered. Children age five or under ride free.

A number of properties on the west side of the Strip are connected by free trams that run roughly every 10 minutes. There's one that runs between Excalibur and Mandalay Bay, from 9 am to 12:30 am; one that runs between The Mirage and Treasure Island, from 9 am to 1 am, extending until 3 am on Friday and Saturday; and one that stretches from Monte Carlo through CityCenter to Bellagio, from 8 am to 4 am.

Contact Las Vegas Monorail Company. ☎ 702/699–8200 ⊕ www.lvmonorail.com.

▌ TAXI TRAVEL

Taxis aren't allowed to pick up passengers on the street, so you can't hail a cab New York–style. You have to wait in a hotel taxi line or call a cab company. If you dine at a restaurant off the Strip, the restaurant will call a cab to take you home.

After some rough spots in the early days of serving Las Vegas, the process of using both Uber and Lyft has become much smoother. Uber Pool, X, XL and Select are available, and Lyft Line, Lyft, Plus and Premier).

Both Uber and Lyft are allowed to both drop off and pick up at McCarran International Airport. Use the app on your phone to book them. The pickup spots at the airport are on Level 2 of the Terminal 1 parking garage and the Valet Level of the Terminal 3 parking garage. They are not allowed to pick up at the arrivals or departures area of either terminal.

RIDE-SHARING SERVICES IN LAS VEGAS

All the major Strip resorts are served by both Uber and Lyft, but there's a designated ride-sharing pickup/drop-off area, and it's generally not near the taxi stand. Just ask a hotel employee if you can't spot it. There also are designated pickup/drop-off locations at large events, such as the Electric Daisy Carnival and Life Is Beautiful festival, and event spaces such as T-Mobile Arena. Be aware that rates can fluctuate rapidly, especially in the cases of holidays and special events, when surge pricing may be in effect. And surge pricing can happen almost anytime on the weekends or during large conventions. Anecdotal evidence suggests that pickup time estimates aren't always reliable in Las Vegas because of traffic and lights.

FARES

The fare is $3.50 on the meter when you get in and 23¢ for every 1/12th mile, or $2.76 per mile (there's also a $32.40 per-hour charge for waiting). Taxis are limited by law to carrying a maximum of four passengers, and there's no additional charge per person. No fees are assessed for luggage, but taxis leaving the airport are allowed to add an airport surcharge of $2. There's also a 3% excise tax on all rates and fees.

The trip from the airport to most hotels on the south end of the Strip should cost about $16 to $20, to the north end of the Strip about $22 to $29, and to Downtown about $24 to $27.

Ride-sharing applications can provide either cheaper or dramatically more expensive service depending on surge pricing.

TIPPING

Drivers should be tipped around 15% to 18% for good service *(see Tipping in Essentials)*. Some drivers can't accept credit cards (and those who do usually add a surcharge); all drivers carry only nominal change with them.

SUGGESTED ROUTES

Drivers who take passengers through the airport tunnel without asking are committing an illegal practice known as "long-hauling." You have every right to ask your driver about the routes he or she is using; don't be afraid to speak up. If you have trouble with your cabdriver, be sure to get his or her name and license number and call the Taxicab Authority to report the incident. ■ TIP➔ Be sure to specify to your driver that you don't want to take Interstate 15 or the airport tunnel on your way to or from the airport. This is always the longer route distance-wise, which means it's the most expensive, but it can sometimes save you 5 to 10 minutes on the trip if traffic is heavy on the Strip.

Contact **Taxicab Authority.** ☎ *702/668–4000* ⊕ *taxi.nv.gov.*

Taxi Companies Desert Cab. ☎ *702/386–9102* ⊕ *www.desertcabinc.com.* **Whittlesea Blue Cab.** ☎ *702/384–6111.* **Yellow Checker Star.** ☎ *702/873–2000* ⊕ *www.ycstrans.com.*

ESSENTIALS

■ BUSINESS SERVICES AND FACILITIES

Las Vegas is one of the nation's leading convention destinations, and all the town's major hotels have comprehensive convention and meeting-planning space and services. Among the best business centers in town are those run by the chain FedEx Office, which has several locations throughout the area. Two outposts on the Strip include The Cosmopolitan of Las Vegas (Level 3, West End Tower) and Mandalay Bay (Level 1, South Convention Center).

Contact FedEx Office Print & Ship Center. ⊠ *Cosmopolitan Hotel, 3708 Las Vegas Blvd. S* ☎ *702/207-2724* ⊕ *www.fedex.com.*

■ DAY TOURS AND GUIDES

BOAT TOURS

The *Desert Princess*, a 275-passenger Mississippi River–style stern-wheeler, cruises Lake Mead. Tours include a 90-minute, narrated Mid-Day Sightseeing or seasonal champagne brunch cruise, and a seasonal two-hour dinner cruise.

Tour Operator Lake Mead Cruises. ⊠ *Lake Mead marina* ☎ *866/292-9191* ⊕ *www.lakemeadcruises.com.*

BUS TOURS

Gray Line and several other companies offer Las Vegas city and neon-light tours; trips to Red Rock Canyon, Lake Mead, Colorado River (rafting), Hoover Dam, and Valley of Fire; and longer trips to different sections of the Grand Canyon.

Tour Operators Gray Line Tours. ☎ *800/472-9546* ⊕ *www.grayline.com.*

HELICOPTER TOURS

Helicopters do two basic tours in and around Las Vegas: a brief flyover of the Strip and a several-hour trip out to the Grand Canyon and back.

Tour Operators Maverick Helicopter Tours. ⊠ *6075 Las Vegas Blvd. S* ☎ *888/261-4414, 702/261-0007* ⊕ *www.maverickhelicopter. com.* **Papillon.** ☎ *888/635-7272, 702/736-7243* ⊕ *www.papillon.com.* **Sundance Helicopters.** ⊠ *5596 Haven St.* ☎ *800/653-1881, 702/736-0606* ⊕ *www.sundancehelicopters.com.*

■ HEALTH

The dry desert air in Las Vegas means that your body will need extra fluids, especially during the punishing summer months. Always drink lots of water even if you're not outside very much. When you're outdoors, wear sunscreen and always carry water with you if you plan a long walk.

■ HOURS OF OPERATION

Las Vegas is a 24-hour city 365 days a year. Casinos, bars, supermarkets, almost all gas stations, even some health clubs and video stores cater to customers at all hours of the day and night (many people work odd hours here).

Most museums and attractions are open seven days a week.

Most pharmacies are open seven days a week. Many, though, including local outposts of Walgreens and CVS pharmacy—several of them on the Las Vegas Strip—offer 24-hour and drive-through services.

Shopping hours vary greatly around town, but many stores are open weekdays and Saturday from 9 or 10 am until 9 or 10 pm and Sunday from 10 or 11 am until 5 or 6 pm. The malls and souvenir shops on the Strip and Downtown often remain open until midnight, and some are open 24 hours. Quite a few grocery stores are open around the clock.

█ MONEY

Prices in Las Vegas can be gratis or outrageous. For example, you can get a sandwich wrap or hot dog at one of the rock-bottom casino snack bars (Circus Circus, Four Queens) or from a food cart for $3–$4, or you can spend upward of $30 for a pastrami sandwich at the Carnegie Deli in The Mirage. A cup of coffee in a casino coffee shop or Starbucks will set you back $2 to $5, whereas that same cup is free if you happen to be sitting at a nickel slot machine when the cocktail waitress comes by. A taxi from the airport to the MGM Grand can be as little as $13 if you tell the driver to take Tropicana Avenue and there's no traffic, or can run as high as $27 if you take the Airport Connector and there's a wreck on the freeway. The more you know about Las Vegas, the less it'll cost you.

ATMs are widely available in Las Vegas; they're at every bank and at virtually all casinos, hotels, convenience stores, and gas stations. Casino ATMs generally tack on a fee of up to $6 per transaction (this, of course, is on top of any fees your bank might charge). In addition, all casinos have cash-advance machines, which take credit cards. You just indicate how large a cash advance you want, and when the transaction is approved, you pick up the cash at the casino cashier. But beware: You pay a service charge up for this "convenience"—up to 18% or more—in addition to the usual cash-advance charges and interest rate; in most cases, the credit-card company begins charging interest the moment the advance is taken, so you won't have the usual grace period to pay your balance in full before interest begins to accrue. To put it another way, don't obtain cash this way.

█ PACKING

Although Las Vegas casinos were filled with people dressed to the nines during the Rat Pack era, things have gotten much more casual over the past couple of decades. The warm weather and informal character of Las Vegas render casual clothing appropriate day and night. However, there are some exceptions. A very small number of restaurants require jackets for men, and some of the city's increasingly exclusive and overhyped "ultralounges" and high-profile dance clubs have specific requirements, such as no sneakers or jeans, or that you must wear dark shoes or collared shirts. At a minimum, even if there's no set dress code, you're going to fit in with the scene if you make some effort to dress stylishly when heading out either to the hipper nightclubs or even trendier restaurants (i.e., those helmed by celeb chefs or with trendy followings and cool decor). Just as an example, where jeans and T-shirts might be technically allowed at some establishments, try to wear plain, fitted T-shirts versus those with logos and designs, and choose jeans that are appropriate for a venue (crisp and clean for a nice restaurant, designer labels for a top club). It's always good to pack a few stylish outfits for the evening, and when you're making dinner reservations at an upscale spot or considering a visit to a nightclub, ask for the dress-code specifics. Also, flip-flops are best kept to pool areas.

Although the desert sun keeps temperatures scorching outside in warmer months, the casinos are ice-cold. Your best insurance is to dress in layers. The blasting air-conditioning may feel good at first, but if you plan to spend some time inside, bring a light sweater or jacket in case you feel chilly.

Always wear comfortable shoes; no matter what your intentions, you cover a lot of ground on foot.

█ RESTROOMS

Free restrooms can be found in every casino; you don't have to be gambling in the casino to use them. Many restrooms have attendants who expect tips for fetching you everything from breath mints to hand towels. You're not obligated to tip.

SAFETY

The well-known areas of Las Vegas are quite safe for visitors. With so many people carrying so much cash, security is tight inside and out. The casinos have visitors under constant surveillance, and hotel security guards are never more than a few seconds away. Outside, police are highly visible, on foot and bicycles and in cruisers. However, you should take the same precautions you would in any city—be aware of what's going on around you, stick to well-lighted areas, and quickly move away from any situation or people that might be threatening—especially if you're carrying some gambling cash. When Downtown, it's wise not to stray too far off the three main streets: Fremont, Ogden, and Carson between Main and Las Vegas Boulevard.

Be especially careful with your purse around slot machines. Grab-and-run thieves are always looking for easy pickings, especially Downtown.

Apart from their everyday vulnerability to aggressive men, women should have few problems with unwanted attention in Las Vegas. If something does happen inside a casino, simply go to any pit and ask a boss to call security. The problem will disappear in seconds. Outside, crowds are almost always thick on the Strip and Downtown, and there's safety in numbers. Still, be aware of pickpockets.

Men in Las Vegas also need to be on guard against predatory women. "Trick roller" is the name of a particularly nasty breed of female con artist. These women are expert at meeting single men by "chance." After getting friendly in the casino, the woman joins the man in his hotel room, where she slips powerful knockout drugs into his drink and robs him blind. Some men don't wake up. Prostitution is illegal in Clark County, although it is legal in the rural counties of Nevada.

■ TIP➔ Distribute your cash, credit cards, IDs, and other valuables between a deep front pocket, an inside jacket or vest pocket, and a hidden money pouch. Don't reach for the money pouch once you're in public.

TAXES

The Las Vegas and Reno-Tahoe international airports assess a $4.50 departure tax (which is usually included in the ticket price), or passenger facility charge. The hotel room tax is 13.38% in Las Vegas. Moreover, virtually all hotels on the Strip—and many Downtown—will charge an additional (and outrageous) resort fee of up to $39 per room per night. These fees are sometimes waived, however, for high-tier players-club members or deluxe-room bookings, so be sure to check.

The sales tax rates for the areas covered in this guide are Las Vegas, 8.15%; Arizona, 5.6%; and California, 7.25% (though in the latter two cases, individual counties can and do add their own).

TIME

Nevada and California are in the Pacific time zone. Arizona is in the Mountain time zone and doesn't observe daylight saving time.

TIPPING

Just as in other U.S. destinations, workers in Las Vegas are paid a minimal wage and rely on tips to make up the primary part of their income. A $1 tip per drink is appropriate for cocktail waitresses, even when they bring you a free drink at a slot machine or casino table. On package tours, conductors and drivers usually get $10 per day from the group as a whole; check whether this has already been figured into your cost. For local sightseeing tours, you may individually tip the driver-guide $5 if he or she has been helpful or informative. Tip dealers with the equivalent of your average bet once or twice an hour if you're winning; slot-machine change personnel and keno runners are accustomed to a buck or two. Ushers in showrooms may be able to get you better seats for performances for a gratuity of $5 or more. Tip the concierge 10%–20% of the cost of a ticket to a hot show. Tip $5–$10 for making dinner reservations or arrangements for other attractions.

TIPPING GUIDELINES FOR LAS VEGAS	
Bartender	$1 to $5 per round of drinks, depending on the number of drinks
Bellhop	$1 to $5 per bag, depending on the level of the hotel
Coat Check Personnel	$1 to $2 per item checked; if there's a fee, nothing
Hotel Concierge	$5 or more, if he or she performs a service for you
Hotel Doorman	$1 to $2, if he helps you get a cab
Hotel Housekeeping	$2 to $5 a day (daily preferably, or at the end of your stay, in cash)
Hotel Room-Service Waiter	$2 to $3 per delivery, even if a service charge has been added
Porter at Airport or Train Station	$1 per bag
Restroom Attendants	$1 or small change
Skycap at Airport	$1 to $3 per bag checked
Taxi Driver or Chauffeur	15% to 20%, but round up the fare to the next dollar
Valet Parking Attendant	$2 to $3, but only when you get your car
Waiter	16% to 20%, with 20% being the norm at high-end restaurants; nothing additional if a service charge is added to the bill

▌ VISITOR INFORMATION

Before you go, contact the city and state tourism offices for general information. When you get there, you might want to visit the Las Vegas Convention and Visitors Authority, next door to The Westgate, for brochures and general information. Hotels and gift shops on the Strip have maps, brochures, pamphlets, and free-events magazines—such as *The Las Vegas Guide* and *Las Vegas Magazine*—that list shows and buffets and offer discounts to area attractions.

Anthony Curtis's *Las Vegas Advisor*, a monthly print newsletter and website, keeps track of the constantly changing Las Vegas landscapes of gambling, accommodations, dining, entertainment, Top Ten Values (a monthly listing of the city's best deals), complimentary offerings, coupons, and more, and is an indispensable resource for any Las Vegas visitor. Visit the website (⊕ *www.lasvegasadvisor.com*) for a free sample issue; annual online memberships begin at $37 per year.

VEGAS.com advertises, To Do Vegas Right, It's Who You Know. Part of the Greenspun Media Group, which also publishes the *Las Vegas Sun*, VEGAS.com offers information and instant-booking capabilities for everything from air and hotel packages to shows and tours. About.com has an excellent online "Las Vegas Travel" guide, which includes dozens of original articles and reviews as well as links to many other Vegas resources, as does the "Visitor Guide" page on the website of the *Las Vegas Review-Journal*. The *Review-Journal*'s *Friday Neon* magazine lists information on shows and events, and its annual Best of Las Vegas lists reader favorites in various categories. Visit ⊕ *www.reviewjournal.com* or ⊕ *bestoflasvegas.com*.

One of the oldest sites is the *Las Vegas Leisure Guide*, which is full of hotel, restaurant, and nightlife info. *Las Vegas Online Entertainment Guide* has listings for hotels and an online reservations system, plus local history, restaurants, a business directory, and even some gambling instruction. *LasVegas.com*, the official Las Vegas tourism website, has a little bit of everything going on in Sin City. Find out about events, book hotels, get special deals, and find out other vital travel info; the Las Vegas Convention and Visitors Authority, which runs the site, also broadcasts great deals and updates on Twitter (⊕ *www.twitter.com/vegas*). The City of Las Vegas has its own website (⊕ *www.lasvegasnevada.gov*), which is a great resource for service-related information, including how to pay a ticket or citation. Remember, what happens in Vegas, stays in Vegas.

Contacts About.com. ⊕ *govegas.about.com.* **City of Las Vegas.** ☎ *702/229-6011* ⊕ *www.lasvegasnevada.gov.* **LasVegas.com.** ⊕ *www.lasvegas.com.* **Las Vegas Advisor.** ☎ *800/244-2224, 702/252-0655* ⊕ *www.lasvegasadvisor.com.* **Las Vegas Convention and Visitors Authority.** ✉ *3150 Paradise Rd., Paradise Road* ☎ *877/847-4858, 702/892-0711* ⊕ *www.lvcva.com.* **Las Vegas Leisure Guide.** ⊕ *www.lasvegas-nv.com.* **Las Vegas Online Entertainment Guide.** ⊕ *www.lvol.com.* **Las Vegas Review-Journal.** ⊕ *www.reviewjournal.com.* **Nevada Commission on Tourism.** ☎ *800/638-2328* ⊕ *travelnevada.com.* **VEGAS.com.** ⊕ *www.vegas.com.*

MARRIAGE LICENSES

If you plan to get hitched during your Vegas stay, you might want to check out the Clark County website for necessary marriage license information.

Contacts Clark County. ☎ *702/455-0000* ⊕ *www.clarkcountynv.gov.*

INDEX

PHOTO CREDITS

Front cover: John Kellerman / Alamy [Description: The Strip and Venetian Hotel, Las Vegas, Nevada]. 1, MGM Mirage. 2, Travel Pix Collection/age fotostock. 5, Carol M. Highsmith/Library of Congress via Wikimedia Commons. **Chapter 1: Experience Las Vegas:** 8-9 Travel Pix Collection/age fotostock. 16 (left), Tomasz Rossa. 16 (top center), MGM Mirage. 16 (top right), Coleong | Dreamstime.com. 16 (bottom right), Hervè Donnezan/age fotostock. 17 (left), CityCenter Las Vegas. 17 (top center), Brent Bergherm/ age fotostock. 17, (bottom center), Kobby Dagan/Shutterstock. 17 (right), MGM Resorts International. 18, Helio San Miguel. 19, Pictorial Press Ltd/Alamy. 20 (left and right), Library of Congress Prints & Photographs Division. 20 (center), wikipedia.org. 21 (top left), Harrah's Entertainment. 21 (bottom left), CSU Archive / age fotostock. 21 (right), Pictorial Press Ltd/Alamy. 22 (left), wikipedia.org. 22 (bottom center), Content Mine International/Alamy. 22 (right), Pictorial Press Ltd/Alamy. 23 (top left), Allstar Picture Library / Alamy. 23 (bottom left), By Carol M. Highsmith [Public domain], via Wikimedia Commons. 23 (right), LOOK Die Bildagentur der Fotografen GmbH/Alamy. **Chapter 2: Exploring Las Vegas:** 25, Gavin Hellier / Alamy. 26, Somchaij | Dreamstime.com. 28, MGM Resorts International. 33, Scott Frances. 36, Maria Lampert / Alamy. 40 Las Vegas Sands Corp. 44, Rubens Abboud / Alamy. 46 LVCVB. 52, Marcin Wichary/Flickr, [CC BY 2.0]. 56, Ed Schipul/Flickr, [CC BY-SA 2.0]. 57 Green Valley Ranch. 59 Judy Crawford/Shutterstock. 61, trekandshoot | Dreamstime.com. 62, Chee-Onn Leong/Shutterstock. **Chapter 3: Gambling and Casinos:** 65, Lise Gagne/ iStockphoto. 74, Greg Vaughn/Alamy. 81, Photo Network / Alamy. 89, Javier Larrea/age fotostock. 91, Danita Delimont / Alamy. 92, Mark Harmel / Alamy. 95, cloki/ Shutterstock. 99, www.imagesource.com. 105, Lee Foster/Alamy. 106, Harrah's Entertainment, Inc. 110, Jeff Thrower (WebThrower)/Shutterstock. 111, M. Timothy O'Keefe / Alamy. 115, Gayvoronskaya_-Yana/Shutterstock. 118, Thomas Hart Shelby. **Chapter 4: Where to Eat:** 123, MGM Mirage. 124, Caesar's Entertainment. 125, (top) Wynn Las Vegas. 125, (bottom) Marie-Louise Avery/Alamy. 126, MGM Resorts International. **Chapter 5: Where to Stay:** 155, Caesar's Palace. 156, Harrah's Entertainment, Inc. 157 (top), MGM Mirage. 157 (bottom), Hard Rock Hotel & Casino. 158, Harrah's Entertainment, Inc. 159, Linq Hotel and Casino. **Chapter 6: Shops and Spas:** 175, Harrah's Entertainment. 176, Asterixvs | Dreamstime.com. 178-79, Grand Canal Shoppes. **Chapter 7: Nightlife:** 201, Douglas Peebles Photography/Alamy. 202, Sander7474 | Dreamstime.com. **Chapter 8: Shows:** 223, Matt Beard Photography. 224, Tomasz Rossa. 229, David Hawe/©BMP. **Chapter 9: Sports and the Outdoors:** 239, Image Source / Alamy. 240, MargaretW/iStockphoto. 243, Station Casinos. **Chapter 10: Side Trips from Las Vegas:** 249, Clicktrick | Dreamstime.com. 250 and 251, NPS. 252, Coleong | Dreamstime.com. 259, Photoquest | Dreamstime.com. 272–73, Paul B. Moore/Shutterstock. 274, Kerrick James. 275, Geir Olav Lyngfjell/Shutterstock. 276 (left), Wendy Holden/iStockphoto. 276 (right), Kerrick James. 277, Alexander Hafemann/iStockphoto. 278, Paul B. Moore/Shutterstock. 279, Kerrick James. 284, MARK LELLOUCH, NPS. 288, Rolf Hicker Photography/Alamy. 290, Rodney Ee, Fodors.com member. **Back cover, from left to right:** Matthew Dixon/iStockphoto; DNY59/iStockphoto; somchaij / Shutterstock. **Spine:** Galushko Sergey/Shutterstock.

About Our Writers: All photos are courtesy of the writers.

NOTES

NOTES

NOTES

NOTES

NOTES

NOTES

ABOUT OUR WRITERS

Joan Patterson is a freelance writer and editor based in southern Nevada, who has also contributed to *Fodor's California* and *Fodor's Complete Guide to National Parks of the West*. She has worked in small-town newspaper production as a reporter, photographer, and news editor, and has been a features writer covering Las Vegas for the *Las Vegas Review-Journal* as both staff member and freelancer.

Heidi Knapp Rinella, the foremost authority on food and dining in Las Vegas, has been with the *Las Vegas Review-Journal* since 1999, and a restaurant critic since 1980 in Florida as well as Nevada. A local judge for the James Beard Foundation awards and a nationally award-winning journalist, she is the author of seven books. She and her family live in Henderson, Nevada.

 Susan Stapleton is a writer and editor based in Las Vegas. She edits *Eater Vegas*, making her an expert on all things food and drink. She's also a regular contributor to *Las Vegas Magazine* as well as the *Los Angeles Times*. When she's not exploring all this city has to offer, she spends her time in the pool she worked so hard to get in her backyard or gardening.

 Matt Villano is a writer and editor based in Healdsburg, California. He contributes to the *Wall Street Journal*, the *New York Times, Sunset*, and *Entrepreneur*. He also serves as senior editor of the Expedia Viewfinder blog from Expedia. When he's not researching stories or working on this guide's Where to Stay chapter (among others), he's playing with his daughters.

 Mike Weatherford came to us well prepared for the task of revising the Shows chapter of this book. He's lived in Las Vegas since 1987, is the author of *Cult Vegas—The Weirdest! The Wildest! The Swingin'est Town on Earth*, and, as the entertainment reporter for the *Las Vegas Review-Journal*, sees all the shows.